VIRGIL AND THE AUGUSTAN RECEPTION

This book is an examination of the ideological reception of Virgil at specific moments in the last two millennia. Following Tennyson's evaluation of Virgil – "Thou majestic in thy sadness | at the doubtful doom of human kind" – Richard Thomas first scrutinizes the Virgil tradition for readings that refute contemporary dismissals of the putative post-Vietnam *Angst* of the so-called "Harvard School," then detects the suppression of such readings in the "Augustan" reception, effected through the lens of Augustus and the European successors of Augustus who constructed Rome's first emperor – and Virgil – for their own political purposes. He looks at Augustus in the poetry of Virgil, detects in the poets and grammarians of antiquity alternately a collaborative oppositional reading and an attempt to suppress such reading, studies creative translation (particularly Dryden's), which reasserts the "Augustan" Virgil, and examines naive translation which can be truer to the spirit of Virgil. Scrutiny of "textual cleansing," philology's rewriting or excision of troubling readings, leads to readings by both supporters and opponents of fascism and National Socialism to support or subvert the latter-day Augustus. The book ends with a diachronic examination of the ways successive ages have tried to make the *Aeneid* conform to their upbeat expectations of this poet.

RICHARD THOMAS is Professor of Greek and Latin at Harvard University. He is the author of *Lands and Peoples in Roman Poetry* (1982), a two-volume commentary on Virgil's *Georgics* (1988) and *Reading Virgil and his Texts* (1999). He has also published more than fifty articles and reviews on Hellenistic Greek and Roman poetry.

VIRGIL AND THE AUGUSTAN RECEPTION

Richard F. Thomas

Harvard University

CAMBRIDGE
UNIVERSITY PRESS

PUBLISHED BY THE PRESS SYNDICATE OF THE UNIVERSITY OF CAMBRIDGE
The Pitt Building, Trumpington Street, Cambridge, United Kingdom

CAMBRIDGE UNIVERSITY PRESS
The Edinburgh Building, Cambridge CB2 2RU, UK
40 West 20th Street, New York NY 10011-4211, USA
10 Stamford Road, Oakleigh, VIC 3166, Australia
Ruiz de Alarcón 13, 28014 Madrid, Spain
Dock House, The Waterfront, Cape Town 8001, South Africa

http://www.cambridge.org

First published 2001

Printed in the United Kingdom at the University Press, Cambridge

Typeset in Bembo and New Hellenic Greek in '3B2' [A O]

A catalogue record for this book is available from the British Library

ISBN 0 521 78288 0 hardback

For Joan, Sarah and Julia,
so often the companions of this work,

and in memory of John Wald
ibi omnis effusus labor

CONTENTS

ACKNOWLEDGEMENTS

I have been fortunate to have had the opportunity to test my ideas on a number of occasions, and to have profited from discussion on those occasions with faculty and students of a number of institutions, in particular the Universities of Colorado, Göteborg, Oslo, Pittsburgh, Washington, Georgetown, Rice, Emory, Boston University, the Vermont Classical Association, the Universities of Florida, South Carolina, and Pennsylvania, Corpus Christi College, Oxford, the University of Florence, and of Venice, the Virginia Classical Association, the University of Tennessee and Bryn Mawr. It is my pleasure to single out those colleagues whose invitations gave me the opportunity to share my ideas on these occasions, namely Ariana Traill, Monika Azstalos, Egil Kraggerud, Hans-Peter Stahl, Michael Halleran, Alex Sens, Harvey Yunis, Peter Bing, Patricia Johnson, Mary Ann Hopkins, Gareth Schmeling, Ward Briggs, Joe Farrell, Stephen Harrison, Emanuele Narducci, Mario Geymonat, Cathy Dougherty, David Tandy and Celia Schultz.

On each of these occasions, and at other times, I was fortunate to have good discussion with more colleagues than I can now remember, some of whom also read and commented on parts of the work. With apologies to those whose contribution I may have omitted (*numeros memini, si verba tenerem*), I would single out, in addition to those just named, Alessandro Barchiesi, Ewen Bowie, Brian Breed, Francis Cairns, Kathy Coleman, Denis Feeney, Don Fowler, Alain Gowing, Jasper Griffin, Albert Henrichs, Stephen Hinds, Christina Kraus, Leah Kronenberg, Christopher Jones, Nico Knauer, Mario Labate, Hugh Lloyd-Jones, Oliver Lyne, Greg Nagy, Robin Nisbet, James O'Donnell, Tim O'Sullivan, Victoria Pagán, Lee Pearcy, Chris Pelling, David Ross, Andreola Rossi, Thomas Schmidt, Zeph Stewart, Sarolta Takács, Richard Tarrant, Mike Tueller, Ariana Traill, Jessica Wissmann, David Wray and Jan Ziolkowski.

I owe a particular debt of thanks for the expertise and industry of Wendell Clausen, Craig Kallendorf, Peter Knox, James O'Hara, Hayden Pelliccia and Christine Perkell, valued friends and colleagues who took on the task of reading and fully commenting on an early draft of the book; it was their detailed and critical response that helped me most to formulate the presentation of this study, and it is my pleasure to acknowledge this valuable contribution. They also saved me from many embarrassments; for those I have not avoided they bear no responsibility. Pauline Hire, who has been my editorial helpmate almost since my day begun, so to say, has all my thanks and all my best wishes for her life after CUP, her thanks not the least because she chose as one of her readers Charles Martindale, than whom there could have been no better judge and critic of a book on Virgilian, or any other Latin, reception. I here also record my thanks to an anonymous Dryden critic whose thoughtful and detailed criticisms led to complete revison of Chapters 4 and 5; I hope remaining criticisms will be tempered by such improvements as I have achieved. I am grateful to have had help in the form of research funds from the Clark Fund at Harvard, and from the James Loeb Trust, and in this connection I thank Matthew Carter for his assistance.

Otherwise my chief debt, after those expressed in the dedication, is to the wonderful students I have been fortunate to teach and work with over the past years, for it is they who have most helped me to test and shape my ideas about Virgil: to the Harvard graduate students and undergraduates, to the students of the Harvard Summer School and Extension School, among them John Wald, and to the school teachers who participated in my NEH Summer seminar on Virgil in 1995. It has been my pleasure to discover with these groups just how vital, relevant and immediate a poet is Virgil.

PROLOGUE

As one long convinced that much of the power and the beauty of
Virgilian poetry lies in the profound qualifications of the poet's vision
of the political and cultural worlds that his poetry engages, I used to
be uncomfortable with the possibility that this view was somehow
related to my opposition to the involvement of my country (New
Zealand at that point) in an illegal and unjust war in Vietnam. Indeed,
as a good classicist, I even felt a little guilty as I read such comments as
"the damage suffered by the interpretation of Roman poetry has
consisted largely of the Vietnam war being imposed on the wars of
Aeneas in Italy."[1] One scholar even responded to some offprints I sent
with the admonition that "it don't help to use the sort of language
that goes back to the worst years of Vietnam or the Spanish civil
war." But since my convictions about the darkness of Virgil's vision,
far from abating, only developed as I read, taught and wrote about
this author, and since I continued to be unhappy with the proposition
that these views were just the product of my days as a Vietnam war
protester, which were after all becoming somewhat remote, I decided
to go looking for my Virgil elsewhere in the Virgil tradition, hoping
that he might have flourished also in other ages. I found him here
and there, but, more importantly, I found him being suppressed and
avoided, replaced by something else, and transformed into what I will
be calling the "Augustan Virgil." E. L. Edmunds, in a review of C.
Martindale, notes that "the hermeneutic approach to a text must
begin with one's own horizon. One's own reading comes first."[2] By
positioning my own reading of Virgil in, and following, a tradition of

---

[1] Galinsky (1992) 32. We are given no representative examples of the golden age of
Virgilian criticism obtaining in 1964 before the damage was inflicted.
[2] Edmunds (1994) 39.

other readings, some of which are hard to recover, I hope to show the pervasiveness of that Virgil, and not just in the imagination of fellow-travellers from the 1960s and 1970s.

"The history of Vergilian scholarship," writes H. P. Stahl, "repeatedly shows how the individual scholar was tied to political and sociological perceptions of his own time."[3] On the next page, on which he too refers to the influence of Vietnam (as grounds for dismissing the non-Augustan Virgil), he will answer his own question about the morality of the character of Aeneas by referring to Turnus' and Dido's having "sinned against the divine order of the universe" – a phrase I would be interested to see put into Virgilian Latin![4] Against the usual assumption that it is the darker reading of Virgil that is the modern construction, much of this book will attempt to demonstrate that the Augustan Virgil is likewise a political and sociological construction, and is potentially no more exempt from the creative manipulations and transformations of reception than the non-Augustan Virgil. We will see that experiences other than Vietnam, such as French and English imperialism, Prussian expansionism, Italian and German nationalism, fascism and Nazism all play a role in the construction.

By "Augustan reader" I mean a reader who sees the writings of Virgil as endorsements of the aims and achievements of Imperator Caesar Divi filius Augustus (as he would eventually be called),[5] endorsements generated either by Virgil's own political and ideological conviction or by the application of external suggestion, chiefly from his "patron" Maecenas; that is, a reader who takes from Virgil what Augustus himself would presumably have wanted a contemporary reader to take. Although for strategic reasons Augustan readers prefer to label the other way of reading Virgil as "pessimism," I prefer, and will use, the term "ambivalence," occasionally "oppositional," and sometimes "non-Augustan." There are two reasons for my choice (which is not new; the word "pessimism" is not, for instance, to be found in the introduction of my 1988 commentary on the *Georgics*): first, it allows for a duality, even a conflict, and this makes it truer to the poetry of Virgil, as many would agree, and second, because the

---

[3] Stahl (1990) 178. We will return to the issue of contemporary politics and interpretation in Chs. 7 and 8.

[4] Augustan Virgilians tend to level the accusation of Christian anachronism, but the shoe is frequently on the other foot.

[5] On the name, see Syme (1979) 365, 370.

term "pessimistic" is false to the poetic power that Virgil achieves when he looks away, as he so often does, from victor to vanquished, or focuses his lens on the price involved in the establishment of Augustanism. Roman *humanitas* may lack the teleology that makes Christian suffering and darkness tolerable, but that does not deprive such Virgilian moments of their grandeur. "Pessimism," moreover, is a term anachronistically rooted in Augustanism, and colored by modern political ideology, particularly the ideology of the establishment of the 1960s and subsequent neo-conservative Reaganism and Thatcherism. Virgil's political "optimism" would constitute optimism about the achievements and possibilities of Augustus. But there is no Augustus until after the *Aeneid* is under way, and it is reasonable to suppose that it would be long after the death of Virgil that the lasting political achievements of Octavian would compensate for his ruthless and opportunistic earlier years.[6]

Nor am I denying that there was a historical Augustan Virgil, to match and generate the Augustan reader of Virgil. That too is in the nature of ambivalence. But here I quote from an article I wrote a few years ago:

> In legislative terms, that is in terms of requiring single, unitary ideological intent and meaning, there is a huge and qualitative difference between the Augustans and the ambivalents. Put quite simply the latter can live with interpretations of these poems, or at least parts of them, that are directed at uncovering ideologies coincident with those of Aeneas and Augustanism. That, of course, is in large part because nobody would deny that the poetry of the 30s and 20s BC, Virgil's and that of others, participates to a great extent and much of the time positively in the revolution of those years. But the ambivalents also accept such interpretations because it is in the nature of ambivalence that it must work in tension with some other, generally less subliminal, meaning; otherwise it becomes mere pamphleteering and subversion. However, given the position of Virgil (and others) within Augustan society, the Augustan critic cannot accept any ambivalence: the slightest reservations expressed by a "client" of Maecenas open up a Pandora's box which must be kept closed for the preservation of the official

---

[6] For further criticism of this terminology, and of a recent study on pessimism and optimism in the *Georgics*, see Thomas (2000a), and below, Ch. 6, pp. 218–21.

status of the purely Augustan poet. Once one moves from a naive Augustan reading to a complex, ambivalent one, there is ultimately no way for the former to exist, for the latter will undercut it and vitiate its purity, the essence of its existence. So it is, I think, that we must be forbidden to countenance the latter, ambivalent or pessimistic reading.[7]

I shall assume nothing in advance about the relationship between Virgil and Octavian, Virgil and Augustus, Virgil and Horace, Virgil and Maecenas. With respect to Virgil and Octavian/Augustus, in particular, the struggle must be to recreate a series of synchronic readings, to recreate hypothetical worlds in which to situate those readings, for the *Eclogues* a world in which Octavian could have died at some time around 35 BC, between 35 and 29 for any given line of the *Georgics*, and for the *Aeneid* a world in which the Augustan principate ended in 19 BC, half a lifetime or more before it consolidated its words and images, and created the Roman empire and laid the foundations of western civilization. Even Ovid's reference to the *Aeneid* as Augustus' poem (*Trist.* 2.533), however it is interpreted, must be seen as an utterance of 9 AD, a generation after the death of Virgil, during which years the political reception and use of the poem will have helped turn it into "Augustus' poem." That is of interest, as a matter of reception, but that should not be confused with circumstances of composition.

It is my assumption throughout that Virgil's poetry is constantly and unrelievedly grappling with the problems of existence in a troubled and violent world, and that this is the case, before, during and after the political "solutions" to civil discord that he observed as he was finishing the *Georgics*. I will not always or systematically argue for such a reading, but will always assume it, frequently argue for it, and look for the suppression of it in the varied and complex reception of this poet. Some will therefore find critical imbalance here. This is, of course, an occupational hazard of the publishing Virgilian, but it is also, I hope, a sign of the continuing, and even growing, vitality of this poet: he clearly matters to those who are capable of reading him.

There is no single or even consistent theoretical stance in this book. I have tended to look for such help wherever it seemed most applicable

---

[7] Thomas (1990) 66. I think this is the last time I used the term "pessimistic," which I here renounce as an Augustan rhetorical strategy!

and most productive, perhaps, at the risk of self-aggrandizement, like Horace at *Epistles* 1.1.14 (*nullius addictus iurare in verba magistri* "submitting myself to the oath of no master"). It does not much matter, for my purposes, whether what I will mostly call ambiguity (one of the tropes by which ambivalence may be established) is called by others diphony, polyphony, polysemy, competing point of view, or complication of the epic norm.[8] Since I am not much interested in theory detached from hermeneutics, I permit myself an eclecticism here that will strike some as theoretically naive. My methods have tended to be historicist, and they look for their support to philology, broadly defined, so as to include, for instance, narratology, reception criticism, some deconstruction, and an occasional dose of new historicism (p. 166). In places the target is also philology, particularly those manifestations of philology which are most assertive about their ability to establish texts and define meanings so as to create Augustan monophony. This is a nuanced enterprise, but it is hardly new in Virgilian studies: V. Pöschl began his influential study of Virgil by opposing himself to the rationalism of "philology."[9] I will join him in suggesting that positivism and false science have indeed distorted the picture, but will differ in insisting that clarity can come only through broadly defined philology.

In an often quoted epigram, T. Eagleton has noted that hostility to theory "usually means an opposition to other people's theories and an oblivion of one's own."[10] Likewise hostility to philology connotes unawareness or denial of one's own philological connections, and has in recent years been a symptom of political academic anxiety more than anything else. Everyone who talks about literature, particularly literature in a foreign language which has no surviving native speakers, is functioning as a philologist, and insisting on one's status as "literary" or renaming the enterprise "close reading" (which is then regarded as a discrete act, or part-time job) will not obscure that fact.

Particularly in the area of reception it has been of help to return constantly to the words of Virgil, and to scrutinize those words against the meanings that have been assigned to them, as against other

---

[8] See Martindale (1993b) 121–8 on the variety in recent use of critical terminology for expressing "ambiguity." There are of course real distinctions, and I have addressed this in Thomas (2000b), arguing for the unsuitability of "polysemy" to describe ambiguity.

[9] Pöschl (1977) 3–7.

[10] Eagleton (1983) viii.

possible meanings that they might have. Where this approach leads to different conclusions from those that have been part of the critical orthodoxy, it may perhaps be characterized as vaguely deconstructive – a characterization that surprises me less now than it did when it was levelled at me some years ago. C. Martindale has referred to deconstruction "at its best" as a "mode of *defamiliarization*, designed to provoke us into fresh apprehensions of fresh possibilities of meaning."[11] One review of my *Georgics* commentary ended by stating "This is not the poem that I have been reading and rereading" – an utterance which I find quite heartening, since that was really my aim.[12] To the degree that my findings partake of such defamiliarization, but at the same time may be seen to stake some claim to philologically determined stability, I would position myself in what J. M. Ziolkowski has desiderated as "a middle ground between the deconstructive aims of some theory and the reconstructive project of all philology."[13] Ultimately, poststructuralist theory and philology may not be inimical, but rather function together, in which case such theory becomes a part of the philological enterprise.

Philological scrutiny, then, is perhaps the most useful tool for scrutinizing the reception of Virgil. But the procedures are delicate and the path is a rocky one, for at the same time philology, and the excessive positivism that has often accompanied it, have been prominent players in the construction of the Augustan Virgil. I have also tried throughout to relate philological observation to hermeneutics. It is sometimes claimed that the interpretation of large-scale narrative must turn from the detail, from the trees, and keep in mind the forest and its general aspect. The ways in which this is true are obvious and I have tried to avoid becoming preoccupied by philological detail for its own sake – diverting as that may be. But the ways in which that claim is false or misleading are more subtle: criticism which frees itself from attention to detail, particularly when the subject of study is Virgil, is in my view likely to go astray, for the writer starts thinking of the (Augustan) reception of Virgil rather than of Virgil. There is a great deal in that reception to distract the critic from the Virgilian text, not the least Augustus and Rome, or constructions of Augustus and Rome. And the hermeneutic circle becomes a particular likelihood when dealing with the triad Virgil, Augustus, Rome, in which

[11] Martindale (1993a) 36.   [12] Fantham (1991) 167.   [13] Ziolkowski (1990) 11.

group Augustus and Rome have always been the dominant partners, into whose service the poet and his poems are pressed.

Two objections may present themselves at this point: first, it may be doubted that we can ever establish an "original" climate of reading, or that there ever was such a thing; second, and related, it may be felt that I am just replacing one imposed construct with another, claiming that my philology works better than the philology of others. Both are legitimate and raise fundamental critical issues. To the latter I can only say that the proof of the pudding lies ahead, and the test can only come through an eventual judgment of individual examples. To the former, I would respond in similar vein, but also add the fact that although different readings of poetic texts are always possible, and can coexist, it will be useful to explore the potential gap between readings that are historically plausible in terms of the culture that produced the text and those that are demonstrably generated by the cultures that received it. For that reason I will constantly and with sustained scepticism question the role of reception, which is to say the collective interpretations that have accumulated in the last 2000 years.[14] Whether this allows reification of a synchronically legible Virgilian text, and whether that is something we should even be striving towards, will depend in part on the tastes of the reader. But I hope the process of deconstructing the reception, as well as the attempt to construct, will be of interest.

It is a premise of this book that Virgil's oeuvre is ideologically complete and susceptible to interpretation.[15] There will be no tolerance for the position, frequently used to explain away ambiguity or troubling passages, that Virgil would have removed this or that passage. What may be known with some degree of certainty about most of his text is that he wrote what he wrote, and that is what we must read, and read as his work. It may well be that the dynamism of the *Aeneid* lies partly in the fact that he did not have those three years to "polish" it, and if so, it is certainly not the task of the critic, with a fully formed Augustus looking over his shoulder, to do that polishing in his place. This, for instance, J. W. Mackail attempted to do when

---

[14] The connection between interpretation and reader reception is well treated by Kallendorf (1994).

[15] By this I do not mean to deny the ideological complexity that characterizes Virgilian poetry.

he wrote of Aeneas' venture into human sacrifice in *Aeneid* 11: "One can say it is Virgil's [not Aeneas', we note] single lapse into barbarism, and think or hope that the two lines might have been cancelled in his final revision."[16] And as we shall see in Chapter 6, there is a long tradition of critical "emendation" and latterly athetization aimed at turning Virgil into a more truly Augustan poet.

It has been particularly useful, occasionally and again in no organized way, to think in narratological terms, an approach that may help to de-Augustanize Virgil. I have tended to use the term "focalization" at some times, "voice" at others, and though I would agree with Farrell that the voices or focalizations can coexist in unresolved competition (with which Parry too would surely have agreed), the fact is that in this poem the Augustan voice will generally be subverted by the "other" voice or voices.[17] On a very fundamental level, it will be useful, and a corrective, to attend to the identity of the voice in question, something which critics have frequently failed to do. All would agree that identifying the narrative voice with that of Turnus or Mezentius is scarcely a legitimate critical procedure. Given the fact that the *Aeneid* is primarily the story of Aeneas, it may seem more legitimate, prima facie, to identify the narrative voice with the voices of Anchises or Aeneas, but such an identification is still hazardous, for there is always a gap between narrator and character. Statements expressed by characters, even, or perhaps especially, when the character is a figure such as Jupiter, need to be interpreted as representing a particular point of view, and one which can never be simply identified with the point of view of the author.[18] This may all seem obvious, but the fact is that throughout the last two millennia, readers of Virgil have just assumed that the voice of the Augustan character is the voice of the Virgilian narrator and of Virgil himself. Neither of these assumptions is any more legitimate than the assumption that the voice of any particular character in a play of

---

[16] Mackail (1922) 105.

[17] Thomas (1990) 66. Also Farrell (1990) 77–80 for a reformulating of the issue in terms of Bakhtinian polyphony.

[18] See Galinsky (1996) 239–40 for treatment of Jupiter as a quasi-authorial character. In reality the god's words in the passage in question (10.112 *rex Iuppiter omnibus idem* "King Jupiter is the same to all") are deeply troubling, in that Jupiter is *not* the same to all, and had already prophesied the success of Aeneas, whom he will actively support in the duel with Turnus. For good treatment of the "characterful" aspect of Jupiter in these lines, see Feeney (1991) 143–6 and generally 129–87.

Sophocles, Terence or Shakespeare has an identity with that of the poet.

The Virgilian narrative voice, unlike that of Horace, for instance, never makes its point by preaching or drawing conclusions, and even in the *Georgics* does not instruct so much as demonstrate – demonstrate systems, the fates of cultures, the consequences and implications of actions. Virgil lays out the world as it functions, gives us a glimpse of how it might have functioned differently, and leaves his demonstration without gnomic epigram, but rather susceptible to interpretation and frequently to competing interpretations. The reader time and again is left to supply the epigram, and there are frequently more than one from which to choose. In this respect the text of Virgil is intensely ambiguous. And in such a text, point of view or focalization will therefore be worthy of attention.

This book, then, is chiefly about reception, about the attempts, from the time of its publication, to put Virgilian poetry back into a constructed Augustan box which its details and nuances so constantly threaten to break open. In the process, however, it is occupied with constructing or reviving meanings that two millennia of literature and scholarship have largely tried to suppress. The reception of accumulated generations, when it is strong and relatively unified, may establish itself as literary fact, and may become difficult to dislodge, so engrained does it become in the handbooks, commentaries and literary histories, and even in the *apparatus criticus*. That is true of the poetry of Virgil to an extraordinary degree, partly because of its perceived intersection and identity with the outlook of Augustus. That outlook in turn becomes important for European cultural élitism, which constructs an Augustus to whom Virgil is just an appendage. Until recently, the reception of Virgil outside the field of Classics was predominantly Augustanized, in part because vernacular poets and other writers were products of educational systems which never questioned the truth of the Augustan Virgil.[19] And some, such as Dryden, had their own neo-Augustan purposes in mind. In such a situation defamiliarization of the received construction will not easily occur, but I would invite the reader to construct a naiveté about Augustus and "his" poet, at least for the time being.

---

[19] There are notable exceptions, for instance, eighteenth-century England, as Weinbrot (1978) has shown.

Unless otherwise indicated I have provided the translations of ancient and modern works, functional rather than literary or elegant (*excudent alii* ...). Finally, in the words of another Virgilian, "I have tried to give honour where honour is due, although the extent of international literature on Virgil is so great that I cannot be sure that I have succeeded."[20] If this was true in the infancy of the twentieth century, a glance at the bulk of Marouzeau's *L'Année Philologique* available in recent years, not to mention a glance at the several pages of Virgilian listings appearing each year, reveals how difficult is the issue of full acknowledgement; like Heinze I regret inevitable failings. To the degree I succeed I am in debt to the librarians past and present of Harvard's Widener Library, the place where I have had the privilege and delight to spend so much of my life, with various manifestations of Virgil, in recent years.

[20] Heinze (1903, tr. 1993) vii.

Introduction: the critical landscape

> In fact these writers are on the lookout for any double meanings, even where one of the meanings renders nonsense. And so, when someone else speaks, they annoyingly interrupt, and when someone writes, they carry out their tedious and unintelligible interpretations.
>
> AUCTOR AD HERENNIUM[1]

> The time has passed, even in classics, when the assiduous discovery of "ambiguity" and "irony" was tantamount to superior insight and sophistication; these terms should be the scholar's last resort, not the first, nor does their relentless repetition help make the case.
>
> KARL GALINSKY[2]

From the preceding we take two lessons: (1) the possibility for ambiguous readings, and also the execution of such readings, existed and was acknowledged in Virgil's time as in ours; (2) the critical response to the subversion of surface-meaning is always characterized by some form of anger, also then as now. Defamiliarization vexes because it makes our worlds less sure.

Foundational paradigm

"Can one be certain about anything in this poem?" asks James O'Hara[3] during a discussion of the ambiguities of Jupiter's prophecy

---

[1] 2.16 *omnes enim illi amphibolias aucupantur, eas etiam quae ex altera parte sententiam nullam possunt interpretari. itaque et alieni sermonis molesti interpellatores, et scripti cum odiosi tum obscuri interpretes sunt.* Translation based on H. Caplan (1964), as throughout for references to this work.
[2] Galinsky (1991) 478; *contra*, Perkell (1994).
[3] O'Hara (1990) 150.

I

in *Aeneid* 1. With regard to Augustus, and his connection to the promise of a new golden age, the one certainty we have is the prophetic utterance of Anchises:

> hic vir, hic est tibi quem promitti saepius audis
> Augustus Caesar, divi genus, aurea condet
> saecula qui rursus Latio regnata per arva
> Saturno quondam, super et Garamantas et Indos,
> proferet imperium.   (*Aen.* 6.791–5)

> This is the man, this is he who you are frequently told is
> promised to you, Augustus Caesar, offspring of a god, who will
> again found ages of gold in Latium through fields once ruled
> by Saturn, and will carry his power beyond the lands of the
> Garamantes and Indians.

So begins "the panegyric of Augustus delivered by Anchises in book six of the *Aeneid* (791–805), analyzed classically by Norden. In the larger context we find both *auxesis* ["amplification"] and *synkrisis* ["comparison"]: First, the achievements of peace, the re-establishment of the *Saturnia regna*. This historical fantasy contains an explicit comparison of the man Augustus to the god Saturn, a type of comparison which is one of the standard devices for creating hyperbole. Secondly, we have the achievements of war ..."[4] In other words, the passage is Virgil's (or rather Anchises') clearest statement of Augustus' restoration of the golden age, a potent metaphor for *pax Augusta*, and a theme recurring elsewhere in Augustan iconography, for instance on the *Ara Pacis*.

And no other theme was to find a more pervasive afterlife in the reception of Augustus by the subsequent leader cult of Europe, from Nero to Louis XIV to Mussolini. But the "achievements of war" and the furthering of *imperium* through military power sit somewhat uneasily with any traditional notion of *Saturnia regna*, which are usually distinct from and exclusive of warfare.[5] Virgil's presentations of cultural systems are never as clear-cut as critics need them to be. So, for instance, the only other occurrence of the words *aurea saecula* is in the context of Evander's characterization of Saturn's peaceful rule in

---

[4] So Hardie (1986) 257; referring to Norden (1899). Cf. also Ryberg (1958).
[5] See Smolenaars (1987) for an attempt to reconcile Saturnian and Jovian notions of existence, essentially an Augustan hermeneutical enterprise.

Latium, whose termination will be coincident with the coming of war:

> aurea quae perhibent illo sub rege fuere
> saecula: sic placida populos in pace regebat,
> deterior donec paulatim ac decolor aetas
> et belli rabies et amor successit habendi.
>
> *(Aen. 8.324–7)*

Under that king were the centuries they call golden: so it was he ruled the peoples in calm and peace, until gradually there came in its place a worse age, tarnished, and the fury of war and love of wealth.

And conversely there might seem to be something inconsistent between the restoration of a golden, or Saturnian, age and the subjection of the world to Roman *imperium:* it is Jupiter, after all, who is generally and emphatically responsible for granting that power: 1.278–9 *his ego nec metas rerum nec tempora pono: imperium sine fine dedi* "for the achievements of Rome I set no spatial or temporal limits: I have granted them empire without limit." Anchises himself, a little later in *Aeneid* 6, will echo these words of Jupiter: *tu regere imperio populos, Romane, memento* (851). But let us move on to another reminiscence: Anchises' words on his descendant, Augustus, particularly in the phrase *aurea condet | saecula*, recall those of Jupiter on his descendant, Romulus, *Mavortia condet | moenia* (1.276–7) – one will found centuries of gold, the other, martial walls. The golden age of *Eclogue* 4 had excluded war and walls – again the terms of the metaphor seem fluid and in tension if not contradictory.

A further reading subverts even the certainty of Anchises' prophecy, whose language, as is characteristic of prophecy, communicates a profound ambiguity: *aurea condet | saecula* "he will found ages of gold" (792–3). The sense is based on analogy with phrases such as *moenia/ urbem condere*, and it seems a fairly easy one. In fact, however, as the *ThLL* shows, the expression *saecula condere*, involving as it does an expression of time, is virtually unique within the group denoting the founding of cities, states, walls, and the like.[6] And yet this phrase, *saecula condere*, is found elsewhere in the *ThLL*, as it is found elsewhere in Latin literature, once before Virgil, in an author of great

---

[6] *ThLL* s.v. *condere* 153.36ff.

familiarity to Virgil: at Lucretius 3.1090, its sense is precisely the opposite of that "required" in the sixth *Aeneid*: *proinde licet quot vis vivendo condere saecla*, "therefore by living on you may lay to rest as many generations as you wish." The *ThLL* lists this under the lemma "to bring a defined time to a close."[7] The usage seems clearly to be based on the formal phrase *lustrum condere*, "to close out the census period."[8] Lucretius elsewhere expresses the same idea in similar language (1.202 *multaque vivendo vitalia vincere saecla*; 3.948 *omnia si pergas vivendo vincere saecla*) – language which Virgil also modified and used at *Georgics* 2.295, *multa virum volvens durando saecula vincit.* Can he then have been unaware of Lucretius' possible coinage of the phrase *saecla condere*, or of the sense it had for Lucretius? How are we to rule out the Lucretian sense at *Aeneid* 6.792–3? Virgil himself has, at *Eclogue* 9.52, *cantando puerum memini me condere soles* ("I remember as a boy closing out the days with song"), where the gerund *cantando*, as well as the sense of *condere*, may be seen as constituting a reference to *vivendo condere (saecla)* at Lucretius 3.1090.[9] Order may be restored by claiming that it is in Virgil's manner to adopt the language of Lucretius and then effect a semantic shift, but this just confirms the fact that another reading, another meaning, is in play: the most certain Augustan utterance of the *Aeneid* is deeply ambiguous, capable of signifying the termination, not the foundation, of the golden age by Augustus. And Virgil could, with any of us, have excluded that ambiguity by writing *reddet* for *condet*, since this "founding" of Augustus' is to be a restoration (cf. *quondam*).

There is a post-Virgilian occurrence of *saecula condere*, and it holds a parallel ambiguity which may confirm our suggestion. The bulk of Statius, *Silvae* 4.1 is in *prosopopoeia*, a speech in which Janus is made to deliver a lavish encomium of Domitian, including the following (37–8): *mecum altera saecula condes,* | *et tibi longaevi renovabitur ara Tarenti* "along with me you will ?found/?close out a second age, and Tarentum's ancient altar will be reinaugurated." L. Håkanson is clearly right in arguing that Janus is referring to the next *Ludi Saeculares*, of 198 AD, which Domitian and the god will witness together (having

---

[7] *ThLL* s.v. *condere* 152.19–27 *"certum tempus finire."*
[8] *ThLL* s.v. *condere* 152.27–43; 153.38.
[9] Cf. also Hor. *Odes* 4.5.29 *condit quisque diem*; and see Usener (1875) 206 for further examples.

closed out the last one in 88; hence *altera*).[10] "Bring to a close" is the natural sense in Statius, as in Lucretius and Virgil.

Such a reading of the Virgilian occurrence, even when it is rooted in the only other instances of the phrase in classical Latin, will not be easily tolerated in the dominant, Augustan critical tradition, and the reception of the Lucretian intertext is instructive. The *ThLL* shows one way: separate the two phrases and place them under lemmas with opposite meanings, thus bolstering the act of hermeneutics with lexicographical *auctoritas*. Conington, unengaged ideologically, noted openly and honestly: "'Condere saecla' occurs at Lucr. 3.1090, in the sense of living through ages, seeing them to their end, as in E. 9.52. Here it can only mean to establish, like 'condere urbem' &c., though the analogy is not very close." Forbiger likewise observes "Dictio autem *condere saecula* alio tamen sensu legitur ap. Lucr. 1.1103 (1090 Lachm.)." Norden noted: "the formula *condere saecula* (so Lucr. 3.1090 at verse end) is here used in a sense opposite to the original."[11] The "parallel" seems to have become too disturbing for reflection, for the commentaries of Williams and Austin simply suppress any reference to Lucretius; for them, *condere saecula* in Lucretius ceases to function as intertext for *condere saecula* in Virgil. That is the safest course.

Two Virgilian interpreters some years ago grappled with the ambiguity. R. J. Getty was the first clearly to face the possibility that the phrase in question could mean "Augustus will bring an end to ages of gold."[12] He argues that it is no great compliment to say that Augustus will restore the age of Saturn, unlike the implication that Augustus will function as a new Jupiter.

I. S. Ryberg also saw the ambiguity, but also saw the pitfalls of Getty's reinterpretation, which she struggled to avoid: the phrase "hints, with 'flattering ambiguity,' that the founder of the new

---

[10] See Coleman (1988) 77–8, for good discussion of the issues, though we differ somewhat in our translations.

[11] Norden (ad loc.) then tries to avoid having the Lucretian sense subvert the Augustan sense by reference to Deubner's study of *lustrum condere* "to close out a census period" (i.e. to store it away for future reference). Cf. *ThLL* s.v. *condere* 152.19ff. *certum tempus finire*; and 152.27ff. *lustrum condere*; see Norden ad loc.; and cf. Livy 1.44.2 *ibi instructum exercitum omnem suovetaurilibus lustravit, idque conditum lustrum appellatum, quia is censendo finis factus est*. But whatever the etymological realities of the phrase *lustrum condere* (see Ogilvie, ad loc.), it is clear that Livy, writing at the same time as Virgil, understood it as indicating a termination. Cf. Usener (1875) 204–6.

[12] Getty (1950).

golden age will be like Jupiter, the son greater than his father who brought to a close the reign of Saturn. This would be a very subtle compliment, precariously poised between the implication of divinity contained in the comparison with Jupiter and the unfortunate linking of Jupiter with the Iron Age."[13] Precarious indeed, given that in Virgil's own outlook, in the *Georgics* and the *Aeneid*, Jupiter ends the golden age. Getty and Ryberg are better obliterated, and just as Williams and Austin drop the reference to Lucretius, so, for instance, strongly Augustan hermeneutics such as that of Hardie (1986) or Cairns (1989) discusses the lines but does not show awareness of the Lucretian meaning or the interpretations of Getty (who is in Cairns' bibliography) or Ryberg.

Once we have recognized the parallel in Lucretius and the meaning of the model, we may claim inversion of Lucretius' Latin, but we can hardly suppress the *possibility* that a Roman reader, not to mention a Roman poet who had absorbed the poetry of Lucretius, would have thought of the meaning of Lucretius as he read Virgil. C. Martindale has rightly criticized the classicist's tendency to insist that a currently demonstrable meaning must be that adopted by the "original re-ceivers,"[14] but it is even more implausible to suggest that such current meanings could be excluded from such reception. And so, in the current instance, the Lucretian meaning, troubling in its new Virgi-lian context, becomes activated by the reader's recognition of the Lucretian sense of *saecula condere*. When that occurs, we get the fol-lowing possibility:

> This is the man, this is he who you are frequently told is
> promised to you, Augustus Caesar, offspring of a god, who will
> again close out ages of gold in Latium through fields once ruled
> by Saturn, and will carry forth his power beyond the lands of
> the Garamantes and Indians.

Why "again" (*rursus*)? Because such a termination has happened twice previously, once on the universal level at the hands of Jupiter himself in the *Georgics* (1.121–46),[15] but more importantly, from the per-spective of Augustan time, it will have occurred in Italy, where the

---

[13] Ryberg (1958) 129.

[14] Martindale (1993b) 123.

[15] And the relationship between Jupiter and Octavian in the *Georgics* is an intimate one; cf. Thomas (1988) 1.1–42, 562; 4.560–1nn.

race of Latinus, descendant of Saturn, will be supplanted by Aeneas, grandson and agent of Jupiter. Augustus, descendant of the Olympian Venus, and of Aeneas, will continue the civilizing work of his ancestors.[16] But of course ambiguity allows Virgil the response: "That is not what I meant at all. That is not it, at all." To a hyperlogical response that Virgil could not have thought of immediate pre-Augustan Rome or Italy as a golden age, one could offer a figure such as Meliboeus at *Eclogue* 1.67–9: in political life one man's golden age will be another's age of iron. Nor need we see the text as politically subversive in and of itself. Augustus himself may not have objected to the lines with their Lucretian reading: aphoristic as he seems to have been, he will perhaps have had Virgilian quotes for many occasions; but it is worth mentioning the only quote actually ascribed to him is from a speech of Jupiter ("look, 'Romans, masters of the world, a race of toga-wearers!'" "en 'Romanos, rerum dominos, gentemque togatam'"):[17] perhaps Augustus embraced the role Virgil mapped out for him, and not just in the Greek East.

The lines have provided an exemplary range of approaches for Augustan critical control when Virgilian ambivalence is at issue: the reordering of the lexicographer, the denial of Conington and Forbiger, the philological argumentation of Norden, the silence and suppression of Williams and Austin, even the exegetical efforts of Getty and Ryberg, and the corresponding silence of Hardie and Cairns – these are just some of the chains binding the text of Virgil in its Augustan confinement.

Theoretical paradigm[18]

In the course of a discussion of *emphasis*, "the use of language in such a way as to imply more than is actually said,"[19] Quintilian (9.2.64–99) first gives a notorious example from Virgil, on whose meaning or meanings critics are still at odds,[20] then a second from Ovid (*Met.*

---

[16] *Aen.* 1.286 ff. (pace Austin ad 6.792) does not deal in terms of a return to a golden or Saturnian age.

[17] Suet. *Aug.* 40, quoting *Aen.* 1.282.

[18] This section is a condensed version of Thomas (2000b), a synchronic treatment of ambiguity in Virgil, and of the terminology used to describe it.

[19] So *OLD* s.v. *emphasis*.

[20] *Aen.* 4.550–1 (*non licuit thalami expertem sine crimine vitam | degere more ferae*), on whose possible meanings see, conveniently, Austin's commentary.

10.422), and he then focuses his attention on a particular type of this figure, a type

> wherein through a certain innuendo we intend something
> unspoken to be communicated not as an opposite, as in
> "irony," but some "other" meaning which lies hidden and is
> as it were to be found by the reader ... It is used in three
> circumstances: first *if speaking openly is unsafe*, second, if doing
> so is unseemly, and thirdly it is employed for the sake of
> elegance, and brings more pleasure through its novelty and
> variety than it would if directly spelled out.[21] [emphasis added]

This type is identified in particular with rhetorical exercises in the schools, but that does not lessen its potential presence in literary contexts, as has been well demonstrated by F. M. Ahl, in the seminal work on *emphasis* in Roman, and particularly Neronian, literature.[22] Quintilian, in the following discussion of this first type of *emphasis* (67–75), talks of the delicacy of the figure, stressing that it will only succeed if the utterance may be understood in a different way (67 *aliter intellegi possit*); if the danger can be avoided by ambiguity of expression (*ambiguitate sententiae*), the hidden sense will be approved. Some will object that this is not a situation appropriate to the relationship between Virgil and Octavian/Augustus. I will address that issue shortly; for now I am concerned to establish it as a principle of composition recognized in the Greek and Roman rhetorical traditions, and therefore fully accessible to Virgil.

Discussion of this figure is in fact found already in Demetrius' *De elocutione* 282–94, and one example is particularly relevant to our enquiry (291):

> Words are often used with equivocal meaning. If anyone
> wishes to practice this art and to deal in censures which seem
> unintentional hits, he has an example ready to his hand in the
> passage of Aeschines about Telauges. Almost the entire account
> of Telauges will leave one puzzled as to whether it is eulogy or
> satire. This ambiguous way of speaking, although not irony, yet
> has a suggestion of irony.

---

[21] Quint. 9.2.65–6 (genus) in quo per quandam suspicionem quod non dicimus accipi volumus, non utique contrarium, ut in εἰρωνείᾳ, sed aliud latens et auditori quasi inveniendum ... Eius triplex usus est: unus si dicere palam parum tutum est, alter si non decet, tertius qui venustatis modo gratia adhibetur et ipsa novitate ac varietate magis quam si relatio sit recta delectat.

[22] Ahl (1984).

The topic seems to have interested Virgil's friend Philodemus.[23] More importantly, it had made the transition into the rhetorical Latin handbooks before the birth of Virgil, who would have studied and applied it during his rhetorical training in Milan (or wherever he studied), in a period where the dangers of speaking openly will have been demonstrated frequently enough. For Greek *emphasis* the *Rhetorica ad Herennium* gives Latin *significatio*, a term which shifts the focalization from passive to active, from reader to author or speaker: authorial intention is suggested, with the producer creating the sign, a phenomenon only implied in the figure of *emphasis*:

> *Significatio* is the figure which leaves more to be suspected than
> has been specified in the speech. It is produced by hyperbole,
> ambiguity, logical consequence, aposiopesis, and analogy.[24]

So far from being a preoccupation of modern scholars, in the view of ancient theoreticians *emphasis*, Latin *significatio*, is a reality of ancient rhetorical theory and practice, a virtue of speech and a figure to be cultivated. As early as Aristotle, deliberate and intended ambiguity is implicitly a feature of the orator's "speaking correct Greek" (ἑλλη-νίζειν).[25] With reference to Virgil, it is difficult to see why "these terms should be the scholar's last resort, not the first."[26]

While it is true that the existence of a rhetorical theory, even if it has been applied to poetic theory, will not prove the existence of a phenomenon in poetry, nevertheless, in a context in which critics resistant to forms of ambiguity forbid us to find it on the grounds that

---

[23] Philodemus, Περὶ ποιημάτων 5.30.6–12 Mangoni ἡ δὲ σύνθεσις λέξεως ἐναργῶς καὶ ἐμφα-τικῶς τὴν ὑποτεταγμένην διάνοιαν [σ]ημαίνουσα{ν} κοι[ν]ή [γ᾽ ἐσ]τι καὶ λόγου παντὸς ἀρετή{ς} "the composition of words which signifies the underlying thought vividly and forcefully/allusively is something universal and a virtue of every discourse." On this difficult sentence, and for the possible ways of taking ἐμφατικῶς, see Gaines (1982) 77–8; with scepticism from Rutherford (1988) 128–9. Asmis (1992) 402–3 argues that ἐνάργεια and ἔμφασις are opposite and complementary terms, referring alternately to vividness and allusiveness, particularly characteristic of the metaphorical quality of poetry – a position allowed by Mangoni (1993) 302–3. On the relationship of Virgil and his group with Philodemus, see Gigante (1989), (1990).

[24] *Rhet. ad Her.* 4.67 *significatio est res quae plus in suspicione relinquit quam positum est in oratione. ea fit per exsuperationem, ambiguum, consequentiam, abscisionem, similitudinem.* The parallel with Demetrius *De eloq.* 286 suggests that *ambiguum* more closely resembles *emphasis*, while that with Quintilian approximates *emphasis* to *significatio*.

[25] Aristot., *Rhet.* 1407a19.

[26] Galinsky (1991) 478.

the "ancients" did not deal in such matters, it is worth noting the presence of those phenomena in the texts that would have been represented in the educational curriculum of the poet in question. Moreover, Virgil and Quintilian are part of the same world, and Virgil's genius in controlling all the tools of ancient rhetoric needs no argument.[27] It is my assumption throughout that the poetry of Virgil came into being under the first of Quintilian's three circumstances, when a poet of genius operates in a time of political upheaval and uncertainty, and in the context of political danger – again, in Quintilian's words, when "speaking openly is unsafe."

Aulus Gellius preserves an interesting exchange on the subject of intended ambiguity. In discussing the views of Chrysippus and Diodorus, he has the former, an ancient deconstructionist of sorts, claiming that every word is ambiguous, since two or more meanings can be taken away from the same word. Diodorus counters that no word is ambiguous, since no word should be perceived with a meaning different from that intended by the speaker. If that does occur then the issue has to do with obscurity rather than ambiguity. The nature of an ambiguous word ought to be such that the person who uttered it uttered two or more things. But nobody who perceives himself to be saying one thing utters two or more things.[28] That Diodorus can argue thus is clear evidence that Chrysippus and others subscribe to a theory of fully intended ambiguity. This obviously brings up all sorts of issues, but it will be useful throughout to assume a text's intended ambiguity or *emphasis*. As G. B. Conte has put it:[29]

> Certainly it will be difficult, in some cases very difficult, to
> rediscover the true intention of the texts. But without the
> tension that drives us to seek an original intention in the
> literary work, our very relation to these works loses any real
> interest. I see no other protection from the arbitrary incursions
> of many modern interpreters, who may be eager readers but
> whose views are often unconsciously alien to the original
> historical contexts and cultural codes.

---

[27] *Vita Donati* claims (50–3) that he even carried out a court case, though his voice was not up to the job. See Horsfall (1995) 9 on Virgil's oratorical training.

[28] Gellius 11.12.

[29] Conte (1994) 3.

The hidden quality of much of Virgilian ideology is in my view intended (cf. *quod . . . accipi volumus*, in Quintilian's Latin, where the producer of meaning is the subject). At least it is intended on the atomic level of the individual word, phrase and so on. The full global effect of Virgil's poetry, and the force of the accumulation of these utterances, is perhaps a different matter, and may have to do with its acquiring a momentum and dimension that went even beyond those intentions. That full meaning will always be what we construct, but its building blocks are identifiable and susceptible to philological hermeneutics. This global effect is I think what Ralph Johnson, one of Virgil's finest readers, meant when he wrote: "In the *Aeneid* the extreme discrepancy between artistic method and ethical dilemma returns and widens and produces a heartbreaking, disconsolate poem that is too big for poetry, that cannot be constrained by the limits of art and explodes its frame."[30]

Roman boys and men reading Virgil

One refuge of the Augustan reader has always been to invoke "modern sensibility," an impulse, it is claimed, that leads *other* readers to emotions that do not exist in the world before Christ, and to "misread" Virgil under the influence of those emotions. As J. Griffin, standing back from the issue, put it: "Some are tempted to read the *Aeneid* simply as endorsing our modern emotions; others, to dismiss as anachronistic the idea that Virgil expressed any reservations about empire at all."[31]

In Virgilian criticism, "modern" is code for "wrong," generally referring to oppositional readers of Virgil, and of his view of principate, empire and civilization. Such an attitude fails to take into account that all reading is a construction, and we will continuously address the pervasively modern construction that lies at the heart of Augustan readings later on. While we need not think of Dido committing a Christian sin, nor hold Aeneas to the standards of Christ, it is equally a critical shortcoming in terms of the Virgilian genius, and

---

[30] Johnson (1981) 50.
[31] Griffin (1984) 213. For similar distancing see Harrison (1990) xxi: "Some modern readers, more mindful of the darker side of great achievements, have taken a different view."

of Greco-Roman social and philosophical realities, to deny to this poet a complex range of emotional responses on such issues.

H. P. Stahl suggests that Virgil's outlook may be closer to that of the twelfth-century Greek heroic code (whatever that looked like).[32] Why is that any more "objective" or likely than suggesting it is closer to possible outlooks in post-Civil War or post-Vietnam America, or between-the-wars Europe, ages afflicted by demonstrably parallel disasters, and, like the late Roman republic, with civil discord, political upheaval and private and public loss in their immediate experiences? And just as Greco-Roman rhetorical theory allows intentional authorial ambiguity, so, prima facie, does it imply that diverse readings can coexist. Does the *Iliad* simply depict the hero's fame in killing and disfiguring his enemies or practicing human sacrifice? Even if we argue that it does, is that likely to have much to do with a culture (late Republican Rome) whose ethical systems (Stoicism in particular) resemble much more the Christianity that they helped shape than the Homeric code which the *Aeneid* adapts to a very different culture?[33] Stahl again: "The reader (I am not here thinking of the Homeric or Vergilian scholar of the twentieth century AD, but rather of the Roman boy or man who, in the new national epic, learns to admire his emperor's ancestor ...)"; as if that reader were any easier to construct, or had one face. Did a "Roman man" such as Ovid really learn such admiration through the *Aeneid*?

A well-known passage from the Suetonian *Life* (*Vit. Verg.* 44) preserves a valuable if disputed piece of information:

> M. Vipsanius a Maecenate eum suppositum appellabat novae
> cacozeliae repertorem, non tumidae nec exilis, sed ex
> communibus verbis atque ideo latentis.

> Marcus Vipsanius used to call him bastard of Maecenas and
> discoverer of an affected style, not overblown or understated,
> but coming from everyday words and therefore of hidden
> nature.

Although the matter has been much disputed, my own view, like that of others, is that the disgruntled individual is indeed M. Vipsanius

---

[32] Stahl (1990) 181.

[33] Haarhof (1949) 30ff. (viz. 34) on the relation of Stoicism and Calvinism (and on Christianity in general).

Agrippa, a contemporary reader of Virgil who surely read the "new national epic." And even if, following H. Jocelyn, we assume the reaction is from an otherwise unknown Vipranius of the MSS, here we have the reader response of a contemporary Roman "boy or man." We cannot be sure of the precise sense of *cacozelia* here, beyond its vague and broad meaning of "affectation."[34] But Quintilian's definition is of interest: "a stylistic corruption consisting of the use of improper diction, redundancies, obscurity of meaning, feeble arrangement, or a childish straining for synonym or ambiguity."[35] The language is close to that describing *emphasis*, and what Agrippa or Vipranius/Vipsanius seems to object to is the hidden meaning (*latentis*) that occurs through this "defective" use of everyday words (*ex communibus verbis*). Could Augustus' friend and general have had in mind a phrase such as *aurea condet saecula* – everyday words indeed, but difficult and covert when so combined?

I have chosen not to treat Lactantius and Augustine, whose well-known responses to the *Aeneid* are strong Christian readings, particularly the reaction to Aeneas' (or Virgil's) failure of compassion at the end of the poem. At the same time I fully recognize that such Christian readings are embedded in any number of other readings, Augustan or otherwise, that I will be engaging or practicing.[36] In what follows, I have assumed, without, I hope, falling victim to demonstrable and egregious anachronism, that most of the spiritual and emotional responses to the world that are accessible to us were also accessible to Virgil. I take as my justification the closing words of K. W. Gransden's *Virgil's Iliad*:

> The modern reader may invest Aeneas with a greater range of
> insight and choice than he could have possessed for his creator,
> and may also create an implied author with access to value-
> systems which lie in fact beyond the limits of the poem and of
> the pagan world. Yet the reader, importing these, is not, save in
> the narrowest and most scholastic sense, "misinterpreting" the
> *Aeneid*. Indeed, *he may be uncovering a more significant text*, one

---

[34] Cf. Görler, *EV*, s.v. *cacozelia*. Also Jocelyn (1979); Horsfall (1995) 225–6; White (1993) 265, n. 55.

[35] Quintilian 8.3.57 *corrupta oratio in verbis maxime impropriis, redundantibus, comprehensione obscura, compositione fracta, vocum similium aut ambiguarum puerili captatione consistit.*

[36] My reasons here have to do with the fact that these two are ultimately using Virgil for Christian exegesis, rather than aiming at Virgilian exegesis.

that may be related to a greater range of insights into history and humanity.[37] [emphasis provided]

In the final analysis, modernity may in fact coincide with antiquity, for Gransden seems to be prescribing attention precisely to the *Ad Herennium*'s *significatio*, to finding, along with Quintilian and against the discouragement of modern critics that "other meaning which lies hidden waiting to be discovered by the reader" (9.2.65 *aliud latens et auditori quasi inveniendum*).

Writing or reading ambiguity?

In an important article that best lays out the theoretical aspects of Virgilian ambiguity, and situates investigation of it not so much in the theory of antiquity, but rather in that of Empson, New Criticism and post-structuralist criticism, C. Martindale poses and explores the central question "Is the uncertainty of a meaning in the author's control, or in the reader's?"[38] From the perspective of deconstruction in particular, the question and the distinction may not matter much, though Martindale never quite says that. And he is surely right in saying (120) that "texts may, or may not, be 'undecidable,' in a post-structuralist sense, but they are not uninterpretable." And in interpreting ambiguity, I will, for the sake of being able to conduct critical discourse at all, assume the ambiguity is not a result of linguistic accident, but is, much like the intertextual references, part of the poet's artistry. Here I find myself most sympathetic with C. Perkell, who well applies the reception criticism of Stanley Fish to Virgilian ambiguity.[39] Specific instances of ambiguity attain canonical status, as the shared experience of such ambiguity (are they Dido's or Aeneas' tears at *Aeneid* 4.449?)[40] tends to reify it – as does the continual attempt to remove it. At that point the ambiguity is implicitly authorial as much as it is reader-driven.

Finally, as we shall see in the chapters ahead, the number of ambiguities that attach to moments in this poet when the issues of power, loyalty, civilization and the like are at stake forces the reader back to Quintilian's third category and at least to the likelihood of authorially centered political ambiguity.

---

[37] Gransden (1984) 217.   [38] Martindale (1993b) 120–1.   [39] Perkell (1994).
[40] On this, see Martindale (1993b) 120–1.

Fighting in the captain's tower:

(1) What *is* a Classic?

The assumption of classicism has always been the dominant mode of Virgilian criticism, long before T. S. Eliot's 1944 Presidential Address to the Virgil Society set that assumption in stone. That is what happens when a poet is taught in his own lifetime and when his particular style attains a normative status, and becomes a sort of cultural, linguistic and even religious *koine*. From Servius and before him critics have tended to monumentalize Virgil. He is so well known, in part because his epic so early became the central literary icon of Augustanism. But from many perspectives he is stranger and less classical even in the *Aeneid* than he came to be, just as Shakespeare was stranger than he has come to be through four centuries of performance, reading and teaching.[41] A school text, which is what Virgil has been from the beginning, will of necessity establish its own diachronic classicism, which may well be at odds with the synchronic anti-classicism inherent in the realities of its composition.

The strangeness of Virgil, his *audacia*, as he put it, may be related to his Callimachean and Alexandrian (rather than his classical) essence. It is not coincidental that resistance to accepting the Callimacheanism of Virgil is usually coupled with promotion of its classicism and insistence on its optimistic Augustanism. E. Fantham reveals a romanticist core when she writes: "It is no small paradox that [Thomas] praises Vergil so often as 'elegant' and 'artful' yet reads Vergil's recognition of hardship and sorrow as an almost bitter pessimism not just about nature but about human nature."[42] Why is that a paradox? Of what other great artist do we insist on optimism about human nature? And whence the assumption that elegance and artfulness, stylistic phenomena, must be accompanied by optimism? It is surely the perceived, and required, classicism of Virgil, along with the ultimate impact of Augustus on Europe, that leads to such an insistence. The *Aeneid* can be as odd and as aware of its artifice as a poem like Ca-

---

[41] See Bloom (1994) 4 "One mark of an originality that can win canonical status for a literary work is a strangeness that we either never altogether assimilate, or that becomes such a given that we are blinded to its idiosyncracies."

[42] Fantham (1991) 167.

tullus 63 or 64; that awareness may be camouflaged by the traditional
genre of the poem, but it constantly comes through, and subverts the
"sublime" veneer of the poem. For a critic such as G. O. Hutchinson,
Virgil in the *Aeneid* is engaged in a "continuous endeavour for extremes of ὕψος, of intensity, elevation, sublimity," with the result that
"the essential nature of the poem forces out the effects which characterize Hellenistic poetry."[43] And so, in a long chapter on the reception of Hellenistic poetry in Rome, Virgil's poem receives only
one page. I would argue on the contrary that the expectation of
sublimity makes its disruption all the more powerful when that
occurs. This holds in obvious places, with the foundation poetry of
Aeneid 3 or the transformation of ships to nymphs (*Aen.* 9.77–122), at
which point our classicizing or sublimizing traditions cry out "lapse!"
or "unfinished!", but it seems to me true throughout. Particularly
with Virgil's ideology, the critical effort has been towards stabilizing
and classicizing, because the *Aeneid* in particular has had to stand for
Rome, and Rome is the cultural anchor of Europe. Bakhtin sub-
scribes to this reception myth when he asserts, as a way of prioritizing
the novel as the genre of dialogue and resistance, that epic is a genre
in which only the voice of the dominant culture is heard.[44] That is
easily refuted by any number of models, but it is the received view of
epic and of Virgilian epic in particular, and it needs constantly to be
tested. On the levels of style, syntax, words, metrics – and politics –
Virgil tends to be viewed as normative, as being at the heart of the
"classical" Augustan age, although recent scholarship has contested
this status.[45] Normativity is constructed by familiarization, classicism is
a notion that works backwards, is diachronic and retrospective, for
the subsequent tradition could only deal with Virgil by anchoring
him in some fashion, by back-forming classicism onto him.

W. R. Johnson has written of a certain body of poetry in the
Western tradition that he calls "counter-classical," poetry that

> has been too frequently misjudged both as to its nature and to
> its quality by critics whose temperaments and training lead
> them to require of it things it does not offer. This kind of

[43] Hutchinson (1988) 328–9.
[44] Bakhtin (1981) 3–40; see also Watkins (1995) 5.
[45] See Conte (1993) for good instances of the strangeness of Virgil's Latinity; also Horsfall (1995) 225–31; and now O'Hara (1997) 241–58.

poetry is created not to refute the moral experience that
classical poetry reveals but to view that moral experience in
another way. Counter-classical poetry tends to underline
possibilities of disharmony even as classical poetry tends to
underline possibilities of harmony; where classical poetry
attempts affirmations of man's capacities or his perfectibility or
his nearness to God, counter-classical poetry attempts to stress
man's weakness and his limitations; baldly, Homer and Pindar
tend to show us, in quite different ways, human beings who
have regained their health or who are naturally healthy or who
are beyond health or sickness; Ovid and Horace tend to show
us, in quite different ways, human beings who may yet be
saved.[46]

It is telling that Johnson, who has read so well beyond Virgil's classicism, does not adduce Virgil on either side of this divide. His silence
implicitly situates Virgil in the gap between classical and counter-
classical. Indeed, it could be argued that all poetry contains the seeds
for questioning the values that the classical is thought to uphold, and
there is, I think, a more fundamental question that needs to be asked,
namely whether the notion of "classical" is not one that emerges
from a particular set of interpretations, and, like all interpretation, is
really a matter of reception more than anything else.

It is worth citing Eliot's assumptions about the conditions of
Virgil's writing, assumptions which led him to see the *Aeneid* as the
classic *par excellence*: "We expect the language to approach maturity at
the moment when men have a critical sense of the past, a confidence
in the present, and no conscious doubt of the future."[47] All but the
first of these conditions is problematic for Virgil and for the time of
Virgil's writing, but Eliot is just expressing a received and entrenched
view of anachronistic Augustanism, unsullied by the realities of the
years in which Virgil was formed and wrote, an Augustanism created
long after the death of Virgil. It is significant that Eliot's essay appealed to the likes of Hans Oppermann, who published a translation
of it along with other exclusively German, and ideologically interesting, articles in his 1963 "Wege der Forschung" volume on Virgil –
a volume we shall explore in Chapter 7.

---

[46] Johnson (1970) 126.
[47] Eliot in Kermode (1975) 119. For a recent view of Eliot on Virgil, more sympathetic to
the former's engagement than mine, see Kennedy (1995) 73–94.

Eliot's chief focus on the text of Virgil has to do with a passage whose interpretation is far from closed (123):

> But I have always thought the meeting of Aeneas with the
> shade of Dido, in Book VI, not only one of the most poignant,
> but one of the most civilized passages in poetry ... The point,
> it seems to me, is not that Dido is unforgiving – though it is
> important that, instead of railing at him, she merely snubs him
> – perhaps the most telling snub in all poetry; what matters most
> is that Aeneas does not forgive himself – and this, significantly,
> in spite of the fact of which he is well aware, that all that
> he has done has been in compliance with destiny, or in
> consequence of the machinations of gods who are themselves,
> we feel, only instruments of a greater inscrutable power ...

That sounds civilized, as suits a classical, mature poem, but what happens when we look to Virgilian composition in these very lines? Virgil here reworks a mock-epic line of Catullus, a line spoken by a lock of hair and used by Aeneas precisely at the moment when we expect his greatest maturity. Aeneas' famous disclaimer to the shade of Dido "unwillingly, queen, did I quit your shore" (*Aen.* 6.460 *invitus, regina, tuo de litore cessi*) famously invokes the lock's amusing disclaimer to Berenice in Catullus 66.39: "unwillingly, queen, did I quit the top of your head" *invita, o regina, tuo de vertice cessi*. The intertext, once activated, subverts and explodes the maturity and classicism desiderated by Eliot, who was unaware of it. And no amount of hermeneutical activity has been able to remove this powerful subversion. It is indeed in the activation of intertextuality, particularly Hellenistic and neoteric intertextuality, that the *Aeneid*'s evasion and subversion of its own potential classicism is most observable.[48] This may help to explain the relationship between the Augustan reading and resistance to the presence of Hellenistic intertexts.

Graves, of course, more troubled by tyranny as he was, threw Virgil out with Augustus, dismissing him as the toady that he would be from the perspective of Syme's Augustus.[49] But between Eliot and

---

[48] As, for instance, when the Polyphemus of *Aen.* 3.641–83 functions not simply in a Homeric tradition, but is also recognizably informed by the romance Polyphemus of Theocritus, and the adaptation of that figure into *Ecl.* 2's Corydon; cf. Thomas (1996) 239–41.

[49] Graves (1962).

Graves there is a middle ground, which involves examining the very status of Virgil as an Augustan poet. For constructions of Virgil's classicism and his Augustanism are inextricably involved, and subversion of one disrupts the other. The Augustan element was always there, and to that extent Virgil the poet is no subversive: the Augustan triumphs, and, like Augustus, that is all that is left standing at the end of the day, but subversion comes by recognition of the other possibilities present in that triumph.

(2) Virgil as monument

In G. B. Conte's *Latin Literature. A History*, under the subtitle "The overthrow of the epic genre" (443) we find reference to the Roman epic before Lucan as "a monument erected to the glories of the state and its armies." And on the next page, on Lucan and the *Aeneid*:

> Lucan seems to propose a systematic refutation of the model
> by virtually overturning its assertions, a polemical (or
> "antiphrastic," as it has been called) rehandling of Virgilian
> expressions and situations. This new type of allusiveness is
> sustained by a tone of resentful *indignatio* towards the model. It
> is as if Virgil had perpetrated a deception in the *Aeneid*, covering
> in a veil of mystification the end of Roman liberty and the
> transformation of the old Republic into a tyranny. Lucan
> seems to set himself the task of unmasking the deception ...

Lucan as Robert Graves, it seems. No examples are given, and we shall return to the question of the *nature* or *interpretation* of Lucan's Virgilian intertextuality. The fact is that it becomes necessary for critics to stabilize, monumentalize, and broadly characterize the ideology of the model, in order that the subversion by the later poet may be explored. For the scholar of Ovid or Lucan in particular, having an ideologically ambiguous Virgil would only complicate the task at hand. But the reality is that the seeds of subversion are already inherent in that text, which makes the relationships these poets have to Virgil much less simple and simply confrontational, potentially more collaborative.

The view of Virgil as Classic is for many endemic and unquestioned: Averil Cameron writes in the introduction to an essay by Maria Wyke on Roman elegy: "Reading the Roman elegists ... lets us think the Romans are like us, not all serious, grand and noble like Virgil, but prone to romantic passion, liable to make mistakes, even rather absurd."[50] Let us forget about Virgil, of whom (as of Propertius) we know little or nothing, but let us think of the Virgilian Aeneas: Cameron's "prone to romantic passion, liable to make mistakes, even rather absurd" fits pretty well, I would say. J. Farrell has observed of Ovid's *Metamorphoses*: "We cannot comfortably situate the poem in the epic canon alongside the *Iliad* and the *Aeneid*. This judgment reflects not on the quality of the *Metamorphoses*, but on its manifold departures from the epic norm which the *Iliad* and the *Aeneid* much more nearly represent."[51] This is obviously true on the diachronic level, but to imply that the *Aeneid*, from a synchronic perspective, is part of a normative "epic canon" is to miss the possibility of its fundamental departure from, and subversion of the Homeric model, the possibility, again, of its strangeness.[52]

F. M. Ahl is one of the very few scholars to have explored post-Virgilian ambivalence or hostility towards authority without completely implicating the Virgilian text in that authority: "Even if, as I believe, Vergil's vision of Rome, Aeneas, and Augustus is highly ambivalent, the fact remains that those hostile to the Caesars might well be angered at even the remotest suggestion that Rome and the Caesars could be reconciled."[53] This is the space, between open hostility and pure propaganda, that has always been the site of the critical struggle for the hearts and minds of the reader.

(3) The organization of opinion

There has been a curious phenomenon at work in the last decade or so, consisting of generally Augustan readings of Virgil, which, in the same breath that they respond to the non-Augustans, indulge in rhetorical efforts to terminate such inquiries.[54] In a review of J. J. O'Hara, A. Schiesaro notes:

---

[50] Cameron (1989) 111.
[51] Farrell (1982) 235–68.
[52] The Homerist will reply that the Virgilian critic likewise stabilizes his poems, most notably in assuming a consistent "epic code", recreated or subverted by the Virgilian text.
[53] Ahl (1976) 64–7.
[54] The chief target has been Lyne (1987), a work that holds up well under the barrage.

"Pessimistic" criticism had a seminal function when it set out to disrupt the status quo, but additional statements and expansions of this position sometimes appear less compelling now that such criticism has attained so much influence, especially in this country [he refers to the US]. There is no doubt that an escape from the quandaries of "optimism" vs. "pessimism" is long overdue, and this should probably entail no longer asking of Virgil the same set of questions and readily answering them along well-worn predictable methodological lines. More can be said about Virgil than the contrast between "pessimists" and "optimists" seems to suggest, and this should not necessarily be construed as a prescription for bland compromise.[55]

Similarly, D. P. Fowler, in a review of a different book:

The influence of the American approach to Vergilian scholarship is undoubtedly waning and many would like to see English scholarship moving closer to the traditional German approach of scholars like Buchheit and Wlosok (but not Suerbaum [too American?]).[56]

If "many would like to see" English scholarship moving closer to German, they should help it to do so; and if "more can be said about Virgil" than those interested in ideology are saying (and that is obviously true), why not go out and say it? We will return to Wlosok later in this book; she serves a particular function in the rhetoric of the Augustans, as a post-war German (woman) whose voice validates and affirms the German Augustan Virgil of an earlier generation.

Again, C. Martindale, in an article on ambiguity in Virgil, can write "the ambiguity of the *Aeneid* is becoming a somewhat tired trope,"[57] as he looks for a post-Cold War "end of history": Virgil tied to "the dissipations of the contemporary European scene" – which may however look all too much like the familiar "European scenes," whose intersection with Virgil we shall explore in Chapters 7 and 8. He quotes the similar view of D. Feeney: "Asserted hope, with an undertone of pathos; or stressed pathos, with faint background hope – such, in the bluntest terms, are the poles revolving around which mainstream criticism of the *Aeneid* appears to be stuck; we may at

[55] Schiesaro (1983) 265. [56] Fowler (1991) 92. [57] Martindale (1993b) 131.

least be confident that they will be different poles in thirty years time."[58] Likewise, K. Galinsky constantly inveighs against "the inane 'optimism vs. pessimism' sobriquet," while insisting that we feel absolutely comfortable (optimistic?) about the end, or any other part of Virgil's poem, and the justice of its hero's actions.

In all of this there seems to be a curious obliviousness of the fact that critics, while wishing away the topic, in the process engage that very topic, along with its entourage of controversies, and in fully partisan fashion but almost unconsciously so, precisely because of unquestioned assumptions about Virgil's classical and Augustan status. So P. Hardie, one of the most intelligent and prolific Virgilian critics of recent years, who vacillates between hard and soft Augustanism, can write:

> Among twentieth-century critics, attention to the conflict between the pressure to totalize, to finalize, and the pull to leave endings open has concentrated on the political and historical aspects of the *Aeneid*'s epic "definitions," whence the monotonously reductive debate about whether Virgil was really for or against Augustus.[59]

But then on the very same page the same critic can claim that

> Virgil's peculiar construction of an ideology for the present day through the narration of the legendary past attempts to forge a continuity, even identity, between the times of narrated events and narrating. This strategy of course must highlight the vast processes of change that lead from past to present; Virgil's self-imposed task, breathtakingly, is then to persuade us that with Augustus those processes are brought to a conclusion. The poetic symbol of this immobilization of history which, if successful, would indeed make of the *Aeneid* the final epic, is the Golden Age... In mythological terms the singular achievement of Augustus is to realize a repetition of the Golden Age, that dream of primitive plenitude that was forever unattainable in the present until Virgil ran time backwards in the fourth *Eclogue*.

---

[58] Feeney (1988).   [59] Hardie (1993) 2.

But the belief that Virgil (Virgil, not Anchises) and the *Aeneid* enact Augustus' restoration of the golden age is precisely the Augustan orthodoxy, and it is an act of interpretation presenting itself as a fact, and as an alternative to what it calls the "monotonously reductive debate about whether Virgil was really for or against Augustus." And finally, the reality is that it is the "optimistic" reduction that keeps asserting itself, and keeps producing extensive new bibliography. Just from the last few years we have an array of intensely ideological works to choose from, all pursuing various strategies to restore the Augustan reception, all explictly or implicitly responding to the oppositional readings of the last generation.[60]

While it is true that the proposing of intended ambiguity (ἔμφασις) is not in itself necessarily a sophisticated form of criticism (any more than is the investigation of any other rhetorical figure), it is at least equally the case that the suppression and denial of ambiguity, particularly when carried out by critics who have a stake in that denial (i.e. strong Augustan readers), is likewise an unsophisticated critical act, and in the case of Virgil it is generally an act of positivism that attempts to get back to a world that just don't exist, a world in which poetic language is made to be simple, and the significance carried by it monolithic. When the text in question is that of Virgil, the stakes seem to have been particularly high, the anger directed at the ambiguity hunters particularly extreme. It is hard to find parallel reactions to criticism that sees ambiguity in the plays of Sophocles or Aristophanes or the verses of Ovid or Lucan. This book will examine the attempts to stabilize, speculate about the cultural and ideological impulses of the stabilizers, and in the process further suggest both the futility of the attempt and the ways in which it falls short as criticism, and at the same time reveals precisely that the text's Augustan foundation is unstable.

Does the expression of ambivalence diminish the poet? Is doubt and uncertainty less magnificent, less important, less creative than encomium and confidence? Obviously not in the eyes of another poet, who saw the power of the Virgilian vision:

---

[60] For example, Galinsky (1996), Cramer, (1998), Jenkyns (1998), Morgan (1999), to name just four books from the last four years. Indispensable as an exposé of some of this writing is Henderson (1998).

Thou majestic in thy sadness
at the doubtful doom of human kind

It is the need to heroize princes that leads to critical suppression of
that power, and to princes, specifically to the archetypal prince of
Europe, we now should turn.

1

Virgil and Augustus

It is no easy thing to write against one who has the power to proscribe.

POLLIO IN MACROBIUS, Saturnalia 2.4.21

Deeds were prosecuted, words went unpunished.

TACITUS, Annals 1.72 (of conditions
throughout the lifetime of Virgil)

CAESAR: Welcome to Caesar, Virgil! Caesar and Virgil
Shall differ but in sound; to Caesar, Virgil,
Of his expressed greatness, shall be made
A second sirname, and to Virgil, Caesar.
Where are thy famous Aeneids? do us grace
To let us see, and surfeit on their sight.

BEN JONSON, Poetaster

Much that has recently been written about Augustus is simply panegyric, whether ingenuous or edifying. Yet it is not necessary to praise political success, or to idealize the men who win wealth and honours through civil war.

R. SYME, The Roman Revolution (1939) pref.

Critics and Augustus

Duncan Kennedy captures the issue well: "Critics' responses to Augustan poetry are a measure of the *continuing* capacity of Augustan ideology to determine its reception."[1] In the case of Virgil that results in certain necessary assumptions about the poet's view of the *princeps*. So Brooks Otis, though he saw a troubling side to Virgil's Augustan

---

[1] Kennedy (1992) 41.

"propaganda," as he calls it, preserves the following core in his vision of the poet:

> First of all, it seems quite plain that Virgil was himself a
> convinced Augustan. He was clearly inspired by his theme: he
> believed in his own "ideology." He really saw in Augustus the
> type of man who could bring peace out of fratricidal war, order
> from anarchy, self-control from selfish passion, in a sense, an
> "age of gold" from an age of iron. He also saw in Rome the
> paradigm and goal of all historical activity, in Roman *pietas*,
> *virtus*, and *consilium* the only hope of peace and social order, of
> humane behaviour associated with strong government. (Otis
> [1995] 2)

An updated and similar view of the quality of Augustus as a leader implies that Franklin D. Roosevelt and John F. Kennedy may be seen as parallel figures.[2] The invocation of Democratic political heroes, even though they are slightly tarnished, has a preemptive feel to it, and begs a variety of questions.

My concern here will be rather with the ways in which Augustus, or the interpretation and reception of Augustus by Roman historians, fundamentally conditioned by European thinking about contemporary political rulers, has problematized Virgilian criticism. In opposition both to unexamined generalizations about Virgil's encomiastic relationship with Augustus, and to unevidenced assumptions about what Virgil thought about the achievement of the *princeps*, I will look to the role Octavian and then Augustus plays in the poetry of Virgil, as well as to the little evidence we have on their relationship. Throughout I will be challenging, and suggesting a revision of, the view that Virgil is an "Augustan" poet in any sense that has to do with his speaking for the régime, or even with systematically supporting the careful creation of image that Augustus so successfully carried out.

The present study attempts to do what is extremely difficult: to subordinate Augustus to Virgil, to avoid assumptions about Virgil's place in Augustan Rome, and to look more at his creation of images, and at the primacy of those images before they became subordinated to ideas of Augustus, and in that process were subtly altered, selected

---

[2] Galinsky (1996) 18–20.

or otherwise applied. What I am doing would be more surprising were it not for the revolutionary work of Peter White.[3] In a typically understated way, he observes, and demonstrates, the following (p. 99):

> While there may yet be evidence which will bear the inter-
> pretation that Augustus groomed poets to be publicists for his
> régime, it must be conceded that no such interpretation had
> been formulated by the end of the classical period [as evidenced
> by the writings of Dio, Tacitus and Suetonius].

White further argues that "it is the writers themselves who crowd forward with panegyrics, a situation parallel to that which Tacitus discerned among writers of imperial history." Here we will part company to some extent, for in the case of Virgil I will claim that the "panegyric" is muted, and has a particular function within the poet's system of cultural poetics.

What, first of all, do we know of the period in which Virgil wrote, roughly speaking, the period in which the voices of Caesar and Cicero have fallen silent, before the time of Velleius, and in a world where Livy's contemporary history is available only in epitome? Ronald Syme talks of the difficulty of ascertaining how contemporary Romans, of precisely these years, will have viewed the fall of the republic, and where blame will have been assigned:[4]

> The written history of the time has vanished utterly, no
> political speech survives, no pamphlet, no memoirs. Compared
> with what went before and what came after, the Age of
> Augustus acquires the paradoxical dignity of an obscure and
> highly controversial period. Recourse must be had to official
> documents – with due caution; to the Augustan poets – again
> with due caution. And silence itself will be revealing. Important
> truths are often awkward truths, to be covered and disguised,
> from fear, from complicity, or for comfort.

The problem here, of course, is that such a use of literary "sources" is likely to generate at the same time the historical and biographical preconditions with which we then approach the literary text, part of which has been used to establish the historical "truth." If in that process the critical procedures are not plausible, the results for the

---

[3] White (1993).   [4] Syme (1950) 4.

27

critic may be vitiated, but they may at the same time be hard to shake, since they have become part of the otherwise unrecoverable historical infrastructure.

A simple example: Z. Yavetz, echoing Syme, states that Augustus "gradually but consistently ... distanced himself from the memory of Julius Caesar."[5] That is presented as an historical fact, it has weight and plausibility and it paints an immediate and interesting personal, political and historical picture. The evidence? "Virgil could put the major part of the blame for the outbreak of civil war on Caesar without worry." What sort of worry? There is no awareness, at least none is shown, of the fact that it is Caesar's ancestor Anchises, the father of Aeneas, not "Virgil" (and there is at least potentially a difference) who addresses and admonishes his own descendant; nor does Yavetz even refer to the Virgilian lines in question (*Aen.* 6.834–5 *tuque prior, tu parce, genus qui ducis Olympo,* | *proice tela manu, sanguis meus,* "and you first, you have clemency who trace your line from Olympus, throw down your weapons from your hand, blood of my own"), lines which Yavetz does not actually cite, and which he takes in a sense almost *opposite* to the Latin, as if Anchises had said "you were the first to hurl your weapons"; and finally there is a further implication that Virgil would need clearance to have Anchises say such a thing, and that his having done so allows us to formulate a piece of official Augustan policy.[6]

This is how Virgil has been used and abused, again and again, as a historical source in the absence of other documents. In the process, something happens to the poetry of Virgil that makes it secondary to the pseudo-facts it is used to create. What is needed is a constant questioning of the interpretation that has accompanied such uses of "evidence." In short, it would be difficult to imagine an author who has been so consistently identified with the régime in which part of his corpus is written, or whose work has been so casually used as a virtual manifesto for that régime, with so little close attention to what is actually written, who is speaking it, and what the context is. That this occurs in the case of the *Aeneid*, a poem that is at the same time the most influential artistic creation in European literature, is surely one of the great paradoxes of literary history. It is as if one attributed

---

[5] Yavetz (1990) 34.
[6] See White (1988) for another view of the "distance" from Julius Caesar.

misogynism to Euripides on the basis of *Medea* 408–9 (γυναῖκες, εἰς μὲν ἐσθλ' ἀμηχανώταται,|κακῶν δὲ πάντων τέκτονες σοφώταται, "women, utterly resourceless with regard to good, but most skillful architects of every evil"), ignoring the fact that the speaker is Medea herself, on the point of constructing a plan to kill her children.[7] It will be a given throughout these pages that any critical conclusion that infers authorial intention or ideological belief from character speech will be at least potentially open to scepticism.

One of the additional results of approaching poetry with the primary aim of ascertaining historical facts is that there will be no room for ambiguity, a phenomenon the historian will obviously have little interest in identifying or nurturing. The text must be stabilized, turned into a source, which thereby attains evidentiary status: ambiguity would disrupt that process and taint the evidence. The Servian commentary preserves early attempts to establish the normative, Augustan nature of the poem: "the intention of Virgil is to imitate Homer and praise Augustus through his ancestors" (ad *Aen.* 1. *prooem.* "intentio Vergilii haec est, Homerum imitari et Augustum laudare a parentibus"). Once that "fact" is established, certain critical consequences ensue, consequences which are still very much part of our critical heritage, fathered onto Virgil and hard to dislodge.

Some of S. Harrison's remarks in his study of *Aeneid* 10 suggest that we have not changed much since Servius in this area, even though he otherwise shows good critical instincts, for example when he perceives that "Aeneas' war in Italy is ... to some degree a civil war," and that the poem's "most acute difficulties are in fact posed in the scenes of battle, not only in the ambiguous status of the war itself but also in particular in Aeneas' avenging of Pallas, first in book 10 by the slaughter of suppliants, and then at the end of the poem by the killing of Turnus."[8] And yet he draws the line at allowing any implication that Augustus, surely a participant in that "civil war," is to be implicated: "given the tradition of Roman military epic and the circumstances of the *Aeneid*'s composition," he states, any criticism that sees "an ambivalent or negative view of Augustus" as a result of the

---

[7] Presumably the basis of Aristophanes' imputation of Euripidean misogynism lies precisely in such passages. I owe to James O'Hara the observation that Jocasta's words about disbelief in oracles (*OT* 707–25) are taken to imply the same state of mind in Sophocles.

[8] See Harrison (1991) xxvi; Thomas (1992) 138–9.

parallels drawn between him and Aeneas "seems far from credible." That is, Harrison has turned from observations that proceed from the poem (the evidence) to negation of those observations because of assumptions about the circumstances of the poem's composition and the poet's outlook – of which we know virtually nothing.

A further problem that arises when conclusions about Virgil are tied too closely to examinations of Augustus, when a symbiosis of sorts is created between them, is that the very reputation of Virgil rises and falls with that of the *princeps*. Tenney Frank, writing in 1930, in an article entitled "What do we know about Vergil?," adduced as one of the few "facts" of Virgil's life "that he had the wisdom to appreciate the excellences of the Augustan regime." Is that something we *know* or something we *assume*? We will need to see what evidence there is for this claim, but I would also note that the world has seen a lot since 1930, including Syme's revision of Augustus and the historical circumstances that preceded and followed the publication of *The Roman Revolution*. Under such conditions "appreciation of the excellences" of "the last of the war-lords"[9] may seem a less laudable goal. Of course if Virgil is on some levels a propagandist then his reputation will inevitably rise and fall with the reputation of his prince. The question here is whether it is warranted to tie him so closely to that prince.

Scholars also tend to read the climate of suppression that existed in the final years of Augustus' principate, almost thirty years after the death of Virgil, back onto the periods in which Virgil produced much of his verse. P. White shows that although punishments are meted out in the republic and in the early principate against authors or works which threaten Rome's traditional religious institutions, there is no evidence for *maiestas* trials against defamatory literature until around the year 6, possibly 8, AD.[10] We must be careful with chronologies, for two of Virgil's three poems are closer in time to Catullus' calling Julius Caesar a pathic (Poem 57) – and dining with him after a subsequent apology (Suet. *Div. Iul.* 73) – than to Ovid's committing whatever offense won him exile.

The unexamined notion of Virgil as "Augustan poet" is in other ways problematic from the perspective of chronology. There is in general an extremely unhistorical element to Virgilian criticism in this

---

[9] Syme (1950).   [10] White (1993) 149–55.

matter, as scholars project back onto his verse views for which there is no evidence at the time in question. There is an assumption that subsequent objectives, legislation, and the like, were all in the air in the 30s and 20s, and that Virgil gave voice to them. So it is when Virgil has the Sibyl quoting Phlegyas in the Underworld (*Aen.* 6.619 *discite iustitiam moniti et non temnere divos* "by my example learn of justice and not to disdain the gods"), and W. C. Korfmacher, for instance, lists the various moral reforms, religious revivals, and the like carried out by Augustus down to the end of the millennium, then concludes:[11]

> Vergil, to be sure, did not live to see the actuation of these "reforms" – for his untimely death occurred in 19 BC. Yet *he was fully cognizant* of the general aims and purposes of the prince in regard to the state cult; and *his own genuinely religious heart must have rejoiced* at the program, as his keen mind *must have discerned* with Octavian the latent potentialities of such a course towards toughening the moral and political fibres of the commonwealth. *Fully sympathetic as he was* with the principate and the prince, he *may well have been attracted* especially by the spirit of these "reforms," and *this supposition will explain* much in his *Aeneid* and, to a lesser extent, in the *Georgics* and the *Eclogues.* [emphasis added]

The insistent language aims to persuade in the utter absence of evidence, and the core ("fully sympathetic as he was with the principate and the prince") is unquestioningly accepted by most incidental, and even many engaged, Virgilian critics.

The procedure is as follows: an "Augustan" program is hypothesized from the perspective of the end of his principate; Virgil, who is credited, on no particular evidence, with a "genuinely religious heart," is then made a subscriber to those views, and the words of a mythological figure in the Underworld are magnified to the status of an official Augustan/Virgilian reform program. Nowhere is there an acknowledgment that Phlegyas delivers the line, Phlegyas who is first placed in the Underworld by Virgil, and who was punished by Apollo for burning the god's temple – in revenge for the god's raping his daughter (623 *thalamum invasit natae,* "invaded the bedroom of his daughter"). The "justice" that Phlegyas enjoins us to learn is some-

---

[11] Korfmacher (1955–6).

what ambiguous, and the graphically described violence of Apollo implicitly activates Phlegyas' own claims to justice. And we are presumably supposed to see in Phlegyas' words reference ahead to moral reforms in Rome, rather than back to such writers as Pindar and Plato, who point out long before the upcoming Augustan reforms that punishment in Hades teaches us not to transgress in the upper world – a fairly easy paradigm.[12] A finding such as Korfmacher's, then, that Virgil "may well have been attracted especially by the spirit of these 'reforms,'" is both anachronistic and also highly selective as to the image of Augustus it projects. Will Virgil have been unaware of the the *princeps*' nickname for Horace (*purissimum pene⟨m⟩, Epist.* 41 Malc.), or of his poem on Fulvia (*futuere Fulviam*), which ranks in its obscenity with Catullus and Martial? Nor does the moral conduct of Aeneas in Book 4 seem particularly in line with the as yet unenacted reforms, as Ovid would archly point out from exile.[13] In short, we must imagine a truncated history as we read Virgil, imagining the end of history, and of Augustanism, in the year of publication of that work. That is, we must both avoid anachronism and establish synchronism, extremely difficult enterprises, given the centrality of Augustus in the history of Europe. In this connection Yavetz,[14] quoting Tac. *Ann.* 1.10 and Suet. *Aug.* 13, observes "To survive five civil wars, he had to be firm and ruthless, but he must have found out to his distress that he had acquired a reputation as a cruel, vengeful, selfish, and treacherous youth." That reputation was formed in the period in which Virgil wrote two of his three poems and was presumably forming the idea of his epic.

"The personality of Augustus will be best left to emerge from his actions."[15] The Augustan personality that emerges from Syme's examination is well known, has stood up well over the years, and is in essence the premise of this chapter. It is this issue of personality that Yavetz has recently revisited; and the ways in which he pursues his inquiry further problematize the issue for the Virgilian. The crux of his approach, and the basis of his opposition to Syme's scepticism, emerges from the following: "For our purposes, however, it does not matter whether Augustus actually said certain things, whether propagandists spread intentional rumors of one sort or another, or whether

---

[12] See Austin ad *Aen.* 6.619 for references.   [13] See Ch. 2, pp. 74–8.
[14] Yavetz (1984) 2.   [15] Syme (1939) 113.

the public attributed to him certain assertions because they believed that he was capable of making them – just as it does not really matter whether Louis XIV really said, 'L'état c'est moi.' What matters is that those words were attributed to Louis XIV and not to Louis XVI. It is with Augustus' public image that we are concerned. From this point of view, his *dicta* and *apophthegmata* are of primary importance. They reveal very interesting character traits, which, in my opinion, are undoubtedly his."[16]

The argument here involves a certain amount of circularity, and the sceptic might reply that Yavetz, like many others, had been taken in by the public projection; but presumably the historian cannot be concerned just with the "public image" of Augustus, and the Virgilian critic will certainly not be content with it. If there is a gap between that public image and the realities, and if that gap was perceived by the contemporaries of Augustus, then that will be an important fact to bring to an examination of the relationship of the poet to Augustus. Yavetz, although he goes on to show that Augustus was a master of dissimulation, elsewhere however seems rather naive in his approach. He states that we must be wary of using the *dicta* ascribed to Augustus, because "only rarely do we find a word-for-word quotation of what he actually said."[17] One such quotation is to be found at *Dicta et Apophth.* 62, which Yavetz clearly accepts,[18] and which he uses to interpret the "public image" of Augustus. It has to do with the supposedly good opinion Augustus came to have of the younger Cato. Macrobius reports the following (*Sat.* 2.4.18):

> non est intermittendus sermo eius, quem Catonis honori dedit.
> venit forte in domum qua Cato habitaverat. dein Strabone in
> adulationem Caesaris male existimante de pervicacia Catonis
> ait: "quisquis praesentem statum civitatis commutari non volet,
> et civis et vir bonus est."

> One should not leave out his statement in honor of Cato. He
> happened to come into the house where Cato had lived. Then,
> after Strabo to flatter Caesar expressed a negative view of
> Cato's resistance, he said: "Whoever is unwilling that the
> existing system of government be changed is a good citizen and
> a good man."

---

[16] Yavetz (1990) 31–2.   [17] Yavetz (1990) 31.
[18] Yavetz (1990) 30. Cf. Syme (1939) 506–7 on this matter.

To conclude from this that Augustus admired Cato seems to me naive, even perverse. If, as is thought to be the case, the Strabo is L. Seius Strabo, and if this friend of Augustus and father of Sejanus in fact was aiming to flatter Augustus, we will assume he had good grounds for making derogatory comments about the younger Cato; we can assume that he, some other member of Augustus' circle, or even Augustus himself had done so before. But not, presumably, in the house in which Cato had lived, and where Caesar now happened to be. Strabo's *faux pas* was adroitly handled by the *princeps*, whose praise of Cato in fact serves to argue for the legitimacy of the principate, for that had now become the "existing system of government." This event will have been late in the principate, when Cato's "unwilling[ness] that the existing system of government be changed" is ironically appropriated to subvert Catonian republicanism and uphold empire. Also late will be Augustus' "Reply to Brutus on Cato," delivered with other writings at recitations which Tiberius had to finish when the *princeps* tired (Suet. *Aug.* 85.1). The very construction of this "public view" of Cato presupposes another, less admiring one.

Yavetz concludes with qualified divergence from Syme: "I do not think that one should apologize for underscoring Augustus' greatness. An unfriendly presentation misses the point and might be misunderstood. By tactful and patient hard work Augustus succeeded in shaping a new *form* of government, while a great deal of the *content* was left to the personalities of the rulers to come. It is impossible therefore to speak in general terms of the early principate by treating mainly law, institutions, economy, and society without paying adequate attention to the personalities of the various *principes*." Some will prefer to stay with Syme's approach, that "the personality of Augustus will be best left to emerge from his actions." And what about the personality of Virgil? I would modify Syme's statement on that of Augustus by saying that the personality of Virgil, particularly in relation to Augustus, will be best left to emerge from his poetry. But aside from that, what do we in fact know about the relationship between Virgil and Augustus?

Virgil and Augustus

So far my assessment of Augustus is accepting of Syme's view. Where we part company is in the assessment of the poets, specifically of

Virgil. Of *The Roman Revolution* J. Griffin has stated "That great book, among its other merits, gives an interpretation of Augustus and his poets which is hard-headed and highly political."[19] "Augustus and his poets"; the presumption is explicit and entrenched, as indeed it was for Syme. His interest was primarily in history, and in prosopography, an interest in the actions and schemes of political élites, not an interest in poetry beyond using it as evidence for those actions and schemes. Syme puts the matter in a way that many have found (and would still find) acceptable:

> Virgil, Horace and Livy are the enduring glories of the
> Principate; and all three men were on terms of personal
> friendship with Augustus. The class to which these men of
> letters belonged had everything to gain from the new order.
> Both Virgil and Horace had lost their paternal estates in the
> confiscations that followed Philippi or the disorders of the
> Perusine War: they subsequently regained their property, or at
> least compensation. (Syme [1939] 464)

As has recently been noted, "Roman prosopography necessarily is élite prosopography";[20] in an investigation of such a society poets, whether or not we know their social status, will easily and inevitably become mere extensions of that élite. We just do not know the realities of land confiscation or restoration, nor do we know what or who else might have been lost, what impressions made, by the Perusine and other civil wars of Virgil's youth.

It is also interesting to observe where the chapter "The Organization of Opinion" comes in Syme's book – it is the thirtieth of 33 chapters, and is surrounded by examination of historical events occurring years after the death of Virgil. What it has to do with frequently is the *use* to which the poetry of Virgil was being put, precisely with the beginnings of the political and ideological reception and manipulation of Virgil. Augustus, and the reception of Augustus, controls and diverts the Virgilian text.

The manipulation begins in antiquity and is pervasive. Virgil had been dealing in terms of the metaphor of the Golden Age since the Fourth *Eclogue*, whose unnamed and unborn *puer* will not easily be identified with Octavian, *pace* the Berne scholia – an early example

---

[19] Griffin (1994) 43.   [20] Galsterer (1990) 8.

of the Augustan reception. But subsequent use of that metaphor was likely to have been simplified and used by those who would present the Augustan Age as a Golden Age. The Aeneas in the Forum of Augustus or on the *Ara Pacis* is in many ways an interpretation of the Virgilian Aeneas, more archaized than Virgil's character, and ultimately not very similar to him, in short an Augustan representation.[21] And as we shall see in the next chapter, the Aeneas of Horace's *Carmen Saeculare*, a commissioned, Augustan poem, represents an ideological development of and response to the Virgilian Aeneas.

But what are the grounds for thinking, *prior to the act of interpretation*, that the *Aeneid* is somehow part of the Augustan program? The evidence is remarkably scanty. Harrison has grappled with this question, and finds (1) that there is a tradition of Roman military epic in which the exploits of contemporaries are lauded:[22] Ennius ends his *Annales* with the campaigns of M. Fulvius Nobilior; Varro of Atax wrote a *Bellum Sequanicum* treating the campaigns of Julius Caesar in Gaul; Cornelius Severus, a *Bellum Siculum* on Octavian's defeat of Sextus Pompey. He then backs off somewhat: "The *Aeneid* is of course not a narrative of contemporary campaigns"; but tries to rescue the parallel: "but it does include a considerable and panegyrical account of Octavian's victory at Actium." But this passage (*Aen.* 8.675–728), to which we shall return, does not convert the *Aeneid* into the genre of historical encomiastic epics which seem to have abounded at this time. What is significant is precisely the *absence* of such a poem from the corpus of Virgil (see White [1993] 78–82). Nor is the shield simply a "panegyrical account" as we shall see. Harrison also adduces (2) the claim that the poem "is likely to have been written with some degree of patronage from the *princeps*" (xxiv), and in a footnote "Even if the evidence of the ancient *Lives* of Vergil is set to one side, Ov. *Tr.* 2.533 *tuae . . . Aeneidos* suggests that it was in some way "Augustus' poem.""[23] This is indeed a natural way for Ovid to refer to the poem, for by now, around thirty years after the death of Virgil, Augustus and the Augustan program had appropriated the

---

[21] Zanker (1988) 203–4.

[22] Harrison (1991) xxiv.

[23] Stahl (1990) 211 ends his article relying on the same "evidence." This passage is treated more extensively in Ch. 2.

poem; that has no bearing on the present issue, though it will relate to the question of Virgil's reception.[24]

As for the "evidence of the ancient *Lives*," White has shown how slight this is: a notice only in the Servian and Gudian *Lives*, which as White says is suspicious in that it schematizes the Virgilian career: Pollio proposed the *Eclogues*, Maecenas the *Georgics*, Augustus the *Aeneid*.[25] But even if the *Aeneid* was indeed "suggested (*propositam*) by Octavian," that will have next to no bearing on the political and ideological outlook or meanings of the poem, any more than the possibility that Maecenas proposed the *Georgics* could ever have any connection to the meaning of that poem. Augustus is of course central to the *Aeneid*; that has never been contested (though some have tried to distance him from Aeneas when the latter is behaving with brutality or rage). It is the *nature* of his role that is at issue. But in the final analysis, as White has shown: "The evidence that Augustus prompted Vergil to write the *Aeneid* is considerably weaker than the evidence of his interventions with Horace" (White [1993] 133). As for Harrison's claim that the poem was written "with some degree of patronage from the *princeps*," we just do not know whether that is true or what it means in the context of the end of the republic. Nor can the epic of Ennius or Naevius help much in a consideration of the

---

[24] I am grateful to James O'Hara, for referring me to Kavanagh (1990) 318–19, which discusses a notorious event in the 1984 US presidential campaign involving the "meaning" of Bruce Springsteen: "This began with a column by George Will, America's favorite reactionary nerd, lauding Springsteen as a shining example of the American dream – of how hard work, ambition, and the unfettered ability to accumulate wealth can give hope, if not ensure success, to working-class Americans. This version of Springsteen was then worked into a Reagan speech in Springsteen's home state of New Jersey, attempting to appropriate Springsteen, the cultural icon, as a Reaganite kind of guy ... All of the [ensuing] hoopla eventually prompted Springsteen himself to remind his concert audiences that the words of his songs (like 'My Hometown') hardly proclaim the durability of the American dream; to donate concert proceeds to union welfare funds; and to speak to workers rallying against plant closures, telling them 'What goes unmeasured is the price that unemployment inflicts on people's families, on their marriages, on the single mothers out there trying to raise their kids on their own.'"

At stake here was how the vast appeal of an attractive cultural icon, and the wildly popular and pleasing cultural texts (rock songs) he produced, could be appropriated to support specific political and socioeconomic programs." Unlike Virgil, Springsteen was around to reappropriate his texts.

[25] White (1993) 301 n. 10.

37

Augustan question. White's book makes us consider whether our notion of patronage is both derived from and more appropriate to more recent European court poetry, a question to which we will return.

The details of contact between Virgil and the *princeps* are to be found in Suetonius' *Life*. First at 11–13, treating the retiring nature of the poet:

> cetera sane vitae et ore et animo tam probum constat, ut
> Neapoli Parthenias vulgo appellatus sit, ac si quando Romae,
> quo rarissime commeabat, viseretur in publico, sectantis
> demonstrantisque se subterfugeret in proximum tectum. bona
> autem cuiusdam exsulantis offerente Augusto non sustinuit
> accipere. possedit prope centiens sestertium ex liberalitatibus
> amicorum habuitque domum Romae Esquiliis iuxta hortos
> Maecenatianos, quamquam secessu Campaniae Siciliaeque
> plurimum uteretur. (Suet. *Vit. Verg.* 11–13)

> It is certain that for the rest of his life he was so modest in
> speech and thought that at Naples he was nicknamed
> "Maiden," and whenever he was seen in public at Rome,
> where he rarely went, he would escape into the nearest house
> to avoid those following him and pointing him out. Moreover
> when Augustus offered him the property of a man he had
> exiled he could not bring himself to accept it. He owned nearly
> 10 million sesterces from his friends' generosity, and had a
> house on the Esquiline near the gardens of Maecenas, though
> he usually removed himself to Campania and Sicily.

There is no reason to doubt all the details here, and they conspire to present a figure who avoided not only the public, but in particular Rome, and who declined an offer from the *princeps* of confiscated property. The reader thinks of *Eclogues* 1 and 9, and of Virgil's own possible loss, but these are not likely to have generated this detail. His wealth is attributed to the generosity of unnamed "friends" who would seem not to be primarily identifiable with Augustus and Maecenas, whose names we might expect to have figured if they were primarily or exclusively indicated.

We hear of Naples elsewhere, in a fragment of a letter from Augustus to Virgil: *excucurristi a Neapoli*, "you went running out of Naples" (*Epist.* 35 Malc.). This has been plausibly linked to an independent fragment which Malcovati labels, with others, "Ad ignotos," although she finds the linking very probable: *nos venimus Neapolim fluctu quidem caeco*, "we came to Naples on a foamless wave" (*Epist.* 45 Malc.).[26] They come together to form a mild reproof ("we came into town the day after you got out of town"), which would find a parallel with what Suetonius reports Augustus saying to Horace in his *Life* of that poet: *irasci me tibi scito, quod non in plerisque eius modi scriptis mecum potissimum loquaris*, "You should know I am angry with you for not preferring to converse with me in your many writings." In the case of Virgil we would have the possibility, added to others about his avoidance of Rome, that he had left Naples prior to Augustus' arrival.

Suetonius (*Vit. Verg.* 31–2) tells of the famous recitation that included the death of Marcellus (*Aen.* 6.860–86), which caused the fainting of his mother Octavia. The words prior to that are of interest, again recording contact between poet and *princeps*:

> Augustus vero – nam forte expeditione Cantabrica aberat –
> supplicibus atque etiam minacibus per iocum litteris efflagitaret,
> ut "sibi de Aeneide," ut ipsius verba sunt, "vel prima carminis
> ὑπογραφή vel quodlibet κῶλον mitteretur." cui tamen multo
> post perfectaque demum materia tres omnino libros recitavit,
> secundum, quartum et sextum ...

> Indeed Augustus (for he happened to be away on the
> Cantabrian campaign) would demand in entreating and even
> jokingly threatening letters that he be sent "some of the
> Aeneid," in his own words, "either a first draft of the poem,
> or any section of it." But only much later, and when the
> material was finally polished, did he read three entire books,
> the second, fourth, and sixth ...

Again it is hard to see how this detail would be invented; what it suggests is a resistance to the entreaties, as well as a final willingness to read selected books. That selection, moreover, looks very much like a modern college curriculum for "selections" from the *Aeneid*, and we may wonder about Virgil's avoiding recitation from the second half of the poem, with its treatment of the Latin war, which so often resembles civil war, and which in so many ways tracks the progress of

---

[26] The connection was made by Cichorius (1922) 269–71. Peter (*HRR* II, fr. 24) thought this came from Augustus' autobiography (Suet. *Aug.* 85), but Malcovati's view seems preferable: "it seems rather to derive from a letter" (*ex epistula potius fluxisse videtur*).

Augustus' mythical ancestor from aggrieved to aggressor. Also notably absent from Virgil's reading list is the description of Venus' and Vulcan's heavily Augustan work of art, the shield with its Actian centerpiece and triumphant closure. And finally, even if all of these details in the *Lives* are fiction, they are the product of a mind (in antiquity) that seems to be viewing Virgil as in some way resistant to Rome and Augustus. At the very least, we could see the possibility of an ancient critical belief in an ambivalent Virgilian attitude towards Augustus.

That is it, that is the evidence. From it Harrison (and to be fair, his is just representative of the "Augustan" reading) is forced to conclude: "For such a poem [as the *Aeneid*] to be in any way 'anti-Augustan' [not the only alternative to 'panegyric'] would be extraordinary; apart from the improbability of presenting unfavourably the great man who was both his patron and the sole ruler of Rome, Vergil had publicly anticipated praising that same man in heroic epic in his earlier poem the *Georgics* (3.16–39), and the glorification of Augustus in the *Aeneid* is accordingly full-hearted and unambiguous" (xxiv). It is so because – it must be so.

Virgil on Augustus

What does Virgil's poetry say about Augustus? Here is Syme's view, which is fairly typical:

> Virgil was engaged in writing an epic poem that should reveal the hand of destiny in the earliest origins of Rome, the continuity of Roman history and its culmination in the rule of Augustus. As he wrote early in the poem,
>
> > nascetur pulchra Troianus origine Caesar
> > imperium Oceano, famam qui terminet astris,
> > Iulius a magno demissum nomen Iulo.   (1.286ff.)
>
> Later it is not the conqueror of the world but the coming inaugurator of the New Age,
>
> > hic vir, hic est, tibi quem promitti saepius audis,
> > Augustus Caesar, divi genus, aurea condet
> > saecula qui rursus Latio.   (6.791ff.)[27]

[27] Syme (1939) 462.

No mention of voice or speaker (Jupiter in the first instance, Anchises in the second – both ancestors of Aeneas and Augustus), no indication that these lines are delivered by anyone other than Virgil. If this seems unfair, and itself anachronistic in critical expectations, we may turn to B. A. Kellum, who likewise quotes these and other lines from Anchises' speech with no indication that they are spoken by a character.[28]

The appearances of Octavian/Augustus in Virgil's poetry, including the disputed *Eclogue* 8.5–13,[29] as well as the "Caesar Julius" at *Aeneid* 1.286–96 (on which more later), are as follows:

Citation	Voice	Mode of address/context
Ecl. 1.6–10	Tityrus	unnamed *deus* the salvation of Tityrus
Ecl. 1.42–5	Tityrus	unnamed *iuvenis* allows Tityrus to herd
?*Ecl.* 8.5–13	Virgil	unnamed *tu* to be subject of future song[30]
G. 1.24–42	Virgil	Prayer to Caesar, soon to be deified as Jupiter figure
G. 1.498–514	Virgil	Prayer that *iuvenis* Caesar aid a world gone mad
G. 2.170–2	Virgil	Caesar averting *imbellem Indum* from Rome
G. 3.16–48	Virgil	Caesar in temple; his battles to be told; his name to be carried down through the years
G. 4.559–62	Virgil	Great Caesar warring at Euphrates, Virgil *ignobilis oti* studying at Naples
Aen. 1.286–96	Jupiter	Caesar Julius to be received in heaven; Gates of War will be closed, Furor will be tamed
Aen. 6.789–95	Anchises	Augustus Caesar in parade of future Romans
Aen. 8.675–728	Venus[31]	Augustus Caesar at Actium; in triple triumph

It is noteworthy that the poet-narrator's references to Octavian are confined to the *Georgics* and the Eighth *Eclogue* – if that be addressed

---

[28] Kellum (1990) 289–90.

[29] I incline to thinking that these lines address Pollio, not Octavian, but Clausen's arguments for Octavian (1994) ad loc., with bibliography, are compelling.

[30] For the debate as to identity, see most recently Clausen (1994) ad loc.

[31] The description of the shield is presented by a narrator who has Aeneas reading it; ultimately the work is commissioned by Aeneas' mother, Venus, the ultimate producer of its images.

to Octavian. I believe that there is a single and dominant function to all of these passages: each one creates a close identity between Octavian and Jupiter. This is hardly suprising: association with Jupiter, in one's own lifetime, was a long-standing feature of Republican grandiosity, as S. Weinstock has demonstrated in abundant detail.[32] He notes (304) Horace's hesitant comparison of Augustus and Jupiter in *Odes* 1.12 and 3.5, the Greek identification of Augustus with Zeus under a variety of titles,[33] and the numerous instances in Ovid where Augustus is both compared to Jupiter, and said to be Jupiter (e.g. *Trist.* 5.2.46 *si fas est homini cum Iove posse loqui* "if it is lawful for a mortal to be able to talk with Jove").[34] None of the evidence is prior to the *Georgics*, and most of it is in fact from well into the principate. The connection made tentatively in the *Eclogues*, and pervasively in the *Georgics*, at least two years before Octavian had received the name Augustus, constitutes perhaps the earliest extant evidence for the association. And for Virgil, the *princeps* would not so much be compared to Jupiter, as in the Horatian poems; rather, as in the Greek practice, he would *become* Jupiter. There has, however, been a curious resistance to allowing that Virgil made this approximation, although the Latin Anthology attributes to Virgil the hexameter *Iuppiter in caelis, Caesar regit omnia terris*, "Jupiter in the heavens, Caesar rules all on earth" (*Anth. Lat.* 813R) – perhaps indicating that the Virgilian connection was recognized in antiquity. The reason for this modern reluctance may have to do with the ambivalent nature of the Virgilian Jupiter, in both the *Georgics* and the *Aeneid*, an ambivalence which an Augustan reader will not be eager to attach to the prince.

The *Eclogues*

For the sake of argument I will assume the addressee of *Eclogue* 8.11 (*a te principium, tibi desinam*, "from you is my beginning, in you will be my end") is Octavian (also unnamed in *Eclogue* 1). If he is not the

---

[32] Weinstock (1971) Ch. 14 "Iuppiter Iulius".

[33] Weinstock (1971) 304: Zeus Aineiades, Zeus Sebastos Kronides, Zeus Eleutherios (Egypt), Zeus Patroos (Asia), Zeus Olympios (Athens and Asia), Iuppiter Augustus (Cyrene and Dalmatia).

[34] Cf. Weinstock (1971) 304–5 for the numerous instances in Ovid, and for further bibliography; to which may be added G. Luck on *Trist.* 2.215–18 and F. Bömer on *Met.* 15.858ff. This section was much improved by the suggestions of Peter Knox.

addressee, this example just disappears. Indeed, this line is perhaps the best evidence for the identification with Octavian. As scholars have noted,[35] there is a double reminiscence in the words just cited, and in each case we are dealing with absolute rulers, temporal or otherwise: Virgil reworks Aratus, *Phaenomena* 1, Ἐκ Διὸς ἀρχώμεσθα; more fully Theocritus, 17.1 Ἐκ Διὸς ἀρχώμεσθα καὶ ἐς Δία λήγετε Μοῖσαι (the encomium of Ptolemy II). He further suggests a relationship with Jupiter through intratextual reminiscence of *Eclogue* 3.60 (*ab Iove principium Musae*), at the beginning of amoebeans which end possibly with a riddle on Aratus' poem. A secondary reference, close in rhythm, to Homer, *Iliad* 9.97 (ἐν σοὶ μὲν λήξω, σέο δ' ἄρξομαι "in you shall I end, from you begin") seems to complicate by bringing in Agamemnon, but the words that follow make it clear that even here Zeus is very much in the air: 97–9 οὕνεκα πολλῶν| λαῶν ἐσσι ἄναξ καί τοι Ζεὺς ἐγγυάλιξε| σκῆπτρόν τε ἠδὲ θέμιστας, ἵνα σφίσι βουλεύῃσθα "since you are lord of many people and Zeus has given you the scepter and powers of judgment, so you may take counsel for them." As for *Eclogue* 1, there Octavian is a god on earth, at least in the eyes of Tityrus (7 *mihi*). Jupiter is not specified, but he is certainly not excluded, since unspecified *deus* frequently means "supreme being."[36]

Elsewhere in Augustan poetry the temporal ruler occupies a position just below that of Jupiter, as in Homer. Horace in particular is emphatic in following this tradition in the Roman *Odes* (3.1.5–6; 3.5.1–4) and particularly at 3.6.5–6, in a poem whose addressee "Romane" at the very least includes Augustus:

> dis te minorem quod geris, imperas:
> hinc omne principium, huc refer exitum.

Your *imperium* is based on your setting yourself below the gods:
it is from this fact you should ascribe every beginning, to this
every end.

The second line's elaboration is pointed, and, situated in a set of poems replete with allusion to Virgil, looks like a correction, not just of the *Eclogues*, but also of the *Georgics*, to which we now turn.

---

[35] Most recently, and with bibliography (cf. in particular Fantuzzi [1980]), see Clausen ad loc.

[36] *OLD* s.v. *deus*.

The *Georgics*

The five appearances of Octavian in the *Georgics*, all from the point of view of the poet/didactic narrator, are characterized so by J. Griffin: "It is true ... that Virgil has devoted several grandiose passages of the *Georgics* to Octavian's praise."[37] Is this really the case? Or rather, how is this the case? All five passages conspire to identify Octavian with Jupiter. The identification is clearest at the beginning and end of the poem – *a te principium, tibi desinam* ("from you my beginning, in you will I end") from *Eclogue* 8 aptly describes what Virgil will proceed to do in the frames of the *Georgics*. Sure enough, at the beginning (G. 1.4–42) he adapts the rustic prayer of Varro which begins the *Res rusticae*, but he omits Varro's first deity, Jupiter.[38] The other chief distinction from Varro is the second half of Virgil's prayer, the 19 lines directed to Octavian, which speculate about his future sphere of divinity (land, sea or sky). The possibilities would seem to impinge on the territory of Jupiter. And so Caesar's heir, officially designated *divi filius* years before the *Georgics* were begun, is projected by Virgil as a very replacement of Jupiter. Mynors attributes the absence of Jupiter at the beginning to the fact that he "is now the supreme power who lays down the rules of the game, and cannot be invoked to assist the players."[39] Why not? That gives all the more reason to direct a prayer to him (24–42). The absence of Jupiter in the first half of the prayer, then, may be explained by his presence in the second half – in the person of his descendant Octavian.

Then there is the end of the poem, with Virgil writing in Naples, Caesar warring in the East:

> Caesar dum magnus ad altum
> fulminat Euphraten bello victorque volentis
> per populos dat iura viamque adfectat Olympo.

> while mighty Caesar strikes like lightning at the deep Euphrates
> and after winning gives out laws among willing people and sets
> out on the road to Olympus.

---

[37] Griffin (1984) 193.

[38] See Thomas (1988a) I, 68; Mynors (1990) 1–2 notes the omission, which he interprets as indicating Virgil's viewing the god as the force that controls the action of the poem, and cannot therefore function as one of its actors. The first point, which is true, need not lead to the second.

[39] Mynors (1990) 2.

The conflation of Octavian with Jupiter is deep and unavoidable, *pace* Mynors, who again attempts to dissuade us from making the connection: (324) "It would be a mistake to see an allusion here to Jupiter the thunder-god, any more than in *Aen.* 12.654, where 'fulminat Aeneas armis.'" But if, on plausible philological grounds, we *do* see such an allusion, then we will reject this denial of meaning (itself an interpretative act), and we are likely to bring the identification to our larger reading of the poem. And the fact is that Jupiter can likewise be projected plausibly onto the figure of Aeneas at *Aeneid* 12.654.[40]

Octavian and Olympian Zeus

Now to the center of the *Georgics* (3.12–39) with its elaborate temple, representing the *Aeneid*, as most critics agree.[41]

> et viridi in campo templum de marmore ponam
> propter aquam, tardis ingens ubi flexibus errat
> Mincius et tenera praetexit harundine ripas.
>
> (G. 3.13–15)

And on the green plain I shall set up a marble temple beside
the water, where the great Mincius wanders with lazy
meandering and borders the banks with tender reeds.

In Virgil's vision of literary history his projected poem will replace the epinician of Pindar and Callimachus.[42] Once again Jupiter is discernible, being mentioned in connection with statues that are to appear, and that anticipate the divine and human genealogies that will become important in the *Aeneid*:

---

[40] See Hardie (1986) 51; Jupiter is for Hardie an unambiguously positive force and stabilizer of the universe; see also Thomas (1988a) II, 240. For the possibility of an intertextual link to Callimachus' *Hymn to Zeus*, see Thomas (1993) 211–12.

[41] The objection, that Virgil states he will sing of the battles of Caesar, when he in fact sings of Aeneas, is a distraction; the *Aeneid*, although not historical epic per se, is very much about the battles of Caesar, and not just Actium on the shield.

[42] See Thomas (1988a) at 3.1–48 *passim*; also Henderson (1995) 104–8; 129 n. 11; Thomas (1998) 103–8. The tradition had generally failed to see the presence of Callimachus, particularly before the discovery of the *Victoria Berenices* (i.e. Wilkinson). And even after it, some would try to deny this new intertext; so Balot (1998), on which see Thomas (1999) 9–10, n. 13.

stabunt et Parii lapides, spirantia signa,
Assaraci proles demissaeque ab Iove gentis
nomina Trosque parens et Troiae Cynthius auctor.

(G. 3.34–6)

There will be statues of Parian marble, lifelike effigies, the
offspring of Assaracus and the names of the race derived from
Jove, and father Tros and Cynthian Apollo, Troy's founder.

That race should stretch from Jupiter to Octavian. But there is a more
fundamental nexus. L. P. Wilkinson has noted the basic connection:

> The Mincius should be his Alpheus, and beside it,
> corresponding to the temple of Zeus at Olympia, he would
> build in imagination a poetic temple for Caesar, who was at
> that moment dedicating a real one to Divus Julius, adorning it
> with sculptures of symbolic import corresponding with those
> designated for the already rising shrine of Apollo on the
> Palatine.[43]

The Roman temples are relevant, but in one detail we need to
stay with the Greek architectural models, which the inhabitants of
Olympia and Nemea are in the poet's programmatic vision quitting
so as to attend Virgil's temple. At issue is Virgil's chief occupant,
Octavian (3.16 *in medio mihi Caesar erit templumque tenebit*). Heyne
thought this referred to a statue placed in the temple or in front of it,
La Cerda to the medial position of Octavian within a statuary
group.[44] If Virgil knew the site of Olympia, either from autopsy or
some other means,[45] he will have known at least as much as we do
(from the remains and from Pausanias 5.10–12) of that wonder of the
ancient world, the temple of Zeus at Olympia.[46]

Octavian and Agrippa seem to have been restoring the temple in
the 30s (following an earthquake of around 40) – activity of which
Virgil will possibly have been aware. The temple of course contained
Phidias' great enthroned Zeus on a base inside the middle of the

---

[43] Wilkinson (1970) 287–8.

[44] See Mynors (1990) ad loc.

[45] I have suggested elsewhere (Thomas [1983]) that Virgil's placement of a peplos at the
center of Dido's temple frieze (*Aen.* 1.479–81) could reflect knowledge (whether or
not from autopsy it is hard to know) of the Parthenon frieze.

[46] We know less of the temple of Zeus at Nemea, since its roof had fallen in by the time
Pausanias got to it (15.2).

temple (*templumque tenebit*), as well as a central Zeus in the middle of the great east pediment (*in medio*), above the ramp and main entrance.[47] This would accommodate both Heyne and La Cerda on 3.16 (*in medio mihi Caesar erit templumque tenebit*). There was, moreover, an active tradition of Roman association with this central Zeus iconography. Mummius had added yet another Zeus on the same eastern side, to the right of the entrance ramp, and the Olympian enclosure (Altis), with its great altar of Zeus in the center, was, naturally enough, crowded with statues of the god, dedicated by states and by individuals.[48] In front of this same eastern end of the temple was found part of an inscription of Julius Caesar,[49] who consciously began to cultivate Olympia. At least from the year 36, Octavian emulated this activity, and he is named in three separate inscriptions, two of which were likewise found at the same eastern end of the Zeus temple.[50] One of them is clearly written between the years 40 and 27, since Octavian is designated *imperator*, but not yet with the name Augustus.[51]

This location, then, was a favored locus of Caesarian attention, and it also has further associations with the opening of *Georgics* 3. On either side of the pediment's central Zeus are Pelops and Oenomaus, each with a team of horses and chariot, depicted as they are about to compete for Hippodamia, who also figures on the pediment, beside Pelops. The Altis also had shrines of Pelops[52] and of Hippodamia;[53] the temple of Hera is said to have been dedicated by Hippodamia, in gratitude for her marriage to Pelops.[54] On one of the turning posts was a depiction of Hippodamia about to crown Pelops for his victory.[55] At *Georgics* 3.6–7, this story belongs to the hackneyed Greek

---

[47] See Gardiner (1925).
[48] Pausanias 5.22.1.
[49] Cf. Curtius (1890–97) 5.365 [Γάϊο]ν Ἰο[ύλι]ον Καί[σαρα ... | Λικί]νιος [... τὸν σωτῆρα|- καὶ] εὐερ[γέτην].
[50] Gardiner (1925) 158.
[51] Curtius (1890–97) 5.367 τὸ κοινὸν τῶν Ἀχαιῶν|Αὐτοκράτορα Καίσαρα Θεοῦ υἱὸν|ἀρετῆς ἕνεκεν καὶ εὐνοίας,|ἧς ἔχων εἰς ἀτὸ διατελε ῖ,|Διὶ Ὀλ(υ)μπίῳ. The date of the second is unclear, since there seems to have been space to accommodate the name Augustus (Σεβαστόν): 368 [Αὐτ]οκράτορ[α Καίσαρα] Θεο[ῦ υἱόν] ...
[52] Pausanias 5.13.1–8.
[53] Pausanias 6.20.7; 5.22.2.
[54] Pausanias 5.16.4.
[55] Pausanias 6.20.19.

past from which Virgil will free himself with his new "temple:" *Hippodameque umeroque Pelops insignis eburno | acer equis*, recalling Pindar's first *Olympian*, perhaps Callimachean epinician as well, and, I would now suggest, the iconography of the very Olympia that is envisaged as emigrating to Mantua. Likewise the twelve metopes of this same temple record the labors of Heracles, prominent among the themes rejected by Virgil: *Georgics* 3.4–6 *quid aut Eurysthea durum | aut inlaudati nescit Busiridis aras?* The Alpheus river, which in Virgil's account will be deserted as the competitors make their pilgrimage to the banks of the Mincius (G. 3.19–20), is also depicted on the east pediment, along with its tributary, the Kladeos, or so Pausanias (5.10.7) identified the figures lying at the two margins of the pediment. In the imagination of Virgil, Olympian Zeus has been transformed into Roman Caesar, himself a thinly veiled Jupiter.

Another building in the Olympian Altis is of relevance. The restoration of the Metroon at Olympia, which would be appropriated by the Julio-Claudians, was presumably carried out after the writing of the *Georgics*. The inscription on its architrave is from some time after 27 BC, a dedication by the people of Elis to "Son of a God, Caesar Augustus, savior of the Greeks and of the whole world."[56] As for the Metroon and its statuary:

> in it was placed a colossal statue of Augustus, the torso of
> which was found close to the temple. The emperor was
> represented in the guise of Zeus, with sceptre and thunderbolt,
> and the statue, which was two and a half times life-size, must
> have filled the whole space at the back of the tiny cella.[57]

Virgil had brought the temple of Olympian Zeus to the Mincius, and replaced its central Zeus with a central Octavian; can it be that the words *in medio mihi Caesar erit templumque tenebit* are somehow connected with the exporting of Augustus, the new Jupiter, back to the middle of a temple at Olympia? In general the possibility that Virgil helped shape, rather than reflect, Augustan policy is a distinct one – though the poet has his own purposes for making these connections.

The georgic Octavian makes two other appearances, one in a prayer at 1.498–505, which seems distinctly pre-Actian, that the

---

[56] Curtius (1890–97) 5.366 Ἠλῆῖοι Θεοῦ Καίσαρος Σεβαστοῦ σωτῆρος τῶν Ἑλλήνων καὶ τῆς οἰκουμένης πάσης.

[57] Gardiner (1925) 161.

iuvenis (cf. the designation at *Eclogue* 1.42, in the middle line of that poem) be permitted to come to the help of a world gone out of control; and again, at 2.170–2 in a context open to an ambivalent reading, and recognized as ambivalent in antiquity, where he is addressed (2.170) as *maxime Caesar*.[58]

> et te, maxime Caesar,
> qui nunc extremis Asiae iam victor in oris
> imbellem avertis Romanis arcibus Indum.

and you, most mighty Caesar, who now victorious on the furthest shores of Asia turn away the unwarlike Indian from Roman citadels.

The appearance at the end of *Georgics* I deserves some attention. A metaphor for the primal guilt that plays itself out in civil war, Laomedon's perjured reneging on payment to Neptune and Apollo is compensated sufficiently by the shedding of Roman blood (501–2). Virgil continues:

> iam pridem nobis caeli te regia, Caesar,
> invidet atque hominum queritur curare triumphos,
> quippe ubi fas versum atque nefas ...   (G. 1.503–5)

With earlier commentators, I assume a large ellipsis: "For long now has heaven begrudged us your presence, Caesar, complaining that you care for triumphs among men [as you are compelled to do], inasmuch as right and wrong are inverted among them [i.e. among mortals]."[59] Mynors reveals another nuance, also supplying extra material: "if he stays, triumphs (which will be followed by peace) are certain. But is not the world so far gone that this would be waste of a good man? The gods may well think so."[60] But perhaps Conington's puzzlement is more to the point: "there is something strange in the expression 'human triumphs,' unless we suppose the poet to intend some still more extravagant compliment."[61] If the kingdom of heaven resents Octavian's attention to *human* triumphs (the genitive is extremely marked), that may suggest it wants him to turn to *divine* triumphs, and of those the triumph of Jupiter over the Giants would be the most obvious one.

---

[58] See Thomas (1988a) I, ad loc.   [59] See Thomas (1988a) I, ad 1.503–5.
[60] Cf. Mynors (1990) ad 1.504.   [61] Conington (1898) ad 1.504.

The *Aeneid*

The appearances in the *Aeneid* all serve to approximate Augustus to Jupiter. This study began with the possibility, and the critical reaction to that possibility, that Anchises' words at *Aeneid* 6.791–4 may suggest that Augustus will close out the age of gold, precisely the traditional function of Jupiter, as recorded at *Georgics* 1.121–46.

As for the other clear appearance of Augustus, on the shield of Aeneas (*Aen.* 8.678–81), the Olympians, Neptune, Venus, Minerva, Mars and Apollo, are ranged against Anubis and the monstrous gods of the East, repulsed in their attack on the realm of Jupiter.[62] Critics have long seen this as an updated, appropriately Egyptianized, Gigantomachy, demonizing the forces of the east. What has not, to my knowledge, been noted is the fact that it is the only extant version of the motif from which Jupiter or Zeus himself is absent. So Horace puts the god stage center in his Gigantomachy of *Odes* 3.4.42–64 (42–4 *scimus ut impios | Titanas immanemque turbam | fulmine sustulerit caduco* ... "we know how he destroyed with flying thunderbolt the enormous band of unholy Titans").[63] Nor will it do to say that Jupiter has too central a role in the poem to be depicted, particularly since his appearance on the shield, like that of Venus, Neptune and the rest, would be outside the narrative scope of the poem's major action. We will look in vain, then, for Jupiter himself, that is, unless we care to find him, again in the Actian middle (8.675–7), in the figure of his descendant, standing high on the poop deck: *hinc Augustus agens Italos in proelia Caesar* ... As in the first explicit reference to Octavian at *Georgics* 1.21–42, so here in the last to Augustus, the presence of Caesar is coupled with the absence of Jupiter.

All of which prepares us for a more problematic instance, from Jupiter's prophecy at *Aeneid* 1.286–8:

> "nascetur pulchra Troianus origine Caesar,
> imperium Oceano, famam qui terminet astris,
> Iulius, a magno demissum nomen Iulo."

---

[62] For good observations on the dark side of the shield, cf. Gurval (1995) esp. Ch. 5 " 'No, Virgil, No': The Battle of Actium on the Shield of Aeneas." For detailed discussion of the reception of the text of the shield, see below, Ch. 6.

[63] Cf. Hardie (1986) *passim*.

"There will spring from fair origin Trojan Caesar, who will
stretch empire to Ocean, his renown to the stars, Julius, a name
descended from great Iulus."

The nomenclature, *Caesar . . . Iulius*, has raised questions as to which
Caesar is involved, and although E. Kraggerud has recently tried to
remove any ambiguity from the lines (deciding for Augustus), as he
himself admits, scholars from Servius to O'Hara, and including
recently Mynors, Kenney ([1968] 106), Austin (1971) ad loc., and
Quinn, have seen a reference either to Julius or have opted for deliberate ambiguity.[64] Unsurprisingly, my own sense is of a deliberate
ambiguity, and I would suggest that for reasons emerging from the
preceding pages, Jupiter is not allowed by Virgil to use the name
"Augustus." Throughout the poetry of Virgil, the identity of the two
is shared.

How to praise a prince

We will best be able to assess the "several grandiose passages of the
Georgics [devoted] to Octavian's praise" (J. Griffin) by first observing a
sampling of late Republican panegyric, from Cicero's *Pro Marcello*,
where Cicero expresses his gratitude to Julius Caesar for approving
the restoration of Marcus Marcellus:

> tantam enim mansuetudinem, tam inusitatam inauditamque
> clementiam, tantum in summa potestate rerum omnium
> modum, tam denique incredibilem sapientiam ac paene divinam
> tacitus praeterire nullo modo possum. (Cic. *Pro Marcello* 1)

> Such great humanity, such unusual and even unheard-of
> clemency, such moderation in a position of supreme power, in
> short a wisdom beyond belief and almost divine, these I can in
> no way pass over in silence.

> nullius tantum flumen est ingeni, nulla dicendi aut scribendi
> tanta vis, tantaque copia quae non dicam exornare, sed
> enarrare, C. Caesar, res tuas gestas possit. tamen hoc adfirmo et
> pace dicam tua, nullam in his esse laudem ampliorem quam
> eam quam hodierno die consecutus es. (Cic. *Pro Marcello* 4)

[64] See most recently Kraggerud (1994) with reference to O'Hara in the same volume,
responding to Kraggerud (1992), which is itself a response to O'Hara (1990) 155–63.

No intellect has such flood of genius, there is no power nor
abundance of speech or writing that can narrate, let alone
embellish, your achievements, Gaius Caesar. This, however,
I insist, and by your leave shall say, that nothing in those
achievements is a source of greater praise than the course you
have taken on this day.

And this praise essentially continues throughout, and in a sense constitutes, the oration. Of its excesses Cicero merely said *pluribus verbis
egi Caesari gratias* ("I thanked Caesar at some length"), as he regrets
only the fact that his so speaking brought him back from philosophical writing into the political arena.[65]

With this model in mind, we can look to the tone of Virgilian
"laudation" in other utterances than those that create a close relationship between Augustus and Jupiter. It is first noteworthy that
Virgil, who uses forms of *laudo/laus* some 43 times, never uses the
form when dealing with Octavian. In the *Eclogues* Varus will receive
praise, though not from Virgil (6.6 *namque super tibi erunt qui dicere
laudes, | Vare, tuas cupiant et tristia condere bella*), the glory of the golden
age is to come in under the consulship of Pollio (4.11 *teque adeo decus
hoc aevi, te consule, inibit*), Daphnis will find honor, a name and praise
(5.78 *semper honos nomenque tuum laudesque manebunt*). In contrast,
when it comes to Octavian/Augustus, Virgil's direct confrontations as
poet/narrator seem somehow muted, never quite providing praise.
For Gallus, songs are to be sung; who would deny songs to Gallus?
(*Ecl.* 10.3 *neget quis carmina Gallo?*). At *Eclogue* 8.7–10, again, for the
sake of argument taking the addressee as Octavian, there is not actu-
ally praise, just publicity: *en erit umquam | illa dies, mihi cum liceat tua
dicere facta? | en erit ut liceat totum mihi ferre per orbem | sola Sophocleo tua
carmina digna coturno?* "Telling of deeds" and "carrying songs," is not
quite the same as telling praises or singing songs about. Or again at
Georgics 3.46–8:

> mox tamen ardentis accingar dicere pugnas
> Caesaris et nomen fama tot ferre per annos,
> Tithoni prima quot abest ab origine Caesar.

> soon however, I shall prepare myself to tell of the fiery battles
> of Caesar and to carry his name in reputation through as many
> years as those between Caesar and Tithonus' origin.

---

[65] Cic. *Ad fam.* 4.4.4.

Would those battles include Perugia? And again *dicere pugnas* ("tell of battles") along with *fama . . . ferre* ("carry in report"). Not very impressive from Virgil, the "Augustan" poet, particularly when juxtaposed with the anti-Caesarian Cicero on Julius. The true encomium of Augustus is to be found in the mouth of his ancestor, Anchises, particularly at *Aeneid* 6.791–807, lines which seem to approximate the *princeps* to Jupiter, making him a god more mighty and more effective at world dominion than Heracles and Dionysus.

Conclusions

We need to scrutinize closely the concept of Virgil as "Augustan" poet, if the epithet is taken to imply that his poetry easily serves to persuade, and may have been in part composed so as to persuade, that a new, just and perfect order had arrived. I would propose that this is largely a post-Virgilian development, that, potentially this status is a creation of the past two millennia, and particularly of certain cultural moments of these two millennia. The present study will explore the ways in which the reception of Virgil has magnified his Augustan voice (a voice which, again, is undeniably present), and has in the process silenced other voices that seem at odds with that Augustan one.

If Virgil himself came to see the uses to which his poem might be put, to see that, in a sense, it was being converted to a text which could be put to uses he had not intended, how might he have reacted? The *Life of Virgil* provides a possible, and famous, answer, one of the most stirring and troubling pieces of information we have about this poet (39–41):

> Egerat cum Vario, priusquam Italia decederet, ut siquid sibi accidisset, "Aeneida" combureret; at is ita facturum se pernegarat; igitur in extrema valetudine assidue scrinia desideravit, crematurus ipse; verum nemine offerente nihil quidem nominatim de ea cavit. Ceterum eidem Vario ac simul Tuccae scripta sua sub ea condicione legavit, ne quid ederent, quod non a se editum esset. edidit autem auctore Augusto Varius, sed summatim emendata . . .

> Before leaving Italy he had arranged with Varius that if anything should happen to him, Varius should burn the *Aeneid*; but the latter had insisted that he would do no such thing; and

so when his health was at the very end he kept calling for his book-boxes, intending to burn them himself; but when nobody brought them he took no specific precautions about the poem. Instead he left his writings to the same Varius, and also to Tucca, under the condition that they not publish anything that he had not himself published.[66] But under the influence of Augustus Varius published [the *Aeneid*] after making superficial corrections.

Small wonder that these words, true or not, inspired the great work of Hermann Broch, in which the dying Virgil tries to prevent his masterpiece from falling into the hands of Augustus. If they are indeed true, and if Virgil's motives were as I suggest, there are grounds for seeing a more complex symbiosis between Virgil and Augustus than is often the case. For every Tityrus, secure in his paternal acres – and it is Tityrus who praises Octavian, not Virgil – there is a Meliboeus leaving for exile. Inevitably one man's *deus* may be another man's *impius miles*. That is in the nature of revolutions. It was in the nature of the Virgilian genius that the two aspects were to reside together and create an ambivalence of fundamental quality. J. Linderski in a valuable article on Mommsen and Syme notes that whatever the differences in their vision of the principate, each of the great historians "detests Augustus but appreciates his achievement."[67] I would like not to close out the possibility that a poet such as Virgil, who, unlike the rest of us, wrote and died before the achievement was fully visible, might have understood the first part of this sentiment, and that it may have been one of the formative elements of his genius.

---

[66] The Loeb translates: "which he himself would not have given to the world"; the following *autem*, and the movement of the citation favor taking *editum esset* simply as subjunctive in indirect speech, not as a potential.

[67] Linderski (1990) 53.

2

Virgil and the poets:
Horace, Ovid and Lucan

Horace and Virgil were old friends.
N. HORSFALL, *Companion* 2, n. 14

Now I gotta friend who spends his life
Stabbing my picture with a bowie-knife
Dreams of strangling me with a scarf
When my name comes up he pretends to barf.
BOB DYLAN, *I shall be free no. 10*

The earliest surviving form of Virgilian reception is to be found in the Latin poets who reacted to him. Intertextuality and allusive art is a form of hermeneutics, and, when engaged with ideological purposes of its own, the alluding text's relation to the source text and its very effect on that text may become complex and difficult. This chapter looks selectively at some of the ways Virgil's poetry was received and manipulated by contemporary or near-contemporary poets. The initial emphasis is on Horace, who offers the most immediate reception of Virgil, and whose reading may, prima facie, be suspected of being the most strongly Augustan available. I have not treated the elegists before Ovid, nor have I taken the inquiry as far as Flavian epic, since Ovid and Lucan seemed to provide sufficient evidence of a reception of oppositional elements in Virgil.

De amicitia

It is my contention here that there are no very good grounds for believing that Virgil considered Horace a great friend, and that further (and more importantly for our purposes) Horace may have been "correcting" Virgil in his allusion to him, and in the process neutralizing the older poet's ambivalence and thereby "Augustanizing" him.[1] In other words, I maintain that Horace may be seen as the first Augustan reader of Virgil.

When critics become angry, as E. Fraenkel did, it is often worth paying attention:[2]

> It has not escaped my notice that from time to time somebody attempts once more to show that the addressee of this Ode is the author of the *Aeneid*. Even if we disregard for a moment the improbability of a much earlier poem being included in the fourth book – fancy Horace addressing the poet Virgil of all men as *iuvenum nobilium cliens* and ascribing to him *studium lucri*, and then publishing the poem after his friend's death. A minimum of common human feeling should save us from the sense of humour that turns Horace, the most tactful of poets, into a monster of callousness.

T. E. Page had previously offered a similar ruling:[3]

> Whoever the Vergilius was to whom this Ode is addressed, it certainly is not the poet ... When we recollect the language used by Horace of him elsewhere ... we shall be able to appreciate the taste of those who here consider that Horace, in a book published after his death, can speak of him as the "client of noble youths," and sneeringly hint at his meanness and fondness for money-making! Martin adopts this view which is worthy of his translation of the Ode.

Fraenkel's and Page's well-known words[4] have in fact failed to divert readers, myself now included, from so convicting themselves of lacking either "taste" or a "minimum of common human feeling" by indeed thinking of the poet when encountering Horace's addressee *Vergili* at *Ode* 4.12.13. Nisbet and Hubbard fleetingly engage the issue (on *Odes* 1.3): "Horace wrote for Virgil an *epicedion* on Quintilius (*carm.* 1.24) and probably an amusing invitation-poem (4.12)" –

---

[1] This should not be taken to imply that Horace is himself consistently or uncomplicatedly "Augustan" in his own ideological outlook, just that in certain places he is a strong Augustan reader of Virgil.

[2] Fraenkel (1957) 418, n. 1.

[3] Page (1883) 441.

[4] For bibliography see most recently Belmont (1980) 1–20; including the article of R. Minadeo (1975–6), which begins also with Page and Fraenkel. Horsfall (1995) 2 excludes 4.12 as referring to the poet.

where "amusing" compensates for the identification and deflects the possibility of poor taste. But there is no consensus on the identification.[5] D. E. Belmont imagines a putative reader, skilled in Latin but a newcomer to Horace, reading through the corpus for the first time:[6]

> [The reader] will eventually come to *Ode* 4.12 and find (if the collection is read in order of publication) the eighth reference out of ten to a certain "Vergilius." The first seven and the last two are uniformly granted to be the poet of the *Eclogues*, *Georgics* and *Aeneid*. So, it would seem obvious, is this reference in *Ode* 4.12.[7]

Indeed it is inconceivable that it did not even occur to Horace that his reader might think of the poet, as for instance Porphyrio did: *Vergilium adloquitur.*[8]

What has worked against the identification with Virgil is the injunction to the addressee, described as "client of the young nobility" (15 *iuvenum nobilium cliens*), to "put aside delays and eagerness for profit" (25 *pone moras et studium lucri*), and so to join Horace's symposium. Most assume the date of composition must be before the death of Virgil, well before publication of the fourth book in 13 BC at the earliest. The options, then, for the tone of these phrases is that they are to be taken as light-hearted banter (so Nisbet-Hubbard and others), or, they are not really negative, but are part of a "splendid light-hearted poem ... sent *privately* to a splendid over-worked poet": "The two 'callous' phrases suggest in fact, that the poem was written while Vergil was in the agonizing heat of composing or even just beginning the *Aeneid*."[9] Virgil is to interrupt this work and come and

---

[5] This may best be seen from Belmont (1980) 5–6, nn. 19, 20, 21, 22. A recent exception since Belmont, though tentative, is Putnam (1986) 205–6.

[6] Belmont (1980) 3.

[7] I am reminded of Housman's (1926, xvii) attack on Buecheler: "We arrive at evening upon a field of battle, where lie 200 corpses. 197 of them have no beards; the 198th has a beard on the chin; the 199th has a false beard skewed around under the left ear; the 200th has been decapitated and the beard is nowhere to be found. Problem: had it a beard, a false beard, or no beard at all? Buecheler can tell you: it had a beard, a beard on the chin."

[8] In the commentary of pseudo-Acron, the critical enterprise is to remove the poet; and so, as Belmont puts it, Virgil "has become reduced to *unguentarius* or to *negotiator* or to *medicus* [or *cliens*] *Neronum*."

[9] Belmont (1980) 12–13; so too, for instance, Duckworth (1956) 313.

relax with Horace. But there would surely remain the fact that Horace chose to publicize the private joke by bringing out the poem in a collection published *after* the death of Virgil, an event on which Horace is silent, although he writes on the deaths of various other acquaintances. It is realization of this difficulty that has caused critics to look for another Virgil.[10]

In a brief note giving further evidence for taking the *Vergilius* of 4.12 as Virgil, R. Minadeo finds what critics (though not Porphyrio) try to avoid through a variety of means: "we must come to terms not only with the certainty that its Vergilius is the poet Vergil, but a Vergil represented, on the face of it, as somehow fallen from Horace's qualified good graces – and this in an ode published years after Vergil's death."[11] This possibility has not been sufficiently explored, even by those who allow Virgil to be the addressee of the ode.

In a well known article, G. Duckworth painted an appealing picture of the two poets:

> Vergil and Horace are preeminent as classical poets and as spokesmen of the ideals of Augustan Rome; also, and equally important, they were close associates and friends, and I am particularly interested in the manner in which their friendship bore fruit in their poetry. We know little about their meetings and discussions, the exchanges of views on literature, religion and politics that they must have had, but we are safe in assuming that such meetings and such discussions occurred not infrequently. And many a time Maecenas was undoubtedly also present.[12]

But what is the evidence for any of this? Although there are many instances of intertextual connection between Virgil and Horace (which may imply hostility, friendship or indifference), it is worth noting that the older poet never names Horace. This may not be particularly remarkable, although it is also the case that Gallus, Varius

---

[10] Putnam (1986) 205–6, n. 13 has a long footnote on the issue, which otherwise does not enter into his discussion of the poem.

[11] Minadeo (1975–6) 163.

[12] Duckworth (1956) 282. For fulsome applause of Duckworth's position see D'Agostino (1971) 129 "Nulla potrebbe imaginarsi di più sublime che quest' amicizia, fatta di comuni aspirazioni, di incoraggiamenti – quelli che Virgilio, rivolgendosi a Mecenate, chiama iussa –, di approvazioni: soltanto i rapporti fra Cicerone e Attico potrebbero offrire un adeguato termine di paragone."

and Varus *are* named by Virgil, who will have known his "close friend" Horace before publication of the *Eclogues*. Neither poet appears in the ancient *Life* of the other poet, although, again, poets such as Gallus, Varius and Tucca figure prominently in connection with Virgil in the ancient testimonia, as the *Life of Tibullus* preserves an epitaph in which Tibullus is "companion to Virgil" (*Vit. Tib.*, *Vergilio comitem*). Indeed, the sole basis for assuming a friendship is the poetry of Horace, and chiefly the poetry of Horace written before the year 35 BC.[13] What then does Horace say about Virgil, or rather, how does Virgil appear in the poetry of Horace, which puts it somewhat differently?

We may set aside one late reference, at *Ars poetica* 53–5, where the text rather than the person of Virgil is at issue: "why does the Roman reader allow new coinages to Caecilius and Plautus, but not to Virgil and Varius?" (*quid autem | Caecilio Plautoque dabit Romanus ademptum | Vergilio Varioque?*). Of the nine other references to Virgil in Horace, five come from the first book of the *Satires*, Horace's first poetic publication. One, at *Satires* 1.10.44–5, is also of literary value, but implies nothing about personal friendships: *molle atque facetum | Vergilio adnuerunt gaudentes rure Camenae* ("the country-rejoicing Muses have given a soft and witty nod to Virgil"). Virgil is part of a canon of poets – Fundanius for comedy, Pollio for tragedy, Varius for epic, Virgil for bucolic, Varro of Atax for satire – to which Horace then attaches himself.

It is in *Satires* 1.5. and 1.6 that Horace most vividly projects a friendship with the character Virgil, and others in Virgil's orbit. Virgil it was (*optimus ... Vergilius*), followed by Varius (*post hunc Varius*), who introduced him to Maecenas (1.6.54–5). These recommenders speak for themselves, and mention of them confirms the fact: it is Horace's status as a poet that induced such figures to work for his elevation. The journey to Brundisium (1.5), anachronistically encountered through a linear reading of *Satire* 1 before the introduction to Maecenas, finds the group together again: Horace had set out with

---

[13] Duckworth (1956) 311 implausibly attributes ethical commonplaces in Virgil to the influence of Horace: "It was not a one-way street and the exchange of ideas was mutual. Vergil honored his friend likewise by incorporating into the Aeneid several basic Horatian concepts, such as the vice of avarice, the need for simplicity and a humble life, the value of moderation and the doctrine of the mean" – hardly themes peculiar to, or invented by, Horace.

Heliodorus, and was joined *en route* by Maecenas (*Maecenas optimus*) and Cocceius (we hear their names twice in six lines), and also Fonteius Capito. At Sinuessa they are joined by Plotius (Tucca), Varius and Virgil, "brightest souls ever produced by the earth, and to whom [all three we assume] nobody is closer than Horace" (39–42). Five lines later Maecenas goes off to play, Virgil and Horace, bound together by Horace even in their minor medical ailments, retire for a nap. Small wonder that the book of *Satires* will close with a catalogue of all of these friends as readers and supporters of Horace, the only critics he cares about: Plotius, Varius, Maecenas and Virgil, Valgius, Octavius and Fuscus (*optimus . . . Fuscus*, the epithet by now seems portable and almost formulaic), both of the Visci.[14] The almost prosaic enumeration of these "friends," in parallel, catalogue style, is worth noting, as is the fact that these formulas accumulate in *Satires* 1.5, a poem which may be seen as a minute epic on the journey to Brundisium; character and poetic effect are to the point, rather than journalism and personality:

Sat. 1.5.27–8	huc venturus erat *Maecenas optimus atque Cocceius*
Sat. 1.5.31–2	interea *Maecenas* advenit *atque Cocceius Capitoque* simul *Fonteius*
Sat. 1.5.40	*Plotius* et *Varius* Sinuessae *Vergiliusque*;
Sat. 1.5.48	lusum it *Maecenas*, dormitum *ego Vergiliusque*;
Sat. 1.6.54–5	*optimus* olim	*Vergilius*, post hunc *Varius*;
Sat. 1.10.81–3	*Plotius* et *Varius Maecenas Vergiliusque, Valgius*, et probet haec *Octavius, optimus atque Fuscus*, et haec utinam *Viscorum* laudet uterque;
Epist. 2.1.247	dilecti tibi *Vergilius Variusque* poetae
A.P. 55	*Vergilio Varioque*[15]

So it is that Horace groups together "la brigata virgiliana," and he includes himself explicitly or implicitly. But is that inclusion verifiable from any other source? Before 1989 we had no evidence on the matter. But we are now able to see this same grouping in a dedication by Philodemus in a Herculaneum papyrus:

---

[14] For its use in this sense cf. *OLD* s.v. *optimus* § 8, and esp. Cic., *Att.* 12.21.1.

[15] Brink (1971) 144: "here *Vergilio Varioque* seem to echo mockingly *Caecilio Plautoque* in the same place of the line."

ταῦτα μὲν οὖν|ἡμῖν ὑπέρ τε τούτων καὶ κα|θόλου τῶν διαβολῶν
ἀρέ|σκει λέγειν, ὦ Πλώτιε καὶ Οὐά|ριε καὶ Οὐεργίλιε καὶ Κοϊντί|λιε·
Philodemus, PHerc. Paris 2.18–23

This then is what we would like to say on these matters and
on calumnies in general, O Plotius and Varius and Virgil and
Quintilius.

The same formulary (with the addition of Quintilius Varus), but
where is Horace? M. Gigante concludes from this that Philodemus,
who never cites Horace, nevertheless knew *Satires* 1; that the fragment was therefore written between 35 and 24 (the death of Quintilius); and that Horace, who also cites Philodemus in the same *Satires* 1
(1.2.121), was not included by the philosopher in the literary group of
which Virgil was the spiritual leader.[16] Varius, notably, appears eleven
times in the corpus of Horace, one time more than Virgil, and nor-
mally in Virgil's company; we will however search the secondary literature in vain for accounts of the "friendship" of Horace and Varius
that might match those connecting Virgil and Horace; Varius interests
us less because effectively he does not exist for us. It is Horace, and
only Horace, who tells us that he, Varius and Virgil (only in *Satires* 1,
and never Virgil on his own) were closely connected.[17] The concentration of these names in *Satires* 1 has the effect of validating and se-
curing Horace's own place in the world, of giving it a social as well as
a poetic context in which to operate. A friendship may have existed
among them all, even outside the strong and intimate poetic voices
that Horace creates in the *Satires*, but that possibility should not be
used to control interpretation of poetry written up to two decades
later, in contexts much changed from that of the early- to mid-30s.

Between the years 35 and 19, in the 16 years up to the death of
Virgil, there are exactly two explicit references to Virgil in the writings of his great friend: no mention in the *Epodes* or in the second
book of the *Satires*, and nothing in *Epistles* 1, a work in many ways on
the subject of friendship, and one which addresses Maecenas and a
good fifteen or so other friends and acquaintances, including the poet

---

[16] Gigante (1990) 10–13. He considers the style of Philodemus to be derivative from that
of Horace.

[17] For a good general treatment of Horace's "image-management" in *Satires* 1, see Lyne
(1995) 14–20.

Tibullus, if he be the Albius of *Epistles* 1.4. Virgil is named twice in the great lyric publication of 23 (*Odes* 1–3), twelve years and a political sea-change after *Satires* 1 (*Odes* 1.3; 1.24).[18] If in *Satire* 1 Horace is at pains to bring himself close to Virgil, the opposite seems to emerge from these two odes. Distance and difference are in the air, though the critics allow the image crafted by Horace in *Satire* 1 to endure, and to continue as a prerequisite to reading Virgil in the lyrics.

First, *Ode* 1.24, a lament on the death of "Quintilius," a friend it would seem of Horace's (perhaps Quintilius Varus, the constructive critic with that name at *A.P.* 438–44), and also of Virgil's, as the central stanza shows:[19]

> multis ille bonis flebilis occidit,
> nulli flebilior quam tibi, Vergili.
> tu frustra pius, heu, non ita creditum
> poscis Quintilium deos.

> His death was mourned by many worthy people, mourned by none more than you, Virgil. You, pious to no avail, alas, you ask the gods to give back Quintilius, not entrusted on such terms.

Virgil is apostrophized, as the secondary addressee of the poem (and this is the sole direct address to him in *Odes* 1–3). And even this somewhat oblique address shows none of the warmth Horace demonstrates to other addressees throughout his corpus, not just Maecenas, but also the Albius (Tibullus) of 1.33, the Septimius of 2.6 or the Pompeius of 2.7, to name just a few. Nor is the substance of the message to Virgil one particularly suggestive of friendship or even proximity: the death of Quintilius shows the futility of Virgil's *pietas*. Whether or not that refers to the prominence and function of *pietas* in the forthcoming *Aeneid*, there is no particular warmth or consolation here. For those who invoke the rules of the *consolatio* to justify the delayed and oblique role of Virgil in this poem, the response is simple: look to Catullus 96, to Cicero or Pliny if you want to see how a friend consoles a friend.

---

[18] Again, for the time being, I intentionally separate naming from intertextual matters.
[19] Cf. the Κοϊντί|λιε of the Philodemus dedication.

"*Animae dimidium meae*"

We are left then with *Ode* 1.3, the propempticon to Virgil, called by
Horace *animae dimidium meae* ("half of my soul"). But apart from that
phrase, the tone of 1.3, as of 4.12, has given readers pause. Somehow
a poem which spends eight lines addressing a ship which is enjoined
to deliver Virgil, its human cargo ("ship, you to whom the debt of
Virgil was entrusted, I pray deliver him in sound condition to Attic
territory"), and then proceeds into a diatribe of 32 lines against the
impiety, folly and audacity of travel by sea (the precise activity of
Virgil in the poem), somehow such a poem has seemed problematic.
Nisbet and Hubbard make the case against it: "The poet may protest
his affection for Virgil, but he shows none of his usual tact and charm;
there is not a hint of Virgil's poetry, and it is wrong to argue, as some
do, that the ode's sombre and religious tone is directed specifically
towards the recipient. The second part of the poem is equally unsatisfactory; one expects a Horatian ode to veer widely, but here the
trite and unseasonable moralizing seems out of place in a poem of
friendship."[20] Another strategy is the suggestion that terms such as
impiae (23), *vetitum nefas* (26) *stultitia* (38), *scelus* (39) may in fact not be
pejorative, or may not be meant seriously.[21]

If, with Quinn, we take Horace to mean "without whom life is not
worth living" (or something like that) and then just project that
paraphrase onto a historical relationship between the two poets (based
on Horace's manipulations in *Satires* 1), this ode will remain a
mystery, or worse, a failure. But if we are unencumbered by pre-
suppositions about the historical relationship between the two poets,
alternatives offer themselves. The traditional resistance to allowing
Hellenistic poetry the place it so clearly has in the formation of the
Roman poetic genius will nowhere be stronger than when the best

---

[20] Nisbet-Hubbard (1970) 44–5. The expression of critical dissatisfaction is old; for critical
surveys, see Elder (1952) 140–3; updated by Campbell (1987) 314–15. Youthful clumsiness may also be invoked, as by Nisbet-Hubbard: "The poem may have been written
early, when Horace was still trying to surmount the technical difficulties of writing
Latin lyrics."

[21] So Elder (1952), in an article which is in other ways attractive. His attempts to see these
terms as positive are precisely parallel to those of other scholars who minimize the
criticism inherent in the labels of 4.12.15 (*iuvenum nobilium cliens*), and 25 (*pone moras et
studium lucri*).

evidence that Virgil and Horace were "soulmates" is in jeopardy. Latinists who try to elucidate this poem are happy to paraphrase *animae dimidium meae* according to their preconceptions about the two poets, when they might have started with the fact that the phrase precisely parallels a phrase in *Epigrams* 41 Pf. of the poet Callimachus, whom Horace engages constantly through the *Odes*.[22]

Callimachus in *Epigrams* 41 is in love; "half of my soul" (ἥμισύ μευ ψυχῆς – the same three words, in Greek), he says, still breathes, the other half is gone, unclear at first whether stolen by Love or Hades. Knowing his own pederastic tastes, the poet answers in the affirmative his own question "Has it gone again to one of the boys?" "That must be it." That Horace knew this epigram, and the version of it by Lutatius Catulus (ap. Aulus Gellius 19.9), is not to be doubted.[23] Indeed, Nisbet and Hubbard refer to the Callimachean intertext, as well as to an adaptation of it by Meleager *A.P.* 12.52.1–2: οὔριος ἐμπνεύσας ναύταις Νότος, ὦ δυσέρωτες,|ἥμισύ μευ ψυχᾶς ἅρπασεν Ἀνδράγαθον "the south wind, blowing fair for sailors, O ill-starred lovers, has snatched off Andragathon, half of my soul."[24] This latter is a modified propempticon, and of homosexual orientation, a nuance that Nisbet and Hubbard exclude from the Horatian context by citing as a distraction Euripides, *Orestes* 1045–6 and Aristotle, *Eth. Nic.* 1168b 6, neither of which has the ingredient ἥμισυ, which so clearly confirms the Callimachean and Meleagrian intertexts in Horace's poem. On one level then, Horace's designation is playful and allusive, possibly also allusive to Virgil's purported sexual tastes ("he had quite a passion for boys," *libidinis in pueros pronioris*, Suet. *Vit. Verg.* 9)?[25] In the resistance to this possibility we are perhaps dealing with what Shackleton Bailey, in another not unrelated context, has referred to as "evidence smothered by emotion."[26]

---

[22] Cf. Wimmel (1960) *passim*.

[23] Cf. also Cic. *N.D.* 1.79 on Catulus' liking for a Roscius.

[24] Nisbet and Hubbard (1970) on 1.3.8. Peter Knox adds Asclepiades 17 Page (= *A.P.* 12.166), its context ungendered, but presumably pederastic given its appearance in Strato's *Musa Puerilis*.

[25] See Jenkyns (1998) 6–15 for scepticism about the evidence for Virgil's homosexuality, whose basis in reality cannot be proven or disproven.

[26] Shackleton Bailey (1982) 74, in an absolutely convincing, and little-quoted, demonstration that homosexuality was a possible option, even for the likes of Cicero. He refers (72, n. 19) to the "semi-hysteria" of R.Y. Tyrrell: "according to [Tyrrell] 'Cicero never speaks but in terms of abhorrence' of 'that crime which it is a shame even to speak of,' a state-

In short, Horace's phrase is to be seen as a literary *tour de force*, not a sentimental profession of affection. Its further significance becomes clear when we proceed to the second part of the poem, the extensive attack on those who (like Virgil) have the audacity to take to sailing. If the phrase *animae dimidium meae* may be seen to reside in a literary tradition, specifically a Callimachean literary tradition, we may combine this fact with one critic's suggestion concerning the second part: lines 9–40 constitute a warning to a poet who has undertaken an epic venture, that he sails on dangerous seas.[27] To introduce such a warning in the setting of an intensive Callimachean introduction would surely be highly pointed, and makes perfect sense in a collection which is about to adapt the Callimachean *recusatio* to a new lyric setting (*Odes* 1.6). Just as Virgil had earlier adapted Callimachus (*Aet.* 1. fr. 1) in his sixth *Eclogue* (*cum canerem reges et proelia* ...), so will Horace, in the sixth poem of *Odes* 1, set his own refusal to engage in encomiastic epic: Virgil's friend Varius, he who "does heroic epic better than anyone" (*Sat.* 1.10.43–4), can do such things, Horace will not. *Odes* 1.3 may be seen as a playfully emulative – but definitely emulative – engagement with the Virgilian poetic career.

Horace in post-Virgilian Rome

Let us imagine, then, a world in which Virgil and Horace, the former generally avoiding Rome, the latter at home there along with Maecenas and Augustus, are not necessarily in close or very frequent contact. Let us further imagine the death of Virgil in 19 BC, and move on to observe the ways in which Virgil figures in the poetry of Horace after that year. On the one hand we have a poem, definitely published after the death of Virgil (*Odes* 4.12) which seems to tease or

---

ment hardly consistent with passages (Nat. *d.* 1.79, *Off.* 1.144) cited in his own footnote. For Tyrrell, Cicero had to abhor homosexuality, just as he had to believe firmly in personal survival after death, never mind what he himself wrote on these matters."

[27] First suggested by Basto (1982) 30–43; then supported by Pucci (1991). The way for this interpretation was laid by Elder (1952), who, however, saw the second part of the poem as a positive metaphor of Virgil's poetry; by Cairns (1972) 235; also in a very brief note by Hahn (1945) xxxii–xxxiii, which proposes that Horace is teasing Virgil (who had inveighed against seafaring in *Ecl.* 4) for now going on a trip – a real trip however. Neither Basto nor Pucci develops the Callimachean angle, which to my mind really strengthens their case.

even chide a "Vergilius" with *studium lucri* ("eagerness for profit") and the pursuit of client relationships with young nobles. And then we have the *Epistle to Augustus* (2.1), one of Horace's last works, and a work of particular interest here in that it involves treatment of Virgil in a letter (albeit literary) to Augustus, a potent and charged combination.

What has been little remarked on in *Epistle* 2.1, and what links its Virgil to the Virgil of *Odes* 4.12, is the fact that here too we find reference to venal matters, to remuneration dispensed to other poets, specifically to Virgil and (again) Varius. The orchestration of the closing of the epistle (245–70) is carefully crafted. Horace first (245–7) makes a transition from Alexander, whose poets were not worthy of him, to Augustus, whose poets are of a different stripe; the gifts, unspecified (*munera*), these latter received did credit to the ruler:

> at neque dedecorant tua de se iudicia atque
> munera, quae multa dantis cum laude tulerunt,
> dilecti tibi Vergilius Variusque poetae.
>
> *Epist.* 2.1.245–7

> But neither is your judgment of them to their discredit, nor the
> gifts which they carried off to the great glory of the donor, I
> mean the poets Virgil and Varius, beloved of you.

Let us for the time being ignore the scholiastic response to these lines, which naturally tells us how much the two poets were paid, neatly the same amount, each a million sesterces.[28] If we can resist what the scholiasts could not (and many of us cannot), and if we ask instead what Horace's purposes are here, we see that Virgil, Varius, and the genre Horace imputes to them, encomium, function as negative exempla in the rhetoric of Horace's own self-depiction. For Horace now shifts the argument: sculpture of famous men is not superior to

---

[28] The scholiastic construction of these amounts can be recovered; ps.-Acro, ad loc., is the starting point: *propterea quia iam singulis his donaverat Augustus deciens sestertium* ("because Augustus had already given to each of these a million sesterces"); for Varius the occasion of the donation was easy, the production of the *Thyestes* (in 29 BC): *pro qua fabula sestertium deciens accepit* ("for which play he got a million sesterces"). The occasion for Virgil is more difficult to find, so it is usually tied in to the famous recital of *Aen.* 2, 4 and 6 reported in the *Lives*, though the Suetonian *Life* is silent on the issue of remuneration: Serv. ad *Aen.* 6.862 *qui (Vergilius) pro hoc aere gravi donatus, id est massis* ("for this he was rewarded with heavy copper, i.e. ingots") – Augustus would have been less lavish with Virgil, then. For the references see Brink (1982) 252; also Jocelyn (1980).

literary encomium. Implication: Virgil and Varius received *munera*, and were therefore (paid) encomiasts, whose art was comparable, but superior to (say) that of the paid artists of the (soon to be built) Ara Pacis (248–50):[29]

> nec magis expressi vultus per aënea signa,
> quam per vatis opus mores animique virorum
> clarorum apparent.

> Features fashioned in bronze statues appear no more life-like
> than do the character and courage of famous men in the work
> of the bard.

Horace is now positioned to scrutinize his own place in this system of writing "encomium," and we soon see the rhetorical function for this emphasis on *munera* and the link to the "encomiasts" Virgil and Varius: obviously had Horace the power to write encomium he would do so, since not only would this please Augustus, but he would presumably be rewarded – with the assumption, presumably as false as the assumption that Virgil was given a million sesterces for making Octavia faint, that the writer of *sermones* (lyric is not mentioned) toils away unrecognized (250–9):

> nec sermones ego mallem
> repentis per humum quam res componere gestas,
> terrarumque situs et flumina dicere, et arces
> montibus impositas et barbara regna, tuisque
> auspiciis totum confecta duella per orbem,
> claustraque custodem pacis cohibentia Ianum,
> et formidatam Parthis te principe Romam,
> si quantum cuperem possem quoque; sed neque parvum
> carmen maiestas recipit tua, nec meus audet
> rem temptare pudor quam vires ferre recusent.

> My preference would not be to compose *sermones*, which crawl
> along the ground, but rather exploits, and I would tell of

---

[29] We are not to pause at this point to ask ourselves precisely how much of the *Eclogues*, *Georgics* or *Aeneid*, or, for that matter, how much of Varius' *De morte* or *Thyestes* qualifies as encomium in any way equivalent to political statuary, or when compared, for instance, to actual encomium such as the *Panegyricus Messalae* or the *Laus Pisonis*. Suffice it to say Horace knew the difference. There is no reliable evidence that Varius wrote a Panegyric to Augustus; cf. Cova (1989) 82–5; Courtney (1993) 275 is inclined also to dismiss the notion.

geography and the course of rivers, citadels built on mountain tops, and foreign realms, and wars completed throughout the world through your auspices, and bolts closing the temple of Janus, guardian of peace, and Rome feared by Parthians in your principate – if my ability was up to my desire; but neither does your majesty admit a little poem, nor does my inadequacy dare try a subject which is beyond my strength.

That was a way of putting it: we are in the territory of *recusatio*, since Horace is now able to plead his inability to produce epic, encomiastic or otherwise, as in *Odes* 1.6 framing his refusal in terms of his wish to avoid detracting through his incompetence from the honorand's praise. Virgil's and Varius' receipt of *munera* is to the credit of Augustus, since they are competent encomiasts; were Horace to try such a genre, in which he would of course prove incompetent, the issue of remuneration would become embarrassing (267 "lest I blush for being rewarded with a fat gift," *ne rubeam pingui donatus munere*). And what Callimachean would want a "fat" gift? Virgil and Varius are foils for Horace's own self-depiction, just as Varius on his own had been a foil to the chief *recusatio* of the *Odes*, where it was Agrippa who was to receive the praise (1.6.1–2 *scriberis Vario fortis et hostium | victor* ... "Varius will write you up as a hero and vanquisher of foes ..."). That Varius did not write an encomium of Agrippa is irrelevant; all that matters is that Horace should not do so (5–9 *neque haec dicere ... conamur, tenues grandia* "we in our slenderness don't try to say big things like these").

What do the recused encomiastic topics of Horace's catalogue (251–6) have to do with Virgil's poetry? There in fact seems little that is related: Horace talks of geography and potamography, of citadels set on mountain peaks and of foreign realms.[30] But the penultimate of Horace's topics has seemed more Virgilian (253–5):

> tuisque
> auspiciis totum confecta duella per orbem,
> *claustraque custodem* pacis cohibentia *Ianum*

---

[30] Brink perhaps felt this want when he compared *Aen.* 8.722ff. (captive races in Augustus' triumph) to *Epist.* 2.1.253 *barbara regna* and *G.* 3.474–5 *aerias Alpes et Norica* ... | *castella in tumulis* (where plague struck) to *Epist.* 2.1.252–3 *arces | montibus impositas* – "though in a different context." In neither case, however, do we find either shared diction or shared context!

War ended throughout the world, and the closing of the gates of Janus. Scholars point to the *Res gestae*, and to the Augustan propaganda of universal peace figured through the metaphor of the gates.[31] Virgil had set this propaganda in the future, as prophesied by Jupiter (*Aen.* 1.294 *claudentur Belli portae*), but in the reality of the poem's narrative time, of course, the very opposite occurs (*Aen.* 7.607–22; cf. 620–2 *regina deum ... Belli ferratos rumpit Saturnia postis*), and they remain open throughout the poem. Pointedly it is to this more elaborate treatment Horace in fact looks, particularly, as Porphyrio saw, to 7.609–10, at which point, for Virgil, the gates are about to burst open:

> centum aerei *claudunt* vectes aeternaque ferri
> robora, nec *custos* absistit limina *Ianus*

> A hundred bolts of bronze and the everlasting strength of iron
> close them, and the guardian Janus never leaves the threshold.

Rudd notes that "at the end of *Georg.* 1, Virgil had hoped that the young (Augustus) Caesar would save a war-torn world ... here that task is presented as accomplished"[32] – something that cannot quite be said of the narrative time of Virgil's *Aeneid*.

Horace's deflected encomium, then, proceeds from the Virgilian text, but it represents a fulfillment or concretizing of a possibility in Virgil. To the extent that those interpretations are then back-formed onto Virgil himself, we are observing the correcting of Virgil from an Augustan perspective, a process in which Horace played a key role, perhaps the key role. It is by no means my contention that Horace is in any way a propagandist for Augustus, and there are good grounds for seeing a great deal of his own verse as both independent of and even ambivalent about what was happening in the Rome of Augustus.[33] At times, however, in his later poetry Horace seems in relation to the Virgilian text to be working behind a strongly Augustan mask.

Nowhere is this more true than in Horace's performance poem, the *Carmen saeculare* (17 BC), whose images were among the most

---

[31] Aug. *Res gestae* 13.
[32] Rudd (1989) 118–19.
[33] See e.g. Putnam (1990) *passim*.

nakedly Augustan Horace would produce.[34] In the words of Fraenkel, "The *Carmen saeculare* is in fact the first great milestone on the road over which the *Aeneid* was to travel through the centuries."[35] The voice of the régime comes through most clearly in this poem, significantly the only poem quoted in its entirety in Zanker's *The Power of Images in the Age of Augustus* – for the poem indeed amounts to an Augustan image.[36] At one point Horace writes:

> quaeque vos bobus veneratur albis
> clarus Anchisae Venerisque sanguis,
> impetret, bellante prior, iacentem
>   lenis in hostem.   (Hor. *Carm. saec.* 49–52)

Grant whatever the famous scion of Anchises and Venus prays for, with offering of white bulls, he who bests the warring enemy, then treats him gently when subjected.

The *clarus sanguis* is momentarily ambiguous, until the next stanza for the first time in the poem specifies Augustus, rather than Aeneas (the subject of the preceding stanzas). So the stanza realizes a metamorphosis or progression from Aeneas to Augustus. Be that as it may, as the commentaries note, there seems to be a reference to Virgil's famous lines, and specifically to *Aeneid* 6.853 "*parcere subiectis et debellare superbos*" ("to spare the subjugated and war down the haughty").[37] What for Virgil was an injunction delivered by Anchises (not, again, by Virgil)[38] to an unspecified *Romanus* (Aeneas? Augustus? the generic Roman?) to do what Aeneas will not be able to do in the last lines of

---

[34] There is a world of difference between the occasion and function of the *Carmen saeculare*, which never alludes to its own status as command performance, and the *Letter to Augustus*, which does (*Epist.* 2.1.1–4); with the latter belong the lyrics on the Alpine victories of Drusus and Tiberius (*Odes* 4.4, 14).

[35] Fraenkel (1957) 375; also cited by Moritz (1969) 179; he also quotes Kytzler (1961) 151–67 (*Sat.* 2.1.8–15 = *Aen.* 2.8–15).

[36] Zanker (1988) 169–72.

[37] Fraenkel (1957) seems to want to minimize the presence of Virgil here ("Horace in all probability is not borrowing from the Aeneid"), although he is right to point to other similar utterances, particularly in Cicero (376, n. 3).

[38] Historians have been particularly oblivious to the issue of voice, or point of view, when mining Virgil for "evidence" on "his" view of the age. Anchises seems to me to be issuing an order here, and the sentiment is not one that we can simply attribute to Virgil. Hammond (1965) 147 goes even further: "[Augustus] would surely have echoed – if indeed he did not inspire – the familiar lines of Vergil." I would agree that Augustus' rhetoric may have inspired the lines, but that is a different matter.

the *Aeneid* (spare the subjugated), has been converted by Horace into a piece of Augustan propaganda, delivered at an Augustan ceremonial occasion.[39] Anchises' words have been carried out; clemency has been applied by the descendant of Venus and Anchises. Horace's lines may in fact be seen as one of the very early, Augustan uses of the text of Virgil, but its nuance is very different from that of the original.

Horace's engagement with the *Aeneid* is confirmed by the appearance of Aeneas himself at *CS* 41–4, which was interpreted in antiquity in connection with Virgil's poem. The stanza in question is a mini-*Aeneid*, but with notable detail:

> cui per ardentem sine fraude Troiam
> castus Aeneas patriae superstes
> liberum munivit iter, daturus
> plura relictis

> the group (of Trojans) for whom chaste Aeneas, unhurt
> through burning Troy, survivor of his country, built a path of
> freedom, destined to bequeath more than those left behind.

The commentators take *castus* as the equivalent of *pius*, and although that is not unreasonable, the shift is also open to interpretation. The *ThLL* includes Horace's instance with other examples of this religious shade of meaning;[40] but will a Roman reader, or listener, two years after the publication of the *Aeneid*, not have thought of *Aeneid* 4? Horace seems indeed to be negating and correcting the Dido episode (she never appears in his poetry), or at least any moral complicity on the part of Aeneas. This will have satisfied Augustus, as will the greatest poetic lapse of the corpus, lines 17–20 of this same commissioned poem: *diva, producas subolem patrumque | prosperes decreta super iugandis | feminis prolisque novae feraci | lege marita* ("bring up our progeny and bring success to the edicts of the senate concerning the marrying of women and the matrimonial legislation which will be productive of new offspring")!

The stanza reveals another possible engagement with the *Aeneid*. As distinct from all modern commentators, one native Latin speaker allowed two meanings to the phrase *sine fraude* (41): "without suffering harm" (of Aeneas), or (Troy fell in flames) "without treachery":

---

[39] Though see White (1993) 124–5 for the somewhat muted encomium of Horace's poem.

[40] *ThLL* s.v. *castus* 565.26

ARDENTEM SINE FRAUDE TROIAM aut ut Troia non
proditione (*cf. Porph.*) videretur eversa, sed fato, aut "sine
fraude" "sine laesione," ut (*carm.* II 19, 20):

> Bistonidum sine fraude crines

Non "sine fraude ardentem," sed "sine fraude iter munivit"
Aeneas. Quidam enim putant Aeneam patriae superstitem
fuisse, quod iuxta quorundam opinionem crimine proditionis sit
damnatus (Porph.) Pseudo-Acro ad *CS* 41

ARDENTEM SINE FRAUDE TROIAM either that Troy be
seen as overturned not by betrayal but by fate, or *sine fraude*
means "without damage," as in *Odes* 2.19.20: "the hair of the
Bistonides without harm." Not "burning *sine fraude*" but
Aeneas "built a way without being harmed." For some think
Aeneas survived his fatherland because in the view of some he
was condemned with the charge of betrayal . . .

The Servian tradition also records that the *Aeneid* alluded to the tradition, implied by Livy, and dating back at least to the fourth century
BC, that Aeneas survived the fall of Troy precisely by betraying it,[41]
and moreover Servius long ago made precisely the point I am making
here:

> hi enim duo Troiam prodidisse dicuntur secundum Livium,
> quod et Vergilius per transitum tangit, ubi ait "se quoque
> principibus permixtum agnovit Achivis," et excusat Horatius
> dicens "ardentem sine fraude Troiam," hoc est sine proditione.
> (Servius ad *Aen.* 1.242)

> According to Livy these two (Aeneas and Antenor) are said to
> have betrayed Troy, which Virgil on the one hand touches
> upon in passing when he says "he recognized himself mingled
> with the Greek chieftains," but which Horace exonerates by
> saying "Troy burning without treachery," that is "without
> betrayal."

In the Servian commentary, then, an ancient reader confirms the
point of view of the Virgilian Turnus, that there is room for a position
that sees Aeneas as a traitor (*Aen.* 12.15 "*desertorem Asiae*"). Further,
this same reader saw Horace in Augustus' secular hymn establishing
what would doubtless be the Augustan position against subversive

---

[41] For bibliography on this see Casali (1995) 60, n. 3. See also below, pp. 78–9.

possibilities in the texts of Livy and Virgil. No wonder that modern Augustan critics reject the possibility, none more emphatically than Ritter, who has an interesting reaction to Servius' allowing a prepositional phrase to qualify the words that surround it: "Remarkably Servius on *Aen.* 1.242 reads the words *ardentem sine fraude Troiam* together and takes 'sine fraude' to mean 'without betrayal,' evidently seduced by useless polymathy and blind to the truth. The same error afflicts the scholiasts, though Acron at the same time mentions the true meaning of the passage."[42] We are back with the critical anger with which we began, and the source of the anger is the same – the defence of the Augustan meaning.

Image control: Ara Pacis Augustae

The secular hymn finds a kindred artifact in the Ara Pacis, whose details will also have been specified by Augustus or by those representing and sharing his interests. Verbal detail and visual detail are both open to interpretation, and recent works, for instance by Castriota and Elsner, in fact debate the precise meaning of the Ara Pacis, each arguing for the fluidity or deconstructibility of that work and its images.[43] While images may be unstable and hermeneutically open in the same way that literary texts are, there is a far greater possibility for control and stability with the production of a particular image of a character than occurs in an epic poem in which that same character has multiple appearances and is described, is assigned emotional and physical responses, is involved in action and speech, and so on. At some level we may imagine the sculptors of the Ara Pacis were instructed, as a result of Augustan policy, "let's have on the right hand panel of the west façade a pious, bearded Aeneas sacrificing a sow under an oak tree; let's get the *penates* in there, and make sure everything looks ritually correct: give him two young sacrificial assistants; we'll make the connection stronger by having Iulus (or is it trusty Achates?) stand behind Aeneas." If so, the result could not be

---

[42] Ritter (1856) 408–9 "Mire Servius ad Aen. 1.242 iungit ardentem sine fraude Troiam, idemque sine fraude accepit 'sine proditione' ... scilicet inutili πολυμαθίαι seductus a vero et caecutiens. Idem error scholasticas vexat, quamquam Acron simul veram memorat loci sententiam."

[43] For the hermeneutics of the Ara Pacis in general, see Castriota (1995); Elsner (1995) 192–210.

anything other than occurred, an official, Augustan, icon, with a deeply religious, pious Aeneas functioning as he should. Let us assume, with less confidence that this describes a historical reality, but for the sake of argument, that at some level, some time after Actium, a suggestion was made to Virgil: "let's have a poem that celebrates Aeneas' founding of Rome, referring to the *penates*, stressing his *pietas*, and connecting him across time to Imperator Caesar." That is obviously what the *Aeneid* "is," but it is not a sufficient description of the poem to the same degree that our description of the right hand panel of the west façade of the Ara Pacis is generally accurate and sufficient. That sculptural image, like the *Carmen saeculare* of Horace, was produced after the death of the author of the *Aeneid*; it was voted in 13 BC and completed in 9, in an age when that poem had, as Ovid would put it some years later, become "Augustus' *Aeneid*." And just like the *Carmen Saeculare*, the image on the Ara Pacis represents an Augustan interpretation and manipulation of Virgil's poem. It is also worth noting that this vital, founding ritual, Aeneas' sacrifice, a central piece of Augustan iconography, received at the hands of "Augustus' poet" a perfunctory couplet, lacking in ritual elaboration or narrative detail: *Aen.* 8.84–5 *quam [suem] pius Aeneas tibi enim, tibi, maxima Iuno,* | *mactat sacra ferens et cum grege sistit ad aram* ("indeed pious Aeneas sacrifices her to you, greatest Juno, to you, bearing the sacred objects and he sets her with her young at the altar").[44]

"It's your poem now"

> Vergilium tantum vidi.
>
> (Ovid, *Trist.* 4.10.51)
>
> I only knew Virgil by sight.

Ovid was twenty-four years old when Virgil died. It was around thirty years later, in the context of his own relationship to the prince, that he referred explicitly to Virgil, as opposed to the Virgilian text, which had always occupied him.[45] H. P. Stahl writes:[46]

---

[44] The elaborate account of Dionysius of Halicarnassus (1.56–7) makes an interesting contrast.

[45] For the probabilities of publication date of Ovid's earlier work, see with bibliography Knox (1995) 1–6.

[46] Stahl (1990) 211.

The poet [Virgil], at the time of his death, considered his epic
unfinished and unpublishable (he planned three more years of
polishing). Nevertheless, Augustus personally saw to it that
the work *was* published. He must have felt that his interest
was sufficiently rewarded. This, at least, is the way Ovid
understood the situation. In addressing Augustus (*Trist.* 2.533)
he calls Vergil "the . . . author of *your Aeneid,*" **tuae** . . .
Aeneidos auctor.

So too S. J. Harrison, for whom the *Aeneid* "is likely to have been
written with some degree of patronage from the *princeps*" (xxiv), and
who notes "even if the evidence of the ancient *Lives* of Vergil is set to
one side, Ov. *Tr.* 2.533 *tuae . . . Aeneidos* suggests that it was in some
way 'Augustus'' poem."[47]
And so it does, but when in the thirty years between Augustus'
saving the poem from the flames and the publication of the *Tristia* did
it become *his* poem? And what does this have to do with the status of
the poem before its appropriation, up to the time when its poet lay
dying? Are all parts of the poem Augustus', or just the Augustan parts?
In this regard Ovid's words need more scrutiny than they have received from the Virgilian critics:

> bella sonant alii telis instructa cruentis
>   parsque tui generis, pars tua facta canunt.
> invida me spatio natura coercuit arto,
>   ingenio vires exiguasque dedit
> et tamen ille tuae felix Aeneidos auctor
>   contulit in Tyrios arma virumque toros,
> nec legitur pars ulla magis de corpore toto,
>   quam non legitimo foedere iunctus amor.
>   (Ovid, *Trist.* 2.529–36)

Others sound wars equipped with bloody weapons, and some
sing your deeds, some your son-in-law's. Nature, spiteful, has
limited me to narrow scope, and given my talent slender
strength, and yet the blessed author of your *Aeneid* brought
arms and a man against Tyrian beds, nor from the whole corpus
is any part more read than that where love is joined in
illicit pact.

---

[47] Harrison (1990) xxiv and n. 10.

There is something quite strange about the expression *ille tuae felix Aeneidos auctor*. I find no parallel for *auctor* in the sense of *scriptor* with an objective genitive of the title (e.g. *Aeneidos*, annalium, etc.) which is then specified as belonging to a second party.[48] In this sense *auctor* has more the sense "originator, initiator, cause, source" as at [Tibullus] 3.1.15 *per vos* [sc. *Pierides*], *auctores huius mihi carminis, oro* ("by you I pray, causes of our song") or [Virgil] *Culex* 12 *Phoebus erit nostri princeps et carminis auctor* ("Phoebus will be our leader and initiator of our song"). Ovid could easily have written *iste tuus*, but that is not what he meant.[49] The effect of Ovid's *tuae* is to create a gap between Virgil and the *Aeneid*, a gap into which Ovid puts Augustus: "Virgil is the *auctor*, but it's *your* poem now."[50]

This gap is widened by the context of Ovid's lines, which, of course, constitute another *recusatio*, pleading in the first couplets an exiguous Callimachean nature as the cause for writing elegy and not wars (*bella sonant alii* 529). Ovid has a good defense of his erotic verse: "I wrote lascivious verses, it is true, and yet the fact is (*et tamen*) that *felix auctor* of your *Aeneid* also directed his *arma virumque* against Tyrian boudoirs, that is the most widely read part of the poem." Here, in classical antiquity and in a poem addressed to Augustus, the duality of the *Aeneid* is emphatically sounded. A. Barchiesi has dealt well with these lines, pointing to the sexual overtones of *arma*, unavoidable in combination with *toros*.[51] S. Casali also points to the moment at which the arms of the Virgilian Aeneas will be brought *in Tyrios ... toros*: *Aen.* 4.507–8 *super exuvias ensemque relictum* | *effigiemque toro locat* ("and on top Dido sets on the couch his clothes, the sword he left and his likeness").[52] This can be taken further, for there is an even closer engagement with Virgil: Ovid inverts and alludes to a sexual ambiguity from *Aeneid* 4 itself, involving precisely the same narrative moment, namely the sexual union of Dido and Aeneas: Dido's first five words at *Aeneid* 4.19 (*huic uni forsan potui succumbere*) momentarily

---

[48] The use of *auctor* + genitive of title is anyway quite rare; cf. *ThLL* s.v. *auctor* 1210.76 ff., where the closest parallel is perhaps from Suet. *Iul.* 56 *Alexandrini belli ... incertus auctor est.*

[49] *Iste tuus* need not be pejorative: cf. *Am.* 1.8.57 (banter); *Met.* 7.820 (positive); 13.117 (some contempt); *Pont.* 4.8.7 (neutral).

[50] Barchiesi (1994) 18 "appropriata dal discorso augusteo (tuae)."

[51] Barchiesi (1994) 19; also Adams (1982) 17, 21, 224; cf. Ov. *Am.* 1.9.25–6.

[52] Casali (1995) 67.

present themselves as a sexual fantasy ("under this one alone could I have lain"),[53] until the line ending *culpae* forces a correction of the referent of the unmarked masculine-looking *huic uni*, naturally taken as referring to Aeneas, the central subject of her thoughts and obsessions. And so we end up taking *succumbere* figuratively rather than literally: "give in to this one sin" which will, of course, consist of lying beneath that one man. Ovid mirrors and inverts this process as he begins *contulit in Tyrios arma virumque,* where *Tyrios* looks momentarily nominal, *arma* literal – "he brought arms and a man against the Tyrians." The line ending *toros* forces a similar correction of the referent of *Tyrios* and likewise moves *arma* from literal to figurative, but reversing the direction: the epic moved from indecorous and erotic *emphasis* back to epic decorum, while the elegist begins sounding epic but ends revelling in fully established erotic innuendo.

Barchiesi suggests Virgil's epithet *felix* is in contrast to *Tristia*, written in compensation for Ovid's own mistake in producing the *Ars amatoria*.[54] We might add that *Tristia* 2 itself begins by referring to the poet's earlier verses as *infelix cura*; and *Tristia* 1.2, Ovid's autopropempticon reflecting on the anger of Caesar, prays to the gods of sea and sky for safe passage into exile:

> quamque dedit vitam mitissima Caesaris ira,
> hanc sinite infelix in loca iussa feram.

> And allow me, unlucky, to carry into the prescribed places this
> life which the most gentle anger of Caesar has granted me.
> (61–2)[55]

In short, Ovid is the opposite of Virgil, unlucky in his love poetry. Virgil on the other hand was lucky: Augustus got what he wanted from him, and Virgil got away with the rest. Small wonder the exile was not revoked, but let us not confuse what Ovid was doing with evidence for the relationship of Augustus with either Virgil or the composition of the *Aeneid*. All that *tuae . . . Aeneidos* suggests, and it does so suggest, is that (1) by the time of Ovid's exile, and in the view

---

[53] *OLD* s.v. *succumbo* 2a. The point was made by Clausen (1987) 41–2 and n. 11, though I see the ambiguity of the verb as having more of an etymological force ("lie under") than occurs with his "perhaps I might have yielded to this one – sin."

[54] Barchiesi (1994) 18.

[55] Cf. also *Pont.* 1.5.69 where his Muse, though *infelix*, will be content with a Getan rather than Roman theater.

of Ovid himself, the Augustan reception had occurred, the *princeps* had appropriated the *Aeneid* and given it the status of an "Augustan" poem separate from its *auctor*; and (2) an ancient reader could well see the ways in which its Augustan status was able to be subverted by drawing attention to its own oppositional material.

Intertextuality: Ovid and the collaborating narrator

"We cannot ignore, however, the total absence of any criticism of Aeneas' action [at the end of the *Aeneid*] in the non-Christian ancient *Aeneiskritik*, which was rather copious."[56] Is that so? We have already seen that the case of *Tristia* 2.529–36 constitutes precisely such an awareness with regard to the Dido question: the Virgil of *Aeneid* 4 is, under the lens of Ovid and with the oppositional Virgil's help, at odds with the Augustan Virgil. The topic of intertextual connection between Virgil and these later poets is a huge one, and I will select just a few examples where a problematic aspect of a Virgilian passage is activated in the later text. In each case there is a hermeneutics in the alluding text amounting to affirmation of the problematic aspect. In some cases recent critics have preferred to stabilize the Virgilian source text and see simply subversion, correction or destruction in the alluding text, but such a procedure requires a monolithic under-reading of the model that is false to the subversive potential already in Virgil. Where Ovid or Lucan are "anti-Virgilian" they may be so only in targeting the Augustan version. The other Virgil supplies them with the tools.[57]

S. Casali and P. E. Knox have recently contributed excellent treatments of Ovid's allusions in *Heroides* 7 to Aeneas' separation from Creusa at *Aeneid* 2.711, where the hero's injunction has seemed to some to be lacking in conjugal charity (*et longe servet vestigia coniunx* "and let my wife follow our steps from a distance").[58] The later reception of this line will be discussed elsewhere; here the concern is with Ovid, whose Dido, as Knox notes, is unambiguous in her charge against Aeneas: 83–4 *si quaeras ubi sit formosi mater Iuli | occidit a duro sola relicta viro* ("in case you should enquire into the whereabouts of pretty Iulus' mother, she's dead, left alone and deserted by her hard-

---

[56] So Galinsky (1988) 322.   [57] Paratore (1950) 498.
[58] Casali (1995) 59–62; Knox (1995) 21–2.

hearted spouse"). That puts the matter unequivocally; it does so, I would argue, and Knox has observed,[59] as an activation of a reading already possible in the model.[60]

"Virgil is everywhere in Ovid."[61] Ovid's engagement of the *Aeneid* in the *Metamorphoses* is a complex and large topic. What seems clear is the fact that, as in the *Heroides* so in his epic, Ovid draws attention to troubled or ambiguous aspects of Virgil's poem. Some scholars have taken the brevity with which Ovid treats the Virgilian aspects of Aeneas' story as evidence that he was not engaging with its conflicts and ideologies. So Galinsky, for whom Ovid is "merely telling the story *aliter*," and "restricted himself to presenting an outline of the *Aeneid*, choosing, at various length, one or two of the main episodes of a given book of the *Aeneid* and not entangling himself in the rest."[62] I would argue rather that the very starkness and brevity of much of Ovid's *Aeneid* allows the poet to engage ideologies in a particularly intense way. I would argue thus on the grounds that it is virtually impossible to imagine a poet's writing about Aeneas within a generation of the *Aeneid*'s publication without having some degree of engagement with that poem, and without the reader constantly reflecting on the relationship between the two. After all, the *Aeneid* was by now presumably a school text and a classic.

Ovid's *Aeneid* opens with the fall of Troy and with Aeneas carrying his father (13.625 *venerabile onus*) on his shoulders. So far quite traditional, though not so what follows, perhaps (626–8):

> de tantis opibus praedam pius eligit illam
> Ascaniumque suum profugaque per aequora classe
> fertur ab Antandro

> From all the wealth there the pious one chose that booty (i.e. Anchises) and his own Ascanius, and is borne from Antandros across the seas in exile fleet.

Galinsky comments: "Ovid's desire to tell the story *aliter* is reflected by his allusion to a tradition, different from that used by Vergil, according to which the Greeks granted Aeneas an honorable departure from Troy with whatever possessions he cared to choose, and he chose his father." A connected variant of that tradition, appearing in

---

[59] See Knox (1995) 221.   [60] On this topic generally, see Perkell (1981).
[61] Barnes (1995) 257.   [62] Galinsky (1975) 219, 225.

Lycophron (*Alex.* 1263–4), has Aeneas abandoning wife, children and father when he is permitted to leave Troy.[63] And not unconnected to that tradition is the one we have already touched on, that has Aeneas betraying Troy.[64] Virgil may even have alluded to that tradition, reflected as we saw in Aeneas' compromising position on Dido's temple (Serv. ad *Aen.* 1.488). So when Ovid has Aeneas selecting his father as *praeda*, and leaving Troy with him and Ascanius, but with no mention of Creusa, and with the question of why Aeneas is granted safe conduct left hanging over the situation but otherwise unaddressed, it may well be that the ambiguities of the Virgilian text are being activated and intensified. In Ovid's reference to Anchises and Ascanius (*praedam . . . Ascaniumque suum*), we may detect an echo of Aeneas' reference at *Aeneid* 2.729 *pariter comitique onerique timentem* ("fearing equally for my companion and my burden") – no word of Creusa. As Casali well notes, Ovid seems to be indicating that even in Virgil the details are open to differing interpretation, particularly since the account of Creusa's loss is there entrusted to the voice of Aeneas, not the narrator, and it is "un racconto un po' confuso."[65] That being so, Ovid's intertextuality has collaborative effect; he brings out what was already there in Virgil.

It is significant that neither Dido nor Turnus, whose words are so central a feature of the *Aeneid* and of the conflicting sympathies evoked by that poem, utters a single word in Ovid's *Metamorphoses*.[66] That is not accidental, nor is it just a result of the brevity of their appearances, though it may help explain that brevity. The fact is that the narrator of the *Metamorphoses* speaks for the two, and he does so in such a way that he participates fully in the point of view of the two characters, whose point of view is quietly but strongly represented throughout. First, the story of Dido:

> excipit Aenean illic animoque domoque
> non bene discidium Phrygii latura mariti
> Sidonis: inque pyra sacri sub imagine facta
> incubuit ferro deceptaque decipit omnes.
>
> (*Met.* 14.78–81)

---

[63] See Casali (1995) 61.

[64] See Casali (1995) 60 and n. 3.

[65] Casali (1995) 61, with reference to the discussion of this account even in antiquity (Serv. ad *Aen.* 1.711; 743; 746.).

[66] As Lavinia has nothing to say in the Aeneid.

There the Sidonian queen took in Aeneas to her heart and her
home, she who would not handle well the divorce of her
Phrygian husband: on a pyre built under the pretext of sacrifice
she fell on a sword and herself deceived deceived everyone.

Bömer ad loc. notes the allusion to Juno's sarcastic words at *Aeneid*
4.103 *Phrygio servire marito*, but, following Lamacchia, is able to deny
any authorial ambivalence to the Ovidian site by claiming that *decepta*
is strictly the focalization of Dido: it is one thing to have Juno be
ironic in this matter (as in the Virgilian instance), quite another to
allow a narrator to be so (as in Ovid). Casali has dealt with this in the
most recent, and the best, treatment available on Ovid's *Aeneid*.[67] We
also are told that *mariti* in Ovid means "partner," not "husband," on
the basis of *Aeneid* 4.35: *[Didonem] nulli flexere mariti*. But there the
word clearly means "candidate to be husband" not "partner." At
Heroides 7.69 the Ovidian Dido refers to her status as a spouse of
Aeneas (*coniugis . . . deceptae*), as had the Virgilian Dido at *Aeneid* 4.172
(*coniugium vocat*). Indeed whereas the Virgilian narrator had reserved
coniunx for the shade of Sychaeus,[68] at *Metamorphoses* 14.81 the Ovidian narrator seems to be siding with both Didos, for *decepta* in line 81
confirms Dido's view of her desertion from *Heroides* 7, thereby unambiguously assigning responsibility to Aeneas, and affirming Dido's
sense of her treatment at *Aeneid* 4.330 (*non equidem omnino* **capta** *ac*
deserta *viderer*).[69]

The end of the *Aeneid*, and specifically the clash of Aeneas and
Turnus, is generally deflected in *Metamorphoses* 14.445–580. The
Callimachean Ovid narrates the epic action with the utmost brevity,
and expatiates on two insets, the mission of Venulus to Diomedes
(457–526) and the story of the magical Phrygian ships (530–65) –
each with its metamorphosis. The remaining narrative, encompassing
the second half of the *Aeneid*, from the departure from Circe's island
to the death of Turnus, amounts to 23 lines (447–58, 527–31, 568–
73), but two details in those lines are of note.

---

[67] Casali (1995) 66–70. I read Casali's article while revising this chapter, and have profited
greatly from it, both in its details and in its coincidence with my own thinking about
the early reception of Virgil.

[68] As noted by Knox (1995) 214.

[69] Barnes (1995) 264, n. 72 holds that *decepta* "is not necessarily pejorative"; and that it
"could be referred to Ovid's own reworking of Virgil's subject, *Her*. 7.69." But the fact
remains that it may be pejorative and may refer to the *Aeneid*.

A central issue of the *Aeneid*, and of Turnus' culpability, centers on the Latin warrior's relationship with Lavinia. Amata favors the match (*Aeneid* 7.56–7), the narrator identifies Turnus as the prime suitor (7.54–6), and even the prophecy of Faunus which finds that Lavinia is to marry an outsider concedes that marriage arrangements are under way (7.97 *thalamis neu crede paratis*). Amata will cling to the slight ambiguity that allows her to point to the Argive ancestry of Turnus (7.367–72). The Ovidian narrator in fact affirms the point of view of Amata and Turnus with emphatically straightforward words: (14.450–1) *bellum cum gente feroci | suscipitur, pactaque furit pro coniuge Turnus* "war is taken up with a fierce race, and Turnus rages on behalf of his betrothed bride." Since the very wording echoes the argument of Turnus at *Aeneid* 9.138 (*coniuge praerepta*) and Juno at *Aeneid* 10.79 (*gremiis abducere pactas*), the Ovidian version may then be seen as giving narratorial authority to Turnus' viewpoint, even if that viewpoint, in the words of one critic, is an "attempt to pervert the course of history."[70] Bömer (ad 14.451) provides a way out by first quoting *ThLL* IV. 343, 49ff., where *coniunx = sponsa* or *amica* (*ThLL* does not actually cite the Ovidian example), and then presenting his own lemma: *Non quae est, sed quae esse cupit* ("not in reality, but wishing to be"). We have seen such lexicographical hermeneutics before, and will see them again.

But of course the easiest way out would be to see all of this as constituting the focalization or point of view of the character, who does not speak but whose thoughts are presented by the narrator: Dido (thinks she) is deceived (*decepta*), suffering (what she sees as) the divorce of her Phrygian husband (*discidium Phrygii latura mariti*), and Turnus rages on behalf of (the person he thinks is) his betrothed spouse (*pactaque ... coniuge*).[71] There is obviously a level on which such a reading works, but to the extent that the focalization of these characters is in no way "deviant,"[72] but is rather the sole point of view of this narrative, there is also formed a strong bond and even identity between narrator and focalizer. The Ovidian *Aeneid*, built at crucial moments on the character speech of the oppositional figures of the Virgilian *Aeneid*, brings to the narrative foreground the case of those oppositional figures.

---

[70] Hardie (1994) 100. [71] First claimed for Dido by Lamacchia (1969) 7.
[72] On this see Fowler (1990a).

This phenomenon finds its climax at *Metamorphoses* 14.573–80: the death of Turnus (*Turnusque cadit*) is followed by the fall of Ardea (*cadit Ardea*), which leads to the aetiology of the heron (*ardea*), born from the ruins of the city after Turnus had been killed by the "sword of the foreigner" (*barbarus ensis*).[73] At *Aeneid* 7.468–9 Turnus is presented precisely as the defender of Italy against the outsider: *iubet arma parari, | tutari Italiam, detrudere finibus hostem* ("he orders arms to be readied, orders them to protect Italy and drive the enemy from their territory"). And Juno sarcastically echoes him at *Aeneid* 10.74–8: it is shameful that Turnus is attacking the new Troy and standing on his own soil (*patria ... terra*); what of it that the Trojans put their yoke on the fields of others (*arva aliena*)? That Turnus and Juno see things that way is not surprising, although it should also be said that their position is a defensible one in the context of the *Aeneid's* action. But even the strongly Virgilian voice of the exordium at *Aeneid* 7.38–39 refers to the Trojans as *advena ... exercitus* ("foreign army"). And at *Metamorphoses* 14.573–80 the Ovidian narrator again affirms this position of Virgil, the Virgilian Turnus and Juno, subverting Aeneas, but not the *Aeneid*, which contains the seeds of its own subversion. Ovid's *barbarus ensis* has also been referred to the Sibyl's scornful prediction at Tibullus 2.5.48 *iam tibi praedico, barbare Turne, necem* ("already I predict your death, barbarous Turnus"), which captures the same moment in the story.[74] If so, it seems reasonable to suggest that Ovid is correcting Tibullus' (or his Sibyl's) strongly Augustan reading of the end of the *Aeneid*, as the authoritative narrative voice engages and refutes Tibullus' character.[75]

Lucan

There are two current views of Lucan's involvement with Virgil, again extending from subversion to affirmation.[76] The critical stance

---

[73] See Bömer ad loc. for attempts to emend *barbarus* away. See Casali (1995) 72–6 on the aetiology of the name and the fall of Ardea, and on the ideological implications of the fact that Ardea is destroyed by "pius Aeneas"; 76 on *barbarus ensis*.

[74] See Barnes (1995) 265, n. 73.

[75] For the generally positive reception of the Augustan *Aeneid* in Tib. 2.5, see Ball (1975) with bibliography.

[76] Cf. Thompson and Bruère (1968); more recently Narducci (1979); Henderson (1988); Masters (1992); Martindale (1993a) 48–53; Quint (1993) 131–208. Martindale realizes the difficulty of the terrain: (48) "Lucan's anti-Virgilianism is by now a commonplace";

depends, to some extent, on critical attitudes to oppositional voices *within* Virgil. Indeed some recent works on Lucan clearly have a stake in creating a young, brilliant and revolutionary Lucan who can then play the postmodern academic role of destroying Augustus' stodgy old toady, the Virgil of Robert Graves.[77] Such work has tended to create a monosemous Virgil. Promoting the interests and cause of the firebrand, and justifiable hostility to designations of "silver" Latinity, are often the driving forces. But others allow Lucan to have fostered seedlings already germinated by Virgil. A good example of the latter is D. C. Feeney's "Lucan's Underworld," an appendix to an excellent article on Virgil's parade of heroes, to which we shall return elsewhere. A reading of Lucan, *Bellum civile* 7.391–3 which is just seen as oppositional to *Aeneid* 6.773–6, "in glossing over Vergil's qualifications, misrepresents his parade of heroes, and hence inevitably misrepresents Lucan's adaptation."[78] Feeney had found grounds for subversion already in Virgil's own treatment, and thus sees Lucan as teasing out and extending that subversion.

Aeneas, Erysichthon and Caesar

Back to Ovid briefly:

> scelerataque limina Thracum
> et Polydoreo **manantem sanguine terram**
> linquit.   (*Met.* 13.628–30)

he leaves the accursed shore of the Thracians and the land
dripping with Polydorus' blood.

Bömer ad loc. refers us to *Aeneid* 3.60 *scelerata excedere terra*, of the same area, clearly a site of Ovid's allusion. But there is perhaps another reminiscence of Virgil, from a few lines earlier at *Aeneid* 3.41–2, where the violated Polydorus cries out to Aeneas: *quid miserum, Ae-*

---

(49) "We can see more in all of this than overt anti-Virgilianism: Lucan can prompt us into fresh ways of perceiving the *Aeneid* which might otherwise have remained invisible to us." This latter stance, though it works less well in the context of the oppositional image of Lucan, does better justice to the realities of both poets.

[77] Graves (1962). There is a strong element of Romanticism in some of the recent Lucan scholarship, with one scholar even thinking of himself as a young Lucan. Parallels with Senecan drama might suggest troubled poetics more than troubled poets.

[78] Feeney (1986) cf. 17. The Lucan article in Conte (1994) 445–6, a translation of the 1987 Italian version, reads the lines as oppositional to Virgil, rather than collaborative.

*nea, laceras? iam parce sepulto, parce pias **scelerare** manus"* ("Aeneas, why
are you tearing me apart? Spare now one who is buried, spare bringing crime to your pious hands"). I argued in 1988 that the opening of
Aeneid 3 is in fact one of three instances in which Aeneas or his men
do harm to trees, an act with serious sanctions in antiquity, but one
which the Trojans, as agents of the new order, seem to carry out in
the *Aeneid* with impunity.[79] The passage in question involves a double
violation in that Aeneas pulls out shrubs connected to the corpse of
Polydorus, on whose *tumulus* they are growing. Now when Ovid has
Aeneas leave the "land dripping with Polydorus' blood," readers
presumably refer this to the treacherous killing of Polydorus by
Polymestor. But can we really be expected not to think of the results
of Aeneas' actions at *Aeneid* 3.27–9: *huic [sc. arbori] atro **liquuntur
sanguine** guttae | et **terram** tabo maculant* ("from here flow drops of
black blood which stain the land with corruption")? There is a more
immediate way in which Aeneas left the land "dripping with the
blood of Polydorus."

Lucan likewise involved himself in the issue of tree violation, at
B.C. 3.399–452, where he describes Julius Caesar's clearing of a
sacred grove in order to facilitate the siege of Massilia. The episode
seems to have no historical validity,[80] but serves to paint Caesar in a
negative light. Scholars have for some time recognized that Lucan
associates Caesar's acts with those of Ovid's Erysichthon,[81] but it also
seems that Lucan, who was one of Virgil's closest readers and adapt-
ers, has drawn from Caesar's ancestor, the Virgilian Aeneas, in creating his depiction. The grove is presented through an ecphrasis (399,
lucus erat); although ominous, it is sacred, and like the forest of *Aeneid*
6.179–82 has been undisturbed through the centuries (399, *longo
numquam uiolatus ab aeuo)*; Caesar, like Aeneas at 6.183, leads the
attack (433–4, *primus raptam librare bipennem | ausus et aeriam ferro pro-
scindere quercum*); and Lucan, in his description of the felling of the
grove, has a catalogue of five trees (3.440–2) which refers unmistakably to the three-line, five-tree catalogue at *Aeneid* 6.180–2, with
the first line (440, ***procumbunt** orni, nodosa impellitur **ilex***) reshaping

[79] Thomas (1988b). I include part of that discussion in what follows. Masters (1992) 20–9
   treated the matter, but was unaware of my article.
[80] Phillips (1968) 296.
[81] Phillips (1968) 296–300.

Virgil's first (180, **procumbunt** *piceae, sonat icta securibus* **ilex**).[82] It seems reasonable to suggest that Lucan saw, and confirmed, the ambivalent nature of the tree-felling in *Aeneid* 6.

The final and most explicit violation of the *Aeneid* occurs towards the end of the poem; Virgil begins with another ecphrasis:

> forte sacer Fauno foliis oleaster amaris
> hic *steterat*   (12.766–7)

> It happened that a bitter-leaved wild olive tree had stood here, sacred to Faunus

Steterat – the tree stands no more. In this incident the *type* of tree matters. While it stood not only was it a sacred tree (767 *venerabile lignum*), but it was an *oleaster*, or wild olive, and the *oleaster* is the archetypal *wild* tree of the *Georgics,* the tree which in that poem represents the stage before man's propagation arrives, and which stands in opposition to the civilizing ventures of man.[83] Appropriately here at the end of the *Aeneid* the *oleaster* no longer stands, for it has been indiscriminately cut down by the Trojans in their own civilizing ventures; and Virgil unambiguously indicates that it is a violation (12.770–1): *sed stirpem Teucri nullo discrimine sacrum | sustulerant* ("but the Trojans had indiscriminately destroyed the sacred trunk").[84] The motives of the Trojans make sense in terms of military strategy (*Aeneid* 12.771 *puro ut possent concurrere campo* "that they might have a cleared plain in which to fight"), and in fact Lucan, in the sequence to which we have already alluded, ascribes the same motivation to

---

[82] Three of the five trees are common to both passages (mountain-ash, ilex and oak).

[83] At G. 2.314, after man's works have been destroyed by the fire in the oliveyard, only the barren wild olive is left standing: *infelix superat foliis oleaster amaris*. In this poem *felix* and *infelix* respectively define the cultivated and the wild, on a mythical level the ages of Jupiter and Saturn. On this see Thomas (1988a) 1, on 2.303–14, 314. At 2.182 an oleaster growing in the wild, and strewing the ground "with wild berries" *(bacis siluestribus)*, indicates soil suitable for the olive, the cultivated tree which Virgil (falsely) claims needs "no cultivation" (2.420 *non ulla est oleis cultura*).

[84] It is notable that most critics almost completely ignore this incident. Jackson Knight, Otis and Quinn are typical in passing it over completely; Pöschl (1962) 233 mentions it in passing and without concern. Putnam (1965) 189–90 focuses on it, although his concern is chiefly with the demonstration that Faunus is shown as incapable of protecting his own. And Nethercut (1968) has a treatment which, while brief, fully recognizes the force of *nullo discrimine* at 770. The passage is clearly an obstacle to a purely positive reading of the *Aeneid*, and its placement shortly before the disturbing culmination of the poem makes it all the more powerful.

Caesar's sacrilege: *B.C.* 3.426–7 *hanc iubet immisso silvam procumbere ferro; | nam vicina operi* ("this tree he orders to be put to the axe and cut down; for it was close to his operations").

Lucan touched on the issue of retribution, an element uniquely lacking to the Virgilian violation – that, after all, is the point of stories such as Erysichthon's. Here too Lucan seems to be interpreting Virgil. When the sacred grove is felled by Caesar in Lucan's poem, the besieged Massilians rejoice, for they know that retribution must follow such violations: *B.C.* 3.447–8 *quis enim laesos impune putaret | esse deos?* ("for who would imagine that injury to the gods would go unpunished?"). Lucan then responds to what was supposed to be a rhetorical question, and it is a response that looks to the *Aeneid* as much to Lucan's own poem:

> servat multos fortuna nocentis
> et tantum miseris irasci numina possunt.

> but good fortune tends to save the guilty, and only against the
> unlucky are the gods able to carry out their anger.

For Caesar as for Aeneas there is to be no retribution, at least not in the compass of the two epics. I had suggested that the unpunished tree violation of the *Aeneid* was a sign of how the culture of Jupiter works, and further that this theme was to be found in some lines from *Georgics* 2, in which we see the arrival and development of that culture. Virgil is discussing different types of soil; one of the richest types is that converted from woodland:[85]

> non ullo ex aequore cernes
> plura domum tardis decedere plaustra iuvencis;
> aut unde iratus silvam devexit arator
> et nemora evertit multos ignava per annos,
> antiquasque domos avium cum stirpibus imis
> eruit; illae altum nidis petiere relictis,
> at rudis enituit impulso vomere campus. (205–11)

> From no other plain will you see more wagonloads returning
> home with slow oxen; likewise with the land from which the

---

[85] Reckford (1974) 64, n. 4 also invokes these lines, but his reading of the crucial line 2.211 is different from my own. Miles (1980) 132 notes: "The angry plowman does succeed in cultivating his land but only by doing positive violence to it." For other expressions of uneasiness at these lines cf. Betensky (1979) 112; Putnam (1979) 110–11.

angry ploughman has carried off the woodland, and has
overturned groves idle for many years and eradicated the
ancient home of birds; they leave their nests and seek the sky,
but the rough field shines as the plough is driven through it.

This is more than a mere description of the clearing of land: the
ploughman acts in anger *(iratus)* – Servius again rationalizes by suggesting that the anger is justified by the fact that the land has been
unused for so long,[86] but *ira* is nowhere else a positive quality in Virgil.
The expression *nemora evertit* is extremely strong, and again suggests
religious desecration, akin to Ovid's *nemus violasse* of Erysichthon
(*Met.* 8.741) or Lucan's *procumbunt nemora et spoliantur robore silvae* of
Caesar (*B.C.* 3.395); and the whole action is presented from the
viewpoint of the birds whose *antiquae domus* are overturned by their
deepest roots.[87] And *eruere* belongs to the language of sacking cities,
bringing us, again, back to the *Aeneid*, to the famous simile for Troy's
fall at 2.626–31 *(veluti summis **antiquam** in montibus ornum . . . **eruere**
agricolae* "as on the mountain heights farmers have uprooted an ancient ash tree").[88]

Lucan, I believe, found inspiration in the lines and context from
Georgics 2 for the climax and closure of his passage on Caesar's
desecration:

> utque satis caesi nemoris, quaesita per agros
> plaustra ferunt, curvoque soli cessantis aratro
> agricolae raptis annum flevere iuvencis
>
> (*B.C.* 3.450–2)

and when enough of the grove was cut down wagons were
acquired throughout the countryside to cart it away, and since
their oxen were also snatched from the curved plough with the
earth now idle, farmers wept over the loss of the year's harvest.

Lucan has inverted Virgil's image: for Virgil, deforestation, though
disruptive of the natural world, led to productivity, but for Lucan the
plaustra that are associated with that productivity, and the oxen that

---

[86] And he is echoed by Page, for whom the *labor* of the Georgics, as it has been for most
until recently, is a simple and positive ideal whose interests vanquish all obstacles,
physical or moral. Zwierlein (1999) resolves the problem by athetizing the lines from
Georgics 2; see Cramer (1998) n. 954, 1056.

[87] For the implications of *antiquus* in such a context, cf. Thomas (1988b) 266.

[88] The connection is also made by Reckford (1974) 65–7; cf. also Briggs (1980) 33–5.

pull them and the plough, get appropriated away from the farmer, whose land reverts into idleness precisely as a result of Caesar's deforestation. But this can in no way be simplistically thought of as "anti-Virgilian," for Lucan's lines engage and affirm a larger Virgilian theme. For Virgil the world becomes problematic when *labor* fails, when the age of Jupiter stops working, for instance when plague takes the ploughing oxen, with a result much as it would be for Lucan:

> it tristis arator
> maerentem abiungens fraterna morte iuvencum,
> atque opere in medio defixa reliquit aratra.
>
> (*G.* 3.517–19)

> The sad ploughman goes to unyoke the ox which grieves for its brother's death, and leaves the plough stuck in the middle of its task.

Lucan's Caesar, with his connections to both Erysichthon and Aeneas, has the same effect on the agricultural enterprise as Virgil's plague (*pestis*). The death of Virgil's ploughing ox reverberates in Lucan's *raptis . . . iuvencis* (3.452), where the surface-meaning of the verb ("snatched away") hints through the Virgilian death at a deeper, sepulchral meaning. And finally Lucan's image of the farmer weeping over his lost harvest strongly recalls Virgil's warning of what awaits when toil fails in the age of Jupiter: *Georgics* 1.158–9 *heu magnum alterius frustra spectabis acervum | concussaque famem in silvis solabere quercu* "alas in vain will you have to look upon the great heap of another, and in the woods knock down acorns to give solace to your hunger."

Identifying Curio

At *Aeneid* 6.621–4 the Sibyl points out various criminals in the Underworld:

> vendidit hic auro patriam dominumque potentem
> imposuit; fixit leges pretio atque refixit;
> hic thalamum invasit natae vetitosque hymenaeos:
> ausi omnes immane nefas ausoque potiti.

> This one sold his country for gold and installed a lord to rule it; he posted laws and broke them down for a price; this one intruded into his daughter's chamber and forbidden union; they all dared huge sins, and got all they dared.

The criminals have an appearance that is more political and contemporary than mythological, and Servius in fact came up with two identifications, one Greek one Roman:

> **621 VENDIDIT HIC AURO PATRIAM** etiam haec licet
> generaliter dicantur, habent tamen specialitatem: nam Lasthenes
> Olynthum Philippo vendidit, Curio Caesari xxvII. s. Romam:
> de quo Lucanus ⟨IV 820⟩ "Gallorum captus spoliis et Caesaris
> auro."

> **HE SOLD HIS COUNTRY FOR GOLD** although these words
> may be spoken as generalities, they nevertheless have specific
> application: for Lasthenes sold Olynthus to Philip, Curio sold
> Rome to Caesar for 2.7 million sesterces: Lucan says about him
> ⟨IV 820⟩ "captured by Gallic spoils and by Caesar's gold."

For Lucan, Curio is a paradigm of corruption: *B.C.* 1.269 *audax venali comitatur Curio lingua* ("along goes Curio, bold to say anything for money"); and the climactic paradox that concludes *B.C.* 4, in the lines immediately following that cited by Servius,[89] seems to point to Virgil's lines and provide an identification of the earlier poet's criminal:

> ius licet in iugulos nostros sibi fecerit ensis
> Sulla potens Mariusque ferox et Cinna cruentus
> Caesareaeque domus series, cui tanta potestas
> concessa est? emere omnes, **hic vendidit urbem**.
>
> (*B.C.* 4.821–4)

> Others gained the right to hold their swords against our throats,
> powerful Sulla and fierce Marius and the butcher Cinna and
> the house of Caesar more than once; but none of them had the
> power granted to him: they all bought Rome, but Curio *sold* it.

Virgil's *vendidit hic auro patriam* has become *vendidit hic urbem*, now with a name attached. But we need to return the focus to Virgil's reference and the Servian identification. R. G. Austin (ad loc.) sees what is at stake, and reacts accordingly:

> This [Servius' identification], however, would apply a nasty
> insinuation against Caesar in *dominum potentem*, such as Virgil

---

[89] I would guess that Servius' source saw Lucan 4.820–4 as referring to Virgil's lines; this was then abbreviated to citation of the first line.

himself could not have countenanced. In fact there is no
ground for separating the subject of *vendidit* from that of *fixit*
... *refixit* which Servius himself refers to Antony.

We are back on familiar territory: Virgil (or rather the Sibyl) could
not possibly be making a reference to Curio and Caesar because –
well, because Virgil could not possibly do such a thing; it would not
be "Augustan." And of course there is always Antony, onto whom
the allusion can be safely attached, to the exclusion of any other,
less comfortable warlord. There is indeed ancient evidence making
Antony a candidate, and evidence worth pursuing. We need to go
back to Virgil's friend, L. Varius Rufus, and to a precious couplet of
his *De morte*, preserved by Macrobius (*Sat.* 6.1.39 = Varius *De morte*
fr.1 Morel-Buechner = fr. 1 Courtney).

> vendidit hic Latium populis agrosque Quiritum
> eripuit, fixit leges pretio atque refixit.

Macrobius made the obvious connection to *Aen.* 6.621–3. Virgil's
lines again:

> vendidit hic auro patriam dominumque potentem
> imposuit; fixit leges pretio atque refixit

When Virgil alludes so closely to a model, he means us to look carefully, and to look to the differences, for it is in those differences
that significance may lie.[90] As the commentaries point out, Servius
thought Varius' lines referred to Antony mainly because the words
fixit leges pretio atque refixit recalled Cicero *Philippicae* 2.98 (*et de ex-
sulibus legem quam fixisti Caesar tulit?*).[91] The Servian suggestion in fact
seems valid for Varius' couplet in all three details: Antony was ac-
cused by Cicero[92] of selling Roman citizenship to entire communities
(this is the force of *vendidit hic Latium populis*, as Courtney notes), as
he was of grabbing land and posting arbitrary and partial legislation.
But as J. E. G. Zetzel has shown, Virgil, while ensuring that we
will notice the basis of his couplet in that of Varius, has so rewritten it

---

[90] For similar variation of a model which is fully recognizable, see G. 1.374–87, and
Thomas (1988a) 1, ad loc.; also ad 1.377, 378.

[91] See Courtney (1993) 272 for further parallels, including *Phil.* 2.43 (*agros ereptos*).

[92] Cic. *Phil.* 1.24 *civitas data non solum singulis sed nationibus et provinciis universis a mortuo*
(that is, by Antony in the name of the dead Caesar); also 2.92.

as to *exclude* the possibility that Antony is the subject. Only the un-changed third element (*fixit leges pretio atque refixit*) fits Antony, while the rest has been subtly but radically rewritten: *vendidit hic auro patriam* can no longer refer to selling citizenship, but can only refer to betraying one's country for money. Land grabbing is gone, to be replaced by the paid installation of a tyrant, which likewise can no longer apply to Antony, whose designs were that very *potentia* for *himself*. So Antony just will not fit Virgil's lines.[93] But any reader who has come from Varius to Virgil will feel the need to connect *some* specific person to the Virgilian *hic*. Lucan and Servius gave a natural interpretation to Virgil and supplied the name of Curio, and the "nasty insinuation" (only nasty from a strong Augustan perspective) about the deified father of Augustus will stand, not just in a reading of Lucan and Servius, but through them in Virgil as well.

---

[93] See Zetzel (1989) 271, n. 35. The fact needs more prominence. Norden, Austin do not address the issue of the applicability to Antony. Hollis (1977) 188 says of Servius' pro-posal of Curio "I doubt this; it seems to me that Virgil, in describing a whole category of the damned, has widened and generalized his model, leaving untouched *fixit leges pretio atque refixit* to confirm the imitation and recall Varius' reference to Antony." So the reader is expected to recognize a reference to Antony, note that some details do not fit him, but well fit another contemporary figure, with which identification, however, is not to be made. The interpretation of Lucan, Servius and, I suspect, an earlier source, is to be preferred.

3

Other voices in Servius:
schooldust of the ages

This is Virgil's intention, to imitate Homer, and praise Augustus
through his ancestors.

SERVIUS

The Virgil tradition is crowded with lost or threatened voices, always
subordinated to the Augustan voice and frequently unnamed. In
the battle between Virgil and Augustus, Augustus always wins. So
Dryden in his dedication to his *Aeneid* talks of "those" who think this
or that. What endures is Dryden's heavily Augustan "translation," to
which we return later. Similarly modern critics will tend to refer
darkly to "those who make their living by detecting ambiguities," or
to the "damage done by imposing Vietnam on the wars of Aeneas."
Just as Virgil's language, though odd and audacious in its synchronic
manifestation, becomes normative in its reception by grammarians,
who use it as their handbook precisely to create and uphold the
norm, so his political outlook must be clear and univocal – to praise
Augustus through his ancestors. That is an easy message for Servius
to infer, living and writing as he did after centuries of increasingly
autocratic rule, with the divinity of the emperor an absolute given.[1]
The aim here is to identify the presence or the suppression of the
oppositional voice to be found in the early commentary tradition.
The suppression of such voices in the first four centuries of Virgil's
reception has strong similarities to that at the end of the twentieth.

Of the power of the first 400 years of the Virgilian tradition to
create their own construction of Virgil, C. Martindale has well noted
that "Servius was as far from Virgil as we are from Shakespeare," and

---

[1] I will generally use the term "Servius" without distinguishing the complex layers of
authorship involved. In citations italics will be used to indicate the expanded text of
Servius Danielis (DServius).

that we must avoid reifying antiquity as a "time-free zone."[2] As with the philology of Servius, so with his hermeneutics, there is need for caution, but meanings embraced in Servius, as well as possibilities rejected, may also be taken to indicate debate at a much earlier period. In such debate, as in more recent periods, the Virgilian text is still open to a variety of ideological responses. Much of the time we will see that variety being suppressed, with Servius responding more like Horace than like Ovid. But that too is of value, for it may indicate an early and pervasive organization of opinion, with the scholiastic tradition mirroring the poetic. Almost against its will the Servian commentary tradition is compelled, as it assumes or argues for a simply positive view of Virgil's relationship with Augustus and Augustanism, to refer to a voice, otherwise suppressed, that may have had a different view of the matter.[3] In the same way Varro's theological views survived thanks to Augustine, as a consequence of the Christian writer's polemical citation of them.[4]

Octavian, the evictions and the oppositional voice

There is no need here to rehearse the evidence, or the lack of it, for Virgil's having lost his land to the veterans of Antony or Octavian.[5] All that matters here is that Eclogues 1 and 9 are and were read as indicating such a loss, and that the commentary tradition collaborated in such a reading. At Eclogue 2.73, a context which has nothing to do with the issue at hand, Servius reports two views:[6]

> YOU WILL FIND ANOTHER ALEXIS IF THIS ONE SPURNS YOU
> another Alexis, i.e. another pretty boy very much less likely to
> spurn. And some people want there to be a Virgilian allegory
> here, so that we understand "you will find another emperor" if
> this one rejects your petition for your property.

---

[2] Martindale (1993b) 122–3.
[3] Bowra (1933–4) 9–10 briefly touches on ancient criticisms of Aeneas, showing "that criticism existed quite different from the deferential applause of the poets."
[4] Here see MacCormack (1998) 199–200.
[5] See with good bibliography Horsfall (1995) 12–13.
[6] INVENIES ALIVM SI TE HIC FASTIDIT ALEXIN alium Alexin, idest alium puerum formosum, qui te minime spernat. et volunt quidam, hoc loco allegoriam esse antiquam in Augustum, ut intellegamus, invenies alium imperatorem, si te Augustus contemnit pro agris rogantem.

So Servius identifies unnamed critics (*quidam*) for whom it was not ridiculous to see in these lines a possibility of anti-Augustan allegory intended by the poet (*antiquam*). Servius himself proceeds to reject such a possibility, but only for the present lines: "sed melius simpliciter accipimus hunc locum: nam nihil habet, quod possit ad Caesarem trahi" ("but we are better to take this passage straightforwardly: for there is nothing about it that can be referred to Caesar"). But even Servius allows the possibility of opposition to Octavian, as he continues: "illud vero paulo post paene aperte dicetur in Augustum Caesarem ⟨9.5⟩ 'quoniam Fors omnia versat'" ("though a little later there will be almost open criticism of Augustus Caesar ⟨9.5⟩ 'since Fortune brings complete reversal'").

And on *fors omnia versat* at 9.5 we find an obviously related comment: "nisi hoc ad personam rusticam redigas, aspere contra Augustum dictum est, cuius felicitatem, sicut omnia, dicit posse mutari" ("unless you just refer this to the rustic character, there is a harsh criticism of Augustus, whose luck, the speaker says, can like everything else change"). The comment is of interest in that it brings up the issue of voice and focalization, allowing neutralization of the political dimension by stipulating that Moeris' comment be that of purely pastoral character. It is however questionable whether critical insistence on the point of view of a character can ever completely neutralize the political reading. If this is true of the Augustan point of view of Anchises in Book 6, with which Virgil or a contemporary would obviously have been able to identify, then it is also potentially true of the words of Moeris in *Eclogue* 9 – or of Numanus Remulus at *Aeneid* 9.598–620. But Servius' comment also allows the evictor, the new *possessor agelli*, to be Octavian, on whom Moeris then wishes the same reversal of fortune that he himself has suffered: 9.6 *hos illi (nec quod **vertat** bene) mittimus haedos* ("these goats we send him (may it not turn out well)." Here in Servius, then, we may detect competition between the Augustan and the oppositional voice.

Making up rules

It was stated in the introduction that in a sense philology has generally been complicit in creating the Augustan interpretation of Virgil. And although all hermeneutics must proceed from philology, there should be constant skepticism of philology when it creates philological rules that seem devised for the hermeneutics of the moment. This is a general fallacy of the philologist, and Servius practiced it as skillfully as any modern classicist. A few years ago F. Cairns, wishing to minimize the fact that Aeneas at the end of the poem was overcome by *furiae* and *ira*, held that while *furor* occurs "always with a negative force," *furiae*, in that they are found (elsewhere in Virgil) with *iustae*, can even when occurring without such an adjective be less negative.[7] As I pointed out in 1991, Servius produced the exact reverse rule.[8] The grammarian was dealing with *Aeneid* 4.474, where, unlike at the end of the poem, the non-Augustan figure (Dido) is overcome by *furiae*. This leads to the following: "et quidam 'furorem' pro bono et innocenti motu accipiunt, 'furias' semper pro malo" ("and some people take 'furor' as a good and blameless emotion, but 'furiae' always as a bad one"). Servius and Cairns had different needs, and so formulated different rules.

So strong is the allure of the hermeneutic circle that Servius even seems to invent meanings for words which would otherwise lead away from the Augustan reading. P. E. Knox has recently pointed to Servius' strategies for disallowing the narrative voice of the *Aeneid* from designating Olympians or Trojans as "savage" (*saevus*).[9] At *Aeneid* 1.4 the epithet is reduced to the meaning "big" (*magnam*, of Juno), at 1.279, "harsh" (*aspera*, of Juno), at 1.99, "big" (*magnus*, of Hector), at 12.107, "brave or big" (*fortis . . . vel magnus*, Aeneas), at 11. 910 "brave" (*fortem*, Aeneas). This last instance can also be neutralized by ascribing it to the focalization of Turnus, but Knox is surely right (232, n. 28) to insist that this does not eliminate the narrator's participation in that point of view. At 2.616 we further find syntactical gymnastics, as line-end nominative *saeva*, modifying Athena, is impossibly connected to ablative *Gorgone*. At 12.849 *saevi* (of Jupiter) is made conditional through interpretation:"id est cum saevit; neque enim est Iuppiter semper saevus" "i.e. when he rages; for Jupiter is not always *saevus*" – the option of glossing with *fortis/ magnus* is not available here, since that only works where action is involved. At 6.824 *saevumque securi* (of Torquatus) is made to be metaphorical to avoid creating the image, in line with Livy's account, of Manlius Torquatus' beheading of his son with an axe ("nam securi non animadvertit in filium").

---

[7] Cairns (1989) 83–4.   [8] Thomas (1991a).   [9] Knox (1997).

The tendentiousness of Servius' philology is fairly obvious in the preceding instance, and the modern lexica essentially ignore his proposal for the meaning of *saevus*. At other times, however, Servian philology is of a more nuanced type, and has succeeded in influencing the lexicographical tradition, which has by and large shared in the Augustan outlook of Servius. A good and much-discussed instance is to be found at *Aeneid* 12.7 where Turnus, about to face Aeneas, is compared to a lion wounded by the weapon of a *latro*. Servius notes "modo venatoris" "just a hunter," a suffix to and excision of the gloss found in the fuller version of DServius: LATRONIS: *insidiatoris, a latendo* " 'brigand,' from 'lying hidden.' " Again we see ameliorating dialectic in the scholiastic tradition, which is also reflected outside that tradition in various hermeneutic strategies for avoiding an identification of Aeneas as "brigand": the focalization is solely that of Turnus and not the narrator; the tenor/vehicle boundary is a solid one, with the details of the simile not participating in the narrative; the *latro* is not to be identified with Aeneas, just with the Trojans in general. Servius, however, chose a more drastic strategy: the normal sense of the word is not meant here, it just means hunter.[10] The *ThLL* was convinced, assigning the Virgilian example to a category of its own: *audacius de venatore* ("[Virgil] more daringly of a hunter").[11] The *OLD* had a more subtle approach, with a category under the general heading of "brigand" defined "of predatory animals; also of a huntsman." Under that lemma we find references to Phaedrus 1.1.4 (wolf), Pliny, *Nat. hist.* 10.108 (hawk) and – *Aeneid* 12.7. The aim of the entry is that the two prior instances neutralize the Virgilian site, but this is hardly convincing, for Phaedrus and Pliny are both describing brigand-like activities through the metaphor in *latro*. In particular Pliny's *speculatur occultus fronde latro* provides the gloss familiar from Servius (*occultus* = *a latendo*). The only basis for the desiderated meaning is the need for an Augustan reading; the grammarians and lexicographers struggle valiantly, but the effort fails to neutralize the complexity of the Virgilian word, and the effort itself becomes revealing.

[10] See Putnam (1965) 153–4, particularly for reading the word through the lens of Turnus.

[11] See *ThLL* s.v. *latro* 1016.10–12.

Muted debates

At *Aeneid* 4.245, Virgil describes Mercury and his wand (*illa fretus agit ventos et turbida tranat | nubila*, "relying on this he drives the winds and floats across stormy clouds"). DServius had some trouble with the line, or rather with one word:

> **245.** *AGIT VENTOS* not "calls" or "crosses"; for *and floats across the stormy [clouds]* comes next; is it then "leads and controls" as in (G. 4.510) *charming and leading tigers*, which also gives us "paedagogos"? or "shuts out and drives away," as in (G. 2.130) *and from the limbs drives out the black* — and so on? or "pursues" as in (2.265) *was driving the scattered Trojans*? or "steers them," so that they do not bend back their course, as in "steers the horses," because he is carried by them? — for he has just said *carry him together with the swift wind.* Or does *agit* mean "acts"? Sallust has "acts between the contests of tyranny and freedom."[12]

Much ado about nothing, or about very little, one might say; but this internal monologue is noteworthy in that it well shows the critic's acute sense of the possibility of linguistic slippage. Parallels are adduced from elsewhere, both from the text of Virgil, and even from outside it. The lemma may be seen as recording the traces of a polemical debate, in this case grammatical rather than ideological, as constituting a collective treatment of the issue at hand, with developments and reactions all quite evident. The opening negation (*non*) strongly implies that there is a gloss (*"vocat" aut "transit"*) in play. Servius then explains his rejection (*nam*) and gives five possible meanings (also already in play, or ad hoc proposals?), with parallels from elsewhere in Virgil or from Sallust, and he ends without reaching a decision.

In other instances the multiplicity of critical voices is more evident, and it is from these that there emerge the views of reading communities, contesting meanings, but with the guardian attempting to

---

[12] *AGIT VENTOS* non "vocat" aut "transit"; nam sequitur et turbida tranat. an ergo "ducit atque moderatur," ut (G. 4.510) *mulcentem tigris et agentem*, unde et "paedagogos" dicimus? an "excludit ac pellit," ut (G. 2.130) *et membris agit atra et reliqua*? an "insequitur," ut (2.265) *palantes Troas agebat*? an "ante se agit," ne reflectant cursus, ut "equos agit," quia illis defertur? — nam dixit (241) *rapido pariter cum flamine portant.* an agit "in actu est"? Sallustius *inter certamina dominationis aut libertatis agit.*

control that community. When Tennyson said of Virgil's art "all the charm of all the Muses often flowering | in a lonely word," he was perhaps thinking of *cunctantem* at *Aeneid* 6.211. Here is Servius on the infamous participle describing the golden bough:[13]

> 211 CVNCTANTEM relative to what precedes: "lingering,"
> because of "greedy," to show that there was such a desire to
> tear it away, that no speed could satisfy him: for we cannot say
> that the bough which follows according to fate "holds back."
> Some refer "cunctantem" to the nature of gold, i.e. "soft,"
> because it is broken away gradually and is pliable. Others take
> "cunctantem" to mean "heavy," as in (*G.* 2.236) "be prepared
> for heavy clods and thick ridges."[14]

A natural meaning of Virgil's *cunctantem* – and it is the meaning that precedes and generates all other meanings – is that the bough hesitated or lingered, that it did not respond easily to Aeneas' eager attempts to break it away (210 *avidusque refringit*). Such a meaning is particularly troubling when set against the Sibyl's words 64 lines earlier (146 *namque ipse volens facilisque sequetur,* | *si te fata vocant,* "for it will follow of its own accord, willingly and easily, if the fates call you"). When so taken, the words have produced for some readers an ambivalence about the whole mission of Aeneas.[15]

The modern bibliography, and the conflicting views contained therein, is extensive and familiar;[16] but here in the commentary of Servius we are given a glimpse of a parallel situation, a glimpse of

---

[13] "Una parola che ha suscitato una bibliografia massiccia," says Horsfall (1991) 26.

[14] CVNCTANTEM aliud pendet ex alio: "cunctantem," quia "avidus," ut ostendat tantam fuisse avellendi cupiditatem, ut nulla ei satisfacere posset celeritas: nam tardantem dicere non possumus eum qui fataliter sequebatur. alii "cunctantem" ad auri naturam referunt, id est mollem, quia paulatim frangitur et lentescit. alii "cunctantem" gravem dicunt, ut (*G.* 2.236) "glaebas cunctantes crassaque terga expecta."

[15] The lines are rendered truly ambivalent by the fact that Aeneas fits neither of the Sibyl's conditions: the branch does not come easily, but it does come, so that Aeneas is not devoid of support from the Fates (147–8 *aliter non viribus ullis* | *vincere nec duro poteris convellere ferro* "otherwise you will not be able to conquer it by any strength nor tear it out with hard iron"). It is a mark of the Augustan reading that it has to explain away *any* ambiguity at a moment like this.

[16] Horsfall (1991) 26 n. 27; to which add Thomas (1988b). Horsfall himself opts for *cunctantem* as an expression of "realismo dendrologico" (= "bending," "pliant," in ring composition with *lento vimine ramus,* 6.137). I am not here concerned to exclude any meaning, merely to observe the ways in which it and others are generated by tensions created by the primary, "natural" meaning.

critical polarities in antiquity. It goes without saying that the Servian position cannot allow *cunctantem* to mean "(actually) holding back," but it is notable that the whole entry is directed towards suppressing such a meaning. Given Servius' stated view (*praef. ad Aen.* 1) that the purpose of Virgil is "to imitate Homer and to praise Augustus through his ancestors," including Aeneas,[17] we should not be surprised to find a silencing of voices that question this meaning, for at *Aeneid* 6.211 praise of Aeneas is precisely the issue.[18] Servius' claim of a meaning for *cunctantem* only relative to *avidus* (*aliud pendet ex alio*) implies an unreported voice which says "*cunctantem* is somewhat strange; the Sibyl prophesied that the bough would come easily if the fates gave their call." For when Servius writes "for we cannot say that the bough which follows according to fate 'holds back'" (*nam tardantem dicere non possumus eum qui fataliter sequebatur*), it must follow that someone had said precisely that. The "natural" meaning ("holds back") is nowhere openly acknowledged by Servius, but it nevertheless informs and generates his whole entry on *Aeneid* 6.211. Likewise the attempt to relate the participle to the softness of gold, or to defuse it into meaning "heavy": these are both attempts to silence the obvious and unstated meaning and its implications. Under this reading, then, the attempt to silence fails, and it draws attention to its own failure to do so, as it does to the potent oppositional meaning.

Heroic expectations

All commentaries are to some extent tendentious, for they all partake in hermeneutics. One of Servius' central thematic preoccupations has to do with the ethical status of Aeneas – he is a *vir fortis*, a "hero," one who is strong, brave, and emotionally self-controlled. The word *heros* is first used of a character in the *Aeneid* at 1.196, of Aeneas as he is about to comfort his shipwrecked companions. Servius remarks: "**HEROS** vir fortis, semideus, plus ab homine habens, ut ait Hesiodus" (*W.D.* 158–60), "**HEROS** brave man, demigod, superhuman, as Hes-

---

[17] Cf. Serv. ad *Aen.* 8.672; 8.678, for detailed claims that glorification of Augustus is the overriding concern of the poem.

[18] This process is a little like reconstructing the opposing arguments from a Ciceronian oration; the process is precarious, but it is possible, and in both cases we can be sure of one thing – the opposing argument did exist.

iod says." The term is also used of others, for instance at *Aeneid* 6.426, where Servius says that the fifth circle of the Underworld is inhabited by *viri fortes*.[19] *Vir fortis* is for Servius a technical term, denoting the hero, or central character of epic, the figure whose mission and exploits are the central focus of the poem.[20]

Servius communicates his stereotypical views of the heroic at a number of points throughout the poem. When Aeneas refers to the difficulty of recounting the fall of Troy with the word *infandum* (*Aen.* 2.3), Servius explains: "quia viro forti victum se dicere et doloris et pudoris est" ("because it is a matter of grief and shame for a hero to relate his defeat"). Likewise, later on in the same book, when Aeneas reports his impulse to throw himself to a patriotic death (317 *pulchrumque mori succurrit in armis*), DServius opines "*ratio viri fortis; quid enim aliud a bono cive et forti amissae patriae posset impendi?*" ("the reasoning of a hero; for what other sacrifice could a good and valiant citizen give his lost country?"). When at *Aeneid* 10.156–7 Virgil has Aeneas' ship at the head of the fleet (*prima tenet*), Servius again provides a commentary: "more viri fortis in principiis est" ("in heroic fashion, he is in the front lines"). Nor is it Aeneas alone who is seen as operating according to such codes. Later in book 10 Juno removes Turnus from the battle-field by having him pursue a phantom Aeneas, since such deception is the only way to secure the removal of a hero: 10.644 "more viri fortis ille fugae praeponeret mortem" ("in heroic fashion he would prefer death to flight"). Again at 12.648 we find the maxim "fuga grande crimen est apud virum fortem" ("for a hero running away is a terrible indictment"). So too Mezentius, when facing sure death, accepts his fate (10.901 *nullum in caede nefas*) in heroic fashion, as Servius again notes: "mori viro forti nefas non est." And when Turnus asks Latinus to let him barter death for glory (12.49 *letumque sinas pro laude pacisci*) Servius' reaction is equally predictable: "vir fortis enim gloriosam mortem praeponit saluti" ("for the hero prefers a glorious death to safety"). Even word order can function to protect heroism; so at 12.935, as Turnus is formulating his final words, Servius notes: "ET ME the order is 'return [me] to my people,' but so as not to seek something that would bring shame to a

---

[19] Here Virgil places Tydeus, Parthenopaeus, Adrastus, and the Greek and Trojan leaders – all said to be *bello clari, Aen.* 6.478.

[20] Cf. ad 6.648; 7.268, 796; 8.441; 10.644; *Ecl.* 3.79.

hero, he uses an interjection, saying '[me] or if you prefer my body robbed of its life.' "[21]

All of these instances constitute a recognition of standard heroic action, and the comments reflect expectations of epic decorum from such figures. Other instances are perhaps more problematic, and begin to suggest a simplification and rigidity about the heroic code precisely when a gap appears between the expectations of such decorum and the details of the poem's action – an essential quality of the *Aeneid*, I would argue.

When Venus reminds Aeneas of his duty to return to Ascanius and forget the burning city, she taxes him with the words *quid furis?* (2.595). The Servian commentary explains: "*either* because it is madness for a hero to throw himself into the killing of a woman: *or 'why are you frantic' in your wish to fight, since you see that your men are dead. A good word to use in calling a hero out of battle*" (Serv. ad *Aen*. 2.595).[22] There remains little doubt that *Aeneid* 2.567–88, the "Helen episode," was not written by Virgil;[23] but Servius thought it was and here interprets the question *quid furis?* in the light of those spurious lines. DServius would seem to be operating along sounder lines, situating the reference to *furor* in the futility of rushing into battle when those one would defend are dead.

Servius applies "rules" about heroism in ways which diminish and flatten the richness of the Virgilian text, precisely by denying to figures such as Aeneas those very human characteristics that make him not like a traditional hero but rather more like us. In other words, Servius tries to argue against, and forbid us from seeing, Virgil's interrogation of traditional heroism, one of the chief factors that contribute to the complexity of our response to his characters. Gods and heroes should not, for instance, be subject to conditions such as fear or grief. When at *Aeneid* 1.61 Virgil refers to Jupiter's having locked up the winds for fear (*hoc metuens*) that they may cause chaos on land and sea and sky, Servius is careful to explain: "so Jupiter fears not for himself but for the earth's elements, lest they be thrown into confusion by the escape of the winds, just as, if you were to say that a hero

---

[21] ET ME ordo est "redde meis"; sed ne ex aperto rem viro forti pudendam peteret, interpositione usus est, dicens "seu corpus spoliatum lumine mavis."

[22] aut quia furor est virum fortem ruere in mulieris interitum: aut "quid furis," cum extinctos socios videas, velle pugnare. et bono verbo usus est, virum fortem a proelio revocans.

[23] See Goold (1970) 101–68.

fears in war, it would not be for himself but for his children" (Serv. ad *Aen.* 1.61).[24]

We meet a similar instance of anxiety about the fear of the hero when Aeneas enters the temple grove at Carthage; the depictions on the frieze allay his fears: *Aeneid* 1.450–1 *hoc primum in luco nova res oblata timorem | leniit* ("in this grove for the first time the appearance of a new situation softened his fear"). This may seem a fairly normal human reaction, but any mention of fear attracts the scholiast's attention:

> 450 TIMOREM many ask why he feared anything after his mother appeared to him: which some explain by saying that Aeneas did not even then believe the person he saw to be Venus, and since she was unknown to him he had grasped none of her words. But the true explanation is this: Venus had said nothing to her son about the ways of the Africans [the current source of Aeneas' fear], just about the saving of the ships. *Or because Aeneas is not to be completely assured by the pledge of his mother,* lest there be nothing left over for the hero to do to achieve greatness and praise.[25]

Again we see the method: multiplicity of unnamed critics question the basis of Aeneas' fear, with subsequent hermeneutics reflected in Servius and DServius aimed at reassurance. Elsewhere, when Aeneas tells of his terror at the shadows as he leaves Troy (2.728 *nunc omnes terrent aurae*), and refers his fear to his responsibility to father and child (2.729 *pariter comitique onerique timentem*), Servius is quick to deflect any imputation of diminished heroism: **2.726** "quasi et vir fortis et pius non timet bellicum timorem, sed naturalem, propterea quia sequitur 'comitique onerique timentem'" ("even a pious and heroic man does not experience fear of war, but of the natural world, which is why 'fearing for his companion and his burden' follows"). DServius is similarly anxious, declaring that fear may be inevitable and appro-

---

[24] ergo Iuppiter timet, non sibi, sed elementis, ne turbentur eruptione ventorum, ut si bellorum tempore dicas virum fortem timere, non sibi, sed liberis suis.

[25] TIMOREM multi quaerunt, cur post visam matrem quicquam timuerit: quod tamen alii sic solvunt, ut dicant, ne tunc quidem Aenean Venerem quam viderat esse credidisse, cuius, ut ipse putabat, agnitae nulla verba perceperat. sed vera solutio haec est: Venus nihil de Afrorum moribus, unde nunc formidat Aeneas, sed de classe liberata dixerat filio. *vel quia non in totum Aeneas matris fiducia confirmandus est,* ne nihil supersit magnanimitati et laudibus viri fortis.

priate in a hero: **2.728** *NVNC OMNES TERRENT AVRAE hic ostendit, etiam fortes viros pro ratione temporis et causarum et debere et decere metuere* ("here he shows that it is necessary and fitting that even heroes should experience fear depending on the occasion and circumstances").

The shedding of tears, and other visible or audible signs of grief, are likewise acts eschewed by the stereotypical hero, and therefore acts whose extenuating motivation Servius feels he must explain. Virgil's first image of Aeneas has struck many readers as being at least unconventional in its initial exposure of the principal character:

> extemplo Aeneae solvuntur frigore membra;
> ingemit et duplicis tendens ad sidera palmas
> talia voce refert: "o terque quaterque beati,
> quis ante ora patrum Troiae sub moenibus altis
> contigit oppetere!" (*Aen.* 1.92–6)

Suddenly Aeneas' limbs go loose with chill fear; he groans and stretching both palms to the stars cries out so: "Oh thrice and four times blessed, whose lot it was to seek death before the sight of their fathers beneath the high walls of Troy!"

Servius makes a distinction that we may well, with reflection, accept: "**INGEMIT** non propter mortem ingemit, sequitur enim 'o terque quaterque beati,' sed propter mortis genus" ("he groans not because of the fact of death – for there follows "Oh three and four times blessed" – but because of the type of death"). But what is important for our purposes is to note the commentator's consistent efforts to create a conventional reading of Virgil's hero. And not only heroes, but even the ghosts of heroes, are permitted to groan only under certain circumstances. As Hector appears to Aeneas and urges him to leave the hopeless situation in Troy, he too groans (*Aen.* 2.288 *sed graviter gemitus imo de pectore ducens*); which evokes the following tendentious hermeneutics from Servius: **2.288** "**GEMITVS** nec enim parvus dolor est viro forti fortem virum fugam suadere" ("it is no small source of grief for a hero to have to persuade a hero to run away").

As with groans, so with tears, permitted for women and boys but not heroes. At *Aeneid* 10.789–90 Lausus reacts with due piety to the wounding of his father (*ingemuit cari graviter genitoris amore, | ut vidit, Lausus, lacrimaeque per ora volutae*). Servius was concerned that we be sure it was Lausus and not Mezentius (794 *ille*) who shed these tears ("non viri fortis, sed filii est considerata persona" "the character in question is that of the son, not the hero"). After the death of Nisus and Euryalus, and particularly after the lament of Euryalus' mother, the Trojans are desolated:

> hoc fletu concussi animi, maestusque per omnis
> it gemitus, torpent infractae ad proelia vires.
> illam incendentem luctus Idaeus et Actor
> Ilionei monitu et multum lacrimantis Iuli
> corripiunt interque manus sub tecta reponunt.
>
> (*Aen.* 9.498–502)

> Their minds were shattered by her weeping, and a sorry groan passed through their ranks, their strength is shattered and paralyzed for battle. As she fuels their grief Idaeus and Actor, on the advice of Ilioneus and much-crying Iulus, seize her up and carry her inside.

Again Servius makes distinctions: *Aen.* 9.499 "LACRIMANTIS IVLI puero dat lacrimas, cui potest sine pudore; viris fortibus tantum dolorem" ("to the boy he assigns tears which carries no shame; to the heroes he only assigns grief"). The realities, of course, are otherwise: earlier in this same book Euryalus' parting words had caused tears among all the Trojans (though admittedly most in Ascanius): *Aen.* 9.292–3 *percussa mente dedere | Dardanidae lacrimas, ante omnis pulcher Iulus* "The Dardanians' minds are shattered and they give forth tears, beautiful Iulus before all others." The fact is that heroes do weep, Aeneas included; indeed even the deified Hercules weeps (*Aen.* 10.464–5 *audiit Alcides iuvenem magnumque sub imo | corde premit gemitum lacrimasque effundit inanis* "Hercules heard the youth and held back a great groan in the depth of his heart and poured forth empty tears").[26]

In all the preceding examples Servius was driven by the principle that heroic behavior cannot involve the demonstration of grief and sorrow, and this is just one of the ways in which the commentary tradition flattens out the poem, reduces its complexity, and makes it more reassuring and less rich than it in reality is, more conforming to critically constructed decorum. This process occurs in particular when the commentary tradition starts showing anxiety about public or

---

[26] On *lacrimae* etc. in the *Aeneid.*, see Harrison (1991) on 10.464–5; also Petrini (1997) 63–5.

official issues, about the character of Aeneas, about Augustus, and about Jupiter, a triad whose cause is the focus of the Augustan reader, ancient or modern.

Vituperating Aeneas

Servius exhibits a consistently defensive attitude towards the character of Aeneas. That defensiveness has as much to do with the grammarian's standardizing the hero as it does with any conscious Augustanism, but that does not matter. The fact is that these commentaries consistently resist any qualification of Aeneas' actions, with the result that they constitute one of the strongest Augustan readings of Virgil. But as in the earlier instances, so here, we may find traces of those voices which generate the defensiveness. At *Aeneid* 6.351–4 the ghost of Palinurus explains to Aeneas that when swept overboard along with the rudder he feared not for himself, but rather for the ship, deprived as it now was of helm and helmsman (353 *spoliata armis, excussa magistro*). Servius' response is protective of Aeneas: (ad 354) "nec de Aeneae peritia desperavit, sed propter perditum gubernaculum" ("he does not despair about the skill of Aeneas, but because of the lost rudder"). It is true that Aeneas took the helm when Palinurus was lost overboard (5.867–8 *amisso . . . magistro*), but to extract from Palinurus' words an implied stigmatization of Aeneas' navigational skills suggests that the Servian tradition was attuned by nature or practice to debate about the character of Aeneas.

Elsewhere indications of such a debate are more explicit, with specific issues debated over an extended period of time and with critics named, not unlike the commentary tradition of the last two centuries.[27] In the archery contest of *Aeneid* 5 Aeneas himself sets up the target for his men to shoot at, a dove tied to the top of the mast of Serestus' ship (487–9). Here is Servius' reaction (ad 5.517):

> One should be aware that this passage was taken from Homer: and so it is not valid to criticize Aeneas for hanging up the bird of his mother. For the sequence was simply translated: and whatever bird he had hung up he would be open to this

---

[27] See Timpanaro (1986) 129, n. 2, on the chronology of Velius Longus and Urbanus, and on this topic generally, see his whole Ch. 5 "Velio Longo, Urbano, Aspro" 129–41.

criticism: for each bird is consecrated to a divinity. Moreover Urbanus says that a mother could be more easily placated.[28]

A series of strategies emerges, reactive to an unelaborated critical voice, dismissively judged *inanis* by the apologetic Servius. But again his wording points us to and recovers the existence of the debate he would have us find worthless; in saying "it is not valid to criticize Aeneas," you necessarily imply that someone has done so, and further demonstrate the vigor of your point of view by minimizing the argument. And what of the strategies for proving critical *inanitas*? Servius' strategy is to invoke the Homeric original: Virgil was compelled to "translate," and any consequences for interpretation in terms of the *Virgilian* poem are accidents and therefore uninterpretable. This is a ploy familiar in modern commentaries on the later parts of the *Aeneid*, when Aeneas starts looking a little too savage, and where actions such as human sacrifice might seem to take him beyond the requirements, or even the bounds, of *pietas*.[29] A further critical rationalization in Servius' note claims that *some* deity had to be slighted since all birds are sacred to some god or other. In other words, the actual bird used is not significant, a claim that will, I suppose, persuade nobody. A third and more ingenious critical move, by Urbanus, makes a virtue of Virgil's choice of the dove: mothers are easiest to placate.

We in fact have further information on these lines; the Scholia Veronensia (ad *Aen.* 5.488) preserve a fuller and more lively critical context for the Servian note:

> Velius Longus: Cornutus comments that [Aeneas] improperly set up as an archery target a bird sacred to his mother. But it is clear that he is just following Homer; but one could likewise complain whatever bird was set up, because each type of bird is sacred to some god or other.[30]

---

[28] sane sciendum hunc totum locum ab Homero esse sumptum: unde inanis est vituperatio Aeneae, quod suspenderat avem maternam. nam et res est translata simpliciter: et quamcunque suspendisset avem, in hanc incideret vituperationem: nulla enim avis caret consecratione, quia singulae aves numinibus sunt consecratae. quamquam Vrbanus dicat, matrem citius potuisse placari.

[29] See Thomas (1992) 139–41.

[30] Velius Longus: adnotat Cornutus, quod indecenter sacram matri suae avem sagittis figendam constituerit. sed videlicet Homerum secutus est; sed et eodem modo quamcunque aliam avem expositam queri potuit, quia singula genera alitum Diis quibuscunque sacrata sunt.

Servius' entry derives from Velius Longus' (?early second century) criticism of the comment of Cornutus (mid-first century), the critic whose name Servius was to suppress, replacing it with the vague *inanis est vituperatio.* Servius then plagiarized Velius Longus (simple Homeric echo; any bird would offend some deity), and added the further, post-Velian response of Urbanus (mothers are easier to appease), whose name, unlike that of Cornutus, is recorded.[31]

In the preceding example the voice of L. Annaeus Cornutus, teacher of Persius and of Lucan, seems to be the ambivalent, or at least the non-Augustan one.[32] Subsequent notices by Velius Longus, and after him Urbanus, further erase the non-Augustan reading, whose author is ultimately consigned to oblivion by Servius (who does name the apologist reader Urbanus). And the fact that Gellius, writing two centuries before Servius, can discuss Cornutus as just one of a number of those writing commentaries on Virgil (2.6.1 *nonnulli grammatici aetatis superioris ... qui commentaria in Vergilium composuerunt*) brings home just how rich and polemically charged that tradition is likely to have been.[33]

It would certainly be of great interest to have more than the handful of observations that survive from Cornutus' commentary on the *Aeneid*,[34] and not just his comments on that poem. Servius and DServius on *Eclogue* 6.9 (*non iniussa cano*) give the following: "NON INIVSSA CANO vel ab Apolline, vel ab Augusto, *vel a Maecenate,* ⟨*ut*⟩ *'te sine nil altum mens incohat' (G. 3.42). et hoc ideo, quia dixerat 'aurem vellit.'* " ("I DO NOT SING WHAT IS NOT COMMANDED either by Apollo, or by Augustus, *or by Maecenas, as in 'without you my mind begins nothing lofty.' And it's because he had said 'he tweaked my ear.'* ") Junius Philargyrius is briefer ("id est a Nymphis vel a Caesare," "i.e. ordered by the nymphs or by Caesar"), but it is again the Verona scholia that allow us both to identify the voices and reconstruct dialogue: "[NON INIVSSA CANO] Cornutus putat hoc ad Musas pertinere, sed illud magis accipiendum: 'Cynthius aurem vellit et admon-

---

[31] On Urbanus, Geymonat (1990); also *RE* 17.983.

[32] See Chapter 2, pp. 83–92 for Lucan as a reader of the *Aeneid*. In general on Cornutus' connection with Persius, see Suet. *Vit. Pers., passim*; also Geymonat (1984).

[33] Cf. Timpanaro (1986) 71–5 on such communities.

[34] The evidence is to be found in Charisius, *Inst. Gram. Lib.* i, 127 Keil (*L. Annaeus Cornutus in Maronis commentariis Aeneidos X ...*); see also Ribbeck (1966) 123.

uit,' scilicet quia iussu Augusti admonitus sit, ut Bucolica scriberet."
("[MY SONG IS COMMANDED] Cornutus thinks this refers to the
Muses, but this is preferable: 'the Cynthian tweaked my ear and
warned me,' presumably because he was warned by order of Augustus to write the *Eclogues*"). The poetical forces (Apollo, Muses,
Nymphs, the latter presumably confused with the Muses, who are at
least in the previous lines of the *Eclogue*) are in competition with the
political (Augustus, Maecenas). Virgil's meaning is not of concern
here; what matters rather is the fact that Cornutus' name attaches to a
view that seems consciously to exclude Augustan inspiration for
Virgilian verse, and that the Cornutan point of view is then denied
by the Servian commentary, which is consistent and unequivocal
in its view that Virgil writes for Augustus. The teacher of Lucan and
Lucan himself seem to have affinities in their response to the text of
Virgil.

Lest we turn Cornutus into a full-blooded oppositional reader of
Virgil, there are indications elsewhere that he participated in supporting an Augustan view of the poem. We have for instance the
infamous tradition, reported by Servius and treated in the last chapter,
in which Aeneas and Antenor survive the fall of Troy through
betrayal of their city to the Greeks: "hi enim duo Troiam prodidisse
dicuntur secundum Livium, quod et Vergilius per transitum tangit,
ubi ait 'se quoque principibus permixtum agnovit Achivis'" ("According to Livy these two are held to have betrayed Troy, which
Virgil alludes to in passing when he says 'he also recognized himself
mixed in with the Achaean leaders'" [Serv. ad 1.242]. Cornutus
argued against such a reading. Servius allows the depiction of Aeneas
in the midst of the Greek leaders (*Aen.* 1.488 *principibus permixtum . . .
Achivis*) to be taken in one of two ways: it is either an oblique reference to his betrayal ("aut latenter proditionem tangit"), or, con-
versely, a sign of his courage, since it is a mark of great courage to
fight in the midst of the enemy. The lemma ends on a different note:
"Cornutus tamen dicit versu isto [2.396] 'vadimus immixti Danais'
hoc esse solvendum" ("Cornutus however says that this is to be explained by the line that goes [2.396] 'on we went mixed in with the
Greeks'"). In spite of the parallel verbs (compounds of *misceo*), it
seems unlikely that the depiction of Aeneas alone with Greeks on
Dido's temple refers to Aeneas and his men in Greek camouflage at
the fall of Troy. What matters however, is that already by the mid-

first century AD Virgil criticism, like post-Virgilian poetry, permits the critical position that the poet alluded to a tradition in which Aeneas betrayed Troy.

Conflicting pieties

T. S. Eliot is but one of the more eloquent critics to have drawn attention to the central and chief quality of Aeneas:[35]

> When Virgil speaks, as he does, of *pius Aeneas*, we are apt to think of his care of his father, of his devotion to his father's memory, and of his touching encounter with his father on his descent into the nether regions. But the word *pietas* with Virgil has much wider associations of meaning: it implies an attitude towards the individual, towards the family, towards the region, and towards the imperial destiny of Rome. And finally Aeneas is "pious" also in his respect towards the gods, and in his punctilious observance of rites and offerings. It is an attitude towards all of these things, and therefore implies a unity and an order among them: it is in fact an attitude towards life.

That *pietas* is the chief ethical condition to which Aeneas is subject is beyond debate, and yet is has also been claimed that at times in this poem "one form of *pietas* may conflict with another."[36] When such conflict occurs, Virgilian ambivalence becomes particularly intense. An infamous instance occurs at *Aeneid* 4.393, where the narrative resumes, following Dido's collapse, with the words *at pius Aeneas* ... Here too we find competing scholiastic voices, those of R. G. Austin and T. E. Page, on whom Austin remarks:[37]

> "Virgil seems unmoved by his own genius, and begins the next paragraph quite placidly *at pius Aeneas!*" – so Page, in words that "every schoolboy knows" and has echoed in examination answers for sixty years, words that are unjust and quite misleading.

Austin then devotes two pages of his commentary to arguing that *pietas* is a quality that brings "pain and sorrow" to the character who is possessed by it (which may well be the case); and so it is that whereas "Dido is an open book" Virgil only gives us "half-glances,

---

[35] Eliot (1951) 142. [36] Harrison (1991) 219. [37] Austin (1955) 121.

half-revelations" of Aeneas: "here is another such glance, and all his misery is there for us to pity." Readers who glance back to the transition from *Aeneid* 4.392–3 may see other miseries, other grounds for their pity. It is the very attempt, which can never succeed, to resolve the conflicting *pietates* and the ambiguities figured in them, that simplifies the complexity of the text.[38]

Harrison's emphasis on the notion of conflicting pieties provides a far more satisfactory and plausible way of looking at the issue, for Virgil's very elaboration of Dido, his constant presentation of the narrative through her eyes, prevents us from a simple focus on Aeneas. Servius, like Austin, works to avoid allowing double or competing pieties, later in the poem when Aeneas, only moments before he kills the young Lausus, states (*Aen.* 10.812): *fallit te incautum pietas tua* ("reckless you are deceived by your piety"). Servius elaborates: "quod credis idcirco me pium tibi veniam posse concedere, quia et ipse pietatis intuitu dimicas pro patris salute. 'tua' autem 'pietas' prudenter est additum, quasi non a parente descendens" "because you believe that I who am pious can grant you pardon, on the grounds that you too are fighting with regard to piety, for the safety of your father. Yet '*your* piety' is added intentionally, as not coming down from his father [i.e. the evil Mezentius]." Where Harrison and others see some irony in the conflict between Lausus' piety and Aeneas' drawing attention to his own piety, Servius is able to keep his focus on the piety of Aeneas, without regard to the other relationships that are disrupted by that piety and that are so emphatically foregrounded in Virgil's narrative.

At the end of the epic, when Aeneas is temporarily swayed by Turnus' final words and just before he sees the baldric of Pallas, Servius (ad 12.940) interprets: "CVNCTANTEM FLECTERE SERMO COEPERAT omnis intentio ad Aeneae pertinet gloriam: nam et ex eo quod hosti cogitat parcere, pius ostenditur, et ex eo quod eum interimit, pietatis gestat insigne: nam Evandri intuitu Pallantis ulciscitur mortem." ("**Aeneas hesitated, beginning to bend to Turnus' words:** everything is directed at the glory of Aeneas: for in that he ponders sparing his enemy he is demonstrably pious, and in that he in

---

[38] There is at least a potential *pietas* relationship between Dido and Aeneas. *Pietas* can be an extra-familial relationship (*OLD* s.v. 3D), and is frequently found in inscriptions of the relationship between husband and wife, a relationship that Dido believes, with some support from the narrative, she has with Aeneas.

fact kills him he bears a mark of piety: for he avenges the death of Pallas out of respect for Evander"). Here is the extreme Augustan reading, and it is certainly a possible reading of Virgil's ending. Aeneas is doubly pious: once for considering sparing Turnus, and again for not doing so. But to maintain it Servius must keep the focus on Aeneas, and take no account of the plea to remember Turnus' relationship with his father, which again leads us towards conflict of pieties at the poem's end. As for Dido, so here for Turnus, the *pietas* on which Aeneas settles is the one that eclipses other pieties and brings with it doom. That doom is required by public, Augustan *pietas*, but that is small comfort to those whose own claims on *pietas* are rejected.

Servius and ambiguity

Servius frequently talks of what we would loosely call ambiguity; his terms are chiefly *ambiguus* and *amphibolos/ia*, but not, however, *polysemus*.[39] Linguistic slippage is permitted by the grammarian, and on the levels of morphology, syntax or larger meaning.[40] When Euryalus falls dying (9.433 *volvitur Euryalus leto*) Servius is unsure about the case of *leto* ("aut septimus aut dativus" "either the instrumental ablative or the dative"). At times, as here, the commentary is fully indeterminate: "it could be A or it could be B."[41] And in such circumstances we also find elaboration of the two possibilities, as at *Aeneid* 6.302: "**VELISQVE MINISTRAT** aut per vela, et est septimus: aut 'velis obsequitur,' et est dativus" ("either by means of the sails, in which case ablative: or 'attends to the sails,' in which case dative"). Here the choice is left to the reader. Elsewhere, however, a distinct preference may be stated, as at *Aeneid* 5.127 ("**TRANQVILLO** melius septimus est, quam dativus," "better ablative than dative").

---

[39] There are differences in the types, but for the *Aeneid*, I note the following references in Servius: 2.31; 3.398; 4.66; 4.209; 6.558; 7.56; 8.76; 8.406; 8.544; 9.350; 9.431; 10.109; 11.523; 11.527; 11.601; 12.446; 12.952. On the distinction with *polysemus*, see Thomas (2000b).

[40] I am indebted to Peter Knox for reference to Bell (1923) 293–303, Ch. 35 "The Amphibole," with abundant examples, and with the specialized definition by the grammarians as "the use of a single word in two different relations in the same clause or sentence."

[41] See also ad *Aen.* 6.558 "**TRACTAEQVE CATENAE** et genetivus singularis potest esse et nominativus pluralis"; 12.511 "**CVRRV** autem aut septimus est, aut dativus *casus* antiquus."

Sometimes we get a glimpse of a community debating morphological and inflexional ambiguities. So at *Georgics* 1.344: "alii hunc locum aliter accipiunt, ut 'miti Baccho' non sit septimus, sed dativus et duo numina intellegamus, Liberi et Cereris" ("some take this passage differently, seeing 'miti Baccho' as dative rather than ablative, so we are to understand two deities, Liber and Ceres"). The unnamed *alii* are by now familiar. Elsewhere identifications occur, and debates are recorded, as on *Georgics* 2.324:

> Asper took this simply, seeing "terrae" as nominative plural;
> but Donatus wants "terrae" to be genitive singular, with the
> meaning "the trees swell with the spring" – "silvae" supplied
> from 323 – "and demand the generative seeds of the earth," i.e.
> the trees swell and seek out the generative seeds of the lands.
> But it is better to follow Asper, and take "generative seeds"
> as the ones we throw, not the ones that the trees draw from
> the earth. We call those seeds "generative" through which
> something is created and grows.[42]

Perhaps because he is taking issue with Donatus, Servius is particularly elaborate here, arguing for a traditional and "simpler" reading of *terrae* as nominative plural; and in this he is of course followed by subsequent commentators.

Between the preceding example, and that on *Aeneid* 5.127 ("TRANQVILLO melius septimus est, quam dativus"), we can detect an intermediate point, where the defeated voice (in this case the voice arguing for the dative), excluded by Servius, is restored by the fuller citation of DServius. When the Trojans land at Delos, they greet King Anius, an old friend of Anchises: *Aen.* 3.83 *iungimus hospitio dextras et tecta subimus.* Probus seems to have been puzzled:

> *In spite of Probus' inquiry as to what was meant by "iungimus
> hospitio dextras" nevertheless* it is ablative case, i.e. through the
> law of hospitality, for "for hospitality" cannot be the sense,

---

[42] VERE TVMENT TERRAE ET GENITALIA SEMINA POSCVNT Asper simpliciter accepit, ut "terrae" nominativus pluralis sit; Donatus vero "terrae" genetivum vult esse singularem, ut sit sensus mutata distinctione "vere tument silvae" – scilicet a superioribus – "terrae et genitalia semina poscunt," id est tument silvae et genitalia semina terrarum requirunt. sed melius Asprum sequimur, ut "genitalia semina" quae nos iacimus intellegamus, non quae ex terra silvae suscipiunt. "genitalia" autem dicimus "semina," quibus aliquid procreatur et gignitur.

since he was already a friend. *Or as some relate "we join hands and go into the house in hospitality."*[43]

Behind Servius' bare statement that *hospitio* is an ablative, thanks to the fuller commentary of DServius we are able to see both the initial inquiry of Probus, as well as traces of the debate sparked by that inquiry. We have now moved from the detection of ambiguity to more polemically charged terrain, where resolution of the ambiguous is at issue.

In all of these cases Servius brought up alternative meanings, but in general settled on one solution or the other. His purpose, as a grammarian, is to establish meaning and therefore to remove amphibole rather than allow it to stand. Elsewhere, however, his wording seems to allow authorial ambiguity, hinting at a double meaning which stays unresolved. So at *Aeneid* 1.69:

> **INCVTE VIM VENTIS** There is a double meaning: for if "incute" means "instill," "ventis" is dative, *that is, their power is small, give them great power*; if however it means "give," "ventis" is ablative and the meaning will be give power to the Trojans through the winds, *that is, instil power in the Trojans through the winds.*[44]

Here we are close to a truly ambiguous reading: each of the options is laid out, and neither Servius nor DServius chooses between them; indeed, the double conditional and the wording *duplex sensus* postulate an authorially intended ambiguity.[45]

The Latin language, with its high degree of inflexion, and particularly poetry with its dynamic manipulation of word order, is extremely fertile of such forms of ambiguity. The Servian commentaries, more frequently than we might imagine given their generally

---

[43] HOSPITIO *licet Probus quaerat, quid sit "iungimus hospitio dextras"* tamen septimus casus est, id est iure hospitalitatis: nam "ad hospitium" non potest intellegi, quia iam amicus fuit. *aut sicut quidam tradunt* "iungimus dextras et hospitio tecta subimus."

[44] INCVTE VIM VENTIS duplex sensus est: "incute" enim si inice significat, "ventis" dativus est casus, *hoc est, parva est eorum, etiam tu eis da magnam vim*; si autem "fac" septimus casus est, et erit sensus: fac vim Troianis per ventos, *hoc est, per ventos vim in Troianos incute.*

[45] Cf. *duplex* ad G. 1.218; 2.98; 3.165, 366; *Aen.* 11.152; 12.74. At G. 4.141 we find the famous claim of DServ. of a "duplex scriptura" (*pinus/tinus*) in the hand of Virgil himself.

positivistic outlook, allow such ambiguity to stand unresolved. Here
are some examples:

Aen. **3.531** *APPARET IN ARCE MINERVAE hic dubium* est, utrum
"Minervae templum," an "in arce Minervae" debeamus
accipere.
It is unclear here whether we should take it as "temple of
Minerva" or "on the citadel of Minerva."
4.66 *MOLLIS FLAMMA utrum "mollis flamma," an "mollis*
medullas."
[Unclear] whether "soft flame" or "soft marrows."
7.56 PETIT ANTE ALIOS PVLCHERRIMVS aut "ante alios
petit," aut "pulcherrimus ante alios."
"Seeks before others" or "most beautiful before others."
8.148 *PENITVS SVA SVB IVGA utrum "penitus sub iuga mittant,"*
an "omnem penitus Hesperiam."
[Unclear] whether "send deep beneath the yoke" or "all
Hesperia to its depths."
8.406 *PER MEMBRA potest ambiguum videri, Vulcani an Veneris.*
Can seem ambiguous, Vulcan's or Venus's.
8.544 *MACTAT LECTAS de more lectas, an de more mactat.*
Chosen in the customary way, or sacrifices in the customary
way.
8.702 *SCISSA* DISCORDIA PALLA *utrum "scissa palla gaudens,"*
an "scissa palla vadit" et seorsum "gaudens"?
[Unclear] whether "rejoicing in her torn robe," or "goes in her
torn robe" and separately "rejoicing."
9.146 *LECTI FERRO utrum "ad ferrum lecti," an potius "acie lecti,"*
ut si dixisset "virtute lecti."
[Unclear] whether "chosen for the sword," or rather "chosen
because of their blade," as if he had said "chosen for courage."
9.350 *DEFICERE EXTREMVM utrum "ignem extremum," an*
"*deficere* extremum."
Unclear whether "last fire" or "finally dying."
9.648 SAEVA SONORIBVS ARMA strepitu terribilia. *et utrum*
saeva arma quae habent sonorem, ut ⟨359⟩ *"aurea bullis*
cingula," an etiam "sonoribus saeva?"
[Unclear] whether "cruel arms which make a noise," as ⟨359⟩
"golden belts with studs," or also[46] "cruel sounding."

---

[46] "Also" (*etiam*) is interesting here in that it implies and allows a true double meaning,
and not just an ambiguity between two distinct meanings.

10.21 INSIGNIS EQVIS *et ambiguum, utrum "equis insignis" an "equis fertur."*
Also ambiguous, whether "distinguished by horses" or "is borne by horses."

10.428 OPPOSITVM *obstantem, fortiter pugnantem. et quidam dubium volunt, utrum "pugnae oppositum," an "nodum pugnae," quod est melius.*
Standing in his way, fighting bravely. And some want it to be unclear whether "standing in the way of battle," or "battle's knot," which is better.

11.523 DENSIS FRONDIBVS ATRVM *utrum "densis frondibus urget," an "densis frondibus atrum."*
[Unclear] whether "hems in with thick foliage," or "black with thick foliage."

11.601 FERREVS HASTIS *quaeritur quid sit "ferreus"? utrum "ferreus ager horret hastis," an "ferreus hastis ager horret."*
A question of what "iron" goes with, whether "the iron field bristles with spears," or "iron with spears the field bristles."

11.751 VTQVE VOLANS ALTE RAPTVM *Homerica comparatio. et utrum "alte volans," an "alte raptum," an "alte fert"?*
Homeric simile. And [unclear] whether "flying on high," "seized on high," or "carries on high."

12.319 ALIS ADLAPSA SAGITTA EST *utrum "alis stridens," an "alis adlapsa"?*
[Unclear] whether "whizzing with wings," or "glided on wings."

12.446 AGGERE TVRNVS *quidam ambiguitatem volunt, utrum ipse Turnus "in" aggere, an venientes "ex" aggere?*
Some want an ambiguity, whether Turnus *himself* "on" the rampart, or *them* coming "from" the rampart.

Most of these examples are easily "resolved"; the ambiguity is only fleeting. But it is instructive to collect them, for in each of these cases Servius – rather, it is worth noting, DServius, in all but one instance – in each case the commentator allows the indeterminacy to stand. The terms *ambiguum* and *dubium*, or the simple option *utrum . . . an* underscore this indeterminacy. This is not to say that DServius did not necessarily believe that in each case Virgil intended one sense or the other; rather that he felt unable, and possibly also unwilling, to resolve the ambiguity. That, however, is not always the case, for there also exist instances of emphatic resolution of ambiguity and of a more active ideological engagement of the figure.

Raising the stakes

Anna's first question to her afflicted sister is a curious one:

> solane perpetua maerens carpere iuventa
> nec dulcis natos Veneris nec praemia noris?
>
> *Aen.* 4.32–3

"Will you alone grieve and be eaten away through all your
youth and will you not know sweet children and the rewards
of love?"

That is how the lines are taken by all modern commentators, who
give parallels for the postpositive second *nec*,[47] but otherwise do not
address the possible meaning without its being postpositive: "will you
not know the sweet sons of Venus and her rewards?" – Cupid and
Aeneas. *Nosco* of "knowing" in the "biblical" sense is amply attested.[48]
Epic decorum will explain Anna's ambiguity, as Quintilian would
attest.[49] If such an ambiguity were possible, following the examples in
my previous section, we might have expected from DServius something like the following:

> **4.33 NEC DVLCIS NATOS VENERIS utrum "natos Veneris", id
> est Cupidinem et Aeneam, et "praemia" deae, an "natos" tuos et
> "praemia" veneris.*

either "the children of Venus," that is Cupid and Aeneas, and
her "rewards," or "children of your own" and the "rewards" of
love.

We in fact get no such entry, but it is Servius himself who preserves
traces of such a comment, which certainly existed in the tradition:
4.33 "alii male iungunt 'natos Veneris' Cupidinem et Aeneam."
"Some wrongly connect Cupid and Aeneas 'children of Venus.'"
This reading, which has Anna referring to Aeneas and Cupid as
brothers – and which does so in the context of an amatory exhortation that Dido succumb to the forces to which she has been subjected
– this is a reading that the Augustan critical commentary must reject.

---

[47] Of the 24 instances of postponed *nec* in Virgil listed by Norden (Anhang III, 405), none
involves the sort of ambiguity we find at *Aen.* 4.33 (5.217, 7.811, 12.630 come closest).

[48] See Adams (1982) 190.

[49] See Ch. I, pp. 7–8.

What is noteworthy is the fact that Servius, while participating in that rejection, preserves the evidence for an ambiguous reading, evidence produced by unnamed readers (*alii*) who read *Aeneid* 4.33 in their own native Latin, and saw an ambiguity in that Latin. Ideologically neutral ambiguity was, as we have seen throughout, frequently permitted to stand unresolved. But when the heroic status of Aeneas is in question Servius becomes more decisive. Ovid, less concerned with that status, may have read the Virgilian line in its subversive sense: his Dido implores Aeneas through his mother and his "brother's weapons, arrows that is" (*Her.* 7.157 *per matrem fraternaque tela, sagittas*).

At *Georgics* 2.495–8 Virgil praises the idealized rustic, and in turn vituperates the life which involves itself with politics, power, discord and public affairs:

> illum non populi fasces, non purpura regum
> flexit et infidos agitans discordia fratres,
> aut coniurato descendens Dacus ab Histro,
> non res Romanae perituraque regna.

> He is not distracted by the people's fasces, by regal purple and
> by discord which drives brothers into treachery, nor by the
> Dacian coming down from confederate Danube, nor by
> Rome's affairs and kingdoms bound to fall.

In the final line it is hard to avoid at least a vague connection between *res Romanae* and *peritura regna*.[50] Servius, however, made an attempt to do so:

> **2.498 NON RES ROMANAE PERITVRAQVE REGNA** Kingdoms,
> that is, of foreigners; for he is saying two things: (a) the rustic is
> unaffected by (i.e. has no political ambitions for) the Roman
> empire, and (b) the rustic is also unaffected by kingdoms
> doomed to perish: for Virgil did not malign the Roman empire.
> Others however want this statement to come from the general
> view that all large powers are subject to dangers.[51]

---

[50] Cf. Clausen (1987) 83–4: "This settled and mature awareness of suffering, of final, irretrievable loss, not excluding (the reader senses) even Rome itself, 'Rome and kingdoms that shall perish,' 'res Romanae perituraque regna.'"

[51] **NON RES ROMANAE PERITVRAQVE REGNA** regna scilicet barbarorum; nam duo dicit: rusticum nec Romanum imperium movet, id est ad ambitum cogit, nec barbarorum regna peritura: non enim Romano male dixit imperio. licet alii dictum hoc velint ex generali venire sententia, quod omnis magnitudo imperii periculis subiacet.

In attempting to steer us away from implicating *res Romanae* with *peritura regna*, Servius in fact does the opposite, for he preserves, with the gnomic "non enim Romano male dixit imperio" a voice which said "Romano male dicit imperio." Servius' commentary is in fact circular in a way familiar from some modern Augustan readings: "Virgil cannot have been criticizing Roman power; therefore [what is] a [fairly obvious] reading of this line that implies as much is impossible."

But we do in fact have here a secular parallel for Augustine's negative and subversive Christian reading of the line.[52] Augustine (*Serm.* 105.7.10) compared it to the famous prophecy of Jupiter at *Aeneid* 1.278–9: *his ego nec metas rerum nec tempora pono:* | *imperium sine fine dedi* ("for them I set neither spatial nor temporal bounds: I have given power without end"). His sermon then becomes dramatic, with Virgil admitting to flattery and falsehood in the case of Jupiter's prophecy: *sed quid facerem, qui Romanis verba vendebam, nisi hac adulatione aliquid promitterem, quod falsum erat?* ("but what was I to do, I the word-merchant to the Romans, other than promise them through this flattery something that was in fact false?").[53] Augustine exonerates the poet of *Georgics* 2, noting of the line under discussion: *[regna] peritura, veritate non tacuit, mansura, adulatione promisit* ("kingdoms 'destined to perish,' he spoke out in truth, 'destined to remain,' he promised through flattery").[54]

Meliboeus is emphatic about the qualities of the soldier who evicts and replaces him (*Ecl.* 1.70–1): *impius haec tam culta novalia miles habebit,* | *barbarus has segetes.* "An impious soldier will hold these well-worked fallows, a barbarian these crops." The use of the epithet caused a flurry of activity, preserved by Servius:

> IMPIVS MILES Meliboeus angrily calls the soldiers "impious,"
> either for occupying his land, or for waging civil war. IMPIOUS
> SOLDIER who bore arms for Antony. IMPIOUS S. because
> he waged and hungers for civil war. IMPIOUS S. Virgil has
> here castigated Octavianus Augustus; he nevertheless has adhered

---

[52] Cf. Hagendahl (1967) 2.416–17, against Augustine's abuse of Virgil; see also Mynors ad loc.

[53] For good discussion of Augustine on Virgil here, see O'Hara (1990) 126–7.

[54] For Dryden's way of dealing with *peritura* see below, pp. 147–8.

to truth: for that soldier by bearing arms and by conquering
others neglects piety.[55]

We can detect at least four voices here, some of which have a political
mission; and significantly the *impietas* involved has been imputed to
both Antony and Octavian. For the fact is, and it is a fact to which
Servius had access, that Octavian was as brutal a land confiscator
and proscriber as Antony or any other figure in the history of that
tumultuous century; and this activity was carried out precisely in the
years in which Virgil was beginning to write his *Eclogues*.[56] Even four
centuries of Augustan reading, then, have not completely removed
the potential of Meliboeus' words to convict Octavian's soldier of
impietas, the very quality whose opposite will be inscribed on the
standard of Aeneas. There will be other Meliboeus's in that poem
too, who do not share in the protection of Trojan *pietas*.

The full force of such political ambiguity emerges in a notice on
Aeneid 6.612, on the sinners in the underworld. *Pietas* is again at issue:
(hic) quique arma secuti | impia nec veriti dominorum fallere dextras, | inclusi
poenam exspectant ("and shut up here there await punishment those
who followed impious arms and did not fear to break their oath to
their lords"). Servius begins with the suggestion that the lines are a
compliment to Augustus (*hoc loco videtur blandiri Augusto*), since they
allude to the Pompeians' taking up the *impia arma* of civil war. But
this does not work, he continues (*non procedit*), for if the *impia arma*
are those of civil war, Augustus and Julius Caesar are also implicated
(*tangit et Augustum et Caesarem*). Moreover, if the reference is to those
who break alliances, then there is a further allusion, since Actium was
won because of 2000 cavalry who crossed over from Antony's side.
And there would be a further insult to Augustus or Caesar, since the
title *dominus* (rather than *pater patriae*) was unpopular. Better therefore
to have the reference be specifically to Sextus Pompey, whose runaway
slaves will fit the sense of Virgil's lines ("melius ergo est ut bellum a
Sexto Pompeio ... gestum accipiamus"). So the scholiastic mentality

---

[55] iratus Meliboeus impios milites dicit, seu quod agrum suum teneant, seu quod civile
gesserint bellum. IMPIVS MILES qui pro Antonio arma portavit. IMPIVS M. quia bella
civilia gessit et desiderat. IMPIVS M. hic Vergilius Octavianum Augustum laesit; tamen
secutus est veritatem: nam miles portando arma et vincendo alios pietatem praetermittit.

[56] For a vivid account of the late 40s in this regard, together with the abundant sources,
see Syme (1939) 187–201, Ch. XIV "The Proscriptions."

struggles to neutralize what looks like a reference to contemporary
political activity in which Augustus could have been implicated.

I conclude with an instance I have treated before, *Georgics* 2.171–2,
a couplet addressed to Octavian and marked by distinct syntactical
ambiguity:

> qui nunc extremis Asiae iam victor in oris
> imbellem avertis Romanis arcibus Indum.

> who now, victorious on the furthest shores of Asia, turn the
> unwarlike Indian from Roman citadels.

Servius read *imbellem* proleptically, without mentioning that it could
have the sense I give it above. His comment is therefore like those
that state that *nec* at *Aeneid* 4.33 is postpositive; the point of grammar
is formed by hermeneutical, and ultimately by ideological, need.
DServius, however, preserves the fuller scholiastic discussion which is
implicit even in Servius' insistence: "**INBELLEM AVERTIS** id est aver-
tendo reddis inbellem. *et aliter: avertis et inbellem facis. an 'inbellem' victum
iam, nec bellantem? ceterum quid grande, si inbellem avertis?*" ("**INBELLEM
AVERTIS** i.e. make unwarlike by turning away. *And otherwise: turn
away and make unwarlike. Or 'unwarlike' = already conquered, and not
fighting? But what is so great about turning away the unwarlike?*").

Once again, we see the efforts to which readers who must sustain a
strongly Augustan view of Virgil must go, as once again Servius omits
and thereby attempts to suppress interpretations that were available in
the tradition with which he was working. There is no way of for-
bidding a proleptic reading, and the proleptic reading seems, and has
seemed, to qualify the Augustan achievement. Servius' cause is one
that has been fought from the very beginning, a cause that has found
new champions over time and throughout the reception of Virgil.
For the guardians of language are also guardians of the Augustan
meaning. But of equal importance is the fact that we have detected,
with the help of the guardians, traces of alternative, oppositional
readings, which, far from being the monster child of post-Vietnam
anti-imperialism, fathered onto a straightforwardly Augustan poem,
were activated by Latin-speaking Roman readers from the very first
century of our era, and no doubt before it began.

4

Dryden's Virgil and the politics of translation

the most noble and spirited translation I know in any language.
ALEXANDER POPE on Dryden's Virgil[1]

the *Aeneid* was evidently a party piece, as much as *Absalom and Achitophel*. Virgil was as slavish a writer as any of the gazetteers.
ALEXANDER POPE, quoted by his friend
Joseph Spence.[2]

"May execration pursue his memory": Virgil in the eighteenth century

In 1685, even more than a decade before Dryden published his translation of the *Aeneid*, Matthew Prior could write in *A Satyr on the modern Translators*:

> If VIRGIL labour'd not to be translated,
> Why suffers he the only thing he hated?
> Had he foreseen some ill officious Tongue,
> Would in unequal Strains blaspheme his Song;
> Nor Prayers, nor Force, nor Fame should e'er prevent
> The just Performance of his wise intent:
> Smiling he'd seen his martyr'd Work expire,
> Nor live to feed more cruel Foes than Fire. (151–8)

Dryden himself, by this time translator of Ovid's *Heroides* (1680), is one of the objects of the satire (23 "In the head of this Gang too *John Dryden* appears"), and it is fair to say that when the 1697 Virgil translation came out, at the end of a century that had seen around thirty partial or complete translations, largely Royalist, of the *Aeneid*

---

[1] *Complete Poetical Works*, ed. H. W. Boynton (Boston and New York 1903) 259.
[2] For details see White (1993) 300, n. 16.

alone, it drove all from the field. So much so that Prior could later write, now in satire against the lack of learning of his age:[3]

> Hang HOMER and VIRGIL; their meaning to seek,
> A Man must have pok'd in the *Latin* and *Greek*;
> Those who Love their own Tongue, we have Reason to Hope,
> Have read them Translated by DRYDEN and POPE.

The English reception of Virgil, particularly in the eighteenth century, is as much as anything the reception of Dryden's Virgil, and in some quarters it continues to be so. As C. Burrow has recently put it: "Someone who has taught us, or someone who has taught someone who has taught us, will have read and absorbed, say, Dryden's Virgil."[4] Another critic has summed up an excellent treatment of Dryden's poem with the following:

> Through his *Aeneis* Dryden honoured his father [Virgil] with
> a work which would be one of his richest gifts to his own
> posterity. With the *Aeneis* Dryden finally brought into his own
> language the Latin poem that had lived in his mind since
> childhood, and had inhabited – as guest and ghost – so much of
> his adult writing.[5]

What are the implications of Dryden's translation for the reception of Virgil? A strong translation such as his was bound to have an effect of some sort. From a political perspective, as we shall see, Dryden tied Virgil closely to Augustus, and the reputation of Dryden and Virgil would suffer accordingly. As H. D. Weinbrot has succinctly put it:[6]

> hostility to Augustus by the major classical historians, especially
> Suetonius and Tacitus, was transmitted to renaissance Florence
> and then much of western Europe; it temporarily submerged
> during the triumph of sixteenth- and seventeenth-century
> royalism, re-emerged in England late in the seventeenth
> century, and by the earlier eighteenth century had become
> entrenched in libertarian commonplaces, historical discussions,
> and practical politics. The years of verbal and printed combat
> during the opposition to Walpole were especially rich in anti-
> Augustanism, as Whig and Tory administration and opposition
> smeared each other with the same brush.

---

[3] On this see Frost (1955) 2.   [4] Burrow (1997) 21.
[5] Hammond (1999) 282.   [6] Weinbrot (1978) 233.

Dryden himself is not unlike Virgil in that both were caught in a transitional time, without the benefit of knowing how history would judge those times and the princes to whom they would be so closely tied. We will return to the issue of Dryden's affiliation (nostalgia for the exiled James II or paraenesis for the new order of William III?), but for now what matters is the eighteenth century's received hostility to Augustus and to Virgil, or rather the received, imperial Virgil who was in part the creation of Dryden.

The eighteenth century shows resemblances to the twentieth in its ideological response to Virgil and Augustus.[7] As Gibbon on Augustus anticipated and influenced Syme, so Pope on Virgil has strong similarities to the anti-authoritarian negative readings of Graves and, to a lesser extent, of Auden.[8] We even find, in Robert Andrews' 1766 translation to Virgil's *Aeneid*, an attitude not unlike that of the current ambivalent reader, somewhat polemically defined by Harrison:[9]

> [Andrews] is everywhere inspired by "the spirit of Liberty" in Virgil, and yet he has nothing but liberal condemnation for Augustus. There is only one way for a mind to reconcile these positions and that is to make Virgil a kind of fifth columnist. This is precisely what Andrews does, but in such waxing and assertive oratory that it would be difficult for any reader not to detect the severity of his desperation. Virgil, it is admitted, is in the position in which his detractors place him, as the poet of a despotic court.

Also resonating with our own times, by the end of the eighteenth century Lucan is the "Bard of Freedom," "Hating with Stoic pride a Tyrant's arms," while Virgil evokes the following: "May execration pursue his memory, who has placed a crown on the brows of a tyrant, that were much too bright for the best of Kings."[10]

That Virgil's stock was low by the end of the eighteenth century

---

[7] The best work on this topic is Harrison (1967), a short piece, and somewhat inaccessible; also important is the work of Erskine-Hill (1983) 234–66 "The Idea of an Augustan Age," and particularly Weinbrot (1978) 120–49 " 'Let Horace blush, and Virgil too': The degradation of the Augustan Poets."

[8] See Ziolkowski (1993) 99–100, 140–1.

[9] Harrison (1967) 6–7; also Weinbrot (1978) 123–9 for vigorous debate in the early- to mid-eighteenth century over the degree of Virgil's flattery.

[10] Harrison (1967) 7 quoting William Hayley (1782) on Lucan, Robert Heron (i.e. John Pinkerton [1785]) on Virgil.

(at least Virgil of the *Aeneid*) is beyond dispute, particularly when compared to the end of the previous century. And Dryden's stock was at a similar ebb, for much the same reason: both had praised princes, and the times were no longer conducive to princes. My concern here will be with the degree to which Dryden converted Virgil into a flatterer, with the way he viewed Virgil and Virgilian poetry through the lens of his own times, whether Jacobite or Williamite, and consequently made Virgil's poem something that it had once not been. The eighteenth-century reputation of Virgil was in my view in part a product of the royalist translations of that poet which burgeoned throughout the seventeenth century and culminate in Dryden's version. To the extent that the eighteenth century is also the site of the genesis of modern classical scholarship, the fixing of the Augustan Virgil in this version has implications for nineteenth- and twentieth-century reception as well. But first, Dryden as a theorist of translation.

"Translation with latitude"

In a well-known passage of the *Examen Poeticum* (1693) John Dryden defends his preference for "paraphrase, or translation with latitude," which occupies a middle ground between the more literal "metaphrase" on the one hand, and free "imitation" on the other.[11] In his *Life of Lucian*, Dryden says the following:[12]

> A translator that would write with any force or spirit of an
> original must never dwell on the words of his author. He ought
> to possess himself entirely and *perfectly comprehend the genius of*
> *his author,* the nature of the subject, and the terms of the art or
> subject treated of. And then he will express himself as justly, and
> with as much life, as if he wrote an original; whereas he who
> copies word for word loses all spirit in the tedious transfusion
> ... [emphasis added]

---

[11] Kinsley (1961) viii. "Sure I am, that if it be a fault, 'tis much more pardonable, than that of those, who run into the other extream, of a literal, and close Translation, where the Poet is constrained so streightly to his Author's Words, that he wants elbow-room, to express his Elegancies. He leaves him obscure; he leaves him Prose, where he found him Verse." On Dryden's theory and practice, see Frost (1955), and for a good brief account, Steiner (1975) 267–70.

[12] Thus Dryden in Watson (1962); included in Schulte and Biguenet (1992) 29–31.

True as that may be, and is, of the aesthetic reception of the translator's work, it immediately points to problematic aspects of translation as interpretation. The potential for a particularly insidious form of hermeneutic circularity is great. And in the "Dedication of the *Aeneis*," Dryden is quite clear about his procedure: "Some things too I have omitted, and sometimes have added of my own. Yet the omissions I hope, are but of Circumstances, and such as would have no grace in *English*; and the Additions, I also hope, are easily deduc'd from Virgil's Sense."[13] We shall soon observe some of those additions.

As C. Martindale has aptly noted: "If translation is inseparable from interpretation, and if reading can profitably be seen as a form of translation, enquiry into translation becomes an important part of the hermeneutic process."[14] Now Martindale is here concerned not so much with actual translation as with conceptualizing what happens when translations take place. Nevertheless, although he does not mention Dryden, his three models map well onto those of Virgil's greatest translator. In Martindale's first model translation identifies a "single, stable meaning" which it then tries to reproduce (Dryden's "metaphrase"); his second model, close to Dryden's "translation with latitude," is one in which the translation "selects and arranges elements that are 'there' in the original." Presumably those elements may with collaboration from communities of readers be judged to be not only "there," but also there. Thirdly, the most radical model, which may parallel Dryden's free "imitation": "On an alternative model, involving a more radical untying of the text, translations determine what is counted as being 'there' in the first place, and good translations thus unlock for us compelling (re)readings which we could not get in any other way" (93).

If we are not compelled by the hermeneutic created by the translation, then how can it continue to have a meaningful relationship to the original? Has not the model ceased to be? Furthermore, and more insidiously, if the original comes to be perceived through the translation, because that translation is a strong version, with claim to poetic and meaningful status of its own (but still posing at least as paraphrase), what happens to a reading that engages the translation alone?

[13] Frost and Dearing (1987) 5.329.
[14] Martindale (1993a) 92, and generally 92–4. He well emphasizes that translation can be used as an interpretive aid in the classroom.

For if translation is (among other things) a form of hermeneutics, it is at the same time a particularly potent and seductive form, since it poses as a paraphrase rather than a description of a poetic text in a way that other hermeneutic enterprises (commentary, interpretive writing, and the like) do not. Translations, then, may exert enormous power over the possible meanings of the original, and may control and direct reading with an authority that is not usually conceded by the reader to those other forms of interpretation or commentary. This applies particularly to translations that immediately become classics (such as Dryden's Virgil) and that are read in ages that identify themselves closely with the culture of the source text (as did the eighteenth century with Augustan Rome).

As P. Hammond has recently noted, Dryden, unlike Milton, wrote no Latin for publication, Hobbes and Locke both wrote in English, and from the Restoration into the eighteenth century Latin generally declined as an international language.[15] In such a setting, Matthew Prior's humorous couplet also conveys the new status of translation, now as a *substitute* for the original: "Those who Love their own Tongue, we have Reason to Hope, | Have read them Translated by DRYDEN and POPE." Hammond elsewhere captures what is great in Dryden's achievement in the context of its own tradition, but also, for the reception of Virgil, what is highly problematic about that achievement:[16]

> Dryden writes a poetry in which the Roman poets are not
> guests but ghosts: in his translations from Virgil, Horace, Ovid,
> and Lucretius he is remaking poems from the Roman period
> which have a strong hold over him because of the wit or the
> philosophy of the original ... In quotation the Latin text enters
> the English in fragments, as a sign of an authority elsewhere but
> at the same time testifying to the power of the modern author.
> In translation the Latin text is banished from the page, but
> haunts every line as we hear echoes of the ghostly original.
> Impossible but necessary, translation provided Dryden with the
> ground which he could fashion for himself, a territory where
> he was free to explore Roman insights about the gods, and
> sexuality, and death, and the loss of the homeland.

[15] Hammond (1999) 42.   [16] Hammond (1999) 21.

Others, Hammond most recently, have explored what Dryden did in his *Aeneis*, and nothing, or little, in these pages is intended to detract from Dryden's achievement as a poet; I am concerned with what he did to the *Aeneid*, and to Virgil's other poems, in the process.

"Comprehending the genius of his author"

If Dryden's procedure for translation involved a latitude that was justified by comprehending his author, as he put it, an inquiry into that comprehension will be appropriate, and we may begin with a contemporary, Luke Milbourne, who in 1698 reacted sharply: "No man can admire Virgil who can't understand him, nor can any man who understands him be pleased with Mr. D.'s translation."[17] At times Milbourne is simply unhappy with the aesthetics of Dryden's translation: "'*And all the* Sylvan *Reign*.' I have heard Mr. D. was once a *Westminster Scholar*. Dr. *Busby*, I doubt, would have *whip'd a Boy* for paraphrasing *omne* nemus so *Childishly*. The *three next verses* are worthy of Mr. D. but unworthy of his *admirable* Author."[18] But Milbourne, a contemporary who was therefore attuned to the political and ideological potential of the translation, at other times provides more valuable information. The "three verses" to which he here objects are Dryden's translation of *Eclogue* 6.11–12: *nec Phoebo gratior ulla est | quam sibi quae Vari praescripsit pagina nomen* ("and no page pleases Phoebus more than that which has the name of Varus at its head"). Here is Dryden's offending translation:

> Thy name, to *Phoebus* and the Muses known,
> Shall in the Front of every Page be shown;
> For he who sings thy Praise, secures his own. (16–18)

The last line, expressing the reciprocity of literary patronage, is presumably what Milbourne objected to as being "worthy of Mr. D." Dryden has given us a line which finds no trace in Virgil's *Eclogue*, cannot be said to be "there" in any sense, but which belongs rather to the circumstances and cultural position of Dryden, not Virgil. Similarly at the end of the *Georgics*:

---

[17] Milbourne (1698) 30.　[18] Milbourne (1698) 72.

Caesar dum magnus ad altum
fulminat Euphraten bello victorque volentis
per populos dat iura viamque adfectat Olympo.

(G. 4.560–2)

Such a theme calls for six lines from Dryden:

> While mighty *Caesar*, thund'ring from afar,
> Seeks on *Euphrates* Banks the Spoils of War:
> With conq'ring Arms asserts his Country's Cause,
> With Arts of Peace the Willing People draws:
> On that glad Earth the Golden Age renews,
> And his great Father's Path to Heav'n pursues.

(4.809–14)

"This is one of Mr. D's *Interpolations* ..." grumbles Milbourne (205), "Mr. D. abuses [Virgil] by presuming to teach him how to Court his *Patrons*." The source of one of the interpolations (i.e. "On that glad Earth the Golden Age renews"), of which there is again not a trace at the end of *Georgics* 4, is *Aeneid* 6.791–4,[19] the familiar lines from Anchises on Augustus and the *aurea saecula*, lines with which this study began. Once a reader has encountered Anchises' line transplanted by Dryden to the final lines of *Georgics* 4, the effect is produced: the poem which began with the transition away from golden age is made to close with the triumphant return of that golden age, utterly false to Virgil's Latin and to his poem. The Virgilian closure is otherwise: Octavian fulminating like Jupiter, laws (absent from the real golden age) created, and the age of toil (the age of Jupiter, and of iron) secured. I might add here that the Virgilian narrator nowhere in the entire corpus with his own voice associates Augustus with the golden age. Posterity consigned Luke Milbourne to the Rare Book Library, while Dryden's "translations" lived on to produce whole genres of upbeat georgics in the eighteenth century, all with the return to a golden age featuring prominently.

Luke Milbourne's literary judgment for the most part need not detain us, and his own translations of Virgil lack any poetic merit of

---

[19] "The sixth Aeneid figures in more than one-seventh of Dryden's Virgilian allusions, quotations or adaptations," Frost and Dearing (1987) 6.850.

their own.[20] But his sense of the political situation is another matter. Quoting Dryden's claim in the "Dedication" that he can speak more freely than French court poets (283), Milbourne (11) throws his words back at him: " '*He can speak what the* French *durst not.*' Yet would not a *French army*, with the P. of W. at the head of it, be very welcome to Mr. D., and, without doubt, they'd make us all *Free Subjects* presently." Or again, imputing nostalgia for the days of James II (35): "Things are mightily altered with him since the days of the *Hind and the Panther,* and the *Defence* of the *Strong Box Papers.* This *tempora mutantur.*"

What of Dryden himself on his comprehension of his author? In "Postscript to the Reader" he distinguishes his own conditions from those enjoyed by Virgil:

> What Virgil wrote in the vigour of his age, in plenty and at
> ease, I have undertaken to translate in my declining years;
> struggling with wants, oppressed with sickness, curbed in my
> genius, liable to be misconstrued in all I write; and my judges,
> if they are not very equitable, already prejudiced against me, by
> the lying character which has been given them of my morals.

These words, and his view of the *Aeneid* and its relation to Augustus, cannot be separated from his own experience in the forty years preceding publication, particularly in 1688. After the Revolution of that year Dryden lost his position as poet laureate and chief court poet, but he never lost his sense that the highest function of poetry was to advise the prince and win the people to him. A Dryden critic has put the matter succinctly: "the persona of Virgil which Dryden exhibits is, like Dryden himself, frankly practical and political. Indeed, he reduces the epic to a commentary on Augustus and his Age which is almost as narrowly topical as *Absalom and Achitophel* itself."[21]

In the lengthy "Dedication to the *Aeneis*," it is inevitable that we connect Dryden's own circumstances to his vision of Virgil, a vision

---

[20] The clergyman published his polemical *Notes on Dryden's Virgil* the year after the appearance of Dryden's translation (London 1698). Time has sided with Dryden's response to Milbourne's jibe that Ogilby's translation was far superior to his own: "For 'tis agreed on all hands that [Milbourne] writes even below *Ogilby*: That, you will say, is not easily done; but what cannot M__ bring about?" Sloman (1985) 239, n. 2.

[21] Proudfoot (1960) 258.

that recalls and validates the ex-laureate's own previous happy state: Virgil, he says:[22]

> proves that it is possible for a Courtier not to be a Knave ...
> Obliged he was to his Master for his Bounty, and he repays
> him with Good Counsel, how to behave himself in his new
> Monarchy, so as to gain the Affections of his Subjects, and
> deserve to be call'd the Father of his Country.

Dryden's construction of the Virgilian political outlook is to be found first of all in the "Dedication," where, on the basis of the positive reference to Cato at *Aeneid* 8.670, he hypothesized that Virgil was a republican at heart, a reluctant supporter of the Augustan régime.[23] Dryden then has Virgil converting fully to the cause: "[Virgil] consider'd it in the Interest of his Country to be so Govern'd [by Augustus]: To infuse an awful respect into the people, towards such a Prince: By that Respect to confirm their Obedience to him; and by that Obedience to make them Happy."[24]

Along with the larger question of Dryden's comprehension of Virgil's *Aeneid* and its political purpose is the enormously complex issue of Dryden's own view of Aeneas, Augustus and other kingly figures in Virgil's poem; also of the parallels and equations he drew between those figures and the kings under whom he had either flourished or was in decline. Dryden's translation constantly evokes contemporary events, even if the nature and function of the evocation is not consistent but is itself ambiguous – not unlike the case of Virgil. P. Hammond well notes of Dryden's enterprise, that it "invites us to recognize both similarity and difference, and to weigh discontinuous correspondences rather than seek a totalizing allegory."[25] At times, as H. Erskine-Hill has shown, Aeneas, particularly from early in the poem, seems to represent the exiled James II; so the very opening of the poem where the single word *profugus* (1.2) becomes "expell'd and exil'd," which is hardly appropriate to the realities of

---

[22] Frost and Dearing (1987) 283.
[23] Recently, scholars have suggested that Dryden's hatred of William III is tempered by republicanism, rather than nostalgia for James II; Burrow (1997); Ross (1984).
[24] Frost and Dearing (1987) 281. Good work has been done on the preface by Zwicker (1984) 62–9, 178–88 and Hammond (1999) 219–28.
[25] Hammond (1999) 225.

Aeneas' flight, and where *dum conderet urbem | inferretque deos Latio* (1.5–6) is expanded in ways that immediately bring into play the British succession:[26]

> and built the destin'd Town;
> His banished Gods restor'd to Rites Divine,
> And settl'd sure succession in his Line   (1.6–8)

"Sure succession" alone would be evocative, even without the punning gloss "Rites Divine," conjuring up those rights of which Charles I as well as James II were stripped.[27] Likewise Hammond has shown how the language of restoration is woven into the motives and desires of Dryden's Aeneas: so at *Aeneis* 2.1066 his Creusa turns her Virgilian model's *illic res laetae* (2.783) into "There Fortune shall the Trojan Line restore"; so Dido to Aeneas: "Were *Troy* restor'd and *Priam*'s happy Reign" (4.451), while Aeneas states his preference "And *Priam*'s ruin'd palace to restore" (495).[28] It is hard through all of this – and the contemporary Milbourne found it impossible – not to hear a Jacobite voice yearning for a second Stuart Restoration. Likewise Dryden's Jupiter is made to allude to a restoration of Catholicism, as he converts the Virgilian *cana Fides . . . iura dabunt* (1.292–3) into "Then banish'd Faith shall once again return" (1.398);[29] the language of banishment, return and restoration is nowhere to be found in the entire prophecy of the Virgilian Jupiter (1.257–96).

Elsewhere Dryden is openly hostile to William and Mary. Among the tortured of Virgil's Underworld are those who commit crimes against family (6.608–9 *hic quibus invisi fratres, dum vita manebat, | pulsatusve parens*). No reader would miss the conversion of the simply familial to the monarchical: 824–5 "Then they, whose Brothers better claim disown, Expel their parents, and usurp the Throne." And a few lines later, Virgil's domestic traitor (6.621–2 *vendidit hic auro patriam dominumque potentem | imposuit*) has acquired a detail that specifies William of Orange: 844–5 "To Tyrants others have their country sold, | Imposing Foreign Lords, for Foreign Gold" – with the anaphora of "Foreign" bringing out what was not there in Virgil.[30] But as Hammond has also argued, Aeneas is not simply a Jacobite allegory,

[26] Erskine-Hill (1996) 203–5.   [27] The pun is noted by Erskine-Hill (1996) 204.
[28] Hammond (1999) 249, and generally 249–60.   [29] Hammond (1999) 254–6.
[30] For these connections see Proudfoot (1960) 201; Erskine-Hill (1996) 206.

and in that he was not in lineal succession to Priam, his right action elsewhere may serve as an exemplum for how William III should conduct himself as an elective king.[31]

Even more distant events of seventeenth-century history are made to revise Virgil's poem and bring it into contemporary contexts. In 1656 John Denham had published his *Destruction of Troy*, a translation of lines 1–558 of *Aeneid* 2.[32] Although not an extreme Royalist early on in the Civil War, he attended on Charles I, and seems to have been close to him, and he deplored the regicide in a 1650 poem: "By his untimely Fate, that impious Stroke, | That sullied Earth and did Heaven's Pity choke."[33] It was perhaps in the early 1650s, while he was in contact with the exiled Prince Charles, that Denham was both working on his *Aeneid* translation and involving himsef in the Royalist cause.[34] It is significant that his *Destruction of Troy* in fact ends at 2.558, with another headless Monarch, with the corpse of Priam on the Trojan shore: "On the cold earth lies th' unregarded King, | A headless Carkass, and a nameless Thing" (547–8). It is hard to imagine Denham's choice to have Troy end at this point was entirely unconnected with the recent death of Charles I. And so it is that Dryden's intertext at this point is noteworthy. Dryden is indebted to Denham as to many of the other Royalist translators, and he mentions him favorably in the Dedication. In fact, as Venuti has noted, Dryden "absorbed more than eighty lines of it in his own version."[35] For the death of Priam he in fact borrowed from Denham, with slight alteration: "On the bleak Shoar now lies the abandoned King, | A headless Carcass, and a nameless Thing" (2.762–3). What is more noteworthy is that at this point, uniquely in his entire translation, even though he takes many lines over from predecessors, Dryden has a footnote: "*This whole line is taken from Sir* John Denham." Could the footnote be drawing attention to the historical reference implicit in Denham's translation?[36]

---

[31] On this see Hammond (1999) 225–6.
[32] Parts of it, and parts of his translation of *Aen.* 3, were in fact written as early as 1636.
[33] *An Elegie upon the Death of* Lord Hastings 31–2; for these details on Denham, see Banks (1928) 6–9; O Hehir (1968) 54–82.
[34] See Banks (1928) 15–16; O Hehir (1968) 101–8.
[35] Venuti (1995) 64.
[36] For a somewhat different reading of the footnote, see Hammond (1999) 239–40.

Royalist French theory

From the point of view of reception, it matters little whether Dryden was writing with nostalgia for James II or as an adviser to William III, and the two are not mutually exclusive. For the eighteenth century, the Whig ascendancy and the proliferation of the Tacitean view of Augustus and Augustanism, all that mattered was that Virgil's poem had become a poem depicting and exhorting right action by the prince and urging the obedience of his subjects. Dryden's vision for this function came from France.

Père René le Bossu

"Impartially speaking," says Dryden, "the *French* are as much better Criticks than the *English*, as they are worse Poets" (Dedication 287). Le Bossu is such a critic, author of *Traité du Poème épique* of 1675, a work much read in England both in French and in English, into which it was translated (by the mysterious "W. J.") in 1695, when Dryden, who knew it in the French, was translating the *Aeneid*.[37] A. F. B. Clark has noted the oddity of the British obsession: "one of the strangest phenomena in the strange annals of neo-classicism is the history of le Bossu's reputation; for this man, who represents that literary *régime* at its woodenest, is most quoted in England of all the French critics."[38] All one need really know of this work is its central premise, which resides in its very definition of epic, a definition that ill fits *any* epic poem of classical antiquity, but would be readily embraced by Dryden: "epic is an artistically produced discourse, whose function is through instruction to form morals disguised beneath the allegories of an important narrative, which is recounted in verse in a manner which is plausible, entertaining and spectacular."[39]

Peter White has demonstrated just how much of our view of ancient Roman patronage is in fact a whole-cloth creation of the seventeenth century, chiefly shaped by the court of Louis XIV, and by le Bossu in particular.[40] As White notes, le Bossu "held that Vergil

---

[37] For a good, brief assessment of le Bossu, see Clark (1925) 243–61.

[38] Clark (1925) 243.

[39] "L'Épopée est un discours inventé avec art, pour former les moeurs par des instructions déguisées sous les allégories d' une action importante, qui est racontée en vers d' une manière vraisemblable, divertissante et merveilleuse."

[40] White (1993) 95–109.

wrote in order to justify a change of government" (101), not just to praise Augustus, as Servius had held. Le Bossu, constantly using Virgil as his paradigm, talks of the epic poet's need to instruct the prince, and his related drive to urge the people to act in obedience to the prince. As White points out, Dryden took only the second part of this theory, that the poet (Virgil/Dryden) writes to urge obedience to the government of the prince (Augustus/James II or William III), in whose interests it is "to be so Govern'd." White discusses the modification of French thought by English political and literary writers in the eighteenth century, and we can see in the politicizing of literature and the rise of the Press the ways in which propaganda in a modern sense took hold, and was then back-formed onto Virgil, with the help of Dryden's new classic. Consequently by 1735 Pope could say "the *Aeneid* was evidently a party piece, as much as *Absalom and Achitophel*. Virgil was as slavish a writer as any of the gazetteers."[41] The Augustan Virgil was thus firmly entrenched in England by the early eighteenth century, and his ideological status would rarely be questioned until the middle of the twentieth. And it is also the case that in generally literate non-classical circles, the Augustan Virgil remains the orthodoxy. His popularity might rise and fall depending on the political outlook of the reader, but his ideological position, which John Dryden helped to create, has rarely been doubted.

"*Spencer* wanted only to have read the rules of *Bossu*: for no Man was ever Born with a greater Genius, or had more knowledge to support it." So Dryden in his Dedication (323), again in a discussion of the superiority of French theory and of its role in guiding the political program of the poet. Luke Milbourne's voice is of interest in this setting (26): "Mr. D. used to talk in Days of Yore of an *Heroic Poem* to the *Honour of* Charles II. Had it ever been finished, doubtless Mr. *Bossu's Rules* would have appeared in every line."

As we look to the means whereby Dryden so emphatically and so effectively produced a poem to match his own political horizons, it is worth recalling his operating principle from the Dedication:[42]

> I have already said from Bossu, that a poet is not obliged to
> make his hero a virtuous man; therefore neither Homer nor
> Tasso are to be blamed, for giving what predominant quality

---

[41] White (1993) 106, quoting Pope's friend, Joseph Spence.
[42] Frost and Dearing (1987) 5.287–8.

they pleased to their first character. But Virgil, *who designed to form a perfect prince,* and would insinuate that *Augustus, whom he calls Aeneas in his poem,* was truly such, found himself obliged to make him without blemish, thoroughly virtuous; and a thorough virtue both begins and ends in piety. [emphasis added]

We will return later to the ways in which Dryden went about the task of making Virgil's Aeneas "a perfect prince," a character "without blemish." But first a second French critic, this one an editor and commentator.

Charles de la Rue

J. M. Bottkol, in a study defending Dryden's scholarly strategies for constructing his translation, writes as follows:[43]

> For Virgil he used almost exclusively another volume of the Dauphin's library, the very popular edition of Ruaeus ... he sat with a favorite edition before him (Prateus [Juvenal], Ruaeus [Virgil], Casaubon [Persius], or Cnipping [Ovid]), read the original carefully, often the Latin prose *Interpretatio,* and invariably studied the accompanying annotations.

Ruaeus' edition may have been popular, but we should not lose sight of the function of his edition, as of the Delphine editions in general: to instruct the prince. Unfortunately the lavish Latin hexameter *Epistola* is only to be found in the first edition (Paris, 1675), for it is a good specimen of encomium and sycophancy, and indicates well how Ruaeus (de la Rue, a Jesuit)[44] would handle any ideological ambigu-

---

[43] Bottkol (1943) 242–3; Dryden also used existing translations, from which he liberally borrowed, in the case of the Earl of Lauderdale's with some infamy. Cf. Proudfoot (1960) *passim.* Since my concern is with the reception of Dryden's translation, I do not here distinguish where he adopts the wording of those predecessors, some of whom are also imposing Royalist readings on Virgil. On Dryden's liberal use of prior translation (not unusual for the day) see Proudfoot. We shift from moral ideologies to political ones. Whether or not all the details in Dryden are of his own invention, or borrowed from one of his predecessors, the text becomes "Dryden," and its influence is not diminished by the previous voices that silently inhabit it. For a stemmatics of Dryden's use of other translations, see MacPherson (1910) 74–95 – a Scotsman writes a German dissertation about translations of a Latin poet into English! Dryden ("Dedication," Frost and Dearing (1987) 5.325) talks about his differences with Ruaeus.

[44] For the sake of consistency with them, I have followed Dryden, Milbourne and contemporaries in using the Latinate name.

ities. It also shows how the Virgilian relationship to Augustus is tail-
ored to fit the French court: Louis should not envy the fact that Virgil
was encomiast for Augustus, he too will have a Maro for every war he
fights (*totque tui quondam, quot erunt ea bella, Marones*).

Milbourne on a few occasions refers to Dryden's dependence: 73
"Ruaeus and others to whom Mr. D, is *blindly gathered*"; 122 "as
Mr. D's *Dictionary* may teach him, or his friend *Ruaeus*'s Notes"; 145
"*The thin leav'd Arbute hazle*. Here Mr. D. is misled by *Ruaeus*, who
misunderstanding the *Arbutus*, made *horrida* signifie *thin-leav'd*; but
Virgil's sense is *The true Nut is grafted on the prickly Thorn*." Dryden
worked with Ruaeus' text and commentary, but for the reader of
Dryden's translation the commentary recedes and becomes invisible,
which leaves the "translation" with greater authority, seeming to be a
representation of Virgil, but in fact representing the no longer visible
arguments, often quite flimsy, of a commentator charged with producing a Virgil most congenial to the training of the prince. A famous
example, and one we saw Servius struggling to neutralize, has Virgil's
prince plucking the resistant golden bough:

> corripit Aeneas extemplo avidusque refringit
> cunctantem, et vatis portat sub tecta Sibyllae.
> (*Aen.* 6.210–11)

> He seiz'd the shining bough with griping hold,
> And rent away, with ease, the ling'ring gold.
> (Dryden 6.303–4)

The offending *cunctantem* is done away with; worse, it has been replaced with its virtual opposite – Aeneas tore it away "with ease" as
the Sibyl had said he *should*. The justification is presumably to be
found in Ruaeus' commentary, which draws from the rationalization of Servius: "How is it '*lingering*' when the Sibyl had said 'it will
follow easily if the Fates call you?' The problem is solved by the
word 'eager;' for to an eager person things which are quite swift seem
slow."[45]

Ruaeus' commentary could be usefully studied in a comprehensive
way as a text providing the hidden voice of the exegete in Dryden's

---

[45] Ruaeus on 6.210: "quomodo *cunctantem*, siquidem dixerat Sibylla: *facilisque sequetur,
Si te fata vocant?* Nodum solvit vox ista *avidus*: quippe avido citissima quaeque tardiora
videntur."

rewriting of Virgil, but one more example will suffice here.⁴⁶ At the
beginning of *Aeneid* 11 Aeneas sets up the trophy of Mezentius' arms,
including his breastplate, whose twelve perforations suggested to
readers as early as Servius a ritual desecration of the corpse by each of
the twelve Etruscan cities – from which Mezentius had asked Aeneas'
protection at the end of Book 10. Virgil's lines are quite specific:

> aptat rorantis sanguine cristas
> telaque trunca viri, et bis sex thoraca petitum
> perfossumque locis, clipeumque ex aere sinistrae
> subligat atque ensem collo suspendit eburnum.

> (*Aen.* 11.8–11)

Ruaeus' discussion at least starts out objectively, but soon becomes
desperate:⁴⁷

> perfossumque: Mezentius had received only two wounds from
> Aeneas: one in the groin (10.785), the other in the neck (907).
> Whence then those twelve holes in the breastplate? Servius
> suspects that after his death the Etruscans in their anger inflicted
> many blows on him, as with Hector and Tydeus. But at his
> death Mezentius had begged that Aeneas not expose him to the
> hatred of his people. I think that the number "twelve" is given
> for any undetermined number.

Dryden presumably saw that twelve was not a plausible indiscriminate
number, but Ruaeus' discussion of the implications of the violation
would seem to have heightened his anxiety about the actions of his
"perfect Hero." His translation removed those implications:

> Above his Arms, fixed on the leafless Wood,
> Appear'd his Plumy Crest besmear'd with Blood;
> His brazen Buckler on the left was seen;
> Truncheons of shiver'd Lances hung between:
> And on the right was plac'd his Corselet, bor'd
> And to the neck was ty'd his unavailing Sword.

---

⁴⁶ Løsnes (1963) 115–57 has studied Dryden's dependence on Ruaeus in a limited way,
skillfully showing that Dryden had access to the second edition (Paris 1682; also Amsterdam 1690; London 1687, 1695).
⁴⁷ "duo tantum vulnera Mezentius ab Aenea acceperat: alterum in inguine, *Aen.* 10.785,
alterum in iugulo, *ibid.* 907. unde igitur duodecim illa thoracis foramina? suspicatur Servius eum ab Etruscis infensis post mortem fuisse multis ictibus appetitum: ut fuit Hector
et Tydeus. oraverat tamen moriens Mezentius Aeneam, ne suorum odiis eum objiceret.
numerum autem *duodenum*; pro quolibet incerto numero, a poeta positum puto."

The "breastplate aimed at and stabbed in twice six places" is diminished to "his Corselet, bor'd" — with the implication that it was Aeneas who bored it. Certainly any trace of desecration is gone, and with it the subtlety, openness and potential for oppositional meaning of the Virgilian original. Critics may argue against the suggestion in Servius; Dryden preferred to remove even the evidence for the discussion.

Jean Regnault de Segrais

Dryden also acknowledges his debt to Segrais, whose translation of Virgil, "avec privilege du roi," was published in two volumes in the years before Dryden began his own, but more importantly in the years in which he held a central place in the English court (Paris 1668, 1681). Dryden will have related in particular to Segrais' preface, which is in the form of a letter to Louis XIV, even more slavish than that of Ruaeus: he directly connects the greatness of the Prince to the valor of the Hero. Were Virgil to come back he would recognize in Louis the reborn Augustus, and so on. The only quality Segrais shares with Virgil, he avers, is "the same zeal for the glory of Your Majesty, that that great man had for the glory of his Prince."[48]

Segrais' preface in fact contains some good material on Virgil's narrative style, on invention, and on other rhetorical aspects of the poem. But when it turns to political aspects, it is a creature of its time:

> Virgil was a subject of Augustus and he lived during the
> splendor of the Roman Empire in the most abundant,
> luxurious and just century that has ever been in the whole
> duration of the Latin language: he spent his life under the reign
> of a prince who showered him with riches and who was one
> of the greatest men one could set forth as an example to
> others.[49]

---

[48] Segrais, "Epistre au Roi": "Mais, SIRE, de toutes les qualitez de Virgile, je n'ay que ce mesme zele pour la gloire de V.M. que ce grand homme eut pour la gloire de son Prince."

[49] Segrais, Pref. 7 "Virgile se trouva sujet d' Auguste, il vescut pendant la splendeur de l' Empire Romain dans le siecle le plus poly, le plus delicat, & le plus juste qui est jamais esté dans toute la durée de la langue Latine: Il passa sa vie sous le regne d' un Prince qui le combla de richesses, & qui est esté l' un des plus grands hommes qu' on puisse proposer aux autres pour exemple."

Segrais in fact, like Dryden in his Dedication, responds to those who think that Virgil in any way vitiated the perfection of his hero, perhaps most strikingly when he states (reasonably) that we should not judge the ancients by the standards of other eras. His example? No need to be concerned about the treatment of Dido (36): "Le divorce passoit à Rome pour une galanterie; & l' Empereur auquel il vouloit plaire, l' avait autorisé dans sa famille." Charles II would certainly have gone along with this, although he did not bother with divorce. We will see in the next chapter that this "courtly" attitude towards divorce makes Dryden, paradoxically, one of the most honest of translators of some parts of *Aeneid* 4. Aeneas' actions did not disturb him; no need therefore to change Virgil.

These, then, were the courtiers of Louis XIV who so influenced Dryden and helped shape his political reading of Virgil. We should not forget that England was at war with France for the entire period that Dryden was writing the translation.[50] And all the while James II, who would outlive Dryden, was living in exile in the palace at St. Germain through the beneficence of Louis. For Dryden, the memory of James, and of the favor he and his brother had lavished on the poet, seems to have lived on through his vision of Virgil and his connection to the French Criticks he so admired, Louis' own Augustan writers, Ruaeus, Segrais and le Bossu, all of them, with Dryden, truer "Augustan" writers than Virgil ever was. It may also well be the case, as Erskine-Hill has claimed, that "Dryden sees Aeneas as a 'monitory ideal' to William III, and a hero who served to highlight the sufferings, piety, and destiny of the exiled Stuarts."[51] But again the ambiguity of Dryden's specific associations is immaterial for the issue of reception of Virgil. What matters here is what Dryden did to Virgil's "Augustus, whom he calls Aeneas in his poem."

The perfect prince: Dryden's Augustus as Aeneas

Whatever the contemporary function of Aeneas, Dryden's view of his hero is beyond doubt, both in the translation and in the dedication, where as we saw he merged Aeneas and Augustus, and defined them so:[52]

---

[50] War of the Grand Alliance (1689–97).   [51] Erskine-Hill (1996) 205.
[52] Frost and Dearing (1987) 288.

> Virgil had consider'd that the greatest Virtues of *Augustus*
> consisted in the perfect Art of Governing his People; which
> caus'd him to Reign for more than Forty Years in great
> Felicity. He consider'd that his Emperour was Valiant, Civil,
> Popular, Eloquent, and Religious. He has given all these
> Qualities to *Aeneas*.

Virgil gives Aeneas Piety first, "knowing that Piety alone comprehends the whole Duty of man towards the Gods; towards his Country, and towards his Relations."[53] Next he assigns him Valour "in a
Heroical Degree." In this he follows Segrais, with whom he agrees
that heroes, literary and historical, weep, including Achilles, who
"went roaring along the salt Sea-shore, and like a Booby, was complaining to his mother, when he should have reveng'd his Injury by
Arms."[54] But when Aeneas is struck by fear of the storm in the first
scene in which we see him, Dryden knows that "his fear was not
for himself, but for his People." His actual translation editorializes
accordingly:

> extemplo Aeneae solvuntur frigore membra;
> ingemit et duplicis tendens ad sidera palmas
> talia voce refert ...   (*Aen.* 1.92–4)

> Struck with unusual Fright, the Trojan Chief,
> With lifted Hands and Eyes, invokes relief.   (1.135–6)

The effect of "unusual" is remarkable, given that as readers we have
no standard by which to judge Aeneas, at least on the linear reading
that Virgil assumed, and that Dryden breaches in this couplet. The
addition of the word constitutes a powerful embedding of tendentious hermeneutics into the poem. Protecting Aeneas' conventional
heroism is the mission here; gone is the powerful metaphor *solvuntur
frigore membra*, gone the power of those words to resonate when they
recur, at the other end of the poem, applied to the victim Turnus
as he falls to the sword of Aeneas (12.951), gone also the sense that
Aeneas in the storm is, like us, human and *not* perfect, the most Virgilian aspect of heroism.

A focus on these qualities in the *Aeneis*, particularly where the
actions of Aeneas might be called into question, is quite instructive,

[53] Frost and Dearing (1987) 288.   [54] Frost and Dearing (1987) 290–2.

for Dryden's creative manipulations, in line with the theory expressed in the Dedication, are thereby put into practice. Dryden embellishes so as to add such qualities where they were either more muted or absent from Virgil. So Virgil's *insignem pietate virum* (1.10) becomes "so brave, so just a Man" (1.14);[55] at 1.111 *miserabile visu* is "(A horrid Sight) ev'n in the Hero's view" (1.163); and when Aeneas emerges from his cloud and addresses Dido (594–5), with no help from the Latin Dryden has "And thus with manly Modesty he spoke" (1.833). Aeneas' depiction of his own actions in Book 2 has the hero speaking with anything but modesty. At 2.314–17, Aeneas acts with frenzy (*arma amens capio*), resolving to rush the citadel and seek a beautiful death:

> arma amens capio; nec sat rationis in armis,
> sed glomerare manum bello et concurrere in arcem
> cum sociis ardent animi; furor iraque mentem
> praecipitat, pulchrumque mori succurrit in armis.

As Harrison has noted, "Dryden's hero proceeds almost meticulously with conscious purpose, and not through fear, rage, or desperation."[56] Dryden ennobles Aeneas, assigning him courage, patriotism, and honor, none mentioned by Virgil, while removing the troubling *furor iraque*:[57]

> With frenzy seiz'd, I run to meet th' Alarms,
> Resolv'd on Death, resolv'd to die in Arms:
> But first to gather friends, with them t' oppose,
> If Fortune favor'd, and repel the Foes:
> Spurr'd by my courage, by my Country fir'd
> With sense of Honour, and revenge inspir'd. (2.423–8)

A few lines later in response to Panthus' report of Troy's destruction, Aeneas rushes into combat:

---

[55] It is notable that Aeneas is *iustus* in the *Aeneid* only once, in the words of Ilioneus (1.544–5 *quo iustior alter | nec pietate fuit, nec bello maior et armis*), words which Dryden perhaps imports to the narrative voice at the poem's beginning; kingly justice is more an issue for Dryden than for Virgil.

[56] Harrison (1969) 157, and 152–9 for Dryden's hero as a response to the lack of courage of Virgil's Aeneas.

[57] Cf. also at the end of the poem, where Virgil's *furiis accensus et ira | terribilis* (12.946–7) becomes "Then rowz'd anew to Wrath, he loudly cries, (Flames, while he spoke, came flashing from his Eyes)."

talibus Othryadae dictis et numine divum
in flammas et in arma feror, quo tristis Erinys,
quo fremitus vocat et sublatus ad aethera clamor.

(*Aen.* 2.336–8)

Again, Dryden interpolates on behalf of his perfect prince, who is now "well-born" and "undaunted," with the final line editorializing by replacing the recklessness of Virgil with patriotic purpose:

I Heard; and Heav'n, that well-born Souls inspires,
Prompts me, thro' lifted Swords, and rising Fires
To run, where clashing Arms and Clamour calls,
And rush undaunted to defend the Walls.

When Aeneas and the remnants of his group are drawn by the noise to Priam's palace (2.437 *protinus ad sedes Priami clamore vocati*), once more Dryden's additions underscore the heroism of the speaker:

New Clamors from th' invested palace ring:
We run to die, or disengage the King.

Dryden's second line is not only absent from Virgil; it is refuted by the plot of Book 2 since Aeneas neither dies nor disengages the king.

Scholars have noted Dryden's emphasis on Aeneas' *pietas*,[58] un-surprising given his treatment in the Dedication. It is often inserted into the text where it was at best implied by Virgil (2.766 "My Father's Image fill'd my pious Mind" for 2.561 *subiit cari genitoris imago*).[59] Likewise in Dryden's Book 12, when an arrow is shot at Aeneas, we have "A winged Arrow struck the Pious Prince" (482); likewise at 719 "The Prince, whose Piety ..." and 850 "And stretching out to Heav'n his Pious Hands." The point is not that Aeneas is impious, rather that the repeated insistence produces an emphasis and consistency absent from the original.

Where Aeneas' actions might seem excessively violent or disruptive of the *pietas* of other characters, Dryden protects his hero. At *Aeneid* 10.808–32, for instance, Virgil recounts Aeneas' slaying of the young Lausus, whose downfall is his *pietas* for his own father; and Dryden is at pains to disengage Aeneas: *Lausum increpitat Lausoque minatur* (810)

---

[58] On this subject see Garrison (1992) 234–47 and *passim*; also Hammond (1999) 261–71.
[59] This in fact translates 10.824 *mentem patriae subiit pietatis imago*, the moment following Aeneas' slaughter of Lausus, who died for his father: see below.

has become "And thus to Lausus loud with friendly threat'ning cry'd" (1148). Lausus does not desist, and savage anger swells up in Aeneas: *nec minus ille | exsultat demens, saevae iamque altius irae | Dardanio surgunt ductori* (812–14). Dryden interpolates a humane Aeneas:

> Nor thus forborn
> The Youth desists, but with insulting Scorn
> Provokes the ling'ring Prince: Whose Patience try'd,
> Gave Place, and all his Breast with Fury fir'd   (10.1151–4)

At 10.815–19 Aeneas drives (*exigit*) his forceful (*validum*) sword through the youth and buries (*recondit*) it completely in him; the sword's point (*mucro*) goes through (*transiit*) the light shield, too light for one who threatened so, and it also goes through the tunic his mother had woven from soft gold (*transiit ... tunicam molli mater quam neverat auro* 817–18) – the sense of quasi-sexual violation and of fragility crushed by overwhelming force is unmistakable.[60] Dryden begins by brilliantly shifting the agency to the sword:

> And lifted high the flaming Sword appears:
> Which full descending, with a frightful sway,
> Thro Shield and Corslet forc'd th' impetuous way.
>
> (10.1156–8)

This is followed by a more subtle change. Even this unattached sword is not permitted to go through the tunic the mother wove; that is unmentioned until we see the blood come out, and as far as Dryden's version reveals it is neither made of soft gold nor even punctured:

> The purple Streams thro' the thin Armor strove,
> And drench'd th' imbroider'd Coat his Mother wove.

The effect is still pathetic, but the violence of the Prince, and his violation of the mother's loving token, is greatly reduced in the process.

Dryden will not even allow other characters to question Aeneas' piety. Just before delivering her curse on Aeneas, Dido attacks him for his breaking faith:

> See now the promis'd Faith, the vaunted Name,
> The Pious Man, who, rushing through the Flame,

---

[60] See Adams (1982) 19–22 for the metaphorical status of weapons (*mucro* incuded).

Preserv'd his Gods; and to the *Phrygian* Shore
The burthen of his feeble Father bore!   (4.857–60)

The first line convicts the hero of breaking his word to Dido (as she sees it), as with "see now" she contrasts this behavior with his earlier piety in rescuing Anchises from Troy. But Virgil's Dido had a more fundamental and devastating charge:

> en dextra fidesque,
> quem secum patrios aiunt portare penatis,
> quem subiisse umeris confectum aetate parentem!
> (*Aen.* 4.597–9)

For Virgil's Dido Aeneas' present actions are in no way out of character, for *aiunt* "implies that Aeneas' *pietas* was all a traveller's tale."[61]

Misquotation

P. Hammond writes of the way Dryden's quotation, cited from memory, often becomes neo-Latin: "These 'misquotations' are not signs of an unscholarly carelessness, but creative refashionings of texts which had long ago lodged in his memory and become transposed into something new."[62] This rewriting of the model achieves a text that fits the perfection in his hero – almost like a form of *cento*. In a discussion of the unqualified heroism of Aeneas in the preface he downplays the fact that Jupiter tips the balance by sending the Dira against Turnus and Juturna; he maintains it is a metaphorical sign of the greater strength of Aeneas, and of the inevitability of Turnus' death. In the course of this he twice quotes Turnus' words to Aeneas, obviously from memory (Dedication 316, 317):

> "non me tua turbida virtus
> terret" ait; "dii me terrent et Jupiter Hostis"

"It is not your wild valor that terrifies me," he said, "the gods and a hostile Jove terrify me."

Thereby even Turnus is made to confess the courage of Aeneas. The problem, of course, is that Virgil wrote:

---

[61] Austin (1955) 175.   [62] Hammond (1999) 56.

> non me tua fervida terrent
> dicta, ferox; di me terrent et Iuppiter hostis (12.894–5)

In the Virgilian reality, at the end of the *Aeneid*, *virtus* in the face of the Dira's assault is ascribed to Turnus (12.913 *quacumque viam virtute petivit*), something which Dryden will not allow (12.1319–20 "whatever means he try'd | All force of Arms, and points of Art employ'd" – not quite *Virtus*). Dryden has rather assigned the quality to Aeneas, and has Turnus acknowledge it, when it was never in Virgil's Latin. Virgil's "boiling words" have become Dryden's "turbulent valor," and Turnus' designation of Aeneas as *ferox* has been quietly dropped, replaced with a metrical filler (*ait*). Whether the misquotation is willful or accidental the effect is transformative of Virgil.[63]

Erasing ambiguity

For Dryden literal translation of the model is to be avoided, for it "leaves him obscure."[64] But what if he was obscure in his original? Another translator, more than a century later, would answer that question:[65]

> The obscurity one often finds in the writings of the ancients –
> *Agamemnon* presents an excellent example of this – is a result
> of the brevity and the boldness with which thoughts, images,
> emotions, memories, atonements, as they come out of the
> impassioned soul, are linked together with a disdain for any
> mediating connective sentences. As one thinks oneself into the
> mood of the poet, into his time, into the characters he puts on
> the stage, the obscurity gradually fades and is replaced by an
> intense clarity.

That may be an admirable aim in a translator, but these words also expose the hermeneutical pitfalls of thinking oneself into the mood of the poet and in particular into his time. The clarity which emerges,

---

[63] Oddly, Dryden's actual translation is further confused (12.1295–6) "No threats of thine my manly mind can move: | 'Tis hostile Heav'n I dread, and partial Jove"; Turnus now claims for himself a "manly mind"; *ferox* is still missing. Cf. also the translation of Mezentius' words to the victorious Aeneas (10.900–1), where even an enemy is not allowed to use a negative epithet (*amare*) of our perfect hero: *hostis amare, quid increpitas mortemque minaris? | nullum in caede nefas, nec sic ad proelia veni.* "Why these insulting words, this waste of breath, | To souls undaunted, and secure of death?"

[64] Cf. Kinsley (1961) viii.

[65] Von Humboldt (1816) 59.

and which replaces the apparent obscurity of the original, may be more constructed by the translator than that very obscurity which he first experienced.

True to his sense of Virgil as the poet of a wholly beneficent prince, Dryden was constantly at pains, even outside the *Aeneid*, to remove any hint of ambiguity in the Virgilian depiction of Rome or of Octavian. So in the first *Eclogue*, where we find Meliboeus evicted from his pastoral realm, there is a clear indictment of what is unmistakably a Roman soldier, and we saw the Servian commentary struggling with the identity of that soldier (Octavian's or Antony's?) (70–2):

> impius haec tam culta novalia miles habebit,
> barbarus has segetes. en quo discordia civis
> produxit miseros: his nos consevimus agros!

> An impious soldier will take possession of these well-tilled
> fields, a foreigner of these crops – look to what point of misery
> has strife brought the people: for such as these have we sowed
> our fields!

It is hard to separate *impius . . . miles* from *barbarus*, and indeed from the perspective of Meliboeus the three words almost form a single entity. But Dryden easily broke up the group (97–9):

> Did we for these barbarians plant and sow?
> On these, on these, our happy fields bestow?
> Good heav'n! What dire effects from civil discord flow!

The tricolon is most effective, and gives a good sense of the original Virgilian pathos and indignation; but the *impius miles*, the soldier of Rome, the displacing veteran of Servius and the whole biographical tradition, is gone, to be replaced by a generic "barbarian," who offers the reader evasion of the more troubling implications in *miles*.

A similar moment comes in the *Georgics*, at the end of Book 2, where the idealized life of the farmer is contrasted in Virgil's well-known priamel with those of rulers, politicians, and military figures (495–512). Nothing perturbs the man who knows the gods of the country – neither the vagaries of political life, nor regal trappings, not civil strife or Dacian uprisings, nor "the affairs of Rome and kingdoms which must fall" (498):

> non res Romanae perituraque regna

147

We will recall Servius' attempt to keep *peritura* completely uninvolved in *res Romanae*; as he said "non enim Romano male dixit imperio."[66] Against this attempt Latinity fairly easily attaches both nouns *apo koinou* to the participle; in other words we seem to be dealing with a potential ambiguity. Dryden's rewriting is brilliant: he was able to maintain the balance of the Virgilian line, but at the same time to neutralize it from the perspective of ideology (711–12):

> Nor with a superstitious fear is awed,
> For what befalls at home, or what abroad.

"At home" and "abroad" preserve the the balance of original, though antithesis is stronger, and *peritura* is reduced to the ideologically anemic "befalls," a word with no meaningful connection to "fall" in the sense meant by *peritura*. Dryden has given us *domi militiaeque*.

Again, at *Georgics* 2.170–2, we find rewriting and antithesis used to remove ambiguity:

> et te, maxime Caesar,
> qui nunc extremis Asiae iam victor in oris
> imbellem avertis Romanis arcibus Indum.

> and you, greatest Caesar, who now, victorious on the furthest
> shores of Asia, turn the unwarlike Indian away from the
> citadels of Rome.

We have already discussed this passage in its Servian context;[67] here is Dryden's solution (237–40):

> And mighty Caesar, whose victorious arms
> To furthest Asia carry fierce alarms,
> Avert unwarlike Indians from his Rome,
> Triumph abroad, secure our peace at home.

The final line, again involving the antithesis "abroad" and "at home," is an interpretation of the Virgilian passage. Where the original has Octavian at the ends of the earth, somewhat oddly (as it seemed to DServius, not just to some of us moderns) averting the unwarlike, in a scenario that is at least ideologically open, Dryden offers a way out *via* "defensive imperialism" ("Triumph abroad, secure our peace at home") – which is fine so long as we recognize that this is an inter-

---

[66] See Ch. 3, pp. 118–19.   [67] See Ch. 3, p. 121.

pretation, not just a translation or representation. He has offered us
something that not all readers will agree was "there" in the Latin.

Turnus and the end

Following the lion-simile at the beginning of the twelfth book,
Turnus blazes, his violence growing: *haud secus accenso gliscit violentia
Turno* (12.9). Dryden responds:

> So Turnus fares; his Eye-balls flash with Fire
> Through his wide Nostrils Clouds of Smoke expire
>
> (12.15–16)

And again, following his pledge to bring down Aeneas:

> Thus while he raves, from his wide Nostrils flies
> A fiery Stream, and Sparkles from his Eyes.   (12.157–8)

At least "eyes" are in the Latin, but whence the "wide nostrils"
emitting "Clouds of Smoke" and a "fiery Stream?" The effect is first
of all to tie him more closely to the animals of three similes juxtaposed to these passages (lion and bull), particularly since Virgil at
12.115 describes the horses of the Sun as having lifted nostrils (*elatis
naribus*), for which Dryden gives "From out their flaming Nostrils
breath'd the Day" (176). Indeed Dryden creates his own examples of
"trespass" by blurring the demarcation of tenor and vehicle. But the
effect also verges on the grotesque, which may be the intention, and
another possibility presents itself. Watkins has noted that Turnus in
the Middle Ages was equated with the Devil, a connection that is
made, for instance, in Maphaeus Vegius' "Thirteenth Book of the
Aeneid."[68] Dryden surely could have known this tradition, and if he
did, he may well have had in mind a familiar intertext. At *Paradise
Lost* 10.272–81, Sin and Death share an exchange prior to leaving the
Gates of Hell and passing into the world. Death is compared to a
carrion bird:

> So saying, with delight he *snuffed* the smell
> Of mortal change on earth. As when a flock

---

[68] Watkins (1995) 108, quoting Vegius *De Perseverantia Religionis* I.iiii.x *Tum priusque
[Aeneas] promissam latio quietem assequatur turnum id est dyabolum infestum habet* "Then
before Aeneas gains his promised rest in Latium he meets his enemy Turnus, i.e. the
Devil."

Of ravenous fowl, though many a league remote,
Against the day of battle, to a field,
Where armies lie encamped, come flying, lured
With scent of living carcases designed
For death the following day, in bloody fight;
So scented the grim feature, and upturned
His *nostril wide* into the murky air,
Sagacious of his quarry from so far.

Dryden may already have played on Milton's lines, with his translation of the love-crazed mares of *Georgics* 3.274:

The Mares to Cliffs of rugged Rocks repair,
And with *wide Nostrils snuff* the Western Air
(Dryden, *Georgics* 3.430–1)

Whether animalized or diabolical, Dryden's Turnus is here transformed.

The end of Virgil's *Aeneid* is one place where many readers have found it difficult to sustain Dryden's paradigm of a "thoroughly virtuous" Aeneas, and where Augustan criticism has struggled most keenly to keep the genie in the bottle. Turnus has seemed to such readers to die in a way that at least shifts attention and even sympathy away from Aeneas, resulting in a complicating of the ethical status of the close. Other responses to the end will occupy us in Chapter 9; for now here is Dryden's version:

ast illi solvuntur frigore membra
vitaque cum gemitu fugit indignata sub umbras.
(*Aen.* 12.951–2)

The streaming blood distain'd his arms around:
And the disdainful Blood came rushing thro' the wound.

Vita indignata, that moving and vivid phrase, has become "disdainful blood," a reversion to the characterization of Turnus at his most brutal – a characterization absent from the end of the poem. It combines powerfully in paronomasia with "distained" in the preceding line.[69] But it does more than that: as with "befall" as a representation

---

[69] Noted by Corse (1991) 25. For different readings of these intratexts, see Erskine-Hill (1996) 213–15 and Hammond (1999) 238–9. Neither is aware of Corse's study and neither treats the death of Camilla, which is central to my view of Dryden's purpose, on which more below.

of *peritura*, so here "disdainful" misrepresents and exploits its linguistic connection to *indignata*. And *cum gemitu* is gone, omitted.

Now it is well known that Virgil had also used the poem's last line for the death of Camilla (11.831), thereby creating one of the most powerful pieces of intratextuality in the poem. The "thoroughly virtuous" Aeneas is uninvolved in Camilla's death, however, and so the great poet Dryden is free to match Virgil's poetry, which he does:

> In the last Sigh her strugling Soul expires,
> And murm'ring with Disdain, to Stygian Sounds retires.

Dryden in fact talked about the phenomenon of Virgilian repetition, as Corse has noted:[70] "Dryden says, in his Dedication, that he 'found it very painful to vary Phrases, when the same sense' returned upon him; he excuses himself, however, by referring us to Virgil: 'Even he himself, whether out of necessity or choice, has often express'd the same thing [thought or sense] in the same words' (5:333–34)." It may thus seem odd that in the case of the deaths of Camilla and Turnus, where we have the fairly rare phenomenon of precise Virgilian repetition extending over an entire line, Dryden should fail to do precisely what he apologizes for being about to do. So important was it for him to deny to Turnus the pathetic Virgilian death he permitted to Camilla.

As Corse has noted, Dryden does however ally the dying Turnus to another warrior, notably the dying Mezentius;[71] the parallel is clear and close:

> The Crimson Stream distain'd his Arms around:
> And the disdainful Soul came rushing thro' the Wound.
>
> (10.1312–13)

It is worth considering the Latin describing the death of Mezentius, since it is clear that the verbal approximation of Mezentius to Turnus is a creative act performed by Dryden, not by Virgil:

> haec loquitur, iuguloque haud inscius accipit ensem
> undantique animam diffundit in arma cruore. (10.907–8)

---

[70] Corse (1991) 25–6.

[71] Corse (1991) 25; he is not interested in ideology and seems mainly concerned with the fact that Dryden took the phrase "disdainful Soul" from Spenser's *The Fairie Queen* (2.11.42).

Here is the origin for the phrase "distained his arms," an expression to be found in the Latin describing the death of Mezentius, but nowhere in that at the end of *Aeneid* 12. Dryden's revision unites these adversaries of Aeneas and at the same time through the words "disdainful Blood" characterizes them in ways absent from the Virgilian text. My guess, moreover, is that the use of "disdainful" ultimately comes not from the Latin *indignata* at the end of the poem (although there is an etymological connection there), but rather from the opening characterization of Mezentius in the catalogue of Book 7, where the Etruscan warrior is designated *asper . . . contemptor divum Mezentius* (647–8), which Dryden rendered thus:

> Mezentius first appear'd upon the Plain:
> Scorn sate upon his Brows and sour Disdain,
> Defying Earth and Heav'n.

Dryden's brilliant ending convicts Turnus of "guilt by association." Virgil's poem had it otherwise.

Readers who encountered their Virgil *via* Dryden will have found him familiar and domesticated, that is familiar to their own literary, linguistic and cultural context. L. Venuti has recently developed the theory of translation presented by Friedrich Schleiermacher who in 1813 argued for essentially two opposed methods of translation: "Either the translator leaves the author in peace, as much as possible, and moves the reader towards him; or he leaves the reader in peace, as much as possible, and moves the author towards him."[72] Virgil finds little peace in John Dryden's translation; he is moved to the reader's and the translator's territory, and the disruption of Virgil was all the greater for Dryden's belief in the contiguity of his own and Virgil's societies. Venuti puts it so:[73]

> Translation is the forcible replacement of the linguistic and
> cultural difference of the foreign text with a text that will be
> intelligible to the target-language reader . . . Whatever difference
> the translation conveys is now imprinted by the target-
> language culture, assimilated to its positions of intelligibility,
> its canons and taboos, its codes and ideologies. The aim of
> translation is to bring back a cultural other as the same, the
> recognizable, even the familiar; and this aim always risks a

---

[72] Venuti (1995) 19–20, quoting Lefevere (1977).   [73] Venuti (1995) 18.

wholesale domestication of the foreign text, often in highly
self-conscious projects, where translation serves an appropriation
of foreign cultures for domestic agendas, cultural, economic,
political.

The domestication and appropriation of Aeneas as seventeenth-
century prince is only part of the story of Dryden's translation. It is
time now to see how he deals with Dido, the foreign, eastern queen
of Carthage.

5

Dido and her translators

The wife of one who is to gain his livelihood by poetry, or by any labour (if any there be) equally exhausting, must either have taste enough to relish her husband's performances, or good-nature sufficient to pardon his infirmities. It was Dryden's misfortune, that Lady Elizabeth had neither the one nor the other; and I dismiss the disagreeable subject by observing, that on no one occasion, when a sarcasm against matrimony could be introduced, has our author failed to season it with such bitterness, as spoke an inward consciousness of domestic misery ... When his wife wished to be a book, that she might enjoy more of his company, "Be an almanack, then, my dear," said the poet, "that I may change you once a-year."

SIR WALTER SCOTT, *Life of Dryden*[1]

November 17 (1878). Sunday. Today, am so delighted to be at home, with my wife and babies and my fire and my Virgil, and to go to church, and to go to bed.

Journal of JOHN D. LONG[2]

The reception of Dido is the richest aspect of Virgilian reception, and the one around which the Augustan battle has perhaps been fought most intensely. Early on in his book, *The Specter of Dido: Spenser and Virgilian Epic*,[3] John Watkins spells out the theme of the work, whose modest title conceals the fact that it is in reality a broad study, not just of Spenser's reception of the Virgilian Dido, but of the entire reception of Dido from Ovid to Spenser: he vividly recreates the complex and polemically conflicting transformations through which Dido went, under her own name (the vernacular romance

---

[1] Sir Walter Scott, *The Life of John Dryden*, ed. B. Kreissman (Lincoln 1963) 77, 386.
[2] Long (1956) 146.
[3] Watkins (1995).

tradition), under various disguises in Christian epic, in humanistic correctives and constructions, and ultimately in the *Faerie Queene*, where she paradoxically became a model for the Virgin Queen:

> As medieval and Renaissance commentators, allegorists, editors, homilists, storytellers, poets, painters, illustrators and tapestry-makers judged Dido's abandonment, diverse and often competing notions of what constituted Virgilian writing developed. By the late sixteenth century, imitations of her tragedy responded not only to Virgil's text but to the long history of its cultural reception.

I do however take issue with Watkins's comprehension of Virgil and the *Virgilian* Dido, for he presupposes a fully-formed, anachronistic, and heavily Augustan Virgil, that is the Virgil created by the tradition, who writes always with an eye on the *princeps*:[4]

> A particular coincidence of antifeminism and Hellenophobia at the Augustan court encouraged Virgil to present Dido's repudiation as an image of his ambivalence to Homer. Just as Aeneas reveals his *pietas* by abandoning Dido, Virgil establishes himself as Augustus's laureate by stigmatizing Homer's indulgence toward Odysseus's affairs, his championship of ingenuity over truth, and his narrative digressiveness as incompatible with Roman values.

There is much that is asserted here and that will seem unfamiliar even to Augustan readers of Virgil, but Watkins has a familiar purpose: the Virgilian meaning must be stabilized before, and in order that, the subsequent tradition may be set in motion. Watkins is nevertheless too sensitive a reader not to see how the Virgilian Dido, and readers' sympathy for her, threatens the fabric of an Augustan reading:

> Although Virgil's sympathetic treatment of Dido's death has been taken as a critique of the imperial values necessitating her abandonment, it actually enhances rather than subverts his didactic project. The more we sympathize with Dido, the more we identify with Aeneas in confronting the exacting nature of destiny. As a fundamentally didactic work, the *Aeneid* challenges its readers to explore their emotional responses to the fiction in terms of higher truths.[5]

[4] Watkins (1995) 6.   [5] Watkins (1995) 6.

This is partially true, until one returns to the end of Book 4, the opening of Book 5, and the encounter in the Underworld in Book 6, where Virgil himself prevents pure didaxis, as admiration for Aeneas' fortitude in leaving Dido is diminished by the echoes of her tragedy. Watkins in fact follows in the path of T. S. Eliot, whose "model [in 'What is a Classic?'] was Aeneas, 'the man in fate' who must abandon Dido as the gods command. Eliot, though, does not consider, as Virgil did, the woman's anguish."[6] An Augustan reading will always attempt to subordinate Dido to Aeneas, but it will also just as surely fail to convince that the heroism of the latter is the only lesson of the episode.

Watkins's establishment of the Virgilian outlook is also negligent of details of narrative voice, details that are far from trivial. At one point he states: "Virgil stigmatizes Aeneas's neglect of his future destiny for a passing moment's satisfaction" (20). Here and elsewhere he equates Virgil and the voice of the Augustan character, in this case Mercury and, through him, Jupiter. It might be uncontroversial to state that the voice of Jupiter largely coincides with that of Augustus, but it is another thing to assume that that voice, to the exclusion of others, is identical with the poet's. If I claim "Virgil stigmatizes Aeneas as a deserter of Troy" (12.15), my reader will instantly note that it is Turnus who lays that charge; it has been my insistence throughout that equal attention needs to be paid to point of view. Dido's story is a demonstration of what is necessary in an Augustan world. In that context Mercury and Jupiter certainly pass judgments; Virgil, the producer and director, displays other possibilities.

The ordering principle of Watkins's work is antithesis: pagan/ Christian, vernacular/humanist, and so forth. And although he opposes Ovid to Augustine, he also deals with a fundamental antithesis that pervades the reception – that between Ovid and Virgil himself. So of Ovid in the *Heroides*: "by eliminating the divine decrees and the epic narrator's presumably objective pronouncements [these go unspecified], he suppresses the means by which Virgil justified her abandonment." The Ovid/Virgil antithesis that is the basis of all subsequent polarizations is itself an Ovidian construction that is created by monumentalizing and stabilizing the Virgilian original, which is then open to subversion. In the *Heroides*, including *Heroides* 7 (Dido

---

[6] Gordon (1998) 408.

to Aeneas), Ovid uses his own elegiac language to effect the subversion, but he also uses the archetype of that language, the language of neoteric epyllion, as evidenced in Catullus 64, which is itself reworked in *Heroides* 10 (Ariadne to Theseus). When Ovid effects this construction he blurs the fact that Virgil's Dido was constructed from the same material: the desertion of Ariadne by Theseus, unambiguously a desertion for Catullus, can be suppressed by the reader of *Aeneid* 4 only with some effort. The fact that the Ovidian version is already present in the Virgilian gets lost in the subsequent conflicts between Christian and pagan readings, allegorical or pedagogical traditions and vernacular romance, translation and vernacular epic. The only true tragic Dido is the Virgilian one, who is subverted and simplified in Ovid's intertextual and intergeneric play.[7] The critical and the poetic traditions, satisfied only by black and white, have frequently missed the fact that both shades are present in the Virgilian archetype.

While in the Christianized post-Fulgentian allegorizing tradition the Augustan reading also persists without competition from the vernacular romance tradition with its particular focus on the tragedy of Dido, eventually the two clash. As others also have noted, Dante, for instance, in opposing the courtly tradition, makes Dido fully responsible, removing the role of Cupid; and Petrarchan humanism undercuts the heroine status of the Dido romance. Indeed Petrarch himself may have persuaded Boccaccio to move from his earlier compassionate presentation of Dido, as evidenced in the Italian poems, the *Elegia di Madonna Fiammetta*, the *Filocolo*, and the *Amorosa visione*, to the sterner Petrarchan/Augustan view found in *Africa* and in Boccaccio's later Latin works.[8] So too Spenser reworks the Augustan Virgil in his project of writing the Elizabethan epic to match his received view of the Augustan *Aeneid*. The chaste Dido of the historical tradition, reworked by Spenser into the figure of Amavia, is a model for Elizabeth herself; she coexists with the concupiscent Dido as Acrasia; Anchises' pagan eschatology, which had always bothered the Christian tradition, from the allegorists to the humanists, is con-

---

[7] See Knox (1995) 20–4.

[8] So Kallendorf (1989), who refers (62–3 and n. 18) to the view of Billanovitch that Boccaccio may be deliberately modulating his voice between that of the vernacular poet and that of the humanist.

verted to Protestantism, Aeneas as Redcrosse Knight is saved by the grace of God, and Turnus, the devil in Vegius Maphaeus' allegory, becomes the dragon in Spenser's new national version.[9] The vernacular, English poem has for the first time accommodated the humanist construction of the Augustan Virgil, in its attempt to recreate the perceived political function of epic.

Humanism carries out this enterprise by textual, philological assertion – and the most intense form of textual assertion is translation, which brings us to Gawin Douglas, Bishop of Dunkeld, and his translation of Virgil into Scottish verse. As Watkins notes (49), Douglas, whose prologue to Book 4 is a good Catholic diatribe against love and against Dido, attacks Chaucer for calling Aeneas a "traytour" to Dido:

> Allas! what harm doth apparence,
> Whan hit is fals in existence!
> For he to hir a traytour was;
> Wherfor she slow hir-self, allas!
>
> (Chaucer, *The Hous of Fame*)

But Douglas also notes that his own animus to Dido "is no more true to the letter of Vergil's text than Chaucer's sympathy." Early translation of Virgil, then, proposes to oppose and correct the vernacular "mythologies," and so control the implicit subversive hermeneutics that come with romance adaptations. Douglas, while writing translation, condemns Chaucer's rehabilitation of Dido.[10] We will do well to study with care translations that openly involve themselves in the Dido question.

Leaving Tudor England, with an authoritative Augustan Virgil translated into both Scottish (Douglas) and English (in the version of Twyne and Pharr), and with a vernacular national poem which has liberated itself from the compassionate courtly romance of earlier vernacular treatments (*The Faerie Queene*), we are in a position to move into the seventeenth century, whose Virgilian teleology at century's end will be Dryden's translation, drawing from Royalist

---

[9] Watkins (1995) 106–12.

[10] Watkins (1995) 49. In the Prologue to Book 4 Douglas admits to the pathos of Dido's death. Douglas does so by claiming (wrongly) that even Augustus wept at this part – a subtle appropriation of the imperial reaction to the death of Marcellus at the end of *Aeneid* 6?

translations produced throughout the century. The Virgil that he constructed, and its Dido, looks more to Dryden's own apparent misogynism and to the Roman Catholicism he shares with Douglas than it does to Virgil. His Dido is a powerful figure, particularly in her rage, a rage which underscores the threat to Aeneas; as a result, however, she loses much of the Virgilian sympathy that has appealed to readers since Ovid. We may approach Dryden's Dido by way of his other female characters, beginning with the speechless Lavinia, onto whom Dryden projects his prejudices.

Lavinia and the "secret satire against women"

Dryden interprets Lavinia's ambiguous blush (*Aen.* 12.64–6) as follows: "though in favour of his Heroe, he never tells us directly, that Lavinia preferr'd Turnus to Aeneas, yet he has insinuated his preference twice before" (in Books 7 and 11). And this has recently been seen as a sign of Dryden's republicanism.[11] On closer inspection, however, the situation is very much otherwise, for Dryden continues in a remarkable and revealing fashion:

> But I am much deceived, if . . . there be not a secret satire
> against the [female] sex, which is lurking under this description
> of Virgil, who seldom speaks well of women . . . The rest
> [besides Camilla, Andromache and Venus – "a better mother
> than a wife"] are Junos, Dianas, Didos, Amatas, two mad
> prophetesses, three Harpies on earth, and as many Furies under
> ground. This fable of Lavinia includes a secret moral; that
> women, in their choice of husbands, prefer the younger of
> their suitors to the elder; are insensible of merit, fond of hand-
> someness, and, generally speaking, rather hurried away by their
> appetite, than governed by their reason. (John Dryden *Notes
> and Observations*, on *Aen.* 12.100–102)

Lavinia is made to be attracted to Turnus, so she may be blackened with the rest of the women in the poem; there is no indication, here or in Books 7 and 11, of her preferences. Misogynism, and not republicanism, is what informs Dryden's interpretation of the blush. And the other women are treated accordingly.

---

[11] Cf. Burrow (1997) 30 "Dryden is sure that Lavinia prefers the indigenous Turnus to Aeneas."

Cassandra

One of the most pathetic moments in Virgil is Aeneas' depiction of the captured Cassandra, hands bound and with her eyes silently imploring heaven 2.405–6:

> ad caelum tendens ardentia lumina frustra,
> lumina, nam teneras arcebant vincula palmas.

In vain stretching out her blazing eyes to heaven, her eyes, for bonds restrained her tender hands.

Dryden's version is an utter transformation, and provides among other things good evidence of how far short rhymed heroic couplets can at times fall as representations of the epic meters of Greece and Rome:

> On Heav'n she cast her Eyes, she sigh'd, she cry'd
> ('Twas all she could) her tender Arms were ty'd.
> (2.548–9)

He has "brought out" of the Virgilian text what was never there ("she sigh'd, she cry'd"), with its parenthesis and rhyme transforming and trivializing Virgil's pathos, and turning it into a "silly precious conceit" as one critic has put it.[12] Cassandra is pathetic in Aeneas' description precisely because, silent, bound and captive in this scene, she is *not* the "mad prophetess" of tradition.[13] We will recall how Dryden had rendered Virgil's first depiction of Aeneas, whose Latin has similarities to the description of Cassandra:

> extemplo Aeneae solvuntur frigore membra;
> ingemit et duplicis *tendens ad sidera palmas*
> talia voce refert: o terque quaterque beati ...
> (*Aen.* 1.92–4)

> Struck with unusual Fright, the Trojan Chief,
> With lifted Hands and Eyes, invokes Relief.
> And thrice, and four times happy those, he cry'd
> That under *Ilian* Walls before their Parents dy'd.
> (1.135–8)

---

12 Proudfoot (1960) 209.
13 Only in Juno's *agon* with Venus at *Aen.* 10.68 is she associated with madness: *Cassandrae impulsus furiis.*

Now we perhaps see where Segrais and Dryden may have found the "eyes" for their translations – in the similar lines on Cassandra?[14] Dryden draws attention to the Virgilian parallelism: "cry'd/dy'd" (1.137–8) is superficially an intertextual anticipation of "cry'd/ty'd" (2.548–9), though the effect is very different in the Cassandra couplet, with its additional jingle ("she sigh'd/ she cry'd/were ty'd"), and with the intrusive parenthesis ("'Twas all she could"). There is, moreover, a subtle semantic shift, not unlike those seen in the last chapter: whereas Dryden turned the silent Cassandra into a sighing, crying figure, he transformed Aeneas' groaning (*ingemit*) into a verb of speech via the ambiguity of English "cry." And what is doubly false to the Latin, Cassandra is assigned *lacrimare*, Aeneas, *gridare*.

Creusa

Dryden even problematizes the rather colorless figure of Creusa, to whom he cannot resist adding an epithet. Virgil has Venus urging her son to return to his family so as to escape with them from the falling city:

> eripe, nate, fugam, finemque impone labori;
> nusquam abero et tutum patrio te limine sistam.
>
> (*Aen.* 2.619–20)

> Haste hence, my Son; this fruitless Labour end:
> Haste where your *trembling* Spouse, and Sire attend:
> Haste, and a Mother's Care your Passage shall befriend.
>
> (2.837–9)

"Spouse and Sire" works well as a concretization of *patrio . . . limine*, but where did "trembling" spouse come from? Conversely, when Aeneas tells of his and the Trojans' trembling and panic after the death of Laocoon (2.228–9 *tum vero tremefacta novus per pectora cunctis | insinuat pavor*), Dryden can manage only "Amazement seizes all" (2.300). Aeneas does not tell how Creusa is lost, speculating that she either went astray or collapsed from fatigue (2.739 *erravitne via seu lapsa resedit*). Dryden, however, in a discussion of Aeneas' piety (he went looking for her), has her "losing his Footsteps through Fear or Ignorance,"[15] and he translates accordingly:

---

[14] See above, Ch. 4, pp. 140–1.   [15] Frost and Dearing (1987) 5.286.

Alas! I lost *Creusa*: hard to tell
If by her fatal Destiny she fell,
Or weary sate, or wander'd with *affright*:
But she was lost forever to my Sight.

Dido and Aeneas

But it is on the reworking of Dido that Dryden lavishes most care, because there is where most is at stake: the perfection of his prince depends on his ability to construct a particular Dido, one who is both more dangerous than the Virgilian text suggests, and at the same time is solely culpable for what befalls her. The Dedication confronts the charge against Aeneas, a charge which is clearly current in Dryden's time and society:[16]

> [Aeneas] is Arraign'd with more shew of Reason by the Ladies; who will make a numerous Party against him, for being false to Love, in forsaking *Dido*. And I cannot much blame them; for to say the Truth, 'tis an ill Precedent for their Gallants to follow. Yet if I can bring him off, with Flying Colours, they may learn experience at her cost; and for her sake, avoid a Cave, as the worst shelter they can chuse from a shower of Rain, especially when they have a Lover in their Company.

Dryden archly uses Dido as an object for contemporary didaxis. He then enumerates the various defenses, his own and others', that piety is the chief virtue, and that Jupiter and piety demand departure from Carthage, as they do; that blame rests with Jupiter, and not with Aeneas or Virgil, that the poem was unfinished. He also suggests that the desertion would have appealed to an anti-Carthaginian audience: "He knew he cou'd not please the *Romans* better, or oblige them more to patronize his Poem, than by disgracing the foundress of that city."[17]

The resulting Dido of Dryden is a complex figure, one who is subject both to his own morality, and to the exigencies of the character of his hero. So, for instance, when Dido wanders about the city, lovesick but presumably aimless, in the tradition of the unrequited lover (4.68 *uritur infelix Dido totaque vagatur | urbe furens*),[18] Dryden

---

[16] Frost and Dearing (1987) 5.294.
[17] Frost and Dearing (1987) 5.298.
[18] As for instance Gallus does (*errantem*) at *Ecl.* 6.64. See Thomas (1979) on this theme.

supplies a purpose to her wandering, in the process removing all decorum from her, even before the fateful union:

> Sick with desire, *and seeking him she loves*,
> From street to Street, the raving Dido roves. [emphasis added]
>
> (4.93–4)

This might be thought to emerge from Virgil's Latin – if she is wandering she must be looking for Aeneas – but her wandering has nothing to do with seeking the beloved. Again, at their very first meeting, when Aeneas literally has a divine epiphany (1.589 *os umerosque deo similis*) as he steps from the cloud and addresses Dido, Virgil's Dido responds naturally enough; she is thunderstruck at the appearance, and at his experience (1.613–14 *obstipuit primo aspectu Sidonia Dido, | casu deinde viri tanto*). Cupid has not yet worked his wiles on Dido, and although the language includes the possibility of an erotic response, it is also a response to his heroism (*viri*). Dryden transforms the Virgilian nuance into an openly and predominantly sexual response, and thereby effects a rewriting of Dido's entire character:

> The Tyrian Queen stood fix'd upon his Face,
> Pleas'd with his Motions, ravish'd with his grace;
> Admir'd his Fortunes, more admir'd the Man;
> Then recollected stood; and thus began ...   (1.866–9)

And so Dryden's queen also becomes a woman "hurried away by her appetite," as he said of Lavinia.

At the last encounter, in the *Lugentes Campi* of *Aeneid* 6, Dryden would again mount his pulpit and turn the Virgilian Underworld into a Christian Hell. Virgil made no distinctions among the dead heroines of his catalogue, those with whom Dido shares this abode; nor does he assign any blame. Indeed, the epithet *maestam* is even applied to Eriphyle, who was killed by her son (characterized by Virgil as *crudelis*) after betraying her husband Amphiaraus.[19] For the Roman poet, the focus is that of the heroines themselves, as well as of the narrator, who shows only compassion towards them. They, first and foremost, are victims, specified by the power that brought them down, and otherwise unjudged (442 *hic quos durus amor crudeli tabe peredit* "those

---

[19] Strictly speaking, she died not for love, but rather from greed for the necklace with which Polynices bribed her into committing the betrayal.

whom hard love had consumed with cruel wasting"). Their horror, moreover, lies in the fact that death brings no release (444 *curae non ipsa in morte relinquunt* "even in death their love-cares do not leave them"). Now Virgil's list goes as follows: Phaedra, Procris, Eriphyle (445), Evadne, Pasiphae, Laodamia (447), with the gender-ambiguous Caeneus receiving almost two lines to close the catalogue (448–9). Dryden rearranges: Caeneus stays at the end, but the rest are paired off: Procris and Eriphyle first, Laodamia and Evadne last, and in the middle, the other two, who in the Latin were named without epithet or any other adornment. Not good enough for Dryden:

> He saw Pasiphae there
> With Phaedra's ghost, *a foul incestuous pair.* (6.604–5)

There is a curious parallel here with an earlier attempt to deny sympathy to the inhabitants of the *Lugentes Campi* ("Fields of Grief"). At the beginning of *Africa* 6, Petrarch treats Sophonisba, an unambiguously negative figure and clearly modelled on Dido. He first consigns her to a place reserved for guilty suicides, and then to the *Lugentes Campi* – for those who died for love. But his variant is transformed from the Virgilian original, by inclusion of a catalogue of the crimes and perversions of the inhabitants.[20]

As we saw with Cassandra, Dryden seems obsessed with the presentation of women giving voice to their distress, and he clearly assigns responsibility to the women whose shades lament:

> The Souls, whom that unhappy Flame invades,
> In secret solitude, and Myrtle shades,
> Make endless Moans, and pining with Desire
> Lament too late their unextinguish'd Fire. (6.598–601)

In Virgil's *Lugentes Campi*, there is no sound, just silence, except for the voice of Aeneas, which receives no answer from Dido; nor does Virgil refer to remorse:

> hic quos durus amor crudeli tabe peredit
> secreti celant calles et myrtea circum
> silva tegit; curae non ipsa in morte relinquunt.
>
> (*Aen.* 6.442–4)

---

[20] For the changes effected by Petrarch in this passage, see Kallendorf (1989) 40–1.

Here those whom harsh love has consumed with cruel wasting
are hidden by remote paths and hemmed in by myrtle woods;
not even in death do their cares leave them.

Dryden has transformed the heroines into clamorous sinners, "lamenting too late" their dire sins. I suspect he may here have looked to Dante, precisely to Canto 5 of the *Inferno*, where we encounter Dido, markedly unnamed (61–2 *l' altra è colei che s'ancise amorosa, | e ruppe fede al cener di Sicheo*).[21] The noise as Dante and his guide approach this group is deafening, and it functions as a *leitmotif* of the entire canto (25–39):

> Ora incomincian le *dolenti note*
>   *a farmisi sentire*; or son venuto
>   là dove *molto pianto mi percuote*.
> Io venni in luogo d'ogni luce muto,
>   che *mugghia come fa mar per tempesta*,
>   se da contrari venti è combattuto.
> La bufera infernal, che mai non resta,
>   mena la spirti con la sua rapina:
>   voltando e percotendo li molesta.
> Quando giugnon davanti alla ruina,
>   quivi *le strida, il compianto, il lamento;*
>   bestemmian quivi la virtù divina.
> Intesi ch' a così fatto tormento
>   enno dannati i peccator carnali,
>   che la ragion sommettono al talento.

> Now the *doleful strains* began to attract my attention; now am
> I come to where *much wailing struck me*. I came into the place
> *mute of all light* which was *bellowing as the sea does* in a storm
> when buffeted by opposing winds. The infernal storm which
> never rests snatches up and drives the spirits: spinning and
> striking them it brings them torment. When they come before
> its downrush, *there are shriekings, weepings and lamentations*; they
> *blaspheme* there the power of God. And I learned that carnal
> sinners who subject reason to desire are to such torments
> damned. [emphasis added]

The synaesthesia of line 28 (*d'ogni luce muto*) draws attention to the lamentation of the place. In the reception and rewriting of Dante and

---

[21] See Watkins (1995) 43 on Dante's sharp diminution of Virgil's sympathy in these lines.

Dryden the tone and the entire nature of the Virgilian *Lugentes Campi* are distorted and transformed to the point that, paradoxically, the compassion that pervades the Virgilian version is eradicated by the "Christian" poets, who substitute moralizing and judgment for compassion and empathy. A "Secret Satire" against women indeed, but whose satire is it?

There are other ways of protecting the perfection of Aeneas. It is true that Dryden's Mercury is as vehement to Aeneas as Virgil's in communicating Jupiter's mandates, for the exigencies of plot require that, and, for instance, the jewelled sword of Aeneas is even elaborated: "A sword with glitt'ring gems diversify'd, | For Ornament, not use, hung idly by his Side." But Dryden has not put Aeneas beyond the pale in this description, for such ornament is possible in the context of Restoration society. Virgil's Aeneas also wears an exotic, full-length purple cloak (*Aen.* 4.262–4):

> Tyrioque ardebat murice laena
> demissa ex umeris, dives quae munera Dido
> fecerat, et tenui telas discreverat auro.

> And a cloak of Tyrian purple hung gleaming from his shoulders,
> which wealthy Dido had made as a gift, weaving fine gold
> into the threads.

Aeneas has "gone native." A jewelled sword was one thing, but a purple cloak, which is so clearly repellent to austere Roman ideals and puts Aeneas into an Eastern context, may have been too much for Dryden (384–5):

> A purple Scarf, with Gold embroider'd o'er,
> (Queen *Dido*'s Gift) about his Waste he wore.

There can be little doubt how Virgil's reader would have responded to the original Latin. What about Dryden's reader? A valuable clue is preserved in the *OED*, from the London Gazette, just a few years before publication of the translation (1689):[22]

> Lost: An officer's scarf with four gold Fringes around the Waist,
> set on Crimson Silk, and a very deep Fringe at each end.

---

[22] *OED* 2659 s.v. "Scarf" *sb.*[1] 1, from London Gazette No. 2445/4, 1689.

This looks like the very "scarf" Dryden gives to Aeneas: the exotic has been domesticated, the effeminate even militarized, and in the process Aeneas has been transformed.

After the encounter in the cave, Rumor reports a mixture of truth and lies, enumerated in four lines of indirect speech (*Aen.* 4.191–4):

> venisse Aenean Troiano sanguine cretum,
> cui se pulchra viro dignetur iungere Dido;
> nunc hiemem inter se luxu, quam longa, fovere
> regnorum immemores turpique cupidine captos.

Trojan Aeneas has arrived, Dido sees fit to join in union with him; now they are luxuriously keeping each other warm through the winter; they are forgetful of their kingdoms; they are the captives of base lust. True to his ambiguity of judgment, Virgil does not distinguish Fama's truth from her lies. But Dryden sorts things out: his translation is nothing short of astonishing, and is powerful in its purging of the Latin's ambiguity and its creation of new meaning, with serious implications for the issue of responsibility that has so occupied readers of *Aeneid* 4 (274–81):

> She fills the Peoples Ears with *Dido*'s Name;
> Who, lost to Honour, and the Sense of Shame,
> Admits into her Throne and Nuptial Bed
> A wand'ring Guest, who from his Country fled:
> Whole days with him she passes in delights;
> And wastes in Luxury long Winter nights:
> Forgetful of her Fame and Royal Trust;
> Dissolv'd in Ease, abandon'd to her Lust.

"*Dido*'s Name" is alone, while Trojan Aeneas, named in the Latin, has become "a wandering Guest"; for Virgil, Dido and Aeneas were both subjects of *fovere, immemores,* and *captos,* while Dryden has her as sole subject: "she passes ... and wastes ... forgetful of her Fame ... dissolv'd, abandoned to her Lust!"

A few lines later Iarbas complains of Aeneas and his effeminate crew. Virgil had Iarbas single out Aeneas in describing his eastern luxuriousness, perfume and clothes:

> "et nunc ille Paris cum semiviro comitatu,
> Maeonia mentum mitra crinemque madentem
> subnexus, rapto potitur."   (*Aen.* 4.215–17)

In this case Dryden changes singular Aeneas (*subnexus*) to plural, so as to share the odium among the Trojans:

> And now this other *Paris*, with his Train,
> Of conquer'd Cowards must in *Affrick* reign!
> Whom, what they are, their Looks and Garb confess;
> Their Locks with Oil perfum'd, their *Lydian* dress.
>
> (4.314–17)

Even when the criticism is in the mouth of an antagonist, it must somehow be muted.

True to his view that *pietas* dictates Aeneas' actions Dryden even conjured it up where there was no sign of it in Virgil. So his response to Mercury, where the Latin gives him the adjective *amens* (4.279): 4.404–5: "The *pious Prince* was seiz'd with sudden fear; | Mute was his Tongue, and upright stood his hair." Of course, Mercury had to visit him again, as a result of which he is described as only *exterritus* (571), which evokes a repetition of the formula: 4.822–3: "Twice warn'd by the Coelestial Messenger | The *pious Prince* arose with hasty Fear." And when the Latin *pius* is applied to Aeneas subsequent to Dido's collapse (4.393), with effects seen by many readers as ironic, Dryden avoids the cognate: 4.568 "But good Aeneas ..." Conversely, at the parallel and intertextually marked point in Book 6, where Aeneas, *casu percussus iniquo* (475), follows and weeps in pity for the shade of Dido, Dryden gives us (6.641–2): "Some pious Tears the pitying Heroe paid; | And follow'd with his Eyes the flitting Shade." This is all so systematic as to constitute a conscious exoneration of Aeneas and focus on his virtue.

Dumping Dido

Translators have dealt in various ways with Aeneas' notorious reflection about how to deal with Dido once Mercury has instructed him to leave (4.283–4):

> heu quid agat? quo nunc reginam ambire furentem
> audeat adfatu? quae prima exordia sumat?

> Ah, what to do? With what sort of address is he to dare get
> around the queen in her rage? What opening preface to adopt?

"Get around," I write, staying with the etymology and in spirit developing the comment of T. E. Page, who glossed "canvass" and elaborated thus: "admirably used here to hint at cunning and treachery."[23] Austin agreed with the gloss, but objected to the elaboration: "Page is wrong ... the sense of pleading or persuading is uppermost."[24] The complexity produced by *ambire* is deepened by the use of *exordia* in the following line, a word which also implies that the art of persuasion is in the offing, particularly through the metaphor of a weaving or the act of rhetorically ordered speech.[25] When complex and metaphorical language loses its nuance, it effectively loses its meaning, as particularly happens with the unannotated translation, divorced from its original. Here is what Mandelbaum offers:

> With what words dare
> he face the frenzied queen? What openings
> can he employ?

This rendition is sensible and vivid (indeed, more sensible, or "easier," than the Latin in many ways), but it hardly represents Virgil's *ambire*: "dare he face" turns Aeneas from active figure to passive, as he is here transformed into a figure searching for the confidence to appear before ("face") Dido in her frenzy, because of her frenzy. Again, that would be a sensible reaction, a sensible portrayal, but it is not the portrayal produced by *ambire*, a word which sets Aeneas' planning in response to the expected fury of Dido.

This transformation, and the effacement, so to speak, of the metaphor denoted by *ambire*, in fact occurred long before Mandelbaum, as may be seen from the rendering of Charles Bowen (London 1889):[26]

---

[23] Page (1894) ad 4.283. The *OLD*, perhaps through *aporia*, omits this instance, although it makes reference to *Aen.* 7.333, where Juno sends Allecto to ensure that "the Trojans not be able to cajole Latinus with marriage (of Aeneas to Lavinia)": *neu conubiis ambire Latinum Aeneadae possint*. So Virgil creates a powerful intertextual web, as the word is used first by Aeneas referring to canvassing his way out of a marriage, and later by Juno who implies he will canvass for one. Austin of course forbids us to make a meaningful connection to 7.333, "where the sense of deception is clear, but the word is in the mouth of Aeneas' enemy Juno." See Hor. *Odes* 1.35.5 and Nisbet-Hubbard ad loc.

[24] Austin (1955, repr. 1963) ad 283.

[25] See *OLD* s.v. *exordium*. The phrase *exordia sumet*, occurs at Lucr. 1.149, where it has been seen as a metaphor for weaving.

[26] For a collection of some of the following translations of *ambire*, as well as some embarrassed translations of *optima* (of Dido at 4.291), see Clausen (1987) 45–6.

Whither, alas! shall he turn? How *face* the infuriate Queen?
How may he dare to approach her? the tale how break to her
    ear?

Various other translators removed or softened the metaphor in various ways:

CONINGTON:	He yearns to leave the dear, dear land. But how to fly? or how *accost* The queen, by eddying passion tost? How charm the ravings of distress? What choice to make when hundreds press?

E. FAIRFAX TAYLOR:
(London 1903)
	Ah! what to do? what opening can he
	    find
	To break the news, the infuriate
	    queen *withstand*?

Another group of translators comes close to preserving the metaphorical essence of *ambire*, and at least employs language that hints at persuasion and pleading (as desiderated by Austin), but without any cunning (the position of Page). In these instances Aeneas emerges as a more or less active force, although the full metaphorical power of the verb is lost:

DAVIDSON:	Ah! what can he do? in what terms can he now presume to *solicit the consent of* the raving queen?
LONSDALE/LEE:	Alas what is he to do? with what address can he now dare to try *to conciliate* the frantic queen? what opening can he adopt?

CRANCH:	And yet alas!
	What shall he do? With what speech
	    shall he now
	Dare to *appease* the raging queen? How
	    first
	Begin to speak?

MORRIS:	Ah, what to do? and with what word
	    may he be bold to *win*
	Peace of the Queen all mad with love?
	    What wise shall he begin?

RICKARDS: But how approach the queen? how frame the words
Of parting, and her fierce resentment *brave*?

RICHARDSON: But O what could he do? How *meet the scene*,
And *brave the passion of* the raging queen?

RICHARDS: What can he do, how *coax* the frenzied queen
Or dare address her, what first opening choose?

JACKSON KNIGHT: But what could he do? How could he dare to speak to the infatuated queen, and *win her round*?[27] What would be the best opening for him to choose?

SALT: What shall he do? How *bring* the infatuate queen
Those tidings? How make preface to such tale?

And then there is Dryden, as often a law to himself. How was he to keep Aeneas "thoroughly virtuous" at this point, where the issue is not whether to leave, but *how* to do so? Dryden has no similarity to the nineteenth- and twentieth-century translators whose enterprise it is to create a passive (and therefore morally less reprehensible) Aeneas:

DRYDEN: What should he say? Or how should he begin?
What course, alas! remains, to steer between
Th' offended lover and the pow'rful queen?

Indeed, "what course to steer" is a brilliant renewal of the metaphor *ambire*, and "between th' offended lover and the pow'rful queen" catches the antithesis in *reginam . . . furentem* as does no other version, and the addition of "powerful" helps justify Aeneas' actions. Dryden's lines, of higher poetic subtlety than most that followed his, catch the ambivalence of Aeneas' plan. Except, of course, that for Dryden there is no ambivalence at all: Dido in his version has been the active force

---

[27] With "round" posing as cognate with *ambire*.

in the affair, and it is Dido who pays. We will recall the words of
Segrais, to the effect that deception and divorce were upheld as court
ideals, and back-formed onto the "Augustan court" as ancient Roman
ideals. Here is how Dryden characterizes the action of the fourth
book:[28]

> She was warm'd with the graceful appearance of the Heroe, she
> smother'd those Sparkles out of decency, but Conversation blew
> them up into a Flame. Then she was forc'd to make a Confi-
> dent of her whom she best might trust, her own Sister, who
> approves the passion, and thereby augments it; then succeeds
> her publick owning it; and after that, the consummation. Of
> *Venus* and *Juno, Jupiter* and *Mercury* I say nothing, for they were
> all Machining work; but possession having cool'd his Love, as it
> increas'd hers, she soon perceiv'd the change; this suspicion soon
> turned to Jealousie, and Jealousie to Rage; then she disdains and
> threatens, and again is humble, and entreats; and nothing availing,
> despairs, curses, and at last becomes her own Executioner. See
> here the whole process of that passion, to which nothing can
> be added.

And finally Dryden gave to Aeneas divine justification not just for
leaving Carthage (which Virgil too had supplied), but even for the
manner in which he left. Mnestheus, Sergestus and Serestus are to
prepare the fleet for departure, and conceal (*dissimulent*) their acts. He
will take care of Dido:

> sese interea, quando optima Dido
> nesciat et tantos rumpi non speret amores,
> temptaturum aditus et quae mollissima fandi
> tempora, quis rebus dexter modus. ocius omnes
> imperio laeti parent et iussa facessunt.   (*Aen.* 4.291–5)

It is hard to feel entirely comfortable about Aeneas in these lines, and
about his use of the language of skulking and dissimulation, but
Dryden provides the means, by introducing divinity, of which there is
no trace in the corresponding Virgilian lines (419–24):

> Himself, meantime, the softest hours would choose,
> Before the love-sick lady heard the news,

[28] Frost and Dearing (1987) 5.297–8.

And move her tender Mind, by slow degrees
To suffer what the Sov'raign Pow'r decrees:
Jove will inspire him when and what to say.
They hear with pleasure and with haste obey. [emph. added]

So Jupiter (one of Virgil's "machines") not only endorses the departure of the Trojans, he is the architect of the manner in which it is
effected![29] Dryden saw the "problem" of Virgil, saw the ways in
which these lines failed to do what an encomiastic epic should do. His
attempt to solve that problem, and to embed the solution into a poem
masquerading as a translation or representation of Virgil, is one of the
strongest achievements of the Augustan hermeneutics of this poet.

Dido, John Davis Long and the naive translation

It is time to introduce a new player, another translator who succeeds
in achieving the activism implied by *ambire* as Page and others take it.
Here is the translation of John D. Long (Boston 1879):

> Alas for him!
> What can he do? with what excuse now dare
> To cheat the queen whose love to madness grows?
> What step the first to take?

Long is in fact the closest we come to a naive reader of Virgil.[30] As
he says in the preface to his 1879 translation, he wrote it while serving
as Speaker of the Massachusetts House of Representatives, in the
course of a year, and without consulting any other translation. The
task reminded him of his schooldays, at Hebron Academy in Maine,
and as a young teenager at Harvard in the mid-nineteenth century (he
graduated in 1857); he had no formal study of Virgil after this, and
presumably not much in any critical way before. A devout Yankee
Protestant, a poet, a lawyer and politician, the father of two daugh-
ters, and a supporter of women's suffrage long before it became a
popular political cause, he seems to make quite a contrast to Dryden,

---

[29] Dryden may have found inspiration in John Denham's *The Passion of* Dido *for* Aeneas
(1668), which begins at *Aen.* 4.276, after the speech of Mercury, and which has:
"He many waies his labouring thoughts revolves, | But fear o'ercoming shame at last
resolves | (Instructed by the God of Thieves) to steal | Himself away and his escape
conceal."

[30] For fuller account of this topic, see Thomas (1995), (1997).

particularly in his attitude to the women in his life. He seems to have had no access to the cultural and ideological reception of Virgil, nor any to the continuing humanistic and philological debates on Virgil. As a result, at times his translation looks parallel to the romance vernacular tradition so emphatically opposed by Petrarch, Spenser and Dryden. Indeed, Long's translation may even be seen as the beginning of a sort of American vernacular; and it may therefore be worth digressing on the cultural formation of the author.[31]

On Monday, July 24, 1848, the nine-year-old John Davis Long, living in the northern countryside of Buckfield, Maine, wrote in the journal he had been keeping since the beginning of the same year: "A cloudy, rainy misty and muddy day. Our school keeps two or three weeks longer. *I have begun the study of Latin* [his emphasis]." For Tuesday, October 17, 1850, now at Hebron Academy in Maine and soon to turn twelve, he notes "Pleasant. I study Virgil ..." This interest continued as he studied at Harvard. Almost thirty years later Long, now a successful lawyer and writer, and having just been elected Speaker of the Massachusetts House of Representatives for the third time, noted in his journal (January 17, 1878) "A quiet day. Buy Bryant's *Iliad* and *Odyssey*. Read a book in the former." Five days later, and, one assumes, as a result of this activity, he records (January 22) "Begin this evening a translation of Virgil. Perhaps I shall finish it and publish." For the next year, we find steady references to his task, interspersed with references to his family, to his activities in his law practice and to the workings of the state legislature, and in 1879 he published his translation, in "living blank verse" as he put it.[32] Long served as Governor of Massachusetts in 1880, 1881, and 1882. In the next years, until 1889, he served in the House of Rep-

---

[31] As I once noted (Thomas [1990] 66, n. 4), in response to a claim that only Europeans could understand the *Georgics*: "I think it is worth pointing out that contemporary America, in its more immediate agricultural roots, in the cultural and racial diversity evident in its foundation and growth (Virgil himself, let us not forget, was an 'immigrant' of sorts), in the tensions of how it should deal with the realities of being a world power, and particularly in its struggling to respond to the great cultural burden which is its legacy, would be much more comparable with the Rome of Virgil than is any contemporary European country." That applies even more for the America of the late nineteenth century.

[32] In his brief preface he notes that "a rhyming version must always be a paraphrase rather than translation, besides offending against classic dignity – like a modern bonnet on the head of Minerva."

resentatives, and ended his public career serving in Washington as Secretary of the Navy under McKinley (March 4, 1897 to May 1, 1902), including some months under Roosevelt, who assumed the presidency after McKinley's assassination on September 14, 1901. McKinley had wanted him as his Vice-President for the 1900 election; had Roosevelt not ridden up the hill in Cuba, a translator of Virgil would have been president of the United States – *at tu Marcellus eris!* Long died in his home in Hingham, Massachusetts on August 28, 1915.

The diary Long kept from his boyhood, and the copious letters he wrote, reveal him to be a most likeable figure, and one well suited to the thought of his author.[33] He was himself a poet, somewhat after the manner of Longfellow, and for current tastes of an overly sentimental bent. Even his journal entries at times have a poetic reach to them. The public façade concealed a depth of spirit that is quite remarkable, and Virgil perhaps helped fashion that depth.

As the years went by, the Virgil he had translated stayed with him, particularly Virgil the poet of loss and grief. While Long was Secretary of the Navy, more than twenty years after his translation came out, he recalls sending the Marines off during the Boxer rebellion (*Journal* p. 253; letter to his younger daughter, Helen Long, July 24, 1900):

> On Sunday last, I took Lt. Washington U.S.N. and Mrs.
> Washington with me in the carriage, to go to the corner of
> Ninth and Maryland Avenue, to see the detachment of the
> Marines, five hundred strong, start for China. There was a large
> gathering of people. The Marines were in the cars, in two long
> sections. The Marine Band was playing. The boys were looking
> out of the windows. The women in the streets were waving
> their handkerchiefs. Major Dickins, who goes in command,
> came up and saw me and I gave him a cordial shake of the hand
> and a blessing. There is something very pathetic and at the
> same time, very stirring, in such scenes. Yesterday, I took my
> translation of *Aeneid* and read the scene where King Evander
> sends troops, under the command of his son, Pallas, to fight the
> battles of Aeneas. After all, it was the same scene over again;
> the same tears of parting, and the same high spirit of the boys

---

[33] Long, *MHS* papers.

that were going to the front. The same parade, in marching
and glistening of arms; the same love and sorrow of mothers,
wives and sisters.

Long's daughter, the recipient of this letter, was in Colorado Springs,
dying of tuberculosis, as her mother had years before; I suspect her
father remembered not only Virgil's Evander and his child Pallas, but
also his own sad situation.

Virgil was acutely attuned to the fragility of memory, and to its
connection with grief, but also to its necessity for the functioning of
history and the survival of poetic and other traditions. In one of the
most famous lines of the poem, Aeneas, an exile from his homeland,
and shipwrecked on a foreign shore, looks to the day, never actually
secured in the Virgilian vision of history, when remembrance of
misfortune will bring even pleasure: 1.203 *forsan et haec olim meminisse
iuvabit* "Some day | May yet be happier for remembering this" (Long).

And in the last lines of the poem, it is the memorial of the dead
Pallas, the baldric that Turnus despoiled from the surrogate son of
Aeneas, that prevents what Aeneas almost achieved, Christian mercy
in a poem written two decades before the birth of Christ: *oculis post-
quam saevi monimenta doloris exuviasque hausit* ... "No sooner drank
Aeneas' eyes that sight – | The spoils that called to mind so keen a
grief" (Long). I know of no better, no more accurate, translation of
the line. A final example: at *Aeneid* 2.12, at Dido's request, Aeneas
begins his story of the fall of Troy, and wanderings in exile, in spite of
the difficulty he is caused by recalling the calamity: *quamquam animus
meminisse horret luctuque refugit* ... "e'en though my heart | Aches at
the memory, and with grief relucts" (Long). An anonymous (the
usual practice) reviewer in *The Golden Rule Magazine* 4 (August, 1879)
no. 8, otherwise favorable, takes issue with Long's version: "the idea
of 'shuddering at the thought,' which is intended in the Latin *animus
meminisse horret* is entirely misrepresented and lost in Mr. Long's
'aches at the memory.'" I disagree. Long has shifted the metaphor,
which has a not atypical Virgilian strangeness to it (how does a mind
"shudder"?). Aeneas' difficulty is caused precisely by the ache that
comes from the memory – note that the reviewer would remove
Virgil's crucial mnemonic indicator, *meminisse*, which Long did
represent.

Virgil was twenty years old when Caesar crossed the Rubicon and

swept down through Italy; it would take another twenty years before
there would emerge a glimmer of the security – relatively speaking –
that was to come. John Davis Long was two years older, twenty-two,
when the storming of Fort Sumter, South Carolina, sparked the war
between the states. His civil war was shorter, but no less memorable.
Moeris, the poet-shepherd of Virgil's ninth *Eclogue*, is evicted from
his farm by the victorious veterans settled there in the years of Virgil's
young manhood – perhaps reflecting the poet's own, or his father's,
eviction by Antony's or Octavian's soldiers: "our songs," sings Moeris,
"have as much power amid the weapons of Mars, as do Chaonian
doves at the coming of the eagle." By the end of the poem, Moeris
loses memory of song and his very voice, just as he loses his Arcadia:

> "omnia fert aetas, animum quoque. saepe ego longos
> cantando puerum memini me condere soles.
> nunc oblita mihi tot carmina, vox quoque Moerim
> iam fugit ipsa." (*Ecl.* 9.51–4)

> "The years carry off everything, including even memory. I
> remember as a boy I'd often put long suns to sleep with song.
> So many songs now gone from my mind, now even his voice
> itself flees Moeris."

His song will return when Menalcas, the master singer, returns; but
the poem ends before that time can come.

Civil war and memory come together also for Long, as the following speech, given twenty years after the war began, two after the
publication of the Virgil translation, brings out; here too, Virgil is on
his mind:[34]

> As I look, veterans, upon your faces, your thinner ranks, your
> brows on which time is writing in plainer lines its autograph,
> true, indeed, I know it is that the number of the survivors is
> fast diminishing, and that with the close of the century few will
> remain. But they will all still live in the works that do follow
> them, – in a civilization better because purified by the searching
> fire from the dross of human slavery and political inequality,
> and in a country lifted up to a higher plane of justice, mercy
> and righteousness. They will live, too, in history, – in the

---

[34] Long (1895) 82, Memorial Day, May 30, 1882 before Grand Army Posts of Suffolk
County, Mass.

history of a patriotic people, pictured in pages more graphic
than those of Plutarch or Macaulay, in the songs of poets who
shall sing a nobler than Virgil's man, and an epic loftier than
the Iliad.

For Long as for Virgil the memory that connects father to child and
child to father is that which is most poignant, as we see with the
death of his daughter. In 1901, in his home town of Buckfield, "The
Zadoc Long Free Library" opened; in memory of his father Long
himself contributed "2,500 well chosen volumes," as he records on
August 17, closing with pride and full of memories: "It is an exquisite
day, dedicated more than my pen can write to the memory of my
father and mother. A sacred day to me." A month later McKinley had
fallen to the assassin's bullet; two months later Long's daughter Helen
was dead at age twenty-six. He writes on the last day of the year:

> As I look back, the one prominent figure before all others
> constantly in my mind and before me is little Helen. Then
> President McKinley.

Such death, of the child before the parent, also of the parent, is what
disrupts memory, what creates oblivion. In this focus, Long resonates
with Virgil, particularly with the end of the *Aeneid*, but really with
the whole of that poem. Two entries in Long's diary show the intensity of this type of memory; both have to do with *monimenta*,
memorials, of Long's beloved father, Zadoc, and both have to do
with music and poetry, as was the case with the shepherd Moeris.
Neither is included in Margaret Long's selection from her father's
journal; perhaps they were too difficult for her – *animus meminisse
horret*. One, from 1875, is a form of poetry:[35]

> Received a valentine from Geo. F. Emery, Esq., of Portland,
> Maine, in the shape of an old letter, written Valentine's Day,
> February 14, 1855, twenty years ago, by my dear father to
> Judge Emery of Paris, Maine, father of Geo. F. These two men
> were friends from boys, and often corresponded and visited.
> Father's letter is in his plain and neat handwriting and contains
> a copy of his pretty verses on his "old violin." When I looked
> at the familiar characters, the signature, how all the dear old

---

[35] Mayo (1923) 135–6.

home and past rushed over me!... I could see the wintry scene,
the snow, the white roofs, the frozen river, the lonely streets,
the snug sitting room with its fire, father's nervous fingers on
his pen, mother with her work and angel face, the journals
and newspapers on the table. I must then have been home on
college vacation.[36] How they loved me, and did and hoped for
me! How few days ago it seems! How trite and commonplace
all the words we use to describe such memories, and yet how
deep they go into the springs of feeling. Father and mother and
Zadoc [his brother] are dead. I am in middle life and in new
scenes, in new relations, among new people, hard at work,
ambitious, eager, struggling. The family is scattered, the old
home is gone, the hearth is cold. There are strangers in the
sacred places. And we drift on like straws upon a torrent, always
vainly looking back and trying to cheat ourselves into the
belief that it is not all gone – all past – never, never to return.
I loved and still love my father and mother. It is a constant
sorrow to me that I can never mention their names to sympathi-
zing ears. Perhaps my baby will some day like to hear of them.

A second one, written while the translation was in proof, I found
in Long's diary in the Massachusetts Historical Society:[37]

> 1879 Boston March 9 Sunday. This afternoon go to rooms of
> T. H. Howe, a composer, and hear Mrs. Howard sing a song
> he has composed to dear father's words "My old violin." I
> thought it very sweet – perhaps the words misled me. Poor
> father wrote them perhaps 20 or 25 years ago in the old sitting
> room. I recall it all. I put them in my little volume of poems,
> where Howe saw them. And now, father dead, a stranger sets
> them to music and perhaps, if the song is popular, many a voice

---

[36] In contrast to Long's joy in his parents' home, he later claims he was miserable at
Harvard; cf. Long (1908–9) 352: "There was an entire lack, to me, of all moral or
personal influences. I look back with a certain pathetic commiseration on myself, un-
warmed for the whole four years by a single act or word expressive of interest on the
part of those to whom my education was entrusted ... No instructor or officer ever
gave me a pat on the shoulder physically, morally, or intellectually ..." By the time he
gave his paper, things seemed to have improved: (353) "I meet young men today from
Harvard, touched and toned by the personal influence of men whose names readily
occur to you, and I feel it would have been of priceless value to me if only in those days
some such man could have taken me by the hand, or even by the ear, if only half a
dozen times in the whole four years."

[37] Long, *MHS* Papers, *Journal* 1876, Dec. 12–1883, Jan. 6.

will sing them and they will become familiar. Realized now are the last two lines: —

> A sorrowful touch on the hearts shattered strings
> That soon will respond nevermore

Dead and cold now many a year has been the heart that was so full of love for me, its strings shattering till it broke. Perhaps it responds in heaven.

We in fact have the letter, written seven years earlier, in which Zadoc thanks his son John for including the poems in his volume:[38]

> Dear Johnny:
>   I received your daily favors which are no small comfort to me. I like to know how you are, & what you are doing, and how you are doing, every day, as if I were with you.
>   Julia Matilda [White, niece of J.D.L.] came home safe last evening, & brought your pretty little volume of poems, *Bites of a Cherry* [1872], a very unexpected favor. I thank you for the honor of dedicating them "To my Father." I have read the book through this morning. I see you have inserted my poem, "My Old Violin" to gratify me. The book contains only a small part of your best poetry; but I am pleased with it.
>
> Aff. yours
Zadoc Long

Later in the year (September 19, 1872), just six months before his death, Zadoc asked John to return the actual "old violin," which the latter had taken, in exchange for a "better" one that he had given his father:[39]

> It is an old acquaintance, its familiar tone is pleasanter to my ear than that of any other ... The *old* fiddle will, in some measure, relieve the loneliness of my confinement, carry me back to earlier & happier days, the days of your infancy, when I charmed you to sleep with "Sweet Home," & "Kate's Rambles," and other old tunes ...

Margaret Long prints Zadoc's poem immediately after this letter; the sentimentality is again characteristic:

---

[38] Long (1956) 127.   [39] Long (1956) 128–9.

My Old Violin

While evening's dim folds round me gather fast,
And the chill breezes chant a low moan,
My fancy is busy with scenes of the past,
As I sit by my fireside alone.

The group that once cheered me affection recalls;
Beloved ones I ask, where are they?
My own voice comes back from the echoing walls,
And sadly repeats – Where are they?

A sound like a serenade, plaintive and sweet,
An almost inaudible strain,
Now rises and swells into tones more complete,
Now sinks away softly again.

It seems like a spirit of many a lay –
A voice from the past that I hear
In lingering cadences dying away,
On memory's faltering ear.

Or the music of dreams in the stillness of night,
By some spirit guardian sung; –
'Tis the air through the cracks and the vibrations slight
Of my old violin all unstrung.

How many a cherished remembrance it brings
Of dear friends and pastimes of yore;
A sorrowful touch on the heart's shattered strings
That soon will respond nevermore.

And finally John D. Long's own poem, *At the Fireside* (May 1877), which gives its name to the slim volume of poems published in 1892. Long connects his four-years-dead father to his four-year-old daughter, in a poem that at first seems sentimental and technically strained,[40] but which gains power when put in the context of Long's poetics of memory and in the context of his father's poem, to which

---

[40] Is the postposition in line 2 ("me near") part of a frame concluded by the one two lines from the end ("did he") – a stylistic oddity designed to connect his father Zadoc to his daughter Margaret? Long notes on September 13, 1874, his fourth wedding anniversary: "Father died in Winchendon on Feb. 3, 1873. Our baby, Margaret, was born on October 28, 1873." Margaret's mother, incidentally, died of tuberculosis on February 16, 1882, as would her sister Helen. Long's journal breaks off and is silent in the several months leading up to his wife's death (Journal 151).

there are clear intertextual bonds. Zadoc's lonely fireside is crowded once again:

At the Fireside

At nightfall by the fireside's cheer
My little Margaret sits me near,
And begs me tell of things that were
When I was little just like her.

Ah, little lips! you touch the spring
Of sweetest sad remembering,
And heart and hearth flash all aglow
With ruddy tints of long ago.

I at my father's fireside sit,
Youngest of all who circle it,
And beg him tell me what did he
When he was little, just like me.

Dryden and Long: comparative voices

I hope that what has preceded first demonstrates some of the ways in which Long, in his outlook, in the turmoil and civil discord of his formative years, in his attitude to loss and to the fragility of memory, may be considered at least on the face of it to have been suitable as a translator of Virgil. But, more importantly, unlike engaged translators such as Dryden, unlike the professional classicists who translated Virgil in the nineteenth century, and unlike us, Long was an utterly naive reader of Virgil. He looked at no translation before completing his own, is unconnected to political models with which to connect Virgil and Aeneas, obviously read no secondary literature, and he therefore provides a valuable paradigm of a reading uncluttered by the ideological debris of Virgilian reception. Long's restricted horizons of expectation will be of interest as we read his Dido.

It was also memory of Virgil and his boyhood love of Virgil and Latin poetry that brought Long back to the poet. And in the preface to the *Aeneid* he harks back to those days:

Perhaps some will read this. If so, they will renew, as I after
twenty-five years have done, not only the kindly acquaintance
of this Roman story-teller, but the happy morning of the
school-boy's shining face and eager heart.

The translation has a short preface, containing one curiosity of judgment, at least in the first (1879) and second (1880) editions (it was removed from the third): "... the Aeneid is an immortal poem, though the world could better lose it than a psalm of David or the higher reach of moral sentiment which is suggested in a verse of Whittier." As a review, from *The Parisian* (July 10, 1879) and clipped by Long, notes: "Such being the opinions of Mr. Long on the merits and comparative value of Virgil, we are astonished that he should have undertaken a translation at all, but still more astonished that he should have produced such a hearty and honest rendering." At any rate, by the third edition, the comparison with Whittier and the *Psalms* had left the preface. Moreover, in a letter to his daughter Margaret, written thirty years later in 1910, his view of Virgil seems more mature, though this too perhaps no less controversial:[41]

> I am reading Bryant's translation of the *Iliad*. I do not care
> greatly for the *Iliad*. Virgil is much superior. He copies the
> battles & the fighting, but he abounds in real tenderness, in
> better study of the human heart, in more picturesqueness
> of natural scenery, in reaching the common humanity, as
> true today as then. The *Iliad* is so repetitious. Homer is no
> Shakespeare & does not deserve his repute. If he were not the
> earliest of poets, he would not be one of the most conspicuous.

John Long's translation is not much known nowadays, I suppose, and there is plenty of competition, but his reputation for representing a true sense of Virgil is well-deserved, and is noted by a number of reviews. In this context some remarks from his preface are noteworthy:

> It is accidental if coincidences with other translations occur,
> none of which had I seen before finishing my own. On
> examining some of them, I am convinced that a rhyming
> version must always be paraphrase rather than translation,
> besides offending against classic dignity – like a modern bonnet
> on the head of Minerva. The most faithful translation is of
> course the best; and in mine I have tried – not hesitating now
> and then at an anachronistic rendering – to bring out in to-
> day's phrase, so far as I could, the force of all the Latin words.

[41] Long (1956) 319.

Long's view is as far from Dryden's as could be, and this indeed almost sounds like a response to Dryden, both to his theory and his practice.

Perhaps some of Long's experience has to do with his treatment of Dido, which in its sympathy and empathy is closer to that of Virgil than is Dryden's version, and those of most translators, particularly up to Long's time. A case in point: at *Aeneid* 4.522–33 comes the famous passage in which man and nature all sleep, while Dido lies awake:

> nox erat et placidum carpebant fessa soporem
> corpora per terras, silvaeque et saeva quierant
> aequora, cum medio volvuntur sidera lapsu,
> cum tacet omnis ager, pecudes pictaeque volucres,
> quaeque lacus late liquidos quaeque aspera dumis
> rura tenent, somno positae sub nocte silenti.
> [lenibant curas et corda oblita laborum.]
> at non infelix animi Phoenissa, neque umquam
> solvitur in somnos oculisve aut pectore noctem
> accipit: ingeminant curae rursusque resurgens
> saevit amor magnoque irarum fluctuat aestu.
> sic adeo insistit secumque ita corde volutat ...

First Long's version of the entire passage (697–713):

> 'Twas night; and weariness o'er all the earth
> In peaceful slumber sank to rest. No breath
> Was in the woods or on the fitful sea.
> It was the time when, half their circuit o'er,
> The stars began to fall; when fields and flocks
> Lay still, and birds were nestling 'neath their wings
> Of many hues; when all that lives within
> The water depths, and all that in the fields
> And forest dwell, under the silent night
> In deep sleep lying, dreamed all care away,
> And human hearts forgot that life is toil.
> But not the aching heart of Dido. Ne'er
> In slumber resteth she, nor in her breast
> Nor on her eyes the blessing of the night.
> Her soul is dark; her love springs fresh again,
> And wild with every gust of passion beats.
> So now she ponders and her heart o'erflows ...

Now Dryden's version of the closing five lines of the Virgilian passage:

> All else of Nature's common gift partake;
> Unhappy Dido was alone awake.
> Nor sleep nor ease the furious queen can find:
> Sleep fled her eyes as quiet fled her mind.
> Despair and rage and love, divide her heart;
> Despair and rage had some, but love the greater part.
>   Then thus she said within her secret mind ...
>
> (4.767–73)

When looked at side by side the two passages reflect precisely the tension observed throughout the reception of Dido. Long has given us a fully sympathetic Dido whose feelings and pain are intensified, and this particularly in the transition from the sleeping world of nature to the wakeful Dido. Long perhaps softens lines 531–2 *ingeminant curae rursusque resurgens | saevit amor magnoque irarum fluctuat aestu*, since "angers" are generalized to "passions," but the mix of sympathy for Dido and threat posed to Aeneas, *both* of which are in the Latin, is maintained. Dryden, as always, emphasizes the element of danger to the hero, thereby subordinating the voice of Dido to that of Aeneas: *regina* is nowhere in the Latin, but Dryden's "furious queen" keeps before us, even at a moment when Dido's emotions are very human and may evoke sympathy, the fact, true but not specified by Virgil at this moment, that she is a queen. As Proudfoot has noted of the final couplet (771–2): "Dryden is always apt to end his verse-paragraphs unworthily in the *Aeneid*, but this is one of his worst performances."[42]

Dryden and Long can also be seen as competing readers in their treatments of the fateful meeting in the cave, a passage that strikes many readers as at least partially indeterminate in the moral and ethical judgments it enables us to create, particularly in assessing the degree of Dido's responsibility. Was it a wedding or did she just call it one? If the latter with what justification?

> speluncam Dido dux et Troianus eandem
> deveniunt. prima et Tellus et pronuba Iuno
> dant signum; fulsere ignes et conscius Aether

---

[42] Proudfoot (1960) 212; Hopkins (1986) 163.

conubiis summoque ulularunt vertice Nymphae.
ille dies primus leti primusque malorum
causa fuit; neque enim specie famave movetur
nec iam furtivum Dido meditatur amorem:
coniugium vocat, hoc praetexit nomine culpam.

(*Aen.* 4.165–72)

Here is the translation of Long, striving for exactitude (213–23):

But Dido and the Trojan chief
Seek the same cave. Primeval goddess Earth
And Juno, goddess of wooing, give
The signal. Lightnings flash, the very air
Glows conscious with this wedlock, and the nymphs
Flit shrieking on the mountain top. That day
The seed of death and woes to come was sown.
It matters not to Dido what is said,
Or what the look, for now no more she thinks
Of blushing for her love, but says his wife
She is, and hides her slip beneath that name.

We might object to "slip" for *culpa*, but "slip" could at least refer to
the sexual act carried out in the cave, and so is true to Virgil's text,
albeit as a piece of Victorian, or better, Yankee, deflective euphe-
mism. In general, this is a faithful version of the Latin. As poetry it
pales when set next to Dryden, whose liberties with the Latin, however, go in a different direction, beyond simple nuance (239–50):

The Queen and Prince, as Love or Fortune guides,
One common Cavern in her Bosom hides,
Then first the trembling Earth the signal gave;
And flashing Fires enlighten all the Cave:
Hell from below, and *Juno* from above,
And howling Nymphs, were conscious to their Love.
From this ill Omen'd Hour, in Time arose,
Debate and Death, and all succeeding woes.
The Queen, whom sense of Honour could not move,
No longer made a Secret of her Love,
But call'd it marriage; by that specious Name
To veil the Crime, and sanctifie the Shame.

Dryden's rewriting is violent and radical. Whatever the status of the
relationship in Roman law – and Aeneas' denial of marriage will deal

in such legalistic terms (338–9 *nec coniugis umquam | praetendi taedas aut haec in foedera veni* "I never held out a groom's marriage torches, that was not the pact I entered into") – whatever that status, Virgil in the narrative of 165–72 clearly described some sort of divinely sanctioned or naturalistic ceremony: Aether and Tellus are present and complicit; these two themselves represent on the level of myth the ultimate, generative union between Sky (*Aether*), and Earth (*prima . . . Tellus*).[43] The element of heat (*ignes*) is also present. Virgil had already depicted the union of Sky and Earth, in the *Georgics*,[44] and their presence at the union of Dido and Aeneas is surely pointed. It is noteworthy that at *Georgics* 2.325, treating an ideologically unmarked reference to the union of Sky and Earth, Mynors' Oxford Classical Text prints *Aether*, here at *Aeneid* 4.167, *aether*. The two passages are clearly related, and I take the difference as an editorial attempt to remove an authoritative divine witness from the union. Juno is also there in her capacity as the bride's escort to the marriage chamber (*pronuba*). This could be seen as focalized by the narrator or by Dido, but either way it is there in the Latin, and, like Tellus and Aether, is present in Long's version ("goddess of wooing"). Taken together the cosmic forces and divinities in attendance justify Dido's calling it what she does, a marriage.

Dryden would have none of this: "Hell from below, and Juno from above, | And howling nymphs, were conscious to their love." Where "Hell" came from is not clear; perhaps from *Aether* (!) which has in any case disappeared, and along with it the whole nexus we saw in Virgil of a naturalistic representation of the union. Juno has been stripped of her epithet, *pronuba*, so there may be no mistake about the legitimacy of Aeneas' later denial of the status of marriage: 4.489–90: "Much less pretended to the Lawful Claim | Of Sacred Nuptials, or, a Husband's Name." Dryden, having here deprived Dido of *pronuba Iuno* by giving "Juno from above," will later give us "Thou Juno, Guardian of the Nuptial Vow" (4.873), when Dido includes in the

---

[43] One thinks of Heaven and Earth on the breastplate of the Prima Porta Augustus, where the function is also to provide a cosmic context and legitimacy for the human subjects in the center of the scene.

[44] G. 2.325–6: *tum pater omnipotens fecundis imbribus Aether | coniugis in gremium laetae descendit*, an adaptation of Lucretius 1.250–1 (*postremo pereunt imbres, ubi eos pater Aether | in gremium matris terrai praecipitavit*).

curse *conscia Iuno* (608).[45] So the goddess of nuptial vows, in the re-working of Dryden, is stripped from the narrating voice at the union of Dido and Aeneas, and joins Hecate, the Furies, and other forces of darkness, present there only in the voice of Dido! We again remember Dryden's views of matrimony.

Through this rewriting Dryden well sets up his climax:

> The queen, whom sense of honour could not move,
> No longer made a secret of her love,
> But called it marriage; by that specious name
> To veil the crime, and sanctify the shame.　　(4.247–50)

The complexity and ambiguity of the Latin is gone. Dryden may have followed Lauderdale (as he often did):[46]

> She's neither moved with decency nor Fame,
> Nor longer strives to hide her secret Flame,
> But gilds her Crime with Wedlock's specious name.

But he did have available to him the less extreme version of Stapylton:

> for neither forme doth Dido move
> Nor fame, nor now she meditates stolen love,
> Wedlooke she cals't, pretexting with that name
> Her fault.

For Dryden then her *culpa* has become her "crime" and she is fully aware that the name of marriage is "specious." But *culpa* is surely the sexual act, hidden over by the fact that she considers herself married. Indeed, she had anticipated the fateful incident in the cave, when, wrestling with her passion, she said to Anna:

> si non pertaesum *thalami taedaeque* fuisset,
> huic uni forsan potui succumbere *culpae*
>
> > > (*Aen.* 4.18–19)

Marriage and *culpa* paired again, now in her words, not her thoughts: "if the notion of marriage had not become repugnant to me, to this

---

one I could have succumbed, to this one fault."[47] What temporarily restrains her from the sexual act (*culpa*) in that first passage is aversion to marriage; when she commits that act, it will be in the context, at least to her mind – and that is her tragedy – of partial justification through the marriage she believes she has entered.

I will not reargue the status of these lines, whose real and pervasive ambiguity G. Williams has treated.[48] I find his conclusion ("The decisive fact is that Virgil always portrays Dido as really convinced that she is married to Aeneas") convincing, and it further follows that in Virgil, though not in Dryden, Dido was given every indication by the rulers of the cosmos that it was a marriage. Dryden's removal of Aether, and of Juno's nuptial epithet, are precisely what allow his simplification: "But called it marriage; by that specious name | To veil the crime, and sanctify the shame."

[47] Long in fact gets the line wrong, and is tricked by Virgil's word order: 4.24–5 "To him, but only him, I might perhaps | Be weak enough to yield." See pp. 76–7 on this line.
[48] Cf. Williams (1968) 379–80.

6

Philology and textual cleansing

usurers squeezing crab-lice, pandars to authority
pets-de-loup, sitting on piles of stone books,
obscuring the texts with philology,
 hiding them under their persons,
the air without refuge of silence,
 the drift of lice, teething,
and above it the mouthing of orators,
 the arse-belching of preachers.
  EZRA POUND, Canto XIV, *A Draft of XXX Cantos*

The Augustan Virgil, firmly established in the ancient, medieval and early modern reception of Virgil, was inherited by the nascent science of classical philology in the eighteenth and nineteenth centuries. In many ways the classical philologist is merely an updated Servius, and whatever the specialized title, grammarian, humanist, translator, textual critic or commentator, this figure has functioned as the agent in the assertion of the Augustan Virgil, confident in his ability to establish the true Virgil through the "objective" and "scientific" process of emendation. The hermeneutic circle is evidenced by universal faith in the validity of the "Servian default," holding that the purpose of the *Aeneid* was "to imitate Homer and to praise Augustus through his ancestors." The attitude spilled over into treatments of the *Eclogues* and *Georgics*. The mission of the editor followed as a necessary consequence of this condition, and its effects are still with us today, indeed they are resurgent, as we shall see. The *Georgics* must be made to celebrate the glory of toil, the *Aeneid* that of Augustus – anything that interferes with the clarity of such messages will need attention. The Augustan philologist proceeds on one of two fronts, though from a single base which may be articulated as follows: "It is Virgil's intention to have meant A; he therefore cannot have written B, which is at odds with A; he therefore must have written C." This is very much parallel to hermeneutic mutings of undesirable meaning, for instance the denial that the "Vergilius" of Horace *Odes* 4.12 could be Virgil, or the claim that *latro* just means "hunter" at *Aeneid* 12.7, but, like strongly Augustan translation, it is a particularly forceful mode of Augustanizing, in that it takes the evidence for its opposite out of play, or at least relegates it to the critical apparatus at the bottom of the page. And finally the textual critic has generally seen himself as the purveyor of the highest order of objective and scientifically based truth, and the rhetoric of his voice, still now validated by its authoritative use of Latin in the preface and apparatus, depends not just on philology, but also at times on intimidation and even bluster.[1]

In this connection, I would maintain that such emendation, even when ultimately rejected by the subsequent tradition, may have had an effect in ways that we can no longer fully calculate. For a critical text is a collaborator in articles, monographs, handbooks and encyclopaedias, which then establish their own traditions, independent of the textual tradition and potentially immune to the ultimate readjustments and corrections it may undergo. Such readings were published, read, some believed at least for a time, and all of them helped to reshape Virgilian ideology, just as a line of Dryden continues to reverberate even after its independence from the Virgilian Latin is recognized. And if the other forms of Augustanizing of the Virgilian text have been going on since antiquity, then untraceable emendation is likely to have occurred from the earliest stages – possibly in the editorial activity of Varius and Tucca themselves.

Removing wine stains

The process is not confined to the *Aeneid*; rather, Virgil's whole text must be Augustanized. The final technical material from *Georgics* 2 is a

---

[1] Even if the offending reading is accessible in the apparatus criticus, for many readers, particularly neophytes, it thereby suffers an immediate loss of stature, and particularly in an authoritative edition; given the prevailing climate of Augustanism (in e.g. the entire nineteenth century and most of the twentieth) the act of reviving the non-Augustan reading may be a risky one – even when there is no MS evidence for the conjecture. This will perhaps help to explain why credence was given to conjectures whose tendentious basis now elicits a smile.

curious sentence, which has evoked a full range of critical responses. These lines (2.454–7) close out treatment of the ways man may propagate and control trees, chiefly the vine, which therefore serves as the paradigm of cultivated, versus naturally occurring, trees (for instance the olive, in Virgil's fiction).[2] Here, then, is what Virgil says about the vine, or rather its product:

> quid memorandum aeque Baccheia dona tulerunt?
> Bacchus et ad culpam causas dedit; ille furentis
> Centauros leto domuit, Rhoecumque Pholumque
> et magno Hylaeum Lapithis cratere minantem.
>
> (G. 2.454–7)

What of equal note have the gifts of Bacchus produced?
Bacchus has even given grounds for fault; he it was that drove
the Centaurs mad them tamed in death, Rhoecus and Pholus,
and Hylaeus who threatened the Lapiths with a huge crater.

The ambivalent reading of these lines is also the primary reading: the product of man's toil (and most of Book 2 has been occupied with describing this toil) is stigmatized as causing madness and death. The attempt to evade that clear implication began even before Servius, who himself saw the sense of the lines, designating them a *vituperatio vitis*, a "censuring of the vine."[3] Yet the grammarian also records an early critical attempt to "fix" the lines, to have them say something less subversive of the didactic enterprise of the poem: some, he says, read *et quae* for *aeque*: "why mention also the gifts that Bacchus has brought"? Here are some other "solutions": Page's solution was to offer no comment at all, Conington thought that Virgil lost control, as in his enthusiasm for natural trees "he is carried away into showing that they are superior to the vine"; R. D. Williams thought "the final lines are playful"; Otis called them a "splendid conclusion"; while Wilkinson at least noted "the lines seem an odd and unsatisfactory conclusion to Book 2." And so they are, if we persist, against the evidence provided by the text, with a view of the *Georgics* as simply extolling the ethics of cultivation and toil. But nothing fixes the problem as well as the procedure of Peerlkamp and Forbiger, who simply excised all four lines from the text, as so often without any

---

[2] See Thomas (1988a) vol. 1, 19–21.
[3] On 2.397, referring to 2.455; cf. Ross (1987) 141–5; Thomas (1988a) vol. 1, ad 1.242–3.

justification from the MSS. And now we find Robert Cramer following Otto Zwierlein, and also excising the lines.[4]

Closing unstable doors

It is particularly at moments of ambiguity, and ambiguity involving ideology, that we see Augustan philology working most actively. A case in point is the infamous close of *Aeneid* 6. I do not much need to occupy myself with the critical struggle to explicate these lines in ways that leave us completely comfortable about the choice of gate; the excessive examples of that struggle have generally been held up to the criticism that they deserve, and R. J. Tarrant has put it well: "The oblique connection of Aeneas and *falsa insomnia*, however it operates, must have a negative effect; the associations of deception, illusion and unreality are disturbing, even ominous."[5] Here are the lines:

> sunt geminae Somni portae, quarum altera fertur
> cornea, qua veris facilis datur exitus umbris,
> altera candenti perfecta nitens elephanto,
> sed falsa ad caelum mittunt insomnia Manes.
> his ibi tum natum Anchises unaque Sibyllam
> prosequitur dictis portaque emittit eburna,
> ille viam secat ad navis sociosque revisit. (*Aen.* 6.893–9)

There are twin gates of Sleep, one said to be of horn, through which true shades are given easy egress, the other finished in shining, white ivory, but the Shades send false dreams to the upper air. After speaking Anchises follows his son there and the Sibyl too, and sends them out the gate of ivory, he speeds his way to the ships and rejoins his companions.

That is how most texts of the poem have the lines, but that was not always the case. In 1867, A. Nauck found a way to cleanse this part of the text – he just removed the first four lines (893–6), leaving us with an abbreviated exit:

> et quo quemque modo fugiatque feratque laborem.   892
> his ibi tum natum Anchises unaque Sibyllam   897

[4] Cramer (1998) 133, n. 566; Zwierlein (1999) 107, n. 1; see below, pp. 218–21.
[5] Tarrant (1982) 53; for a summary of views see Otis (1959) 173–9; for bibliography see Horsfall (1995) 146, n. 14.

prosequitur dictis portaque emittit eburna,   898
ille viam secat ad navis sociosque revisit.   899

The lines, we are told, are interpolated by a scribe who added the
Homeric gates (*Od.* 19.562–7) to Virgil's poem. And so these troubling gates – horn and ivory both – are removed, and with them goes
the need to explain away Aeneas' mode of exit. Off Aeneas goes out
of the Underworld, and back to his mission. But wait! Where did that
ivory gate come from (898 *porta . . . eburna*)? Nauck will take care of
that: Virgil obviously wrote (the non-word) *Avorna*, so we can get rid
of the now incomprehensible ivory, but keep the line in which it was
found, since that is needed as a link back to the narrative that will
resume in Book 7.

Nauck's article is relentless in its self-confident positivism: he
argues vigorously for the later insertion of the Homeric original.[6] This
involves a somewhat tortuous use of logic and probability: Homer's
most prominent and expert successor did not adapt Homer; other,
lesser figures did, and from that tradition an interpolator inserted the
lines into Virgil; this all occurrred by early in the second century AD,
since several (presumably native Latin-speaking but incompetent)
grammarians were under the impression that the lines were Virgilian.
Nauck, further exercising his ingenuity, is then forced to argue that
Horace, *Odes* 3.27.41–2 and Propertius 4.7.87 were written with an
eye to the *Odyssey*, but the latter would seem to presume the Virgilian model (*piis . . . portis; pia . . . somnia*), while the former ([*imago*]
quae porta fugiens eburna | somnium ducit), like much else in *Odes* 1–3, is
likely to have been produced with a pre-publication knowledge of
the Virgilian lines. Nauck's emphatic and almost personal insistence
is also a model of its kind, aimed at convincing – or bullying – the
recalcitrant: "nobody seems to have noticed that several things about
these lines just don't fit; the expression in *verae umbrae* (894) is inept;
even more inept is 896, where scarcely a single word fails to give
offense . . . the lines are due to a ridiculous and hasty interpolator."[7]

Why bother with an interpolation, so transparent in its motivation,
proposed over a century ago and not registered, for instance, by the

---

[6] Stated first in Nauck (1867, repr. 1965) xl; then more fully argued in Nauck (1869–74).
[7] Nauck (1867, repr. 1965) xl.

Oxford Classical Text? Partly because it was proposed by a considerable scholar, and is therefore of some interest from the perspective of the history of scholarship, but also partly because it did convince others. We will never know how many others, but it was, for instance, good enough for another considerable scholar, the most significant nineteenth-century editor of Virgil. Otto Ribbeck bracketed 893–6, and in 898 politely printed *averna* in place of Nauck's *Avorna*. His appreciation was tersely stated in the apparatus: "893–6 *spurios esse persuasit Nauckius Mel.* III 89 *sqq.*"[8] And so one of the major critical editions of Virgil, an edition in use through much of the nineteenth and twentieth centuries, contained a version of the *Aeneid* that implied there were no gates of horn and ivory in that poem, no troubling exit for Aeneas.

But only philology can correct such philological excesses, and Norden's 1903 commentary on *Aeneid* 6 rejects Nauck and Ribbeck. Similarly, the editions of Mynors and of Geymonat resist the allure and threats of Nauck and Ribbeck; they restore the gates, the latter in addition recording ad loc. the excessive taste for interpolation-hunting by Ribbeck ("quae erat fere omnium illius aetatis philologorum libido").[9] Still, the questions remain: how many others were convinced by Nauck? And in what ways was their conviction disseminated, and so contributed to the tradition of cleansing the non-Augustan voice of Virgil, in handbooks, commentaries, and in the classroom? Will Nauck and Ribbeck re-emerge at some point from the apparatus of Geymonat?

Some time after writing that sentence in draft, in the last stages of this project, I became aware that the re-emergence had indeed occurred. In fact three of the most recent contributions on this passage show that as we closed the twentieth century we were not far off from the nineteenth in this respect. The first, a more precise bit of knot-cutting, would have us change *veris* in 894 to *falsis*, and *falsa* in 896 to *vera*. After a little cleaning up (*sed* to *qua* or *hac* in 896), we're

---

[8] Ribbeck (1894–5, repr. Hildesheim 1966). He was less polite in arguing, with Bentley, against the "inane arguments" of those who wanted to retain the final line of the book (901), though he has not persuaded editors since Norden – except for Zwierlein (1999) 166.

[9] Geymonat (1973) ix.

on our way to sunny Italy, or so the author would wish.[10] But the attempt fails utterly.

And as for Nauck, surely enough, in 1996 Arne Jönsson and Bengt-Arne Roos,[11] finding that "it is a little bit surprising that Nauck's and Ribbeck's suggestion has had so little impact on scholarship" (25), and believing that Aeneas, after being filled "with a passion for the future glory of his race" (21) by the words of Anchises, should be permitted to "leave the Underworld without any more ado" (27), propose to resurrect Nauck's remedy. Their only new basis, other than a strong belief in the familiar, wholeheartedly Augustan status of the poem that is always the basis of such tampering,[12] has to do with the distance (four intervening lines) between *his . . . dictis* (897–8) and the words of Anchises to which this expression refers (direct speech ending at 886, reported speech at 892). Their finding, in raw statistical terms, is correct: "our conclusion must be that the separation of *his . . . dictis* in 6.897–8 from its correlate does not correspond to Vergil's usage in *any* other passage." But that is because this passage is not like *any* of the passages after which *his dictis* and related terms appear, for the description of the Gates of Sleep is an ecphrasis, a narrative parenthesis that puts the action, time and syntax of the narrative on hold. Like any parenthesis it has syntactical invisibility, allowing resumption of the narrative as if it had never been there. Likewise, at the beginning of *Aeneid* 6, in the ecphrasis that functions as a frame with our passage, Aeneas and his men come beneath (13 *subeunt*) Apollo's temple. The ecphrasis of the temple doors follows in the next line (14 *Daedalus, ut fama est . . .*) and continues for twenty lines, until Daedalus' hands fall as he fails, in mid-line, to depict his son's fall (33 *bis patriae cecidere manus*). There then follows a sentence whose subject is never stated: "they would in fact have read through every-thing, had not . . ." (33–4 *quin protinus omnia | perlegerent oculis*). Does the reader have any hesitation in identifying the subject with that of *subeunt* 20 lines earlier, in line 13? Likewise the subject of *miratur* at *Aeneid* 8.730 (Aeneas) does not need to be stipulated, since the reader

---

[10] Cockburn (1992) Evidently (see 364 n. 9) the author was encouraged in this enterprise by his teacher A. J. Woodman, who apparently preferred slightly different ways of playing around with the lines, but to the same effect.

[11] Jönsson and Roos (1996).

[12] Anchises has also filled Aeneas with information about the limitations of Rome (847–53), and the youthful death of the hoped-for heir (868–86).

elides the 103 lines of shield description (626–728) and takes this verb at 730 as an anaphora with *miratur* in 619. Just so the reader will easily connect *his . . . dictis* at *Aeneid* 6.897–8, across the four-line ecphrasis on the Gates to the almost 150 or so lines of speech, direct and indirect, the longest by far in the poem, that have made up the last part of the book, and that concluded immediately before the four-line parenthesis.

Jönsson and Roos add their own twist to this "emendation": the lines were originally written to follow 6.282–4 (for which the MSS offer no support), then "they were transposed afterwards, by Vergil or by someone else, to the end of the song. . . , but never properly adjusted to their new context." But if Virgil put them there, then what is the issue? That is where he finally wanted them, that is where he put them. As for somebody else's transposing them, what parallels do we have for such a transposition?

The third attempt, not surprisingly, is that of Zwierlein, who follows Nauck in removing not only 893–6, but also 901 and 900.[13] O'Hara's final response to Cockburn is worth quoting here:[14]

> If one's view of the *Aeneid* is incompatible with the transmitted
> text, it is clear that one of the two must be changed. Careful
> thought should be given to the question of which one that
> should be.

Even when the lines are rescued from the trimmers, for instance by philological corrective at the hands of Norden, their ambiguity may be defused by philological hermeneutics. W. Everett got it right, proclaims Norden, Virgil means no more than "before midnight": the Sibyl and Aeneas entered in the morning and emerge before midnight.[15] Nauck and Norden are in fact in parallel positions: each through his own false philology is attempting to Augustanize a text which becomes comfortable only when so violently treated. Horsfall resorts to *indignatio*, a familiar tool of the trade. For him West's view of *Aeneid* 6 as straightforward "political panegyric," represents "robust common sense," while the likes of Boyle and the rest of "the most pessimistic interpreters" convict Virgil and themselves of "rank bad rhetoric and sheer clumsiness in handling the reader's expectations."[16] Which will you be then, sensible or clumsy? Philological nicety also

---

[13] Zwierlein (1999) 236, n. 6; 456; 587.   [14] O'Hara (1996) 333.
[15] Norden (1970) 348.   [16] Horsfall (1995) 146–7.

comes in: *falsus* "need not signify 'lying', though it can ... [it] can also mean 'unreal' (of a deceiving appearance)."[17] But what would that mean in the context of the Gates? In the end Horsfall, whose opening reference and polemic on this "endlessly discussed question"[18] promised more, suggests that "we need to distinguish the Gate's normal traffic (whether or not we claim to understand exactly what that is) from Aeneas who in no way corresponds with it. Much has been seen and known: it may be that Virgil is telling us that parts of that experience are more solidly based in history or literature than others." At the end of the day, though, the reader returns to the quieter reality at the end of *Aeneid* 6 (though not in Peerlkamp's or Ribbeck's edition),[19] and there finds little closure – the gates are wide open, and beyond them stretches the second half of the poem with all its shadows and all its reservations.[20]

Polishing up the shield

The great shield of Aeneas, which renews and Romanizes that of Achilles in the *Iliad*, has a powerful narrative function, linking Aeneas down through his own history to the greatness of Rome and to her "greatest" battle, Actium. The shield is the product of Vulcan, commissioned by the divine ancestress of the Caesars, and as such its vignettes, and particularly its centerpiece, are appropriate Augustan symbols, formations of the Augustan voice at its strongest.[21] And yet, here and there, the images by which we and Aeneas recognize Rome's future greatness, the reputation and fates of his descendants that he lifts up on to his shoulders (8.731 *attollens umero famamque et*

---

[17] Horsfall (1995) 147.
[18] It is symptomatic of the Augustan reader that the non-Augustan reading is what despoils forests-full of trees and wastes the time of the reader, while the "response" is reluctant and compelled.
[19] Nor presumably in that of Zwierlein.
[20] For some of the limitations and qualifications of the Virgilian view of history, see Zetzel (1989) 282–4; also Molyviati-Toptsis (1995).
[21] From a narratological point of view, ecphrasis exists in a state of "nesting," or narrative indentation, its point of view always potentially distinct from the primary narrative voice. This is, I think, particularly the case where the narrator draws attention to the creative act of the producer in the narrative, as happens both in the Homeric shield and throughout the account of Vulcan's shield: 628 *fecerat ignipotens*; 630 *fecerat*; 637 *addiderat*; 666 *addit*; 710 *fecerat ignipotens*. Virgil emphasizes the producer as the narrative resumes at 729 *clipeum Volcani*.

fata nepotum), seem perhaps less than straightforwardly glorious: the rape of the Sabine women, committed *sine more* as Virgil comments, 8.635; the quartering of the treacherous Mettius Fufetius (Mettus for Virgil), which Livy at about the same time was characterizing as a uniquely brutal form of punishment in Rome's long, tumultuous history, an act "insufficiently cognizant of the laws of mankind: to others goes the right to boast that their nation preferred gentler penalties";[22] Catiline in Hades paying for his crimes and hounded by the Furies, with Cato the republican foe of the Caesars dispensing laws to the pious.[23]

These images function as part of Rome's momentous future, a future which includes darkness as well as light, in the Roman self-image, as well as in the Virgilian: Virgil's choices are to some extent predetermined by the limitations of that self-image. That said, Virgil (or Vulcan) could also quite easily have assembled a dossier of brighter vignettes, as Macaulay would do in the *Lays of Ancient Rome* – Horatius at the bridge, the death of Virginia, Cincinnatus, all good, unambiguously stirring stuff. The *Aeneid* is not encomium, but here too textual criticism has attempted to make it so, to alter the shield's images and so introduce simplicity and universal light in the place of occasional qualification and complexity. These efforts will not necessarily find many supporters now, but they were thought up by prominent philologists, accepted for publication, registered in the apparatus of an edition, and presumably made their impressions. Here is the second scene on the shield:

> nec procul hinc Romam et raptas sine more Sabinas
> consessu caveae, magnis Circensibus actis,
> addiderat   (*Aen.* 8.635–7)

> Not far from here he had included Rome and the Sabine
> women lawlessly snatched away from their seats in the theater
> when the great circus games were held

---

[22] Livy 1.28.11 *primum ultimumque illud supplicium apud Romanos exempli parum memoris legum humanarum fuit: in aliis gloriari licet nulli gentium mitiores placuisse poenas.*

[23] After this section was already written there appeared Gurval (1995) 209–47, Ch. 5, "'No, Virgil, No': The battle of Actium on the Shield of Aeneas"; and Zetzel (1997) cf. 199–203. Both of these studies of the shield, like the present chapter, represent more ambivalent readings than the strong Augustan reading available in Hardie (1986) 120–43, and esp. 336–76.

Where Virgil had the "lawless" (*sine more*) rape of the Sabine women, Schrader found an easy way out: *raptas sine Marte Sabinas* ("peaceful rape of the Sabine women"). Indeed, the tradition presents the incident, both the rape and the final resolution, as exempt from either warfare or bloodshed, as is clear, for instance, from Livy's account, (1.9; 13) – although he characterizes it as a use of force (1.9.6 *haud dubie ad vim spectare res coepit*). But Schrader's "emendation" does more than record that: it indeed turns the event into a positive, almost miraculous one. Schrader's suggestion was thought sufficiently plausible to find its way into Geymonat's critical apparatus, as did Heyne's *de more*, which gives us the opposite of what Virgil wrote.[24] Nor is such emendation a product merely of modern tampering: in line 636 for *consessu* the Romanus and one ninth-century MS have *consensu*, while another has *concessu*. How these variants came about is a matter of guesswork, but to the extent that they render sense they likewise mitigate the actions of the sons of Romulus, introducing concord, which was anyway to be reached in the Virgilian text, but not until a few lines later (639 *posito certamine*). But the Augustan reader can allow no trace of lawlessness.

In the center of the shield is Actium, with the protagonists depicted, Augustus on one side (678 *hinc Augustus agens Italos in proelia Caesar*), Antony on the other (685 *hinc ope barbarica variisque Antonius armis*). But Antony is given a further detail: 686 *victor ab Aurorae populis et litore rubro* ("victorious from the peoples of the east and from its ruddy shore"). This refers to an earlier success, which will of course be reversed, with some irony, by the end of the battle, or rather in Caesar's triumph which follows it in 29 BC, as *victor* turns to *victae* (722 *incedunt victae longo ordine gentes* "the conquered nations process in long file"). Even so, it is perhaps a curiosity that, in the most prominent artistic representation of the victory that gave Octavian control of the world, the sole instance of the word *victor* should occur apposed to the name of Antony.

Servius in fact had taken notice of the line, and he used a standard piece of Augustan rhetoric to fend off any sympathy or admiration for the enemies of Augustus: Virgil calls Antony *victor* so as to underscore the achievement of the princeps (*ut maiorem hostem Augustus vicisse*

---

[24] Cf. Heyne ad loc., who refers to Schrader's "clever conjectural play."

videatur). This may satisfy most of us,[25] but not all; for instance J. Markland, editor and commentator on Statius, and another prominent philologist of the early part of the nineteenth century, just could not accept *victor* as a designation of Antony. And so, again unaided by the manuscripts, he first emended then interpreted, combining the editorial and hermenutic function into one:[26]

> we should read *ductor ab Aurorae populis*; it would be easy on
> many counts to show that the usual reading (*victor ab Aurorae
> populis*) is not suitable for that passage ... *ductor ab Aurorae
> populis* is said with contempt, and in indignation that a "leader
> from the peoples of the *unwarlike* East" should dare to take up
> arms against Augustus, Agrippa, and the name of Rome.

That would certainly make for an easier reading of Antony from the perspective of Augustan propaganda – the hermeneutical goal of Markland. Now although the shield treats Actium, memory of Philippi further problematizes the reference to *Antonius victor* (Plut. *Ant.* 22.1–2):

> no great achievements were performed by Caesar [Octavian],
> but it was Antony who was everywhere victorious (νικῶν
> πάντα) and successful. In the first battle, at least, Caesar was
> overwhelmingly defeated (ἡττηθείς) by Brutus, lost his camp,
> and narrowly escaped his pursuers by secret flight; although he
> himself says in his *Memoirs* that he withdrew before the battle
> in consequence of a friend's dream. But Antony conquered
> (ἐνίκησεν) Cassius; although some write that Antony was not
> present in the battle, but came up after the battle when his
> men were already in pursuit. Cassius, at his own request and
> command, was killed by Pindar, one of his trusty freedmen; for
> Cassius was not aware that Brutus was victorious (νενικηκότα).

---

[25] Binder (1971) 234: "Die Grösse des Besiegten erhöht die Grösse des Siegers."

[26] Markland (1827) 242 (ad 2.6.3): "Vergilius Aen. VIII, 685 (*Ductor ab Aurorae populis*) ita legendum; vulgo *Victor ab Aurorae populis*: quod multis nominibus isti loco non convenire facile esset probare. *Ducem* vocat Horatius Epod. IX in eadem descriptione: et Ovidius Met. XV, 826 "*Romanique* ducis conjunx Aegyptia, *tedae* | Non bene fisa, cadet": ubi hunc Vergilii locum in animo habuit. *Ductor ab Aurorae populis*, ut, *Pastor ab Amphryso*: et per contemptum haec dicuntur, et indignationem quod *Ductor ab* imbellis *Aurorae populis* arma adversus Augustum, Agrippam, et nomen Romanum sumere auderet."

After a few days had intervened, a second battle was fought,
and Brutus, being defeated, slew himself; but Antony won the
greater credit for the victory (νίκης), since, indeed, Caesar was
sick.[27]

Markland's attempt to remove Virgil's attribution to Antony of the
epithet *victor*, although not convincing, is quite understandable from
an Augustan viewpoint. Augustus himself, perhaps two years before
the *Aeneid* came out, was involved in creating fictions about the vic-
tors and the vanquished at Philippi, and about his own inglorious
part in the battles, in ways that seem to resonate with a possible implication in Virgil's description of Antony arriving at the battle of
Actium.[28]

Sometimes the emendation does not involve alteration of the text,
or at least of its surface. The final scene before the central Actian
image is a somewhat curious one:

> hinc procul addit
> Tartareas etiam sedes, alta ostia Ditis,
> et scelerum poenas, et te, Catilina, minaci
> pendentem scopulo Furiarumque ora trementem,
> secretosque pios, his dantem iura Catonem.
>
> (*Aen.* 8.666–70)

Apart from these he includes even the dwellings of Tartarus,
the high gates of Dis, with the punishment of crimes and you,
Catiline, hanging from a looming crag, with the pious set apart
and Cato giving them laws.

Servius thought Cato the Elder was indicated; for how could Virgil
include Uticensis, who took up arms against Caesar? DServius further
found it inappropriate that a suicide could be dispensing laws to the
pious.[29] There is no recent enthusiasm for this position, however, and
subsequent editors and commentators make the obvious identification
with the younger Cato, particularly given the coupling with Catiline.

---

[27] Loeb translation.
[28] See Yavetz (1984).
[29] Servius ad 8.670: "HIS DANTEM IVRA CATONEM ut supra ⟨VI 841⟩ diximus, Cen-
sorium significat, non Vticensem, qui contra Caesarem bella suscepit. *quomodo enim piis
iura redderet, qui in se impius fuit?*"

The struggle does not end yet, however. Always ready to deal with such "problems," Peerlkamp in 1843 removed the whole sequence from the shield:[30]

> These lines have always seemed to me so out of place that if
> Virgil himself put them here he did so in a moment of critical
> incompetence. Vulcan had depicted on the shield the "affairs
> of Italy, its triumphs and wars" (*res Italas, triumphos et bella*).[31]
> A plot worthy of a hero. There were Romulus and Remus,[32]
> Tullus,[33] Tarquin and Porsenna, Cocles, Cloelia, Manlius, then
> the festivals connected with the greatness of Rome, to which
> he added the Lupercalia, as a nod to Evander. And now *Catiline
> and Cato*? In the midst of these examples of Roman heroism
> could a less fortunate example be found than that of this
> criminal, however much he was punished? The very image of
> the Underworld, which he has described twice elsewhere, is
> less suitable here. If however he had also wanted to touch on
> it here on the shield, he would, I believe, have chosen some
> other Roman, honored in Elysium. The Romans always held
> the memory of *Catiline* in special disgrace, and neither could
> this please Augustus, in that he knew the role played by Julius
> Caesar in that conspiracy. *Catiline* and *Cato* are names from the
> civil war, which Augustus preferred to consign to oblivion.

[30] Peerlkamp (1843) "Mihi quidem haec semper visa sunt hic tam inepta, ut, si Vergilius ipse posuerit, tunc, quum ponebat omni iudicio destitutum fuisse arbitrer. Vulcanus in scuto caelaverat *res Italas, triumphos et bella*. Argumentum viro forti dignum. Erant Romulus et Remus, Tullus, Tarquinius et Porsena, Cocles, Cloelia, Manlius, tum festa cum magnitudine Romani nominis coniuncta, quibus Lupercalia, propter Evandrum, adiecit. Iam *Catilina et Cato*? Poteratne inveniri, inter media fortitudinis Romanae exempla, exemplum infelicius quam scelerati hominis, quantumvis puniti? Ipsa Orci imago iam minus hic convenit, quam bis alibi descripserit. Si eam tamen et in hoc clipeo attingere voluisset, sumpsisset, credo, alium Romanum, in Elysiis honoratum. *Catilinae* quidem memoria rebus Romanis semper habita est summo dedecori, neque hoc gratum esse poterat Augusto, qui sciret, quas partes ipse Iulius Caesar in ea con-iuratione egisset. *Catilina* et *Cato* sunt nomina ex bello civili, quod oblivioni tradi malebat."

[31] This seems to be a rewriting of 626 (*res Italas Romanorumque triumphos*), which easily comprehends the Catilinarian affair, while Peerlkamp's phrase seems to suggest a defi-nition of *res Italas* as including "triumphs and wars" – but excluding, it seems, the *Bellum Catilinae*! It is fairly clear that the word *bellum* appeared in the title of Sallust's work; cf. Ramsey (1984) 5, n. 9.

[32] No mention of Sabine women.

[33] No mention of the quartered Mettus.

And so Virgil, following the "Servian default," will not have written the lines. The textual critic does what he wishes Virgil had done, and consigns (or tries to) Catiline and Cato to oblivion. We might add the evidence of Suetonius, *Aug.* 85.1, that Octavian seems to have gone to the trouble of writing a refutation of Brutus' eulogy of Cato in his "Reply to Brutus on Cato" (*Rescripta Bruto de Catone*), a refutation that he read at a gathering of his friends (*in coetu familiarium*). These readings, moreover, seem to have continued well into the principate.

Once again Ribbeck was nearly convinced by Peerlkamp: he would have liked to excise the lines, but was compelled to keep them by the realization that the words *haec inter* at 671 demand the presence of the Catilinarian scene – Actium is between the world above and the world below, so 666–70 would have to stay.[34] Zwierlein, on the other hand, removes the lines.[35] It has been worth our while to record Peerlkamp's arguments, naive as they may seem to contemporary readers, for his words have a certain validity: the sequence is indeed troubling if viewed purely from the perspective of Augustan propaganda and encomium. If that were all that Virgil's lines amounted to, one must choose one of Peerlkamp's alternatives: the poet was incompetent, or the lines will have to go. The other option, of course, is that even the shield, one of the most strongly Augustan passages in the poem, has a dynamism that goes beyond and deeper than the policies of Augustus.

In a world in which the license granted to textual cleansing of this sort has been much reduced, we encounter persuasive rhetoric, rhetoric that tries to force ambiguity or shadows out of our minds. In the present instance Fordyce's commentary provides a good lesson. He talks of the passage as "hastily bridg[ing]" the early history of Rome and the Actian scenes – "hastily," not "briefly" – and we should therefore not be too concerned with its problematic status, since the poet would clearly have tidied it up, had the Fates given him time.[36] Fordyce ad loc. has one long period, a model of philological rhetoric:

---

[34] Ribbeck ad loc.: "666–70 hinc ... Catonem *additamentum esse grammatici arbitratur Peerlkampus: parum poeta nostro digna esse concedo, sed cf. prol.* 83."

[35] Zwierlein (1999) 230; 456.

[36] Cf. Ahl and Roisman (1996) 16 (of the critical uses of the early deaths of Virgil and Lucan): "any 'contradictions' yielded by a specific reading can be explained away as things the poets would have emended if they had had the opportunity."

The tribute to Cato is in line with the eulogy for which Cicero set the pattern and is no more extravagant, within poetic convention, than the plain prose of Velleius (ii.35.2 "homo Virtuti simillimus et per omnia ingenio diis quam hominibus propior"): that the implacable opponent of Julius Caesar and the uncompromising champion of the lost cause of the Republic, in criticism of whom Augustus himself wrote (Suet. *Aug.* 85.1), should receive this tribute in a prelude to the *laudes Augusti* and the panegyric of the new regime is the less surprising when one remembers that Horace chose to include *Catonis nobile letum (Od.* 1.12.35f.) in a very similar context, a parade of *exempla* from Roman history leading up to a panegyric on the princeps as its crowning glory.

So Horace is invoked in order to make Virgil normative. Here are the lines in question:

> Romulum post hos prius an quietum
> Pompili regnum memorem an superbos
> Tarquini fascis, dubito, an Catonis
>   nobile letum.   (Hor. *Odes* 1.12.33–6)

I am unsure whom to mention first after these, Romulus or Numa's peaceful reign, the arrogant power of Tarquin, or Cato's noble death.

What is noteworthy here is the fact that Nisbet-Hubbard record an almost precisely parallel attempt to sanitize the Horatian text: "Conjectures have been attempted in order to resolve the puzzle."[37] They do not opt for emendation ("*nobile letum* is so applicable to Cato's suicide that one is reluctant to reject the transmitted reading"), but have a note which is pertinent to our Virgilian inquiry: "It is at first sight surprising to find Cato referred to in such glowing terms in a poem in praise of Augustus." The reader is then taken through a series of steps (including reference to *Aeneid* 8.670) designed to reassure and to remove that initial "surprise" – mainly on the grounds that in later years Cato became a generically idealized figure. But the two initial idealizers are Horace and Virgil, and in both cases, without textual interference, uneasiness remains if we are preoccupied with "enco-

---

[37] Hamacher: *catenis nobilitatum [Regulum]*; Bentley: *anne Curti*. Shackleton Bailey obelizes and suspects *anne Tulli | flebile.*

mium of the new régime." In both cases, the fault may lie in the assumptions about the Augustan poets.[38]

Finally, we have the possibility of intertextually determined meaning, where emendation is not an option, and hermeneutics does the sanitizing. Augustus is observing his triple triumph (8.720–2):

> ipse sedens niveo candentis limine Phoebi
> dona recognoscit populorum aptatque superbis
> postibus.

> he himself, seated in the white threshold of shining Phoebus
> recognizes the gifts of the peoples and fits them to his proud
> doorposts.

D. Fowler has treated the lines well, from the perspective of narrato-logical voice and focalization. His stimulus here is in the works of two scholars, the first of whom, D. Gillis, noted a parallel between these lines and those describing the cave of Cacus earlier (8.195–7):[39]

> semperque recenti
> caede tepebat humus, foribusque adfixa superbis
> ora virum tristi pendebant pallida tabo.

> And the ground was always warm with fresh slaughter, and
> pallid with grim decay, the faces of men hung fixed to the
> proud doorways.

The parallelism is strengthened by the fact that Cacus and the shield are both "products" of Vulcan, and so the signs they exhibit poten-tially bring the shared diction into high relief. Fowler, after citing Gillis' claims for the "odious implications" that arise from this intra-textuality, then allows (as "not absurd") A. Traina's strategy for re-jecting Gillis and separating the two passages within Book 8: they are contrastive. Since the Turnus/Cacus parallelism is the operative one, the reader is to see a *distinction* between Cacus and Augustus.[40] That is indeed a possible interpretation, but one that is in competition with that of Gillis, which it does not drive from the field. For the as-

---

[38] Cf. Williams (1980) 13–19, showing that Cato's presence in *Odes* 1.12 is motivated in part by Horace's emphasis, in the context of the marriage of Marcellus and Julia in 25, on *mos maiorum*.

[39] Gillis (1983). He also notes the similarity to *G.* 2.461 *foribus domus alta superbis*. Horsfall (1995) 163 n. 17 refers to this, and the work of S. Farron as "negative allegory, which does not merit a serious reply."

[40] Traina (1988) 1073, following Gransden (1976) ad loc.

sumption that there is a consistent and sustained equation of Cacus and Turnus is a matter of interpretation, and Virgil has not particularly pointed the way towards allowing a contrastive reading. Indeed at the end of *Aeneid* 9, as he makes an attempt on the Trojan camp, Turnus looks more like Hercules than any other character in the poem.[41] To return to the shield, Fowler, playing devil's advocate, offers another strategy for those wishing to "defuse any hint of anti-Augustanism":[42] *superbis* here represents the "deviant focalisation" of the *victae . . . gentes*. Augustus is depicted ambivalently in the eyes of those he has conquered. It may be a slight obstacle for this reading that those *victae gentes* are not mentioned until the next sentence. And the fact would remain that Virgil chose the words that brought this point of view to be represented at such an Augustan moment of the poem. It is moreover generally typical of Virgil that he allows us to hear the voice of the vanquished.

Policing the parade

Particularly since the publication of Paul Zanker's influential book *The Power of Images in the Age of Augustus*, scholars have become increasingly attentive to the propagandistic function of images in the late republic and early empire. The text of Virgil has its own *imagines*, and those too have been reordered where they have seemed to function contrary to the encomiastic purposes that they are supposed to serve. This seems to have happened even in antiquity, for instance in Anchises' famous address to Julius Caesar: 6.834–5 *tuque prior, tu parce, genus qui ducis Olympo,* | *proice tela manu, sanguis meus!* "you take the lead, you be lenient, you who trace your line to Olympus, throw your weapon from your hand, blood kin of mine!" R. Syme drew from these lines his argument that Augustus sought to distance himself from Julius Caesar: Anchises could not be made to address an admonition to his descendant without such detail being pre-approved as official Augustan policy. But as P. White has shown, such policy, based almost exclusively on these lines, can be shown to be a false construction.[43] All of this takes the *Aeneid* away from the realm of

---

[41] See Hardie ad *Aen.* 9.712–13; 715–16. I am grateful to James O'Hara for noting this similarity.
[42] Fowler (1990a) 51.
[43] See White (1988).

propaganda. Not surprisingly, however, these lines have attracted some critical attention, and even in antiquity there was an attempt to avert criticism of Caesar by emending *meus* (that which entitled Anchises to chide Caesar!) to *pius* (Rufinus 59.13). Zwierlein, predictably, removes the entire passage of 826–40![44]

First a precursor of the parade, on which the critical approach is parallel. In the *Georgics'* "praises of Italy", a catalogue of Italians moves from the general to the specific, and culminates in Octavian, warring in the East (2.167–70):

> haec genus acre virum, Marsos pubemque Sabellam
> adsuetumque malo Ligurem, Volscosque verutos,
> extulit, haec Decios Marios magnosque Camillos,
> Scipiadas duros bello et te, maxime Caesar ...

> This land bred a fierce race of men, Marsians, Sabellan youth,
> Ligurian inured to trouble, Volscians with their spits, this land
> Decii, Marii, and mighty Camilli, Scipios harsh in war, and
> you, mightiest Caesar ...

The name of Marius (*Marios*, "men like Marius"?) has caused problems, partly because there is only one prominent Marius, partly for ideological reasons.[45] Some commentators, restricting themselves to hermeneutics, insist that Virgil refers to Marius as victor over the Teutons and Cimbri, and cannot be thinking about his role as subverter of the republic, as a figure generally troubling at a time when civil discord was a very delicate issue.[46] But again, there are those who

---

[44] Zwierlein (1999) 592, n. 5.

[45] Feeney (1986) 6–7 prefers father (*RE* 14, in Supp. 6) and unimpressive son (*RE* 15): "When a pair of exemplary relatives are immediately succeeded by a suspect father and a bad son, the panegyric doubles back on itself."

[46] Livy's view, as it seems to emerge from *Per.* 80, will presumably have been typical: "vir, cuius si examinentur cum virtutibus vitia, haud facile sit dictu, utrum bello melior an pace perniciosior fuerit. adeo quam rem publicam armatus servavit, eam primo togatus omni genere fraudis, postremo armis hostiliter evertit." ("If you were to weigh the man's vices with his virtues, it would not be easy to say whether he was better in time of war or more destructive in peace. The state which he saved by arms he so thoroughly overturned, first as a civilian with every manner of corruption, and finally with arms as in the role of enemy"). Cf. Sall., *Hist.* 1.77.7M (admittedly from a speech) "tumultum ex tumultu, bellum ex bello serunt" "[the followers of Marius] sow turmoil after turmoil, war after war". Even in antiquity, there seem to have been apologists, though from later antiquity when multiple consulships and autocratic behavior will have been less troubling; so Servius, blandly: 2.169 MARIOS Marii multi fuerunt: quorum unus fuit septies consul.

would solve the problem and remove the uneasiness by conjecture. Ready as always, Peerlkamp suggested the unappealing *Deciosque mares*, while Haeberlin traded *Marios* for *Fabios*, Richter *Marios* for *Curios*. Pick your favorite anapaestic-shaped heroic Republican family, and insert it in place of the unsavory *Marios*. Again, the manuscripts do not encourage any of this activity, though Richter thought *Marsos* in 167 might be involved in the "corruption" that justified his removal of what Virgil wrote.

To return to the parade, D. C. Feeney[47] has shown how many of its details are in tension with any sort of clear encomiastic stance towards Rome's future heroes. Anchises mentions the future towns of Latium:

> hi tibi Nomentum et Gabios urbemque Fidenam,
> hi Collatinas imponent montibus arces,
> Pometios Castrumque Inui Bolamque Coramque:
> haec tum nomina erunt, nunc sunt sine nomine terrae.
>
> (*Aen.* 6.773–6)

> These men will found Nomentum, Gabii, and the city of
> Fidena, these will set Collatia's citadel on mountain-tops, will
> found Pometii, Castrum Inui, Bola and Cora: then will these
> be their names, now just lands without a name.

They will, many of them, become ghost towns before or during the time of Virgil's writing. Feeney well says of Anchises' *haec tum nomina erunt, nunc sunt sine nomine terrae* (6.776): "the tenses are intriguingly two-sided, depending on whether one's perspective in time is that of Aeneas, or of Vergil's audience" (7). From the point of view of the narrator (Anchises) and the recipient of the narrative (Aeneas) the line is neutral, excluding any participation by Virgilian or Augustan time. But from that of the poet (Virgil) and the poet's contemporary reader of the *Aeneid* the words *nunc sunt sine nomine terrae* may take on a darker, subversive meaning, since that reader knows these towns, and knows that they have indeed become ghost towns. Through the lens of "free indirect discourse," the glorious Latin towns of Anchises' predictions have already risen and fallen into ruin.

As for the actual parade, as with the shield, some of the names of the heroes and the epithets or details assigned them, from Romulus to

---

[47] Feeney (1986) 12–16.

the young Marcellus, suggest a falling short, ambivalence, or qualification that problematizes the encomiastic assumptions about the passage. N. Horsfall (148–9), though he finds himself "convinced ... less and less" by Feeney's article, nevertheless allows that "the Parade contains figures good, bad and ambiguous," and concludes that "elements of criticism are present, enough to set heroism and merit in high relief: they were not intended to be overvalued out of all proportion." That, it seems to me, allows for the ambiguity that Feeney demonstrates, and is very different from the view of D. West who finds the pageant to be "subtle, whole-hearted and successful panegyric," just as the whole poem is "political panegyric."[48] West in fact allows that Feeney's article "should be read as a corrective to my arguments."

Now to another well-known couplet:

> quin Decios Drusosque procul saevumque securi
> aspice Torquatum et referentem signa Camillum.
>
> *(Aen. 6.824–5)*

> Look at the Decii and the Drusi standing apart, look at
> Torquatus savage with his axe, and Camillus carrying the
> standards.

Feeney notes that "the name Drusus does not occur in a laudatory context in lists of *exempla*. The reference is always to the younger Drusus [M. Livius Drusus, tr. pl. 91 BC], and is always condemnatory." On the evidence of Cicero, *Orat.* 213, Drusus is representative of "sons falling short of their father's standards" (12). Feeney's point may have been anticipated in antiquity, for the fifth-century Vatican manuscript "Romanus" (Vat. lat. 3867) has *Brutosque* for *Drusosque*, as do the scholia to Juvenal, 8.254. While this is perhaps just a mechanical importation from [*ultoris*] *Bruti* at 6.818, it may reflect an early attempt to remove the panegyrically incorrect Drusi.

King Ancus is in the parade, and the brief mention he receives is somewhat curious (815–16): *Quem [Tullum] iuxta sequitur iactantior Ancus | nunc quoque iam nimium gaudens popularibus auris* ("next to him comes over-boastful Ancus, even now too joyful in the people's favor"). The reference is enigmatic and may depend on some un-

---

[48] West (1993b).

recoverable contemporary anecdote, having to do with the plebeian *gens Marcia.*[49] Feeney lays out the "dubious political tradition" connected with this family. And Zetzel (noted by O'Hara) finds the oddity may be one of many which raise "questions of truth and causation essential to historical understanding."[50] Again my present concern is with textual alteration, and we have here another instance. The phrase *nimium gaudens,* along with *iactantior,* implying excess as it does, is oddly critical of the king who, unlike Tullus Hostilius or the Tarquins, is traditionally depicted as a fairly unobjectionable figure. The *recentiores* read *gaudet* at line 816; Peerlkamp took it from there, emending so as to neutralize any tone of criticism: *et qui iam primum gaudet popularibus auris* ("and who now is first to rejoice in the people's favor").

Peerlkamp was in fact particularly active in this part of the poem.[51] Current editions are often silent on his activity, but Ribbeck tended to listen, and frequently admits him at least to the apparatus criticus. At 817–18 Anchises turns from Ancus to the Tarquins:

> vis et Tarquinios reges animamque superbam
> ultoris Bruti, fascisque videre receptos?

> Do you want also to look upon the Tarquin kings and the
> haughty soul of Brutus the avenger, and to see the recovered
> fasces?

Much has been done to avoid the ambiguities that are packed into this couplet, and to separate Brutus from the word *superbam* – the same adjective that caused trouble at 8.721. R. G. Austin (ad loc.) has a good discussion of some of those efforts, beginning with Servius and Tiberius Claudius Donatus who, followed in modern times by Sabbadini (who changed his mind) and Geymonat (with support from correcting hands of the antique manuscripts M and P), sees a strong break after *superbam.* Servius was likewise at pains to insist on this strong break between the two lines. This allows us to isolate Brutus, the first hero of the republic, from the adjective – which anyway is

---

[49] See Austin (1977) ad loc. The detail fits better with Servius Tullius (cf. Dion. Hal. 4.8.3). See also O'Hara (1996) 179.

[50] Zetzel (1989) 282, 284.

[51] Though not as active as at *Aen.* 9.581–663, which he excised as being unworthy of the *ingenium* and *color* of Virgil; Numanus Remulus' invective against the Trojans, and Ascanius' use of the bow, are thereby removed from Virgil's poem!

better applied to (the second) Tarquin. Austin is surely right to reject such separation and punctuation: "This seems quite untenable: it involves a most disconcerting postposition of -*que* (theoretically possible; see Norden, p. 404 n. 4), and destroys the natural rhythm of both lines, besides depriving Virgil of an arresting point."[52] Norden had a particular agenda, to ward off the transferring of *superbia* from the Tarquins to Brutus:

> But it is evident that this interpretation [as translated above] must be wrong. Vergil can only mean, to paraphrase his words in prose: "Brutus took vengeance on the arrogance of Tarquin by recovering the *fasces* and restoring them to the people."[53]

Here is Augustan philology at its most imperious: Virgil can "only have meant" a reading which avoids applying a negative epithet to the first hero of the republic; the grammatical rule is then fashioned to allow that meaning. This is really no different from emendation, as is shown by the actions of Peerlkamp – who at least saw that the Latin had to be changed in order to give Norden's desiderated meaning; so he gave us: *Tarquinios reges animaeque superbae | ultorem Brutum*. I assume nobody believes this, but, again, it made it into the apparatus of Ribbeck.

The connection must be allowed to stand: as we read the couplet and arrive at *animamque superbam* we naturally take it with *Tarquinios*, and are immediately forced to adjust as the next line begins with what demands to be taken as a genitive dependent on *animam*. Austin brings out the ambiguity: "Virgil is torn between admiration for the proud spirit of the man who gloried in the overthrow of a tyrant, and horror at the unbending spirit of the father who had his sons executed; *animam superbam* contains both implications" (252). But Austin continues: "The memory would be sharpened by the memory of another Brutus, an *ultor* likewise: what were Virgil's thoughts of him?"[54] Once that question gets asked, the lines takes on a significance with contemporary implications, for Aeneas is not the only one

---

[52] Austin (1977) ad loc. In fact the Virgilian parallels do not approach the harshness of the hyperbaton that would occur in 6.818.

[53] Norden (1970) 328 "Aber es leuchtet ein, dass diese Auffassung falsch sein muss. Vergil kan nur meinen, um seine Wörte prosaisch zu paraphrasieren: 'Brutus Tarquinii superbiam ultus est fascibus recuperatis populoque restitutis.'"

[54] So too Feeney (1986) 10.

being questioned; so too is Virgil's reader, for whom the question *vis
... fascis videre receptos?*, asked in the context of the name Brutus, will
have resonated in precisely the sort of way that leads to the ancient
grammarians' desire to separate and therefore neutralize these two
lines. With the received text the alternation and competition of point
of view may be represented as follows:

Strong Augustan point of view (Anchises/Aeneas):

vis et Tarquinios reges animamque superbam,
ultoris Bruti fascisque videre receptos?

> *superbam* of Tarquin
> Brutus = ejector of Tarquin
> *fascisque ... receptos* = establishment of Republic

Qualified Augustan point of view (Anchises/Aeneas):

vis et Tarquinios reges animamque superbam
ultoris Bruti, fascisque videre receptos?

> *superbam* of Brutus
> Brutus = ejector of Tarquin
> *fascisque ... receptos* = establishment of Republic

Subversive point of view (republican *auctor*/reader):

vis et Tarquinios reges animamque superbam
ultoris Bruti, fascisque videre receptos?

> Brutus = assassin of Caesar
> *fascisque ... receptos* = recovery of Republic

The brilliance of the Augustan revolution lay in large part in the fiction that it was no revolution at all, traditional *potestas* coupled with
remarkable *auctoritas*, itself a traditional concept.[55] Nothing in Virgil's
couplet is out of step with that fiction.

---

[55] Cf. Aug. *R.G.* 34.3 *post id tempus auctoritate omnibus praestiti, potestatis autem nihilo amplius
habui quam ceteri qui mihi quoque in magistratu conlegae fuerunt*, "after that time I excelled
all in authority, but held no greater power than others who were my colleagues in each
of the magistracies."

Looking out for Aeneas

Emendation, like the other more subtle forms of sanitization with which we have dealt in other chapters, occurs particularly when the character or actions of Aeneas are in question. One brief example is offered when Mercury delivers his message to Aeneas, with understandable, but somewhat unheroic, results: (4.279–80) *at vero Aeneas aspectu obmutuit amens | arrectaeque horrore comae et vox faucibus haesit*, "But Aeneas is frantic and dumbstruck at the sight, his hair stands on end with horror, his voice is stuck in his throat." The second line will recur with intratextual power when Virgil uses it again of Turnus, as the Dira descends on him (12.868). Ribbeck was perhaps unhappy with the parallelism (which he noted); at any rate he bracketed 4.280, betraying his motives "I would like such stupefaction not to occur here" ("Hinc abesse velim tantum stuporem").[56]

Not looking back for Creusa

An infamous example will show how the full force of translation, editing and commentary can come together in the interests of preserving Aeneas' conventional heroic status. Creusa had to stay in Troy, of course, and her understated death allows her to appear later and give Aeneas her blessing, but she was all the more likely to be lost, given the manner in which Aeneas told her to make the departure:

> mihi parvus Iulus
> sit comes et longe servet vestigia coniunx
>
> (*Aen.* 2.710–11)

> Let little Iulus go at my side and my wife far back observe our tracks.

Ovid, whose reading of the lines is the first we have, will have had no doubt about their meaning, as I suggested in Chapter 2. His Dido is quite clear about what happened to Creusa, and who was responsible (*Her.* 7.83–4):[57]

---

[56] Zwierlein (1999) 60, of course, also removes the line.
[57] So Knox (1995) 216: "a scathing remark, casting doubt on Aeneas' story of his desperate search for Creusa in *Aen.* 2.747–70."

> si quaeras ubi sit formosi mater Iuli
> occidit a duro sola relicta viro.

should you ask where the mother of pretty Iulus is, she is dead,
left behind on her own by her hard-hearted husband.

But other readers, at least since Servius, and doubtless before him, have
tried to do something about these lines. Servius wrote as follows:

> **711 ET LONGE** "longe," "valde," ut ⟨1.13⟩ "Tiberinaque longe
> ostia." nam "longe" non potest, quia sequitur "pone subit
> coniunx." et bene ire singulos facit: scit enim multitudinem
> facile posse deprehendi.

> **711 ET LONGE** *longe* "vigorously", as ⟨1.13⟩ in *Tiberinaque longe
> ostia.* For it cannot mean "at a distance" because he later says
> "my wife comes up behind." And he is right to make them go
> individually: for he knows that a crowd can be easily detected.

But they do not go individually, rather in two groups, one of three
and one of one, the second consisting of Creusa, who is to follow
"a long way back." Dryden dealt with the problem fairly easily:

> My hand shall lead our little son; and you,
> my faithful consort, shall our steps pursue

That is, you ignore *longe*, and with it the problems it created; Creusa
simply follows behind, as is culturally appropriate.

A surprising number of translators followed Dryden; *longe*, like
Creusa, just disappears:

J. DAVIDSON (1794)	"little Iulus is linked in my right hand, *and trips after his father with unequal steps: my spouse comes up behind.*"
C. R. KENNEDY (1861)	"My little Son shall travel at our side, | Creusa *from behind our steps pursue*"
G. K. RICKARDS (1871)	"with me shall walk | Ascanius hand in hand; *my wife behind* | *Keep the same track, and mark our footsteps well.*"
W. MORRIS (1876)	"Iulus by my side | Shall wend, and *after us my wife shall follow on my feet.*"

E. RICHARDSON (1883)   "Let little Iulus at my side
                        proceed, | *And Creusa following to our
                        steps give heed.*"

Another group of translators takes up Servius' suggestion, which interprets Aeneas' prescription as sound strategy:

J. CONINGTON (1866)   "My son shall journey at my
                           side, | *My wife her steps by mine
                           shall guide,* | At distance safe."

F. RICHARDS (1928)   "Iulus, keep | Close by me, *at
                           safe distance walk my wife.*"

W. JACKSON KNIGHT (1956)   "Iulus must walk beside me,
                           and *my wife shall follow at a safe
                           distance in our footsteps.*"

One wonders whether this was one of the instances given the stamp of approval by Haarhof, Jackson Knight's South African friend who claimed to be in communication through a medium with the ghost of Virgil, which would provide Haarhof with confirmation of the rectitude of Jackson Knight's translations![58]

A third group of translators is at first sight rather puzzling:

H. HAMILTON (1888)   "Iulus at my side shall have his
                       place | *Creusa following at a little space.*"
H. S. SALT (1928)   "Young Iulus at my side | Shall
                       journey, and *Creusa follow nigh.*"

That is, they seem to say the opposite of the Latin. But Hamilton and Salt are doubtless translating an emended text, and there are many to chose from, again provided by the nineteenth century: Kvicala's *haut longe*, or Brandt's *et lente*, or Schenkel's *atque legens*, or Baehrens' *a tergo*. No modern edition prints any of these however; but any reader who happens on one of the translations enumerated above will lose access to the ambiguity of the Virgilian text. This is a common limitation of all translations, it is true, but this instance provides a useful reminder that ideologically motivated textual criticism may remain influential long after the act itself has been rejected or corrected.

---

[58] Wiseman (1992) 171–209. Wiseman, amusingly, suggests that Haarhof's views may be more reliable than those who see ambiguities in Virgil.

And then we have the voice of the commentator. All commentary is tendentious to some degree, however much it projects its objectivity. At 2.729 Aeneas, now depicting himself *en route*, expresses his fear for his son and his father (but not his wife): *comitique onerique timentem*. DServius records the efforts of some Aeneas protectors: *quidam comiti pro comitibus accipi volunt* "some want to take 'companion' as 'companions,'" thereby having the singular mean "son and wife." But as C. Perkell has noted, this will not account for 2.741 ("I did not look back for her, or turn my attention back to her until ...").[59] R. G. Austin's note on 2.711 is a splendid example of the art of persuasion in commentary, camouflaged as philologically authoritative and capable of closing out hermeneutics. He begins by enlisting those who might be troubled by the line: "**711 longe:** this has been emended in various absurd ways (cf. Ribbeck's apparatus)". So far exercising good critical judgment, he proceeds with philological scrutiny: "*Longe* with *servet* cannot mean more than 'at a distance', 'apart'" (we are not supposed to notice the slight semantic slippage from "at a distance" to "apart"), "otherwise [he continues] *servet* loses its meaning" (not so, "follow his footsteps from a long way back" is a sensible expression); "it must" we are told "be used as it is in ix. 770f. 'uno deiectum comminus ictu | cum galea longe iacuit caput', in the same sort of relative sense that *procul* often has" (*longe* at 9.771 means "far off" – a sign of the violence of the blow – it never has the relative sense of *procul*).[60] Austin proceeds: "In 723ff. Aeneas describes how the instructions now being given are afterwards carried out: the arrangements for Anchises and Iulus are exactly as planned here, and *pone subit coniunx* (725) must correspond to *longe servet vestigia* – and *pone* has no implication of great distance" (but *pone* does not need an implication of great distance; the implication is already there, established by *longe*). Austin closes with reassurance and moderation: "I doubt if too much planning should be read into the line: the arrangement of Creusa is sensible in itself, but it was just a thing that went wrong by a turn of fate that Thomas Hardy would well have understood". Alternatively we may turn to John Davis Long, our naive translator with no Augustan Virgil to create and no heroic Ae-

---

[59] Perkell (1981) 206.
[60] So the statement "Thera exploded with such force that the tidal wave reached as far as Gibraltar" will not easily mean that Thera and Gibraltar are nearby.

neas to protect, who gives us what Virgil gave us, with all its Virgilian ambiguity:

> Little Iulus at my side shall go,
> Creusa on our track and well behind.   (2.893–94)

C. Perkell has noted the distinction between the Virgilian hero in relation to Creusa and Dido, and the Homeric figures, Hector and Odysseus, who in the relationships to their wives (Andromache and Penelope) function in human and sympathetic ways, as well as in accordance with their public duties.[61] One of the great moral difficulties of Virgil's poem comes from the poet's limiting the sympathy and love that Aeneas is permitted to show to Dido and Creusa. That difficulty finds its confirmation in the varied ways in which a whole range of scholars, working in a climate of unquestioning Augustanism, have struggled to alter the meaning of this text. But the text survives the onslaught, and so retains that moral ambivalence and difficulty that gives it so much of its power.

Magnus ab integro saeclorum nascitur ordo

In 1998 R. Cramer published his Bonn doctoral dissertation, *Vergils Weltsicht. Optimismus und Pessimismus in Vergils Georgica*.[62] He attempts in this to restore the view of that poem as a simply univocal encomium of the life of toil and of the world of agriculture. Cramer refers to an important part of his methodology at the end of his preface: "A special difficulty arises from the fact that the state of the text seems by no means as sure as people have at least in this century generally assumed."[63] And so it emerges that Otto Zwierlein, Cramer's *Doktorvater*, who has methodically been reducing the bulk of Plautine comedies to about 70% of the size found in Lindsay's OCT, has now turned his attention to the text of Virgil – *quod numquam veriti sumus*. At the time of this writing, Zwierlein has just published the prolegomenon to his study, so this will not be the place to respond in full. Cramer, however, gives us a preview, following

---

[61] Perkell (1981) 203–10.

[62] Some of this material is taken from my review of Cramer in Thomas (2000a).

[63] Cramer (1998) 3 "Eine besondere Schwierigkeit ergibt sich allerdings aus der Tatsache, dass die Textgrundlage keineswegs so sicher erscheint, wie man zumindest in diesem Jahrhundert bislang allgemein angenommen hat."

Zwierlein, in every instance it seems, bracketing in his index more than 200 lines of the *Georgics'* 2186 lines. I have already indicated where Zwierlein supports Peerlkamp and the other trimmers. His athetizing is not all ideologically based; just confining myself to *Aeneid* 1, he takes out, *inter alia*, the simile of the orator (144–56), the peplos goes from Dido's temple frieze (479–82) and the brilliant simile of Dido as Diana (498–504). These and hundreds of Virgil's best lines are fathered onto Julius Montanus in a study that is bizarre and grotesque.

I here confine myself to one of the newly athetized passages. Unbracketed (mistakenly) in Cramer's index, but now included among these "spurious" lines, are *Georgics* 3.525–47, containing the verses that Scaliger wished he had composed![64] The lines must go because they contain "three remarkably strange passages."[65] Again, we see the classicizing and normalizing of Virgil, who cannot be allowed to be "strange," but must be turned into a hyper-rational logician. But the real motive behind the removal of these lines, and of others so treated, is to Augustanize Virgil's poem, to make his *Weltsicht* more optimistic, and here we are back in the world of Nauck, Peerlkamp and Ribbeck. The end of *Georgics* 3, in particular the fate of the plough ox, the instrument of man's toil in the age of Jupiter, may also be seen as complicating, correcting and even indicting the idealized fictions of the ending of Book 2, the praise of the happy farmer, a passage which has always occupied Augustan or optimistic readers of this poem, to the exclusion of most others.[66] That passage began with a contradiction of the "theodicy," that is with the poet's asserting that the land of its own accord pours forth an easy provision for the farmer (2.459–60 *quibus ipsa ... fundit humo facilem victum iustissima tellus* "for them the earth exceeding just of its own accord pours from the ground an easy sustenance").[67] Within this golden age setting, so

[64] Cramer (1998) 200–2.

[65] Cramer (1998) 201 "drei recht befremdliche Passagen."

[66] For the fictive status of the end of *Georgics* 2, and for its separation from the technical realities of farming, see Ross (1987) 109–48; Thomas (1988a) vol. 1 ad G. 2.458–540, 459–60, 469–71, 513–40. For unconvincing attempts to negate Virgil's poetics of fiction, and thereby normalize and familiarize him, see Jenkyns (1998) 308–10. On this see Thomas (2000a).

[67] Cf. 1.122 *haud facilem ... viam*, and 1.127–8 *ipsaque tellus | omnia liberius nullo poscente ferebat.*

clearly fictional in relation to the realities of the world of Jupiter and of toil, we find the farmer at ease, uninvolved with politics, luxury and warfare (2.458–66, 495–512); he has carefree rest (2.467 *at secura quies*) beside grottoes and living lake waters and valleys, with the gentle mooing of oxen inducing sleep beneath the trees (2.469–70 *speluncae vivique lacus, at frigida tempe | mugitusque boum mollesque sub arbore somni*), he eats the fruits of the trees, leaving banquets and wealth to the corrupt urbanite (2.500–12). He simply moves the earth with his plough, and so supplies the needs of family, oxen and *deserving* steers (2.515 *meritosque iuvencos*).

In short the fate of the ox at the end of the next book, at 3.525–30, can also be read as making a mockery of this dream of rural ease: as we saw, the ox too lived simply, on leaves and grass, not on banquets, nor did any care disrupt its sleep (3.530 *nec somnos abrumpit cura salubris*). But here in the real world of toil, such ethical and moral virtues will provide no protection from plague, and when plague comes, as it indubitably does in Virgil's poem, the ox derives no comfort from shady groves, pastures or crystal streams (3.520–2), its simplicity, its toil and its deserts are as nothing, its gentle mooing induces no sleep but rather resounds through the parched river-valleys and sloping hills, and now as herald of its death (3.554–5 *crebris mugitibus amnes | arentesque sonant ripae collesque supini*). No theodicy here. Toil itself is indicted in the climactic lines 525–6:

> quid labor aut benefacta iuvant? quid vomere terras
> invertisse gravis?

> What help its toil and its good deeds? What help that it turned
> the heavy earth with the plough?

We can ignore these lines, as many readers do, by forming their judgments of this poem from *Georgics* 2.458–540 alone; or we can, now with Zwierlein and Cramer, resort, even in 1998, to textual cleansing. As the latter has written of lines 3.525–47: "In all these cases we entertain with Zwierlein considerable suspicions against the authenticity not only in view of details but also in view of overall conception."[68] And what of the lines that contradict the gentle

---

[68] Cramer (1998) 202 "In allen diesen Fällen hegen wir mit Zwierlein erhebliche Bedenken gegen die Authentizität der Passagen, nicht nur im Blick auf Einzelnes, sondern auch im Blick auf den Gesamtgedankengang."

mooing (*mugitus*) of Book 2, namely the agonized bleating and bellowing of the dying animals at 3.554–5:

> balatu pecorum et crebris mugitibus amnes
> arentesque sonant ripae collesque supini.

The parched river banks and sloping hills resound with the
constant bleating and bellowing of the herds.

Zwierlein and Cramer will take care of that too: verses 554f. "seem to
be a subsequent interpolation."[69] All this activity demonstrates yet
again what is at stake for the Augustan reader of Virgil. It remains to
be seen how many will be convinced by this athetizing renaissance;
not too many, I would imagine.

---

[69] Cramer (1998) 198 n. 767 "scheinen nachträglich eingefügt."

7

Virgil in a cold climate: fascist reception

The new spirit, to which the future belongs, finds its origin in the Orient and is the deadly enemy of pure Hellenism.

U. VON WILAMOWITZ-MOELLENDORFF,
Hellenistische Dichtung I (Berlin 1924) 2

The Hellenic ideal of culture should also remain preserved for us in its exemplary beauty ... The struggle that rages today is for very great aims. A culture combining millenniums and embracing Hellenism and Germanism is fighting for its existence.

A. HITLER, *Mein Kampf* (Munich 1925) 423

- We believe in the future of the Germans.
- We know that the German has powers which designate him to lead the community of the occidental nations towards a more beautiful life.
- We acknowledge in spirit and in deed the great traditions of our nation which, through the amalgamation of Hellenic and Christian origins in the Germanic character, created western man.

COUNT CLAUS SCHENK VON STAUFFENBERG,
from *Stauffenberg's Oath*, some days earlier in the
month of his failed attempt on the life of
Hitler on 20 July 1944

Vietnam to Pasewalk

F. Serpa has written of Virgilian studies: "In studying this poet only through our own contemporary experiences, we run the risk of speaking too much of ourselves, indirectly, of our anguishes and our rationalizing schemes, and too little of him. It is a risk which certain modern critics, even intelligent and original ones, have not avoided."[1] This is quite true, but it is not a critical tendency confined to any place or any time, nor to any particular political or ideological outlook. In short it is far from being applicable only to oppositional or "post-Vietnam" reading, as the contemporary Augustans would like to think of it. For the dominant European reception of Virgil is always inextricably involved with the reception of Augustus. And this Augustan reception, which has endured and entrenched itself for two millennia, and which is threatened by the post-Vietnam reading, this too is a construction of certain political and cultural conditions. The violence of the response to Parry's fifteen-page article,[2] which detects sympathy on the part of an Italian poet for the early peoples of Italy as depicted in the *Aeneid*, has in particular to do with the widespread support, formed and intensified through the middle of the twentieth century, for the Augustan voice as the predominant one, and, in some cultures, as the only one capable of survival. When scholarship, translation, or pedagogy operates in the interests of states that project themselves as inheritors of Augustan and imperial Rome, the stakes are raised significantly, and the ideological commitment of Virgil to Augustus, and implicitly to subsequent European leader-cult, becomes a critical given, with potent implications.

The Augustan reading has always been a support to political authority and dominance, and the pervasiveness of this reading throughout much of the European reception of Virgil has always been a function of élitist, particularly scholarly, communities supporting the interests of the state, be it a monarchy or tyranny. In the 1930s and early 1940s the Augustan reading created an easy link between Virgil and contemporary leader-cult, with varying degrees of subtlety, as we shall see. When the tyranny ended, as occurred in Italy and Germany in 1945, the Augustan reading continued, without the *Zeitgeist* that had nourished it, and without a latter-day Augustus to connect from the third to the first empire. After 1945 Augustus was just Augustus, which perhaps explains the phenomenon of republication from 1945 to the early 1960s of a number of highly ideological classical writings, originally produced (generally from 1933 to 1942)

---

[1] Serpa (1987) 7: "Studiando qual poeta soltanto con le nostre esperienze di oggi, corriamo il rischio di parlare troppo di noi, indirettamente, delle nostre angosce e dei nostri artifici razionali, e poco di lui. È un rischio che alcuni dei critici moderni, anche intelligenti e originali, non hanno evitato."
[2] Parry (1963).

for use in national-socialist curricula. The idea of Europe, that is, outlasts those most intensive and brutal moments of European nationalism. The authors implicated in this period are Homer, Pindar, Plato, Cato, Caesar, Livy, and particularly Virgil, for Virgil has always been made to represent the idea of Europe. This, as we shall see, can only occur if we keep the focus on just a few lines of his poetry, and at the same time keep the leader, Augustus, in the front of the mind.

On the other hand, in the 1960s, the nationalistic and strongly Augustan Virgil was assailed, mainly in American scholarship, by scholars of the so-called "Harvard School", particularly R. A. Brooks, Wendell Clausen, Adam Parry, Michael Putnam, and others, all of whom in different ways explored "troubled" aspects of this poet.[3] It would become convenient for contemporary Augustan readers to identify this voice, anachronistically in most cases, with the voice of the Vietnam protester. This is a convenient rhetorical ploy, and if you can convince that (a) this means that the criticism in question is simply modern in its preoccupations, and therefore wrong; and that (b) the alternative outlook has some sort of direct and unmediated access to truths about Virgil's culture, thought, and poetic purpose, then you can declare victory.[4] For this reason any views undercutting the Augustan voice will best be labeled with the word "Vietnam."[5] Nor am I objecting altogether to that, since my own views, and those of *some* (but not all) of the non-Augustans, were very much formed by reading Virgil in the context of a culture troubled by the exercise of power in Vietnam. The pretense that our views are not formed by such experiences is a fiction. But the European reading, the Augustan reading, is as much a "modern" construction, with repeated layers

---

[3] Most of these works were soon anthologized by Commager (1966).

[4] E.g. Otis (1995) xii, n. 3 "I myself find the Aeneas of Putnam and, latterly, Mr. A. J. Boyle ['The Meaning of the Aeneid: A Critical Inquiry,' *Ramus* 1.1 and 2 (1972): 63–90, 113–51] to be a strange and most un-Virgilian kind of hero, a product not of the Augustan poet but of the Vietnam War and the New Left."

[5] So Calder (1995), reviewing T. Ziolkowski (1993): "For telling criticism of American attempts to adapt Vergil to Vietnam protests add a reference to Antonie Wlosok, etc." Although Wlosok and Ziolkowski both discuss Parry and others, neither of them mentions Vietnam. What is "telling", on the other hand, is what Ziolkowski does say: "[From Gide to Connolly to Lowell to Broch] the writers of the 1920s and 1930s were fascinated by that ambivalence in Virgil's view of humankind that was subsequently defined by Adam Parry in his well-known essay on Virgil's 'two voices'" (238) – the reviewee thus refutes the reviewer! Neo-conservatives are perhaps more obsessed by Vietnam than the residual resisters to that war now to be found in the academy.

added over time, as the modern constructions from which it claims to be exempt.[6]

The post-Vietnam, oppositional American reading was in fact in place before that Asian war nurtured an uneasiness with empire and the abuse of power, well before it did so, as we shall see in the next chapter. Equally important, the oppositional reading flourishes a generation after the end of that war. It has in fact been my experience that younger, post-baby-boomer readers of Virgil, who have little empathy for, and even some hostility towards, the constructed romanticism of my own generation's formative years, are fully capable of reading Virgil as an intensely ambivalent author.

Here I look to the ideological reception of Virgil during the rise of nationalism, fascism, and National Socialism, through the end of World War II, and beyond. In the next chapter we will consider a competing reception, opposition to extreme nationalism and fascism, a cousin of opposition to the war in Vietnam. This too fits quite easily into our broader patterns, for there were other readers, significantly at the margins of Europe, who read Virgil as more recent non-Augustan readers would read him. A survey and assessment of the twentieth-century reception of Virgil may be found in an article by S. J. Harrison, while T. Ziolkowski's *Virgil and the Moderns* is an excellent contribution to the study of reception, particularly literary reception, and particularly between the two wars.[7] The present chapter looks to some more out of the way evidence and is perhaps more focused on ideological issues.

W. M. Calder has claimed that "although generally foreign to Anglo-Saxon practice ... the tendency of Germans to elucidate ancient subjects as commentary on their own times is well known and

---

[6] It is also noteworthy that Johnson (1976) 11, whose own Virgil is probably as close as we get to a post-Vietnam one, and who coined the term "Harvard School," does not associate this group with that war, but rather with the European left, anti-fascism and post-WWII malaise: "[Brooks and Parry] seem not to be listening to Eliot but rather to the news from the Left Bank or to Auden's *The Age of Anxiety* [1944–6], that wild and scandalously neglected masterpiece that captures its era and outlives it. As critically sensitive as the critics of the rival school [Pöschl, Büchner, Klingner], these critics had read their Syme and their Taylor as closely as they read the front pages of their newspapers, and for them the value, much less the grandeur, of the Roman Empire was not taken for granted. For them Pöschl's version of the 'Augustan idea of Rome,' whether inside or outside Vergil's poem, was utterly problematic."

[7] Harrison (1990) 1–20; Ziolkowski (1993) *passim*.

probably a sign of health if not carried too far."[8] And yet the same author, in a review of Ziolkowski's *Virgil and the Moderns*, while applauding (as do I) that author's focus on reception rather than hermeneutics, only allows such focus if that reception produces the "right" meaning.[9] The other meaning is of course to be rejected, along with the cultural setting that "constructs" it, that is. Never mind that neither Ziolkowski nor Wlosok, unlike the reviewer, uses the word "Vietnam" in the pages to which we are referred; what is more telling is the fact that an extreme Augustan reception of Virgil, such as entrenched itself in continental Europe in the middle of the century, is still treated as the default in most traditionalist classical circles. On the other hand, any interpretation that is in part conditioned by a response from the political left will likely be rejected out of hand.

> *"Who reads Virgil these days?"*
> *("You don't want to know!")*

"In 1926 Ernst Robert Curtius sadly affirmed the depressing truth of a skeptical commentary in the *Frankfurter Zeitung* that asked, 'Who reads Virgil today?' ('Wer liest heute Vergil?')."[10] The implied response to his question may have been in part due to the low esteem in which Virgil was held, particularly in the eyes of prominent German classicists of his day, notably the Hellenist Ulrich von Wilamowitz-Moellendorff, who had no great interest in Latin poetry,[11] and next to none in Virgil. He seems not to have studied Latin poets in any way that he remembered either at his beloved *Schulpforte* with its intensive classical curriculum, or at university (Bonn or Berlin).[12] For Wila-

---

[8] Calder (1985) 87–8.
[9] A. Wlosok is frequently evoked as the great bulwark against Parry and the so-called "Harvard School," whose misbegotten anachronisms and hopeless modern sensibilities she is felt to have routed. But I never was too impressed!
[10] So Ziolkowski (1993) 79.
[11] See Schmidt (1985) 369–70; Wilamowitz' letter to Norden is chiefly concerned with metrics. One non-bimillennial piece is Wilamowitz (1885), on the Clitumnus, from the *laudes Italiae*, his translation of which he dusted off, and altered (see below) for the bimillennium. The (unconscious) disservice to Latin studies caused by figures like Wilamowitz has not yet been fully revealed.
[12] I find no reference to Virgil in his account of these periods in his memoirs (Wilamowitz [1928]). His control of details about Virgil's poem is quite weak; see Horsfall (1988a) 129 for some examples.

mowitz, as for many German classicists, Virgil offered only a pale imitation of that "Hellenic" spirit that was so fundamentally a construction of German romanticism and came to be tied up with Prussian and German nationalism in the century before and the decades following the Treaty of Versailles: "Goethe," Wilamowitz claimed tellingly if incorrectly of Virgil, "does not seem to have mentioned him at all. Of course, he is always read in prep-schools; but surely very few have gained from him a lasting influence on their lives" (116).[13] The young Wilamowitz may have been bullied out of any independent interest in Virgil by the bizarre views on this poet expressed in the lectures of his future father-in-law Mommsen, by whom he was so inspired, and to whom, in the words of his student Eduard Fraenkel, he "swore allegiance" at the age of 25. Mommsen strongly disapproved of the *Aeneid*'s concerning itself with "a rather vulgar erotic motive, the love between Dido and Aeneas," as he did of the transformation of the Homeric Hector into "the jealous lover Turnus," finding that "only when Virgil lauds the new imperial government does a warmer tone emerge."[14] This is worthy of his view of the lyric genius of Horace: "Less outstanding [than the *Ars Poetica*] are the actual Odes, which however include some very beautiful poems, e.g., the *Carmen Saeculare*[!]."[15]

As Theodore Ziolkowski has impressively demonstrated, Curtius's question applied only to Virgil in Germany at this time. In Italy, France, England and the United States Virgil between the wars was enjoying a varied and rich reception. Ziolkowski quotes a German scholar to confirm this fact: "Virgil has remained truly alive only in the Romance countries."[16] In Italy that may be due in part to Dante, but it is also the case that Virgil had occupied a central place, in education as in letters, in England and France, particularly in the sixteenth and seventeenth centuries. Whatever the reason, the living

---

[13] See Calder (1988) 116, n. 3 for the correction.

[14] For which see a more skeptical ("we hear with some surprise") Ehrenberg (1965) 623–4: Mommsen thought the deeper meaning of the Dido episode was that in a refined nation a woman would not be willing to fall into the hands of foreigners ("Barbaren")! Those who favor Ovid over Virgil will find no comfort here: he thought that poet's work (the *Amores* and *Ars Amatoria* excepted) to be no more than "learned doggerel."

[15] For this, and for the translation of Mommsen's lecture notes, see Armstrong and Calder (1994) 89–90.

[16] Ziolkowski (1993) 90, citing Hanns Heiss.

influence of Virgil is constant in these cultures throughout recent centuries, and particularly in the early part of the twentieth.[17]

In contrast, as Curtius affirms, the Virgil of Germany between the wars was by and large a school text at best and a limited object of classical scholarship, rather than a dynamic force in the culture of the vernacular. There would be exceptions, some strange, like Theodor Haecker's bimillennial *Virgil. Vater des Abendlands* (1931), "rapidly translated into English (1934), French (1935), Dutch (1942), and Spanish (1945); widely reviewed; and influential ... in the works of T. S. Eliot and Hermann Broch."[18] But by and large Curtius was right to single out German neglect of Virgil. In spite of such neglect, there may be a more depressing response than the one implied in Curtius's question, a response that leads us away from professional classicists and into unexpected and troubling places. C. Riess, for instance, knew of a young student who was reading our poet:[19]

> He buried himself in the study of Latin and Greek, avidly read
> Cicero and Virgil, happily escaped into the fascinating beauty
> of foreign languages, into the grandiose adventures of heroes
> who enacted deeds of physical prowess, feats from which he, a
> cripple, would forever be barred.

After the Great War, Paul Joseph Goebbels, as he then called himself, having attended the Gymnasium in his native Rheydt in the Rhineland, drifted around in eight different universities. He studied History and Literature, particularly Goethe, at Bonn, studied Winckelmann at Freiburg, was at Heidelberg, Cologne, Frankfurt, Berlin, Heidelberg again, Munich, and again at Heidelberg.[20] And it was amidst the romantic beauty of Heidelberg that he went on to produce a 1921 doctoral dissertation entitled *Wilhelm von Schütz als Dramatiker.*

---

[17] Ziolkowski's table of contents (vii) makes the point: along with the "German Bimillennialists," for the Continent we have treatments of the "French Bucoliasts," "The Italian Hermeticists," for England "The *Eclogues* Parodied," "The Modern Georgicists," and "The *Aeneid* Ironized," to name a few sub-headings, and for the New World, "The Political Eclogue," "Virgil with a Southern Accent," and "*Aeneas Americanus.*"

[18] Ziolkowski (1993) 49.

[19] Riess (1948) 5.

[20] Riess (1948) 6.

Ein Beitrag zur Geschichte des Dramas der romantischen Schule.[21] It is a work written on the suggestion of Friedrich Gundolf, whose seminar Goebbels attended, and under the direction of Max Freiherr von Waldberg. Both scholars were Jewish and the former was one of the period's leading literary critics, and chief spokesman and biographer of one of the great oddities of this odd age, Stefan George.[22] Goebbels will have had no access to the *Georgekreis* itself, and was eventually rejected by Gundolf, but he was surely infected by the aestheticism of his teacher: "Goebbels, attending Gundolf's lectures on the German Romantics, was completely captivated by the strange spell which emanated from the works of the Schlegel brothers, of Tieck, Novalis, and Schelling. He became submerged in a world of a hundred years ago."[23] The introduction of the dissertation (available in the library at the University of Heidelberg) connects the spirit of contemporary times with that of early German Romanticism, insisting on reading the past in terms of its applications to contemporary events, and it does so in ways that place history utterly at the service of the *Zeitgeist*:

> But I believe that in literary history as well there is apart from
> the purely historical also a historical-pedagogical method of
> analysis, and in its application an affectionate investigation of
> the small and the smallest authors is absolutely necessary. By a
> historical-pedagogical method of analysis I understand a way of
> treating literature which not only proceeds from the purely
> historical, i.e. to explore how it actually "must have been," but
> in addition also from the standpoint of education for our age.
> Education in this sense does not have to do with trivial notions
> of pedagogy. A historical-pedagogical method of analysis should
> teach us to grasp our age and its spiritual currents in the middle
> of which we stand, should open our eyes to all that proceeds
> around and in us, in short should educate us into modern

---

[21] He received the doctorate on April 21, 1922. After he became Reichsminister for Propaganda official references, including the propagandistic biographies, used a more grandiose, ideologically charged title, *Die geistig-politischen Strömungen der Frühromantik*, cf. Reiss (1948) 8.

[22] Though Gundolf (real name Gondelfinger), like many academics, some even after 1933 (e.g. F. Jacoby), regarded himself as being German rather than Jewish; see Hoffmann (1995) 313, n. 22.

[23] Riess (1948) 8; cf. also Manvell and Fraenkel (1960) 17.

thought. It should provide a connection between the spiritual currents of previous centuries and those of our age. In the spiritual life of our ancestors we should recognize our own virtues and our own failings. Whoever reads the following pages attentively will be able to determine that while they scorn blatant indications of the fact they are written in that spirit.

The spirit of our time and that of early Romanticism are brothers, conceived of the self-same father and brought into the world by the same mother. Both have the same eyes, the same hair-color and the same appearance. But neither one nor the other can boast of being the firstborn.[24]

The biological metaphor is chilling in the light of subsequent events, although Goebbels' anti-Semitism seems to have grown over the years, particularly, perhaps, following the rejection of his manuscript of the novel *Michael* by the Jewish publishing house Ullstein.[25] The introduction to the dissertation shows more than a sense of repeated patterns over time. A creature of his world, Goebbels clearly saw an unbroken spiritual continuity between his own situation and that of early German Romanticism. The connection from there back to

---

[24] Goebbels (1923) 10–11 "Aber ich meine, daß es auch in der Literaturgeschichte neben der reinhistorischen noch eine historisch-pädagogische Betrachtungsweise gibt, und bei ihrer Anwendung ist ein liebevolles Eingehen auch auf die Kleinen und Kleinsten unbedingt erforderlich. Unter einer historisch-pädagogischen Betrachtungsweise literarischer Probleme verstehe ich die Art, Literatur zu betrachten, welche nicht allein vom Standpunkte des Rein-Historischen ausgeht, d.h. zu erforschen, wie es dann nun eigentlich 'Gewesen sei', sondern daneben auch vom Standpunkte des Erzieherischen für unsere Zeit. Erzieherisch in diesem Sinne hat nichts mit dem platten Begriff Pädagogik zu tun. Eine historisch-pädagogische Betrachtungsweise soll uns lehren, unsere Zeit und ihre geistigen Strömungen, in der und in denen wir mitten inne stehen, zu erfassen, soll uns die Augen öffnen für Alles, was um und in uns vorgeht, kurz, soll uns zu modernem Denken erziehen. Sie soll eine Verbindung schaffen zwischen den geistigen Strömungen vergangener Jahrhunderte und denen unserer Zeit. In dem Geistesleben unserer Ahnen sollen wir uns selbst wiedererkennen, unsere Tugenden und unsere Fehler. Wer die nachfolgenden Blätter aufmerksam durchliest, wird feststellen können, daß sie, äußerlich zwar jeden lauten Hinweis verschmähend, in diesem Sinne geschrieben sind.

Der Geist unserer Zeit und der in der Frühromantik sind Brüder, vom selben Vater gezeugt und von derselben Mutter zur Welt gebracht. Beide haben dasselbe Auge, die gleiche Haarfarbe und die ähnliche Haltung. Aber weder der eine noch der andere kann sich rühmen, der Erstgeborene zu sein."

[25] Cf. Manvell and Fraenkel (1960) 19–30 on *Michael* in general, and 24–5 on the possibility that the novel's anti-semitic material may have been interpolated after the initial rejection, and prior to publication in 1929 by Eher Verlag, a Nazi publishing house.

classical antiquity was the most natural and easy to make, as the
Romantics had themselves made it, and it is a connection that would
become profoundly troubling as the turbulent events of the 1920s and
30s took their course.

Goebbels studied both Greek and Latin in Rheydt, shining in the
latter.[26] His authorized biographer wrote of his school years:[27]

> His love of Latin was especially characteristic; the clarity and
> logic of this language appealed especially to the young student.
> Cicero's orations on Catiline interested him greatly.

It was these speeches, according to Bade (who consulted with
Goebbels in writing this book), that taught Goebbels the power of
oratory as a political tool. The claim gains credibility from a speech
Goebbels gave two years before Hitler came to power, which took
its title, "Wie lange noch, Catilina?" (28 February 1931) from the
opening of the First Catilinarian oration. Cicero's harangue aimed at
driving Catiline from Rome is converted into a virulent piece of Nazi
anti-Semitism, urging evacuation of German Jews who "abuse our
hospitality in Germany" ("die in Deutschland unsere Gastfreundschaft
mißbrauchen").[28]

And what of his Virgil? During World War I Goebbels watched
German troop transports crossing the Rhine and heading for the
French front, from which his own disabilities kept him, all the while
deeply affected, it was later claimed, by the heroic heaven of Cicero's
Somnium Scipionis, a set of images that imbued in him an image of
Germany's historical greatness and glory. In 1933 Max Jungnickel, a
Nazi propagandist and writer of highly nationalistic and militaristic
works, produced a "biography" of Goebbels, in which he is at pains
to bring out the Reichsminister's classical background and the application of that background to contemporary events. Of particular
interest is his chapter "The Shadow of Schlageter" ("Schlageters
Schatten").[29] Albert Leo Schlageter (1894–1923) was a World War I
veteran and fighter in the *Freikorps* in the Baltic, Poland and in

---

[26] Cf. Manvell and Fraenkel (1960) 9: in 1917 he got the highest grade "very good" in
Religion, German and Latin, with a "good" in Greek, French, History, Geography,
Mathematics and Physics.

[27] Bade (1933) 6; Heißer (1962) 6.

[28] Müller (1939) 85–7.

[29] For these details see Waite (1952) 237–8; 233–8 for a general account of Schlageter.

French-occupied Ruhr (1918–23), following the Armistice and the Treaty of Versailles. Holder of the Iron Cross first and second class, he was typical of the élite nationalist soldier of World War I, who immediately following that war looked to continue the struggle for the glory of Germany. He joined the NSDAP after meeting Hitler and hearing him speak in Munich in 1922, a fortuitous event for the Party. The next year he would be executed by the French for sabotage in the Ruhr, after blowing up a railway bridge. The Party did not miss this opportunity, and was swift in transforming Schlageter into the Protesilaus of Nazism, the first martyr of the cause: Hitler sent 70,000 SA and 70,000 Hitler Youth to attend his funeral; and on April 20, 1933, Hitler's birthday, Hanns Johst's propagandistic play, *Schlageter*, premiered and became "the first drama to proclaim and celebrate the Third Reich."[30] Goebbels in particular had a personal need for such a martyr, since "he could not do things, but he could talk about them."[31]

It is against this background, then, that Jungnickel has Goebbels translating and reading Virgil (in fact Schröder's translation):[32]

> Later he translates Virgil's *Georgics*, and he happens upon an image of those warlike German times as he reads:
>
> > Wells flowed with blood, and high built cities
> > resounded at night with the vile howling of predatory wolves.
> > Never did lightning appear so often as if from a clear sky,
> > Never did so many baleful comets appear in the heavens.[33]

The lines (G. 1.485–8) come from a passage describing the portents attending the death of Julius Caesar. Jungnickel continues: "For a long, long time he lingers over one small sentence, which suddenly

---

[30] Parkes-Perret (1984) 55.

[31] So Riess (1948) 19.

[32] I have been unable to determine how Jungnickel was able to attribute knowledge or translation of the *Georgics* to Goebbels. In a sense it does not matter whether the inspiration is that of Goebbels or his propagandist, just that a nazified *Georgics* becomes accessible to German classicists at least from the year 1933.

[33] Jungnickel (1933) 39 "Später übersetzt er Virgils 'Georgika' und stößt auf ein Abbild dieser kriegerischen deutschen Zeit, als er liest: Bronnen erflossen von Blut, und hocherbaute Städte | Schallten des Nachts vom schnöden Geheul raubgieriger Wölfe. | Nimmer geschah so oft ein Blitz aus heiteren Lüften, | Nimmer erschienen am Himmel so zahlreich grause Kometen."

rises before him like a heroic distress signal: 'They melt down the farmer's sickle into a sword.' "[34] The application of this line is utterly inverted by Goebbels (or rather by Jungnickel?). What for Virgil was a sign of calamity, a censuring of a world immersed in civil war, is in the eyes of the future Reichsminister for Propaganda a clarion call to heroic arms. Quoting with an eye exclusively on contemporary contexts is a feature of these times.

Goebbels is next linked to Virgil in Bochum, where, after completing his studies in Heidelberg,

> "in a gloomy, foul-smelling hallway, [he] thinks at once of Virgil. And he must repeat softly to himself the lines from the *Georgics*:
>
>> And indeed the time will some day come, when a man hunting in those fields, moving the clods with probing plough, will come upon shields eaten away by foul rust, and when he buries his hoe knocks against empty helmets in the ground.
>
> As he steps out into the street, the bugles ring out."[35]

The lines are those in which the farmer of the future is imagined digging up the buried helmets of the heroes who fell at Philippi.[36]

The final appearance of Goebbel's Virgil comes in Berlin, where Hitler appointed him as Gauleiter on October 26, 1926, the same year in which Curtius lamented that no one was reading Virgil. There Goebbels moved into the squalid rooms that served as NSDAP headquarters, the "opium den" ("Opiumhöhle") as they called it. Jungnickel again: "In the late evenings he sits in the 'opium cellar.' For recreation he reads in his tattered Virgil: 'Do not prevent him,

---

[34] Jungnickel (1933) 39 "Lange, lange hält er bei einem kleinen Satz, der plötzlich wie ein heroisches Notzeichen vor ihm aufragt: 'Sie schmolzen des Landmanns Sichel zum Schwert ein.' "

[35] Jungnickel (1933) 42: "In Bochum, in einem düsteren, stinkenden Hausflur, denkt Goebbels auf einmal an Virgil. Und er muss die Stelle leise vor sich hinsprechen, die Zeilen aus 'Georgika': 'Ja, und die Zeit kommt einst, da wird in jenen Gefilden | Jagend ein Mann, mit schürfendem Pflug die Scholle bewegend, | Schilde, von schäbigem Rost zerfressene, finden und stösst wohl, | Wenn er den Karst eingräbt, im Grund auf ledige Helme' (1.493–6). Als er auf die Strasse tritt, jubeln die Clairons."

[36] The 50 lines from the end of *Georgics* 1 are the only ones that Jungnickel has Goebbels reading (or translating).

the young man, come as savior of an uprooted world!' "[37] Hitler as Caesar, it seems, is the teleology in the triumph of ideology over history and in the crisis that was coming to its fruition.

Again, W. M. Calder III has claimed that "the tendency of Germans to elucidate ancient subjects as commentary on their own times is well known and probably a sign of health if not carried too far."[38] What is too far? Even before the war, E. M. Butler, a scholar of German literature, wondered whether the price paid by individuals in the creation of that strange phenomenon of German Hellenism was too high; her words are worth quoting, for they have implications beyond the suffering of German poets and philosophers, from Winckelmann to George, who are her subject:[39]

> In what other country would the discovery of serenity,
> simplicity and nobility in art have brought about such dire
> results? And where else would the name of the god Dionysus
> have had such a dreadful effect? Had Hinduism, with its strange
> glories and savage horrors, invaded Germany, could it have
> wrought more havoc than Olympianism with its radiant calm?
> The baffling quality of the Germanic temperament stares at us
> out of these questions. But one thing at least is certain: only
> among a people at heart tragically dissatisfied with themselves
> could this grim struggle with a foreign ideal have continued for
> so long. To an Anglo-Saxon mind it seems wasteful, deplorable
> and almost perverse that the beauty of Greek art and poetry
> should have caused so much frantic pain and so little pure
> pleasure. With the exception of Winckelmann none of the
> German Hellenists was really capable of the pagan attitude to
> beauty which Goethe assiduously cultivated and Heine vocifer-
> ously proclaimed. Objective, dispassionate contemplation was
> beyond their powers. They wished to seize and possess Greek

[37] Jungnickel (1933) 55 "Spät abends sitzt er noch im 'Opiumkeller'. Liest zur Erfrischung in seinem zerblätterten Virgil [G. 1.500–7, breaking off before 508 *hinc movet Euphrates, illinc Germania bellum!*]: Haltet ihn nimmer zurück, der jetzt entwurzelten Welten | Als ein Errettender kommt, den Jüngling! Wahrlich wir büßten | Übergenug Laomedons Schuld und Iliums Meineid! | Siehe, schon neidet uns dich die Burg der Himmlischen, Cäsar, | Dich und den menschlichen, armen Triumph, der deiner nicht wert ist. | Hier aber kehren sich Recht und Unrecht untereinander. | Greul und Gewalt ringsum! Längst mangelt aller geziemen | Frond' und Verehrung der Pflug. Wüst starrt von den Bauern verlassen | Anger und Feld."

[38] Calder (1985) 87–8.

[39] Butler (1935) 335–6.

beauty and make it their own; or to outdo it; or failing that to destroy it; or to drag it violently into the present; to unearth the buried treasure; to resuscitate the gods. Small wonder, in view of these violent and undisciplined desires, that the history of German Hellenism has such a painfully sensational side. One murder, one sudden death, two cases of insanity, another of megalomania; and the insidious disease of mythomania undermining nearly all; it is enough to make the merciful regret that Winckelmann was ever born.

The events of the decade following publication of Butler's book only give grounds for strengthening that regret. The extremes of German Romanticism and its formation and distortion of "Hellenism" and ancient heroism carry a great burden. The line from Winckelmann to Nietzsche and George, thence to Gundolf and Goebbels, would only need the ingredients of Hitler and certain political and economic conditions to reach their full potential.

Mussolini, bimillennialism and the American Classical League

But let us move to the year 1930, a year after Mussolini imposed censorship on all works of a political nature, and at about the same time Virgilio Fiorentino published the 20,000 lines of his 27-volume fascist epic, *Le Cantate della Rivoluzione*. Appreciation of pre-war fascism was, of course, not confined to Europe, as those familiar with the hate radio of Father Coughlin would attest.[40] In this same year, 1930, another American, Professor Ralph Van Deman Magoffin, then president of the American Classical League and a topographer of Praeneste, wrote a letter to Mussolini, congratulating the *Duce* on the bimillennium of Virgil's birth. In an article in the *New York Herald Tribune* he was at pains to establish the authenticity of the exchange, stating that he wrote

---

[40] Coughlin picked up on the burgeoning US anti-Semitism of the 1930s, in a post-depression climate which both allowed the economic disasters of those years to be laid at the door of Jewish industrialists, and also identified Jews as a chief component of Communism, his greatest obsession. In all it is hard to distinguish forms of anti-Semitism from the two sides of the Atlantic during this period, at least until rhetoric turned to action – something current US scholarship on notions of collective German guilt might well take into account. On Coughlin see most recently Warren (1996).

to Premier Mussolini, sending it through proper classical diplomatic channels, and enclosing it in a letter to Commendatore Gorham P. Stevens, director of the American Academy in Rome, who forwarded it through Comm. Roberto Paribeni, director general of Antiquities and Fine Arts of Italy.[41]

Paribeni transmitted the Duce's response to Magoffin, vouching for the genuineness of the handwriting and expressing his own belief in the sole authorship of Mussolini's sentiments. The American classicist then gave his own translation – he did not include the Duce's Italian, which, however, he identified as "written in the highly poetic vein of which he is such a master":

> When the strife of factions, the distraction produced by long periods of civil war, and, even more, the avid desire for immediate riches, had taken the Romans far away from the fields, Virgil sang the love for harvests and for flocks, the supplication of the earth which bore the seed, the miracle of the branch that puts forth the first buds of the spring time.[42]
>
> Then, after having sung of the soil, he sung of Heroes. By making illustrious the origin and the eternal destiny of Rome, by giving to the Romans their national poem, he brought them to a consciousness of their high estate and of their greatness, thus fulfilling the highest duty of the poet, that duty which transcends all others.
>
> Love for his country and love for his countrymen: the two great loves of Virgil are the bases of that spiritual movement that we have called *Fascismo*. It is for this reason that Virgil lives and will live – through the millennia – in the soul of the Italian people.
>
> Mussolini

This is, of course, but one of numerous such openly political appropriations of Virgil made in the year which Magoffin, Mussolini, and most others thought to be the bimillennium of the poet's birth.[43] The celebration was pervasive and thoroughly charged with contemporary political meaning, and Virgil was made to share actively in that tradition.[44]

[41] Magoffin (1930).
[42] Mussolini seems to conflate the *Eclogues* and *Georgics* into a single stage.
[43] See Horsfall (1987) 146.　　[44] See Ziolkowski (1993) 18–19; 90–1.

236

Wilamowitz and bimillennialism

Similar reactions were occurring throughout the classically engaged world, including Germany, and a notable example was produced by Wilamowitz. In spite of his views of the poet, in the year 1930, the penultimate year of his life, Wilamowitz did publish in the journal *Deutsche Rundschau* a tribute to Virgil's bimillennium, recently translated by W. M. Calder III – a good service to Virgilian studies.[45] Wilamowitz found the task difficult.[46] He also made several errors of a nature he would have derided in a critic of Greek literature, and which confirm his essential ignorance of this poet.[47] The focus is squarely on Virgil as a national poet, connecting to twentieth-century nationalism, and not much dissimilar from that of Mussolini:

> For the Italy of the Risorgimento, Dante was the prophet of
> *Italia una*. Now the breasts of Italians swell when they think
> of the power and glory of Augustan Rome – whose poet is
> Vergil. Fortunate the people who possess such a national poet
> and know how to draw from the memory of a great past
> strength and hope for the present![48]

The similarities are hardly surprising given that the extreme nationalism at the heart of Italian fascism and German National Socialism coincides, even if accidentally, with the nationalism and militarism of figures such as Wilamowitz, the Prussian aristocrat.[49] Another excerpt of Wilamowitz leads in a somewhat different direction:

> The name by which people called Vergil was Maro, which
> means something like "village mayor," *Schulze*, probably an
> Etruscan word, and Mantua was an Etruscan foundation, but
> that does not necessarily mean that Vergil was of Etruscan
> descent. It would not matter anyway, for he always felt himself
> to be an Italian and his father was a Roman citizen.

---

[45] Calder (1988).

[46] Calder (1977) 290.

[47] For these see Horsfall (1988a).

[48] Calder (1988) 127. See Faber (1983) 244 for an interpretation of Wilamowitz's words with the troubling events of the times.

[49] Canfora (1977).

Calder, who admits "there is something odd about the essay," says of the Etruscan reference: "His view that it does not matter if Vergil was part Etruscan because he thought of himself as Italian reminds us that Wilamowitz knew he was part Polish but it did not matter for he always thought of himself as wholly Prussian."[50] It is true that Wilamowitz is throughout fashioning a Virgilian experience which resonates with his own (particularly on the education of Virgil), but let us not move on too quickly from the denial of Virgil's Etruscan ancestry, which I would see at the very least as one of the "oddities" of the essay, whether its apparent racism has to do with Prussian attitudes to the Poles, or more general Occidental attitudes to the Orient.[51]

Even before 1930 there had been a fascination in Germany with the racial origins of the Etruscans, and it would be only a few years after Wilamowitz's essay that the SS's "Research and Teaching Institute for Ancestral Heritage" ("Das Ahnenerbe"), with the support of the ancient historian Franz Altheim and other classicists, would be considering such questions as examination of the "non-Nordic Etruscan" infiltration of the (Aryan) Roman racial purity.[52] And the author of the Pauly-Wissowa article on "Tyrrhener" (published half-complete in 1943) could discuss the origins of the Etruscans in terms of the shape of their noses![53] It would only be a decade after the death of Wilamowitz that the outcomes of this racism would begin to become clear, and we must be constantly wary of anachronism, but we must also accept the pervasiveness of the attitudes that were gathering force in these years, and should not ignore the fact that state-sponsored "research" carried out by classicists, and particularly

---

[50] Calder (1988) 113.

[51] Compare Schadewaldt's insistence, in 1931, that Oriental features of the fourth Eclogue, which has to be a prophecy for the West, are only a literary motif, "orientalisch nur das literarische Motiv"; (1963) 498–519. This is clearly a response to the thesis of the Jewish scholar, Eduard Norden (1924, repr. 1931), to which Wilamowitz alluded in his 1930 Virgil essay: "Vergil has hid behind a Sibylline Oracle. Hence Jewish Messianic hopes, Egyptian and Oriental speculations are drawn upon"; Calder (1988) 118.

[52] See Dietz (1984) 257–8; also Canfora (1977).

[53] Brandenstein (1943/8) 1917 "they are part of the subspecies from Asia Minor, which had a bony hooked nose (not the fleshy 'six-shaped nose'[!])" ("Vermutlich kamen sie vom Schwarzen Meer her. Ihre Rasse spricht dafür; denn sie gehören der vorderasiatischen Rasse an, und zwar jener Abart, die eine scharfknochige Hakennase besitzt [nicht die fleischige Sechsernase]"). Cf. Calder (1981) 168: "Publications of the period favored approved topics ... [But] most scholars continued writing RE articles." A word-searchable RE would perhaps be revealing.

ancient historians, played some part in strengthening the intellectual underpinnings for Germany's step into the abyss of racism and genocide. Rosenberg and the geneticists were not working in a vacuum.

Although the Germans could not use Virgil quite as Mussolini had done, the *Nibelungen*, which Wilamowitz says "would not exist without the *Aeneid*" (Calder [1988] 115), would partly fill the bill, with or without Wagner.[54] The major enthusiasm German Romanticism allowed for the artificial and secondary Virgil, other than noting the perfection of his style, appears precisely in its admiration for him as a national poet.[55] This admiration increased and progressed in Germany through the middle of the twentieth century, and has never abated: in Germany and in the outlook of those who inherited the nationalistic tradition after the war, the Augustan Virgil has hardly been doubted or questioned.[56] And of course Virgil could be used as a conduit for the spirit of Hellenism, again as constructed by German Romanticism; so, Wilamowitz: "The Roman national epic is an *Aeneid*. The hero derives from Greek saga. It fills the first half almost entirely; in addition the battles on Italian soil are full of episodes of Greek origin; even the names of the warriors on the Trojan side at least, are Greek" (Calder [1988] 120).[57]

Virgilians owe a debt to T. Ziolkowski for his fascinating and learned study *Virgil and the Moderns*, which for our purposes is of particular interest for its pages on Theodor Haecker and German bimillennialism. Haecker's *Vergil. Vater des Abendlands*, published in 1931 (English translation 1934), focuses on the Fourth *Eclogue* from a perspective of extreme, naive, and anachronistic Roman Catholicism. In Haecker's book, and in the work of others of this period, we can see the Christianized Virgil of the Middle Ages, based in Tertullian's *anima naturaliter christiana*, emerging in a world which had recently been the Holy Roman Empire, whose secular successor was Bismarck's Second Empire. This Christian Virgil of German Catholicism is also akin to the Virgil of the Third Kingdom, a concept that

---

[54] See also Schaefer (1936) 205 "[die Aeneis] hat unser mittelhochdeutsches Epos ebenso erst ermöglicht wie das Waltharilied."

[55] See Ziolkowski (1993) 23–6.

[56] An exception is Suerbaum (1981), with further bibliography of his other contributions. See Faber (1983) 248–56 ("Semper Idem") on the unchanging pre-war and post-war situation. I have generally profited from reading the work of Faber.

[57] This is an important strategical step: the Europeanizing of the Trojans.

appealed to German writers of the twenties and thirties, before the National Socialists appropriated and directed it into the distortions of the Third Reich.[58] Paradoxically, the Christian Virgil of Haecker, who was one of the bravest opponents of National Socialism, and the nationalistic Virgil of Mussolini and Wilamowitz become difficult to distinguish, particularly in their focus on the cult of the leader – though the identity of the leaders in question is another matter. So W. Eberhardt in *Nationalsozialistische Monatshefte* for 1935 uses Haecker's book to argue that "political Catholicism has in combination with fascism constructed National Socialism. Rome is the center of both powers."[59]

None of the bimillennial or nationalist works on Virgil bothers with many details of his poetry, and they all tend to focus on these same passages, the "usual suspects," often in utterly tendentious or otherwise peculiar ways. There is little consideration of anything outside the so-called *laudes Italiae* from the *Georgics*; from the *Aeneid* Jupiter's prophecies about Rome from Book 1, Anchises on the characterization of the Romans in Book 6, and Vulcan's depictions on the shield of Aeneas in Book 8. In particular it is almost mandatory for these works to cite *Aeneid* 6.851–3 *tu regere imperio populos, Romane, memento* . . . In Italy we find a particular use of the *Georgics* to get the Italian farmer back on the land, reinforced with newsreels of the Duce swinging the scythe.[60] But it is the vague, unexamined nationalism of Virgil that creates the overriding impression. Wilamowitz, for instance, in 1930 demonstrated his appreciation of Virgil's nationalism by quoting his own 1885 translation of *Georgics* 2.136ff. – with an enthusiastic footnote: "We Germans, in whose blood lies the longing for this land, enthusiastically share his feelings. How much stronger must the passion of a native son be!" He omits some interesting lines from Virgil concerning Italy, including references to the fictional absence of snakes and poison, and, tellingly, the references to the earthworks that keep the (indignant) Tuscan sea out. But most importantly he omits Virgil's final climactic salute to Italy as a Saturnian (peaceful) land: 173–4 *salve magna parens frugum, Saturnia tellus,* |

---

[58] Ziolkowski (1993) 89; also below, pp. 247–52.
[59] Eberhardt (1935) 125 "Politischer Katholizismus hat ihn in Verein mit dem Faschismus aufgebaut. Beider Mächte Zentrum ist Rom."
[60] Foss (1998) 308, with bibliography.

magna virum "hail great parent of crops, Saturnian world, great parent of men." In 1930 the age of Jupiter, the age of iron, is more in the air, it would seem, and so it is that the climax and new conclusion in Wilamowitz's *laudes Italiae*, unlike Virgil's, leaves the focus on Caesar's crushing the unwarlike Indian, a reference which bothered Servius, but seems to have evoked the Prussian enthusiasm of Wilamowitz:

> und du,
> der Grossen Grösster, Caesar, der als Sieger
> an Asiens Rande jetzt den weichen Inder
> zurückscheucht von des Römerreiches Grenzen.

In a note to his translation of the Wilamowitz essay, Calder refers to the *Georgics* passage as "a shortened version with two minimal changes of his translation of 1885 at *Reden* 347–349."[61] Notably the 1885 version indeed included the Saturnian coda:

> Sei mir gegrüsst, Saturnus' heilige Erde,
> du Mutter reichster Früchte in Feld und Wald,
> Mutter von Männern ...

Wilamowitz obviously made a conscious decision to exclude Virgil's peaceful finale from his 1930 publication. H. Dietz has pointed out that "National Socialist ideology was not completely novel but had been prepared before through decades of German nationalism and racism in Germany's élite," and further that "Wilamowitz, soldier in the Franco-Prussian war of 1870–1871, who lost a son in World War I, gave German classics and ancient history through his strong authority a patriotic if not nationalistic characteristic."[62] This is the context in which Wilamowitz would finally read and write on Virgil.

Hans Oppermann[63]

Hans Oppermann was one of the more eager classical supporters of National Socialism, and he was also a Virgilian. He was the author of

---

[61] Calder (1988) 125, n. 12.
[62] Dietz (1984) 256, with further bibliography.
[63] My MS was completed in draft when I saw Malitz (1998), an excellent study of Oppermann's whole oeuvre and actions.

an intensely anti-Semitic 1943 manual for use in the NSDAP[64] entitled *Der Jude im griechisch-römischen Altertum*,[65] a work whose date,
readership, and contents provide a direct link between classical studies
in Germany and the thinking behind the extermination of the Jews.
Oppermann's research blatantly set out to "prove" the superiority of
the Germanic and Nordic races, along with the inferiority of other
races, particularly the Semitic. He particularly believed in the connection between literature and politics, and in his writing on Plato
and on the Augustan poets identified the voice of such authors with
that of the state. It was the duty of the scholar to work on these authors in ways that would contribute to the "great spiritual awakening
of our nation" ("dem grossen Aufbruch unseres Volkes").

In the years leading up to the war, and as late as 1941, Oppermann
published a series of articles,[66] generally repetitious and intensely
ideological, all implicitly or explicitly presenting Rome as a paradigm
for the National Socialist state, particularly Rome from the battle of
Cannae to the defeat of Antony and Cleopatra at Actium, a defeat
which replays the fall of Carthage, openly functioning as a paradigm
for the victory of the Occident over the Orient.[67] Caesar, Livy, and
Virgil are the authors most readily mined, and Oppermann's titles
speak for themselves, as do the periodicals in which they are published: "Cäsar als Führergestalt" "Caesar as leader-type" (Oppermann
1934); "Altertumswissenschaft und politische Erziehung" "Classical
antiquity and political education" (Oppermann 1935); "Die Bevölkerungspolitik des Augustus" "The population policy of Augustus"
(Oppermann 1936); "Volk, Geschichte, Dichtung (Schiller und Vergil)" "Nation, history, poetry" (Oppermann 1937a); "Neuordnung
des höheren Schulwesens und Altertumswissenschaft" "Reform of
the higher educational system and classical studies" (Oppermann
1937b); "Die alten Sprachen in der Neuordnung des höheren Schulwesens" "The ancient languages in the reform of the higher educa-

---

[64] "Nur für Dienstgebrauch!" ("Only for Official Use!") reads the warning above the
cover's swastika and eagle.

[65] Oppermann (1943).

[66] Losemann (1977) 95.

[67] On the reception of the war with Carthage in this period, see the essays collected by
Vogt (1943); many of them are preoccupied with questions of race and racial difference,
particularly with the strength of the "northern" races.

tional system" (Oppermann 1938a); "Das römische Schicksal und die Zeit des Augustus" "The destiny of Rome and the age of Augustus" (Oppermann 1941).

Most of these pieces encode and imply a relationship between Germany and Rome, Hitler and Caesar or Augustus, but sometimes Oppermann is explicit, as at the end of the article ostensibly on Schiller and Virgil. He first notes that the former, alone among the classical German poets, translated Virgil; this was not entirely accidental since the two shared a bond in their ability to connect the historical spirit of the past to the mission of the future; both saw a higher power connecting the destiny of nations ("das Geschick des Volkes"). Then comes the transition and climax:

> In our life we also find the three components: the blood
> relationship of all members of the German nation, the mandate
> of the final fruition of national consciousness which constitutes
> the meaning of its 2000-year history, and the divine command-
> ment. For what occurred in the military hospital in Pasewalk in
> November 1918, and found expression in *Mein Kampf* in the
> simple words "But I resolved to become a politician," is nothing
> other than the bursting forth of such a mandate in the breast of
> the great man. From where else does a person take the power
> to comprehend, sustain and pursue such duties if not from
> above?[68]

In "Die Bevölkerungspolitik des Augustus" he begins with a quote from Hitler's book, elaborating on the claim that popularity must be an essential element of the creation of authority (*Mein Kampf* 579). He then assserts that this insightful and true principle of the Führer can find no better demonstration than in the history of Rome between the Gracchi and Augustus. There ensues discussion centering chiefly on Augustus, on his representing the idea of Rome in its struggles

---

[68] Oppermann (1937a) 81 "Auch in unserem Leben finden wir die drei Komponenten wieder: die blutsmässige Verbundenheit aller Glieder des deutschen Volkes, den Auftrag der endgültigen Volkwerdung, der sich als Sinn seiner zweitausendjährigen Geschichte ergibt, und das göttliche Gebot. Denn was sich im November 1918 im Lazarett zu Pasewalk abspielte und in 'Mein Kampf' mit den schlichten Worten ausgesagt wird: 'Ich aber entschloß mich, Politiker zu werden', – es ist nichts anderes als das Aufbrechen solchen Auftrages in der Brust des grossen Menschen. Woher nähme auch ein Mensch die Kraft, solche Aufgaben zu erkennen, zu tragen und durchzuführen, wenn nicht von oben?"

against the forces of oriental barbarism (Antony and Cleopatra), with due mention of the shield of Aeneas (117–18). Oppermann refers to Augustus' legislation, reform, and building programs as examples of the princeps' policies, with reflections on Augustan policy as "national-römisch" or better "national-italisch" (121), and there is a rather odd discussion of slavery, census-estimates, and the like, resonating with the Jewish census lists in his NSDAP manual. Discussion of race and racial mixing (128–9) leads to rumination about the importance of farming and the land. Sure enough, we eventually arrive at *Aeneid* 6.851–3 (*at tu, Romane* . . .), along with the *Odes* and *Carmen saeculare* of Horace, designated as "the representative expression of the national aspirations significantly indicated and interpreted in the work of art that was created."[69] Ultimately however, from the National Socialist perspective, and when compared to that system, the Augustan outlook is in Oppermann's vision still short of the perfection of National Socialism:

> So Augustus' population policy finds its limitations in the imperfect perception of the racial-biological foundations of the life of the nation, in the imperfect insight into the value of the peasantry, and in the lack of a truly extensive propaganda and national education system.[70]

After the war, in 1963, Oppermann edited a volume of essays on Virgil, published by the Wissenschaftliche Buchgesellschaft and of interest, he tells us, because they represent "three decades" of work on the poet.[71] This was still three years before the West Germans

---

[69] Oppermann (1936) 131 "der repräsentative Ausdruck dieses nationalen Wollens, das im gestalteten Kunstwerk sinnvoll ausgesprochen und gedeutet wird."

[70] Oppermann (1936) 133 "So findet die Bevölkerungspolitik des Augustus ihre Grenzen in der mangelnden Erkenntnis der rassisch-biologischen Grundlagen des Völkerlebens, in der mangelnden Einsicht in den Wert des Bauerntums und im Fehlen einer wirklich großen Propaganda und Volkserziehung."

[71] The entry on Oppermann in Kürschner (1980) 2815 lists his interests as "Roman literature, especially Caesar, Augustan period, reception of antiquity," to which could be added "by National Socialism" ("Röm. Literatur, bes. Caesar, August. Zeit, Nachleben d. Antike"). The biographical sketch at the beginning of his 1958 *Caesar: Wegbereiter Europas*, states that his work apart from that on Caesar treats "various subjects in Roman Literature" ("verschiedene Gegenstände der römischen Literatur"), while "other studies are directed to a more general public" ("Andere Abhandlungen wenden sich an ein allgemeineres Publikum").

elected the ex-NSDAP member Kiesinger as chancellor of West Germany, and in the context of relief brought by almost two decades of post-war life, a relief that would be shattered by the left-wing uprisings of a few years later. I am not aware of any review of Oppermann's volume, which, however, sold well enough to go to a second edition in 1976. The authors and articles chosen are of interest: of the sixteen, a quarter (Oppermann himself, E. Burck, H. Hommel, W. Schadewaldt) were members of Hans Drexler's *Lagerarbeit* group of loosely affiliated academics, whose group investigations were aimed at producing the new curricula. National Socialism was a given for this group as for others: "the National Socialist world-view (*Weltanschauung*) is no dogma, just obvious."[72] The only non-German piece is a translation of T. S. Eliot's "What is a Classic?" which fits fairly well into the new environment.[73] Oppermann's own contribution had come out in 1938, in the series *Auf dem Wege zum nationalpolitischen Gymnasium. Beiträge zur nationalsozialistischen Ausrichtung des altsprachlichen Unterrichts* – the series title is naturally omitted in the the 1963 volume.[74] As in his article on Schiller and Virgil, he concerns himself (more than does Virgil) with race mixing and world dominion. The cult of the leader is apparent: he finds that in Virgil's view the "highest manifestation is the heroic man who leads his people under command from above toward an understanding of their challenge which confronts the past and demands the future, with a will that voluntarily affirms that challenge, all temptations to the contrary, toward its destiny and promise."[75] After the war Oppermann taught in the famous Johanneum Gymnasium in Hamburg (rector 1954–61), where he presumably continued to instruct new generations on the subject of Virgil and Augustus.

---

[72] Losemann (1977) 97.

[73] On Eliot's relationship to fascism, see, with further bibliography, Morrison (1996), Ch. 3 "T. S. Eliot: The Poetics of Failure."

[74] Other works in this series were also republished after the war by the Wissenschaftliche Buchgesellschaft, either completely unchanged, in the case of Oppermann's Virgil, or with some alterations in the case of Drexler (1939); Drexler in particular removed racially oriented material. The series title page was dropped, of course, and it does not seem absurd to suggest that the motive of denazification was behind some of these republications.

[75] Oppermann (1938b) 176.

Another contributor to Oppermann's anthology was Walter F. Otto, head of the Frankfurter Schule der Religionswissenschaft and teacher of the ancient historian Franz Altheim, who became the chief ancient historian in the SS Institute for Ancestral Heritage ("Das Ahnenerbe").[76] Otto himself was more restrained, a devotee of Jaeger's "Third Humanism." Like Wilamowitz, he too was impressed by the *laudes Italiae*, and like Wilamowitz in 1930, he seems to have felt the need to alter Virgil's concluding salute to the peaceful *Saturnia tellus*. His solution was not to omit, but rather to invert the Virgilian ending *via* paraphrase: "I salute you, you great mother of produce, great mother of men [i.e. 173–4] ... who have produced the greatest stock, the greatest heroes and leaders, and you the unrivalled, Caesar" [i.e. 167–70].[77] False to the Virgilian model in a fundamental way, Caesar at war, not the land of Saturn, has become the climax.

Another of Oppermann's authors was the Hellenist and National Socialist booster, Wolfgang Schadewaldt, whose interpretations of Periclean Athens in particular show his eagerness "to elucidate ancient subjects as commentary on his own times."[78] He too, in his Virgil contribution of 1931, quotes *Aeneid* 6.851–3, toward the end of his article, which closes with a discussion of the Roman national spirit, Virgil's role in its formation, and some comments about the German connection (68): "Virgil's poetry is of value to us as the first classical accomplishment of the occidental soul. As such it must not be lost to the German."[79] These words can be read as drawing the parallel between Rome's and Germany's aspirations to world domination. As such they are representative of the subtle ways in which Virgil could be used in these years.

[76] Losemann (1977) 124 and 235 n. 51.

[77] Otto (1931) 78 "ich grüsse dich, du grosse Mutter der Fruchtbarkeit, grosse Mutter der Männer [i.e. 173–74] ... die die mannhaftesten Stämme hervorgebracht hat, die grössten Helden und Führer und den unvergleichlichen, dich, Caesar!" The skillful manipulation of this rewriting is apparent in the suggestion that "Männer" leads to "mannhaftesten," whereas in the Latin the two forms of *virum* are separated by six lines (167, 174).

[78] Näf (1986) 238.

[79] "Vergils Dichtung gilt uns als erste klassische Menschheitsleistung der abendländischen Seele. Als solche muss sie auch dem Deutschen unverloren bleiben."

The Stauffenbergs and Virgil in the secret Germany

As with Haecker, we also see an odd coincidence in attitude even in authors who have little sympathy with the régime. Also in Oppermann's volume is a piece by Count Alexander Schenk von Stauffenberg (Stauffenberg 1943), an ancient historian who dedicated the article to his teacher Wilhelm Weber.[80] Stauffenberg had given it as a lecture in Würzburg on February 23, 1941, and at the time of publication he was serving in the *Wehrmacht*. He was the brother of Claus von Stauffenberg, the leader of the failed conspiracy to blow up Hitler at the *Wolf's Lair* on July 20, 1944. Alexander was the only one of the brothers not to be killed by the National Socialists (he was in Athens at the time and not a party to the plot), though like many of the families of the conspirators he was imprisoned and spent the rest of the war in a concentration camp. He was no friend of National Socialism himself, and in 1937 he had been criticized by Walter Frank for paying insufficient attention to German national issues in his study of Theodoric,[81] who was important in the racial genealogies of National Socialism for "Aryanizing" the Italians. Nor are such things simply a matter of academic discussion. The year before the Wannsee conference consigned the Jewish people to extermination, Hitler himself could claim "the population of Rome had ended by acquiring a great esteem for the Germanic peoples. It is clear that there was a great preference in Rome for fair-haired women, to such a point that many Roman women dyed their hair. Thus Germanic blood constantly regenerated Roman society. The Jew, on the other hand, was despised in Rome."[82]

The strongly European and strongly Augustan Virgil, who was subtly enlisted by supporters of National Socialism, may also be enlisted by opponents of that régime whose obsessions with leader-cult survive their particular opposition to Hitler. Claus Stauffenberg, one of three brothers in this German aristocratic family, connected to the kings of Swabia, seems at first to have enthusiastically approved of Hitler's appointment as Chancellor in 1933.[83] However, he decided

---

[80] Losemann (1977) 79–85.   [81] Losemann (1977) 87–8.
[82] A. Hitler, 21 October, 1941, midday, in Trevor-Roper (1973) 78.
[83] Hoffmann (1995) 69.

by 1942 that the "foolish and criminal" Führer had to be over-thrown,[84] partly because of the disastrous handling of the war on the Eastern Front, where Stauffenberg served in a Panzer division (*Wehr-macht*), but also it seems because of the brutal and ruthless treatment of the Jews and the Poles, which he himself witnessed. But the Stauffenbergs, whose own personal Führer was the poet Stefan George (the "Master" as his circle called him),[85] were also for a strong and dominant Germany, and precisely for a Germany which con-nected well with the nationalistic Virgil who was nurtured by the Italian Fascists and bimillennialist enthusiasts. The brothers, and others of George's circle, had since they came under his influence in 1923 talked, dreamed, and written about the "Secret Germany."

It was Alexander Stauffenberg who in 1945 published *Der Tod des Meisters*, twelve years after the death of George. Claus there appears as "the war-god's lordly herald of the future world, | only enhanced by one eye's sacrifice" – he had lost an eye in battle (also his right hand and two fingers from the left). Claus Stauffenberg's *Oath* was written, with the help of the third brother Berthold, only days before July 20, 1944, the day on which he set the briefcase containing the bomb under the table in the bunker. The rest is well known: a heavy oak support protected Hitler, and by that night, Claus would lie dead, executed against a sand pile in the courtyard of the army headquarters on the Bendlerstrasse, his last words a defiant shout: "Es lebe das geheiligte Deutschland!" ("Long live holy Germany!").[86] It is worth printing the complete *Oath*, which relates to our larger topic:

Stauffenberg's Oath[87]

- We believe in the future of the Germans.
- We know that the German has powers which designate him to lead the community of the occidental nations towards a more beautiful life.

---

[84] Hoffmann (1995) 151.
[85] Hoffmann (1995) *passim*.
[86] See Hoffmann (1995) 355, n. 86 for variants reported by eyewitnesses, and for the strong possibility that Stauffenberg's adjective was not "geheiligte" but "geheime" ("Long live the Secret Germany!") – the Germany of the *Georgekreis*, that is.
[87] Hoffmann (1995) 293–4.

- We acknowledge in spirit and in deed the great traditions of our nation which, through the amalgamation of Hellenic and Christian origins in the Germanic character, created western man.
- We want a new order which makes all Germans supporters of the state and guarantees them law and justice, but we scorn the lie of equality and we bow before the hierarchies established by nature.
- We want a nation which will remain rooted in the soul of the homeland close to the powers of nature, which will find its happiness and its satisfaction in its given surroundings and, free and proud, will overcome the low passions of envy and jealous resentment.
- We want leaders who, coming from all classes of the nation, in harmony with the divine powers, high minded, lead others high-mindedly, with discipline and sacrifice.
- We unite in an inseparable community which through its bearing and actions serves the New Order and forms for the leaders of the future the fighters whom they will need.
- We pledge to live blamelessly
  - to serve in obedience
  - to keep silent unswervingly,
  - and to stand for each other.

The cult of the leader, the hostility to liberalism and democracy, and tacitly to Bolshevism ("the lie of equality"), with the insistence on natural hierarchies, the emphasis on militarism, and the combination of Hellenism and Germanism, with Germany as the ordained leader of the West, these are all characteristic of Stefan George's outlook, which, like the nineteenth-century Romanticism and nationalism that bred it, is in many details hard to distinguish from the system the drafters of the *Oath* aimed to replace.[88] George's belief in a New Order has its roots in the Holy Roman Empire and Bismarck's second Kingdom, and the term "Third Reich," in this historical sense, indicating a golden age of conservative Germanic revival, predates the National Socialist appropriation, which so deeply problematizes an already (differently) problematic concept. George himself

---

[88] Claus was a devout Catholic, which is doubtless the reason for the addition of "Christian" in the third item of the oath. See Hoffmann (1995) 41 for the observation that George's circle was open to Jewish friends before the mid-1920s, at which point it began to change, along with the times.

used a variant as the title for a collection of recent poems in 1928, *Das Neue Reich*.[89] In Stauffenberg's 1944 *Oath* the concept ("Die Neue Ordnung") also suggests continuities, in addition to the obvious discontinuities, with the Third Reich.[90]

George died on 4 December 1933. Although he despised Hitler as not being sufficiently noble or aesthetically fit to represent the new Caesar, his own outlook was not easy to distinguish from many of the nationalistic impulses of the new régime. Hoffmann discusses George's response to the Prussian Minister of Culture, Bernhard Rust, who on 5 May 1933 had tried to persuade the poet to accept a large sum of money and, more to the point, an honorary position in the Prussian Academy for the Arts:[91]

> Stefan George replied on 10 May, in a letter intended for the "attention of the appropriate government department." He refused the honorary position "in the so-called academy," and refused the money, but declared his approval of the academy's "national" orientation. He himself, he said, had administered German literature for half a century without any academy. On the positive side, he continued, he did not in the least deny his "ancestorship of the new national movement and did not preclude his intellectual cooperation."

It would remain to his followers, eleven years later and with the help of hindsight, to try and make the distinction that George could not. And to judge from Stauffenberg's oath, all of the nationalistic Germanism that helped fuel the atrocities of those years seems to have survived intact. As Hoffmann says of the *Georgekreis* after 1933, and after the death of George, "there was a persistent tension caused by similarities between the terminology of the esoteric sublimities of the Master's teaching and that used for the tenets of National Socialism."[92]

I am concerned with how Virgil fares in such a culture, one ostensibly contrary to the naked servility of Oppermann, for instance. It

---

[89] Generally for George's relationship with National Socialism, see Hoffmann (1995) 62–74.

[90] See Ziolkowski (1993) 87–9 for excellent treatment of this theme.

[91] Hoffmann (1995) 66. Earlier in the same year Jewish members, and various other political opponents, had been removed, among them Thomas Mann.

[92] Hoffmann (1995) 75.

is possible that only a strongly Augustan reading can emerge in such a ruler-oriented and anti-democratic culture. Alexander Stauffenberg reproduced the *Oath* in a post-war poem, "Vorabend" ("The Eve"), which only slightly misrepresents the proximity of the attempted coup to the drafting of the oath.[93] He dramatizes the oath by putting it in the responding voices of his dead brothers. He was bitter that they excluded him from the plot, and afterwards expressed the wish that he too could have died for the cause.[94] Stauffenberg's Virgil article in the Oppermann volume focuses on the usual selections of Virgil in the light of contemporary events. There is a powerful identification with the fourth *Eclogue* and with the troubled political circumstances which it reflects as well as with the dream of a new order inherited and elaborated by George. The article clearly refers to Stauffenberg's formative time in the *Georgekreis* – as a young man he wrote poems of a mystical/homoerotic nature to the old poet, which were later "found among Stefan George's papers, . . . folded and soiled at the folds: the poet must have carried them about with him for a long time."[95] Stauffenberg's Virgil article is, like much of the writing about Virgil in this period, preoccupied with the rulers of antiquity to whom Virgil seems to give access (again, Stauffenberg was an ancient historian). It is really about history, about Alexander the Great, Caesar and Augustus, and about world domination and the *duties* that go along with world domination – this last aspect distinguishing it from the more fascistic articles in Oppermann's collection. It ends in high style (196–8): the Romans were the first people of Indogermanic origin to be kindled by the spirit of Hellenism, which they developed in the light of their own national experience and bequeathed to Europe. The conclusion, that empire must depend on the rule of law, also resonates with contemporary events, and with Stauffenberg's apparent disdain for National Socialism. Virgil is almost incidental to the discussion, with the exception of the fourth *Eclogue*. But Stauffenberg used the upper case to shout out the same lines from Anchises' speech that interested so many other nationalistic readers of

---

[93] The poem is in Stauffenberg (1964), published after Alexander's death, in the Stefan George Stiftung by Rudolf Fahrner, a member of the Circle – and at one time of the SA.

[94] Hoffmann (1995) 280.

[95] Hoffmann (1995) 24.

Virgil, to the exclusion of the rest of the poem. Typically, there is no indication that the lines are part of a character speech:

TU REGERE IMPERIO POPULOS, ROMANE MEMENTO
— HAE TIBI ERUNT ARTES — PACISQUE IMPONERE
MOREM,
PARCERE SUBIECTIS ET DEBELLARE SUPERBOS

For Stauffenberg, these lines were directly relevant to the events of recent and contemporary German history, as they had been for Treitschke, the historian of Germany's nineteenth-century consolidation and expansion. To return briefly to Wilamowitz, it is no coincidence that these lines of Virgil were some of the very few that appealed to him. In his 1885 lecture, "An den Quellen des Clitumnus" the veteran of the Franco-Prussian War out of the blue translates *Aeneid* 6.848–53.[96] The last lines go as follows:

> Du Römer, sei der Herr den Völkern allen,
> dein ist die Herrscherkunst: so übe sie,
> und zwing' die Welt, den Frieden zu ertragen,
> den Trotz'gen furchtbar, mild den Überwund'nen.

Virgil's difficult phrase *pacique imponere morem* is here pushed beyond the limits of its Latinity. Virgil did not say "force the world to endure peace"; that is the language of Prussian and German expansion, from Wilamowitz's own military experience, and from the installation of the German emperor at Versailles following the Franco-Prussian War – and before Wilamowitz's experience of the twentieth-century Versailles, which quietly ironizes his "translation."[97]

---

[96] In fact Virgil is only incidental in Wilamowitz's piece, which is really more concerned with Carducci's adaptation of Virgil, from which Wilamowitz took his title ("alle fonti del Clitunno").

[97] For Wilamowitz on the subject of Versailles the year before his Virgil essay, envying the Italians their national poet, see Canfora (1977) 172–3; Wilamowitz concludes "one day there will once again live the spirit of 1813 and of 1914, and one united Germany is invincible and gains justice for itself. In this faith, we the old, who once saluted the German emperor at Versailles, resign ourselves to die beneath the shame of Versailles, trusting in the young and in eternal Germany. *Per aspera ad astra*." ("Un giorno poi vivrà nuovamente lo spirito del 1813 e del 1914, ed una Germania unita è invincibile e si fa giustizia da sé. con questa fede noi vecchi, che un giorno salutammo l'imperatore tedesco a Versailles, ci rassegniamo a morire sotto l'onta di Versailles, confidando nella gioventú e nella Germania eterna. *Per aspera ad astra*."

Karl Vretska, Rudolf Herzog and Hitlerism

As we have seen, much of the writing on Virgil was coded, with Hitler generally only implicitly behind the figure of Augustus – though occasionally explicit, as in Oppermann. Some of the most blatant application of the classical world to contemporary politics, by Oppermann and others, is to be found either in Berve's series *Neue Jahrbücher,* or in *Das humanistische Gymnasium,* which dropped its humanistic epithet in 1936. At stake was the curriculum and the minds of Germany's youth. A case in point is Vretska (1938), "The path to the new gymnasium. An Austro-German's affirmation of education and instruction in the high schools,"[98] which begins with fawning approval of the *Anschluss* (the seizure of Austria) and insistence on the importance of National Socialism for Austria as for Germany, talks of the greatness of the German spirit, and soon turns to antiquity and the lessons and connections it provides for National Socialism: "Greece and Rome are valuable to us today merely from the perspective of racial destiny."[99] Greek is valuable for transmitting to Germany the spirit discerned by Winckelmann; Homer is the first creator of a "nordic-heroic world," the "school of all nordic youth."[100] Rome is valuable for three reasons: its "nordic outlook," which enabled it alone to fashion an imperial state; the fact that through Rome's achievement exchange between Rome and the German people was achieved; and thirdly because the Augustan period in particular provides a notion of civilization that allows a spiritual and political exchange with that of contemporary Germany (118). As for Goebbels, Hitler as Caesar. Virgil is not far off (119):

> still today France struggles as the agent of a Latin civilization
> according to the principle laid down by Virgil: *pacique imponere
> morem, parcere subiectis et debellare superbos.* But we must draw the
> conclusions in our Latin classes. Europe's dialectic between the
> Latin and the German spirit was born in the Rome of
> Augustus; it explains to us why we Germans not only owe

---

[98] "Der Weg ins neue Gymnasium. Bekenntnis eines Ostmarkdeutschen zu 'Erziehung und Unterricht in der höheren Schule.'"

[99] Vretska (1938) 116 "Griechentum und Römertum ist uns heute allein wertvoll als Rassenschicksal."

[100] Vretska (1938) 117: "Homer ist für uns heute der erste Gestalter einer nordisch-heldischen Welt, er ist 'die Schule aller nordischen Jugend' (Aly)."

much to Rome but also had to struggle with her for more than 2000 years with both arms and spirit as our weapons. From this perspective we understand the historical significance of the Führer's words in Rome in which he set the Alps as the future boundary between Germany and Rome.[101]

The teaching of Classics is political, and "we philologists" ("wir Philologen") must be political also. We must think, feel and act politically, serving as preachers for the greatness of Germany, warriors for Germany's world standing, as "not knowledge alone but life and experience lead us and our schools into a new future." Vretska continued after the war in a distinguished career that presumably included the teaching of Virgil.

The 1938 issue of *Gymnasium* marked the *Anschluss* with the following: "We greet our members and friends in Austria with this fascicle, which for the first time in the new greater Germany comes to them as members of the Third Reich, in special affection with the German salute: Heil Hitler! Editor – editorial board – publisher."[102] Throughout these years the editor of *Gymnasium* was Rudolf Herzog, retired classical philologist and archaeologist.[103] The words of Anchises at *Aeneid* 6.851–3 would not be sufficiently aggressive for Herzog's pure Hitlerism. In "Der englische Krieg,"[104] he refers to the valiant but doomed attempt of Prince Lichnowsky, the Kaiser's ambassador in London from 1912–14, to avert the onset of World War I. Herzog further states that the British actions of 1939 followed the words of Juno, the "state deity of Carthage" (England and the semitism thus

[101] Vretska (1938) 119 "Noch heute kämpft Frankreich als Vertreterin einer lateinischen Zivilisation nach dem Grundsatz, den Vergil aufstellte: *pacique imponere morem, parcere subiectis et debellare superbos.* Wir aber haben in der Lateinstunde die Folgerungen zu ziehen. Die Dialektik Europas zwischen lateinischem und germanischem Geist wurde im Rom des Augustus geboren; sie erklärt uns, warum wir Deutsche nicht nur Rom manches verdanken, sondern auch mit ihm durch mehr also 2000 Jahre kämpfen mussten mit den Waffen des Armes und des Geistes. Aus dieser Schau verstehen wir erst die geschichtliche Bedeutung jener Worte des Führers in Rom, in denen er für die Zukunft die Grenze der Alpen als Scheide zwischen Rom und Deutschland zog."
[102] *Gymnasium* 49 (1938) 53 "Wir grüssen unsere Mitglieder und Freunde in Österreich mit diesem Heft, das zum erstenmal im neuen Grossdeutschland zu ihnen als zu Angehörigen des Dritten Reiches kommt, in ganz besonderer Herzlichkeit mit dem Gruss der Deutschen: Heil Hitler! Herausgeber–Schriftleitung–Verlag."
[103] He is not to be confused with Rudolf Herzog the writer and journalist, with whom however he did share an enthusiasm for the National Socialism.
[104] Herzog (1939) 153–4.

linked), which stir the Italians to war against Aeneas: 7.312 *flectere si nequeo superos, Acheronta movebo* ("If I cannot bend the gods above, I shall move Acheron"). This leads *via* citation of Juno's bursting open the Gates of War (*Aeneid* 7.620–22), to remarks about "Punic-English war methods" ("punisch-englische Kriegsart").[105] The theme of Gates of War in turn allows a transition to Ennius, by way of Horace's and Virgil's references to that poet.[106] Herzog then brings up a different type of war, one not for empire but for existence, *via* Cicero's discussion at *De officiis* 1.38, where a distinction is made between enemies such as the oath-breaking Carthaginians on the one hand and on the other a more just figure, Pyrrhus, significantly a Greek, "from Achilles' stock." Cicero here preserves, and Herzog cites, a fragment from Ennius, Pyrrhus' response to Fabricius some time after the battle of Heraclea in 280 BC, when the latter was attempting to ransom captured Roman soldiers:

> nec mi aurum posco nec mi pretium dederitis:
> nec cauponantes bellum sed belligerantes
> ferro, non auro vitam cernamus utrique.
> vosne velit an me regnare era quidve ferat Fors
> virtute experiamur.   (Ennius, *Ann.* 183–7 Sk.)

No gold for myself do I demand, nor should you pay me any price: not trafficking in war but waging war, with iron and not with gold, let us see both decide who lives. With valor let us test whether Lady Chance wishes you or me to reign.

"This is the spirit," resumes Herzog, "which the Führer has brought back to life in the German people. With it we shall be victorious in the war, which for us has to do with our existence, for the enemy with its empire, the war which for the nations will create a true rule of peace – *pacique imponere morem*."[107] Fortunately for the world that "rule of peace" was not achieved.

---

[105] Hostility to "Punic" elements constitutes one of the chief forms of anti-orientalism and anti-semitism in German classical studies. See Vogt (1943) and Dietz (1984).

[106] Hor. *Sat.* I. 4.60–1; Virg. *Aen.* 7.620–2.

[107] Herzog (1939) 154 "Das ist der Geist, den der Führer im deutschen Volk wieder lebendig gemacht hat. Mit ihm werden wir siegen in dem Krieg, der für uns um die Existenz geht und für den Feind um sein Imperium, für die Völker aber ein wahres Friedensrecht schaffen wird – pacique imponere morem."

Plus ça change

After the war Viktor Pöschl, Friedrich Klingner and Karl Büchner, whatever the continuities and discontinuities in their works, all presented an optimistic Virgil whose views were synonymous with those of the state and Augustus its leader. R. Faber has shown that the postwar Virgil of these and other scholars was essentially the pre-war Virgil, the herald of Augustus.[108] But their work, particularly that of Klingner, tended to avoid the nationalistic element and look rather to the inner, spiritual Virgil. Klingner's Virgil in 1944 was in fact more troubled, less Augustan, than the Klingner of 1966, whose focus was less on ideology, and whose tone was more upbeat.

Writing of Pöschl, Büchner and Klingner, W. R. Johnson has connected the post-war European need to re-establish the centrality of Virgil, particularly as the poet of *labor* and *pietas*:[109]

> This is what Büchner and Pöschl needed: a living and authentic
> *Weltdichter* vouching for the authenticity of a dead, and in
> recent times dubious, Weltdichter ... For European classicists –
> and particularly for German classicists – Eliot's recommitment
> to Vergil, his reassertion of Vergil's central place in the image
> of Europe's essential and unending unity was a heartening and
> necessary event.

Again, Oppermann included Eliot's translated essay with his collection of mainly pre-war, otherwise German, articles, including his own, produced for the National Socialist curriculum. This European Virgil was not an innovation of 1945; it was also the European Virgil of the bimillennium, with the necessary adjustments, an amalgam of the spiritual European Virgil of Haecker and the secular European, or rather German, version of Oppermann and Vretska.

We return to Heidelberg. K. Meister, writing in that city in 1948, seems little different from Wilamowitz, Oppermann or Mussolini as the disastrous effects of extreme nationalism had failed to diminish the nationalist reading:[110]

---

[108] Faber (1983); also Serpa (1987).
[109] Johnson (1976) 7–8.
[110] Preisendanz and Meister (1948) 29 "Er bleibt auch uns Heutigen unverloren. Auch wir dürfen aus Vergil Freude und Hoffnung schöpfen, dürfen uns die leuchtenden Worte zurufen lassen, mit denen Aeneas seine Genossen nach dem Seesturm aufrichtet: *Durate et vosmet rebus servate secundis.*"

He (Virgil) remains vital for us moderns. We too may draw joy
and hope from Virgil, let ourselves be addressed by the shining
words with which Aeneas heartens his comrades after the storm
at sea:

Endure and preserve yourselves for favorable times.

These words could have been written in 1930 or 1942, and they show
the power of the Virgilian text to fuel the fires of nationalism, as well
as suggesting Meister's yearning for the Third Reich. The only article
he cites as representative of work "from recent years" on the *Aeneid* is
from 1943/4, by O. Zimmermann, a Heidelberg student of Meister's,
and also of Oppermann's; its code, like that of Meister, is easily pene-
trated, and Hitler is as much on the agenda as Aeneas or Augustus:

> And so we come to the positive definition of the character
> of Aeneas. He is not the hero, he is the political man, the
> statesman, the leader ("der Führer"). When the age and the
> nation ("Volk") of the Augustan period perceives itself as being
> most profoundly comprehended in the *Aeneid*, when it thereby
> secures its sense of self, when in the story of the *Aeneid* Roman
> history and especially the Augustan epoch as its high point
> and its fulfillment gets its metaphysical meaning (as of course
> inversely the Aeneas saga first of all gets its importance and is
> elevated over numberless other foundation sagas through Rome):
> here is the unusual case that an age and a nation discovers
> its poet, as the poet discovers his nation, which heard him and
> entrusted itself to his leadership ("Führung").[111]

The National Socialists passed laws under which the term "Der
Führer" could only be addressed to Hitler. When in the Third Reich
we find it being used of the leading figures, mythical and historical, of
the first empire, it is pretty easy to see what is going on. For back-

---

[111] Zimmermann (1943–44) 46 "Damit kommen wir zur positiven Bestimmung der
Gestalt des Äneas. Er ist nicht der Held, er ist der politische Mensch, der Staatsmann,
der Führer"; 53 "Wenn Zeit und Volk des Augusteischen Zeitalters in der Äneis sich
in seinem Tiefsten verstanden fühlt, wenn es daraus sein Selbstverständnis gewinnt,
wenn in der Geschichte der Äneis die römische Geschichte und besonders die Augusteische Epoche als ihr Höhepunkt und ihre Erfüllung ihren metaphysischen Sinn
erhält (wie natürlich umgekehrt auch die Äneissage erst durch Rom ihre Bedeutung
erhält und über ungezählte andere Gründungssagen hinausgehoben wird), so ist hier
der seltene Fall eingetreten, dass eine Zeit und ein Volk ihren Dichter, aber auch der
Dichter sein Volk gefunden hat, das ihn hörte und sich seiner Führung anvertraute."

ground reading on Augustus, Meister, again in 1948, singled out Karl Hönn's *Augustus und seine Zeit*, (3rd ed. Vienna 1943), whose resonance with contemporary events would be diminished in the fourth edition of 1953, which lacked the third edition's politically charged afterword and is more than seventy pages shorter than the edition recommended in Meister's 1948 introduction.[112]

Nor did Meister's sense of the national applications of antiquity seem to diminish as the years passed. In 1952, in the same series, he produced the introduction and bibliography for Tacitus' *Germania*, a text that had evoked some of the most ideologically transparent scholarship under National Socialism. Meister recommends many of these works in his bibliography (26–7), and his preoccupation in 1952 with racial and national connectedness is apparent:

> On the other hand those who seek knowledge of history have clung to viewing the Tacitean *Germania* as a primary source of information about the Germans. And so today, and precisely today, it deserves its place in the curriculum of the German schools. For it diverts one to pure knowledge about the Germans, whom we cherish as our forefathers, and to an understanding of the first developments of the German nation, and that promotes our thought and action better than glossy illusions of national mythology.[113]

What "thought and action" Meister had in mind goes unspoken, but one suspects, as with the close of his Virgil introduction, that restoration of national strength is one issue.

Nor has Virgil himself fared well from the far left. R. Faber himself rejects the "Harvard Virgil," since his Marxist orientation needs not just a right-wing reception of Virgil, but a right-wing Virgil, too.[114]

---

[112] One gets the impression that these new, sanitized editions, though in part doubtless intended to replace copies lost or damaged in the war, may also have been produced to distract attention from their earlier, problematic avatars.

[113] Meister (1952) 25: "Dagegen haben die, die historische Erkenntnis suchen, daran festgehalten, die taciteische Germania als eine Hauptquelle der Germanenkunde aufzufassen. Und so verdient sie auch heute und gerade heute ihre Stelle im Unterricht der deutschen Schule. Denn sie leitet sie zu echtem Wissen um die Germanen, die wir als unsere Vorfahren lieben, und zum Verständnis des ersten Werdegangs des deutschen Volkes, und das fördert unserer Denken und Handeln besser als glänzende Scheinbilder nationaler Mythologien."

[114] Faber (1983).

From a Marxist perspective the whole tradition is élitist and tainted. The optimistic, Augustan view has been challenged from within Germany only by W. Suerbaum,[115] whose work is rejected with great emphasis, and often without any bibliographical indication to help us look for ourselves.[116] In particular A. Wlosok (who studied with Pöschl at Heidelberg) is used to beat back Suerbaum, for it is one thing for an American to see a non-Augustan Virgil, quite another to allow a European scholar to do so. And so she is, in the words of N. Horsfall, the "wise and sober sympathizer" of Otis, Klingner and Perret;[117] she can then be used to restore the Virgil of European nationalism, to defend him against the assaults of the outsider. If we are to find our other Virgil in Europe at all, then, we will need to go to its edges, where we will find in the voice of the dispossessed an ability to read beyond Augustus and with different ideological frameworks.

[115] Suerbaum (1981) passim; though also in another lifetime, by A. W. Schlegel, before Germans lost the ability to read Virgil as anything but a poet of nationalism and leader-cult; cf. Rieks (1981) 829–32.
[116] Fowler (1991) 92.
[117] Horsfall (1988b) 243.

8

Beyond the borders of Eboli:
anti-fascist reception

Virgil, who was so often able to express his horror of war, would today be silenced in a concentration camp.

THEODOR HAECKER, *Journal in the Night*,
19 May 1940

Don't follow leaders ...

BOB DYLAN, "Subterranean Homesick Blues"

In the middle of the twentieth century, as perhaps in its later reaches, when many readers of Virgil became alienated from the authority of the state, they seemed to acquire the ability to read Virgil with an eye to oppositional possibilities. They did not necessarily reject him as a representative of that authority, as some like Auden and Graves did, but rather they gained access to, and exploited in their own thinking and writing, the ways in which the Augustan Virgil is an appropriation, not always coincident with the Virgil of their own experience. I here offer some case studies of such readings, all through the lens of the dispossessed of Europe, for whom, as for Meliboeus, Orpheus or Turnus, there was no place in the New Order.

Vienna to New York

Within his general appreciation of Hermann Broch's *The Death of Virgil* and of its place in the modernist reception of Virgil, T. Ziolkowski has convincingly demonstrated Broch's general unfamiliarity with classical philology, Latin, and Virgilian scholarship.[1] With that no critic can easily disagree, but does it necessarily lead to the conclusion that when Broch "attributed Virgil's decision to burn the

---

[1] Ziolkowski (1993) 203–22, with bibliography.

Aeneid to metaphysical doubts involving the crisis of values and the illegitimacy of art, he is projecting onto an ancient author modern anxieties that have no basis in history or the extant texts"?[2] Are we any more justified in insisting that Virgil's motivations could only have to do with the poem's lack of finish, as some ancient texts assert?[3] The fact is that we can never know whether Virgil wanted it burned, or if he did, why he wanted it burned. However, we may be confident that in the thirty-two years of Augustan Rome that stretched from the death of the poet to the death of the emperor any view that ascribed the burning to doubts about the poetic enterprise, which would readily imply doubts about the values of Augustan Rome, will not have flourished.

It is true that Broch did not know our poet as a Virgilian scholar would, but his use of *Aeneid* 6.851–3, the same lines that so appealed to National Socialist and fascist readers, shows a greater critical sensibility to Virgil than that demonstrated by many of the professional classicists and ancient historians with whom we dealt in the last chapter, and whom Broch left behind in Europe in 1938. Much of "Earth – The Expectation," the third of the four parts of Broch's novel, consists of dialogue between Augustus and Virgil. Broch's Virgil is at his most agonized as he realizes Augustus has visited him, as he lies sick and dying, to take away the *Aeneid*. This captures the moment at which the work leaves the control of the artist, a particularly disturbing moment for a writer such as Broch, who was imprisoned by the National Socialists in 1938 before he fled to New York and the United States, where he worked on successive drafts of the book as war raged in Europe. Broch knew well the way words can be used by a régime, and this awareness emerges throughout the work, perhaps most powerfully when Augustus tells the poet: "It is no longer your work, it is the work of all of us, indeed in one sense we have all labored at it, and finally it is the creation of the Roman people and their greatness" (313). Uniquely among those critics and readers with whom we have been dealing, Broch, the literary artist, was able to explore a reading of Virgil that did not immediately focalize Augustus and automatically assume that Virgil was a booster for Augustan programs; rather his focus is firmly on his fellow artist, the poet with whom he clearly empathized. It is precisely the ability to

---

[2] Ziolkowski (1993) 221.   [3] For these see Horsfall (1995) 22.

resist and turn away from Augustus that facilitates the non-Augustan reading.

Broch's Virgil pleads to Augustus the "unfinished" state of the *Aeneid* as the grounds against publication. But other reasons emerge, established by Virgil's inner voice, which subsumes the voice of the narrator as Broch effectively becomes Virgil, in a moment of literary brilliance that has the effect of eliding the millennia between the two writers, and eliding the gap between the Caesars under whom each of them lived. At one point Augustus sets a trap aimed at proving that the work is indeed finished and ready for circulation:[4]

> There was a familiar twinkle in Caesar's eye; it was boyish, almost crafty: "Incomplete? is that how you speak of your work, unfinished, eh? So you could have done it better, or should have?"
>
> "It is just as you say."
>
> "A while ago I had to be ashamed of my poor memory, now let me redeem my honor ... I shall let you hear a few of your own verses."
>
> Small and friendly, malicious, yet very boyishly came the wish that Caesar might fail again, although at the same time – oh, the vanity of the poet – a praise-avid curiosity asserted itself immodestly: "Which verses, Octavian?"
>
> And beating time with lifted finger, accompanied by a soft tapping of his sandal, the ruler of Rome, the sovereign of the world, recited the lines:

> "Others I doubt not will hammer the flexible bronze to soft features;
> Skillfully draw from the marble a latent and livelier resemblance;
> Plead with a craftier tongue, each his cause; in tracing the skyway,
> Measure with rods, thus truly foretelling the course of the planets.
> Thou, though, O, Roman, consider as thy task the ruling of nations,
> This be thine art: to found and to foster a law that is peaceful,
> Sparing the vanquished and vanquishing any who dare to oppose thee."

[4] Broch (tr. 1945) 313–15.

The time-beating finger remained uplifted as though
pointing out the lesson that was to be drawn from the verses,
and to be heeded: "Well, Virgil, are you caught in your own
net?"

This was, of course, an allusion, a very transparent allusion,
to the insignificance of the pure work of art, which was
negligible compared to the real concerns of Rome, but it was
too gratuitous; one need not go into that: "Yes, Augustus, that
is how it goes, you have rendered the verses with absolute
fidelity; those are the words of Anchises."

"Is that any reason for their not being yours also?"

"I have nothing to say against them."

"They are flawless."

"And even if they were, they do not constitute the entire
poem."

"That is irrelevant. Just the same I do not know by what
shortcomings the rest of the poem could be considered marred;
you yourself admit that the Roman spirit is above small
deficiencies of form and there can be no question of anything
else ... your poem emanates the spirit of Rome, is not at all
artificial, and that is the important thing ... indeed, your poem
is the very spirit of Rome, and it is magnificent."

What intimations had Augustus of the real inadequacies?
what did he know of the deep incongruity that stamps all life,
the arts before all? how could he judge of artificiality? what did
he really understand of such matters? And even though he
called the poem magnificent, thus flattering the author – alas,
that no one is able to resist this sort of praise –, the praise was
impaired because a person who fails to take note of its evident
deficiencies cannot understand the poem's hidden grandeur!
"The imperfections, Augustus, go deeper than anyone
suspects!"

As Hannah Arendt remarked, Broch's book is in many ways about the
impossibility and powerlessness of literature confronted by tyranny, a
book in which "the dubiousness of art in general became the thematic
content of a work of art itself."[5] This is likewise a fundamental and
undeniable quality of Virgilian poetry precisely when that poetry
registers the point of view of the dispossessed. So Moeris, the singer/
shepherd of the ninth *Eclogue*, his life jeopardized by civil discord,

---

[5] Arendt (1968) 12.

tells us (9.11–13) *sed carmina tantum | nostra ualent, Lycida, tela inter Martia quantum | Chaonias dicunt aquila ueniente columbas* ("but our songs, Lycidas, have as much power amidst the weapons of Mars as they say Chaonian doves do when the eagle comes"). It would be interesting to know whether Broch's knowledge of Virgil extended to this passage or to the beginning of the sixth *Aeneid* and Virgil's depiction there of Daedalus' artistic failure (6.30–3), occasioned by the pain of personal loss and death, a passage, unique in the history of ecphrasis, in which the description ends in the middle of the line – reflecting the unfinished work of art, the emblem of the *Aeneid* that the tradition had Virgil consigning to the flames. Whether or not Broch knew these lines, here was an artist who was writing when writing was dangerous and who saw in the lines of Anchises, which so many of his German contemporaries were using to legitimize the quest of National Socialism for world domination, a potential for something else, a potential precisely for the opposite. Again, we cannot know what was in the mind of Virgil in his last days and hours, but the glimpse provided by Broch may be as plausible as any other. And Broch's imaginings are also true to the ideological complexities of Virgil's poem, as they are true to the tensions inherent in his relationship to Augustus and Augustan Rome.

Fraenkel and Haecker

Like his revered teacher, E. Fraenkel also contributed to the bimillennium of Virgil's birth, just three years before he lost his position in Germany and went into exile in Oxford.[6] The comparison with the essay of Wilamowitz is instructive, for Fraenkel saw beyond the speech of Anchises and European nationalism's appropriation and application of it, to a deeper Virgilian humanity, and he seems to have seen the danger in the German and Italian attitude. As C. Macleod noted: "In a little-known lecture, delivered shortly before he left Germany as a refugee from the National Socialists, he observed how persistent had been the Germans' neglect of Virgil and what this had done to isolate them from European culture and Europe itself."[7] How different from the view of his teacher is Fraenkel's focus on the

---

[6] Fraenkel (1930), referred to by Calder (1988) 115 and Horsfall (1988a).
[7] Macleod (1970).

sadness of Virgil, on Virgil's focus on what is lost: "He does not let his epic close with the ring of triumphant victory, but with the words *vitaque cum gemitu fugit indignata sub umbras*" ("and his life, aggrieved, fled with a groan beneath the shadows").[8] Fraenkel had indeed referred to Virgil's *parcere subiectis et debellare superbos* (*Aen.* 6.853) at the beginning of his piece, but he saw more to Virgil: "but this, important as it is, by no means exhausts the impact of the contents."[9]

Fraenkel could look beyond these lines as none of his fellow countrymen, including his own teacher, seemed able to do. And Fraenkel situated the German neglect of Virgil precisely in German Romanticism, and in the idiosyncratic views of Winckelmann, views that Butler would find so destructive and pernicious in these same years.[10] He lamented that Virgil was known in Germany only by a few tags and although he gave other examples (*quos ego / sic notus Vlixes / timeo Danaos et dona ferentis / Acheronta movebo*) he chiefly had in mind Anchises' words at *Aen* 6.851–3.[11] Fraenkel desiderated a new German understanding of Virgil, not just the Virgil of those few passages from the *Aeneid*, an understanding that might put down its roots in the *Georgics* and in *Eclogues* 4, 9, and particularly 1.[12] Events got in the way. In his assessment of the German neglect of Virgil, Fraenkel was quite close to Theodor Haecker, who put the matter in stronger polemics in his hugely influential *Virgil, Father of the West*, first published in German in 1931, the year after Fraenkel's essay:[13]

> the German is for ever trying to find out the source of things –
> which in itself is good – but in the process he is apt to neglect
> the stream that has come into being from that source and
> which is also *nature* – and this is not so good. The work of
> Virgil is a stream from many sources, yet they are all in him.
> The German imagines that only the source is pure; but the
> stream is pure too – both are real, and he who ignores the

---

[8] Fraenkel (1930) 34 "Er lässt sein Heldenepos nicht in Siegestriumph ausklingen, sondern in die Worte *vitaque* etc."

[9] Fraenkel (1930) 5 "aber dieses, so wichtig es ist, erschöpft die Wirkung des Gehaltes bei weitem nicht."

[10] Cf. Butler (1935) *passim*; also above, pp. 234–5.

[11] Fraenkel (1930) 14 "Primär lebendig sind in Deutschland nur einige besonders einprägsame Formulierungen."

[12] Fraenkel (1930) 38.

[13] Haecker (tr. 1934) 108.

stream and thinks only of the spring becomes deluded, and fails at last even to find the spring.

Haecker then connected this theme to that of Germany's perception of its own origins; although somewhat elliptical, like Fraenkel and Butler he was clearly addressing Germany's constructed Hellenic myth:

> In Aachen stands the chair of Charlemagne … And yet, do the Germans bother themselves about it? – No, they must still be forever searching after their sources, and for starting everything all over again from the very beginning. School children in France, England, Italy, Norway, are taught that the chair of Charlemagne is in Aix-la-Chapelle, which of course must be a French city. When they actually travel to see this chair, they are astonished to find that Aix-la-Chapelle is a German city, Aachen by name. No German has ever troubled to tell them. What do the Germans care? – they must begin at the beginning! But Aachen stands for more than Weimar in the destiny of the German people. There the roots go down into a real, not a fictitious, soil (108).

Fraenkel and Wilamowitz on Virgil

Fraenkel in fact sent a copy of his Virgil article to Wilamowitz, whose article he also read and acknowledged, as two letters from the latter show.[14] In the first (23 October, 1930) Wilamowitz began "Many thanks for your kind reception of my Virgil, which certainly took me a great deal of work."[15] He went on to concede that the first *Eclogue* is a "truly beautiful poem" (his essay had deprecated Virgil's spawning of the trivial genre of later pastoral, and Fraenkel presumably objected). Wilamowitz then talked about the addressee of the fourth (all from the *Eclogues* that really concerned him in the essay) and concluded the letter, responding to his own query about the meaning of the Virgil jubilee: "National comparisons, even where nothing has been said, would be very instructive."[16] Soon after this Fraenkel must

---

[14] Calder (1977) 290, 293.

[15] In Calder (1977) 290 "Lieber Herr College, schönen Dank für Ihre freundliche Aufnahme meines Vergil, der mir allerdings viel Arbeit gemacht hatte."

[16] In Calder (1977) 290–1 "Die Vergleichung der Nationen, auch wo man nichts gesagt hat, müsste recht belehrend werden."

have sent his own 1930 essay, for on 10 January, 1931, Wilamowitz acknowledged it, referring chiefly to a footnote of Fraenkel's that had pointed out that Wilamowitz's characterization of Virgil's poetry as "Kunstfigur" (*Hellenistische Dichtung* II 224) was essentially the same as that made by Voss 125 years earlier, and that both were signs of the "tenacity of the German point of view."[17] Given the great difference in the two scholars' view of Virgil, it is worth quoting Wilamowitz's letter:[18]

> I took great pleasure in your Virgil, particularly the connection
> with Dante [central to Fraenkel's essay]. But a Homerizing epic
> remains a *Kunstfigur* as Herman [*sic*] and Dorothea remains a
> *Kunstfigur*.

In other words, no change since Winckelmann: because Virgil writes in an intertextual relationship with Homer, he is just a technically competent writer, and one who offends against the Romantic outlook.[19] How did Fraenkel react to this virtual admonishment and to the fact that the two so clearly disagreed on the topic of Virgil? We have a clue: after the war, in 1948, Fraenkel wrote his article, "The Latin Studies of Hermann and Wilamowitz."[20] The piece was "of essential importance,"[21] one of the most vivid statements of the continuing importance of a teacher, almost two decades after the death of that teacher – "he is almost among us" said the expatriate Fraenkel. The article was almost comprehensive, treating Wilamowitz on Terence, Horace, Seneca, and so on. But it is astonishing that Fraenkel said only the following of Wilamowitz's Virgilian writings (on which the two had corresponded): "We have no room here to discuss Wilamowitz's contributions to the study of Statius (and his ancient commentators) and *other Latin poets*, but on his attitude to Cicero a

---

[17] Fraenkel (1930) 19, n. 1 "die Festigkeit des deutschen Standpunktes."
[18] In Calder (1977) 293: "An Ihrem Vergil habe ich viel Freude, namentlich die Verbindung mit Dante. Aber eine Kunstfigur bleibt ein homerisierendes Epos wie Herman [*sic*] u. Dorothea eine Kunstfigur bleibt."
[19] My only concern here is the reception of Virgil; obviously Wilamowitz's unparalleled status as a Hellenist is a given, but if we focus on that status we will miss his flawed and influential involvement with Virgil.
[20] Fraenkel (1948) 28–34.
[21] Calder (1977) 277, n. 14.

word must be said" [emphasis added].[22] Fraenkel in effect tried to obliterate the piece.[23]

It is hazardous to speculate about possible reasons for Fraenkel's silence, but speculation is called for. At the very least, I would surmise that, like Calder, he may have found the essay "odd," and even somewhat embarrassing. But we also know of Fraenkel's response to Wolfgang Schadewaldt (whom we met in the last chapter), who had repudiated Fraenkel in 1934, after the so-called "Law for the Reconstitution of the Civil Service" of 7 April 1933 stripped Jewish civil servants of their posts.[24] Schadewaldt later (after the war) sent Fraenkel a book, with the inscription "memor,"[25] to which Fraenkel sent a two-word reply – "et ego." As we have seen, Fraenkel clearly and openly disagreed with his teacher's view of Virgil,[26] but does that really explain his *damnatio memoriae* of it? Can it perhaps be that he saw in Wilamowitz's bimillennial essay, and in the exchange about Virgil that he had with the great man, something troubling, the memory of which became difficult after 1933? It is hard to imagine that Fraenkel would not have asked how his teacher might have reacted to the disastrous laws of that year, and Wilamowitz's Virgil article may have provided disturbing indications. Was that essay better buried along with the Europe whose nationalism had destroyed it and so much else besides?[27]

---

[22] Fraenkel (1948) 33.

[23] This even though Fraenkel does refer to the Horatian piece (1930–1) whose very title alludes to the Virgil essay: "Nebengedanken bei dem Jubiläum Vergils." Those who would explain Fraenkel's omission by the somewhat popular nature of *Deutsche Rundschau* will also need to explain his *inclusion* of the Horace piece, since *Süddeutsche Monatshefte* was similarly popular – for the year in question the end covers sport Löwenbräu advertisements. Equally surprising is the fact that Calder, in his introduction to the very Wilamowitz essay which Fraenkel ignored (Calder [1988] 114), does not mention Fraenkel's omission, although he does there refer to Fraenkel's article as being one of the "two authoritative treatments" of Wilamowitz's Latin studies.

[24] Adam (1972) cf. 51–64 "Das 'Gesetz zur Wiederherstellung des Berufsbeamtentums.'"

[25] Lloyd-Jones (1971) 638, n. 3; also Calder (1977) 297, n. 133.

[26] Fraenkel (1930) 19, n. 1 is clearly critical.

[27] Momigliano (1971) notes "A journey to Israel in 1963 moved him profoundly. He read Goethe to the children of his Israeli pupils, but also became more disposed to admit what at the bottom of his heart he had always known – that his own vicissitudes belonged in the context of millenarian Jewish history." This need imply little about Fraenkel's actual religious practice; cf. Lloyd-Jones (1971) 634, n. 1 on Momigliano's review: "disappointing; the eminent historian has oddly chosen to consider Fraenkel

Walter Benjamin and the response of the left

A third example of an oppositional reading comes from a figure who was neither a novelist nor classicist, but a prolific and brilliant essayist and literary critic. On September 26, 1940 after the fall of France, the German-Jewish writer Walter Benjamin was detained at the Spanish border town of Portbou in the Pyrenées while attempting to flee to the USA. There, in the Hotel de Francia, at the end of September, he chose to take his own life rather than fall into the hands of the Nazis. Eight years earlier, a year before Hitler came to power, and before leaving his homeland for exile in Paris, Benjamin, who had been vacillating between Zionism and Marxism, Palestine and New York, wrote a review of Theodor Haecker's *Vergil. Vater des Abendlands.*[28] Entitled "Privileged Thinking" ("Privilegiertes Denken"), it was written vaguely from the perspective of the left. It also expressed hostility to the Christian appropriation, and it points to fundamental flaws in Haecker's approach, and in the approach of much contemporary German Virgil scholarship: the absurdity of the notion of Virgil as historically proto-Christian (not confined to Germany), and the élitism of the notion of the Western races as superior.

Benjamin pointed to the contrast between Virgil's status at the turn of the century and that which the poet enjoyed at the jubilee, on which various articles "bespeak a very positive assessment of the poet."[29] He criticized Haecker's philological shortcomings, and para-

from the standpoint of orthodox Judaism, in which he took no interest." Calder (1977) 279 n. 27 says of Wilamowitz' greeting to Fraenkel ("Hoffentlich haben Sie doch noch Stimmung das Fest zu feiern und das neue Jahr zu begrüßen"): "That Wilamowitz assumed Fraenkel would celebrate Christmas supports Lloyd-Jones' assertion against Momigliano that Fraenkel 'took no interest'" in orthodox Judaism. Calder seems to have asked Fraenkel's son about his father's beliefs: "Professor Edward Fraenkel emphatically agrees with Lloyd-Jones." It seems to me that Momigliano was not ascribing belief to Fraenkel, but wrote metaphorically: (56) "He studies the Classics as his forbears had studied the Torah, not only for knowledge, but for companionship, simple wisdom and uncompromising truth." Beyond that, the Judaism of Momigliano, and his own Kaddish for Fraenkel, is what is more to the point. Fowler (1991) 95 n. 34 has noted that Fraenkel chose to publish an obituary of Gilbert Murray, who "did more than anyone else to bring him and other Jewish refugees from the National Socialist nightmare to Oxford," in the *Association of Jewish Refugees Information* for July 1957.

[28] Benjamin (1932) 467–74; cf. Faber (1983).
[29] Benjamin (1932) 467, in Livingstone, et al. (1999) 569.

doxically (but rightly I think) situated that author's failures as a very manifestation of the romanticism that Haecker himself criticized in the German obsession with Hellenism: "Haecker's resolute neglect of any secular – in other words authentic – philological study of Virgil prevents him from recognizing such theological arguments for what they are: clichés inherited from the aesthetics of Later Romanticism."[30] Benjamin much preferred Rudolf Alexander Schröder who like Haecker "recognizes the importance of *pietas* for Virgil," but unlike Haecker "can place it in its historical context."[31] He situated Haecker's privileged outlook in that author's rejection of the relevance of Roman religion, for Haecker "solely the province of scientific research," to be discarded in favor of the demands of the "pure spirit." As the title of Haecker's book suggests, it is the spirit of the Occident that preoccupies him, and this is where Benjamin's critical focus turns, as he cites Haecker, the privileger of western man: "the author makes the political implications of his 'idea of humanity' so painfully clear – namely, that radically privileged understanding of non-Western man which is characterized by a combination of exploitation and the missionary spirit."[32]

The thought is throughout somewhat abstract, even more so than Haecker's, but here and elsewhere we get a glimpse of the coming darkness and a suggestion of the abandonment of a true intellectual humanism that might have provided some light in that darkness. Haecker, too, would fall victim to the barbarism whose advent was less than a year away, but Benjamin saw in that author's internal, spiritualized, strongly Occidental Virgil a privileged attitude that would strip the intellectual of his ability to bring humanism to bear on these dark times, futile as that attempt might have been:[33]

> "A humanism emptied of theology will not stand the test of time," the author claims. But to recommend Thomism as a cure for an age whose humanism is intellectually and actually compromised is to take the joke too far. Haecker lives in an ivory tower and spends his time gazing out of the topmost

---

[30] Benjamin (1932) 469, in Livingstone, et al. (1999) 570–1.
[31] On Schröder see Ziolkowski (1993) 80–5. So Benjamin (1932) 469, in Livingstone, et al. (1999) 571.
[32] Benjamin (1932) 469, in Livingstone, et al. (1999) 571.
[33] Benjamin (1932) 473, in Livingstone, et al. (1999) 573–4.

window, belittling things. And the worst of it is that the ground on which this tower has been built is giving way. How otherwise could anyone use the phrase "adventist paganism" as if it were in common use, while not noticing that the future approaching him and all of us is perfectly "adventistic," even when not on the march? How could he describe "a merely philological and aesthetic interpretation of Virgil" as "a false approach, an undermining of civilization, carried out by minds themselves undermined," yet find no words for the barbaric conditions to which humanism of every kind is tied nowadays?

Benjamin desiderated a questioning of what the tradition of Virgil's poetry and inquiry into it have to teach us in an era in which both are threatened by elimination. The reality however was very different: Oppermann and others, in a tradition connecting to Goebbels and antithetical to Benjamin, would restore the "centrality" and "relevance" of Virgil, by converting him into the herald of world domination and subordinating him to the new, rising Augustus.

Syme's fascist Virgil

It is a paradox of Virgilian reception that this poet also fared poorly at the hands of the opponents of fascism and National Socialism. Ziolkowski has captured well the distaste of writers such as Arthur Miller, Robert Graves, or (at times) W. H. Auden for Virgil. However, in each case it was a distaste for an Augustan Virgil, with as little nuance to him as the Virgil of Wilamowitz, but viewed with a different hostility from that of the great German scholar, one formed by hostility to order, authority, nationalism and militarism. The basis for Ezra Pound's anti-Virgilianism, complicated by his support of fascism, was slightly different, residing more in aesthetics. The historiographical basis for this Anglophone hostility is kindred to the anti-Augustan revision of Ronald Syme's *The Roman Revolution* (Oxford 1939), a work that must be seen in the context of opposition to panegyrical assessments of Augustus, which have as much to do with nineteenth-century nationalism and ruler-cult as with the realities of ancient Rome. Virgil suffered in Syme's revision of Augustus, for Syme's reading of the poets generally was a strongly Augustan one, a reading in which the poet became a supporter of tyranny rather than the herald of the golden age.

Sforza's anti-fascist Virgil

Another writer notoriously demonstrates that it is possible to love Virgil and despise Caesar:

> However extraordinary it may appear that not less than a couple of millennia were required for the problem of Virgil to be brought before the general public, we confidently expect that, now that this is done, it will elicit serious and dispassionate consideration. And, moreover, we trust that in due course these views will eventually prevail over the old traditional conception.

So Francesco Sforza, an Italian writing not in Vietnam-obsessed Harvard but in Nicosia, beyond the borders of fascist Italy, towards the end of an article entitled "The Problem of Virgil,"[34] in the words of one critic, "a provocative article ... from which Virgilian criticism has never fully recovered."[35] Sforza's article must by any standard constitute the most extreme and polemical view of Virgil's hostility to Rome and Augustus that has ever been produced. An unannotated Italian monograph of seventy-seven pages, elaborating his earlier views, followed some years later.[36]

The major substantive contemporary response to Sforza of which I am aware was from R. D. Williams, who responded with a single column in the *Classical Review* of 1954. His response is worth reproducing, both for its summary of and reaction to Sforza's views. As emerges from this review, Sforza was as little interested in the Augustan Virgil as Oppermann was in the possibility of its opposite:

> This small volume restates and somewhat amplifies the remarkable interpretation of the *Aeneid* which Sforza put forward in *C.R.* xlix (1935), pp. 97–108. His interpretation carries no more conviction now than then.
>
> He holds that the *Aeneid* is "the most virulent libel ever written against Rome." Virgil, as a lover of Italy, so hated Rome and Augustan despotism that he set out to show in the *Aeneid* the vileness of this authoritarian régime. The circumstances of his life are examined to show that he had every reason to hate Augustus: when the emperor imposed upon him the task of writing the *Aeneid*, he met the

---

[34] Sforza (1935).   [35] Quinn (1972).   [36] Sforza (1952).

unpleasant situation by concealing beneath a façade of
panegyric a vehement invective against Roman tyranny, a
hymn to political freedom. Sforza examines the character of
Aeneas in the poem, and finds him always stupid or villainous
or both, incapable of arousing any emotion in us except
derision and contempt. The Trojans are all odious characters,
while the Italians are admirable throughout. The gods beneath
whose auspices Rome grew to greatness are clearly intended to
appear ridiculous and base. Priam, Evander, and Latinus are
examples of dotard tyrants bringing evil on their peoples: thus
the *Aeneid* is a plea for liberty and the rights of man.

Sforza states these views in the most exaggerated terms
throughout, and again and again presses his argument beyond
the extreme limits of plausibility. (Mezentius becomes an
admirable figure; Virgil is said to have remained faithful to
Epicureanism all his life.) He fails to set Virgil in the historical
context of his times, and he runs counter to all likelihood in
suggesting a hidden meaning of which no contemporary
Roman, and indeed no Roman, seems to have had the faintest
suspicion. Nor is it credible that Virgil would use his talent
for epic poetry to ridicule the heroes of his poem. One may
concede to Sforza just this much, that the *Aeneid* is not pure
panegyric, contains certain elements (the suffering of Dido, of
Turnus, of many others) which do not altogether harmonize
with the vision of the glory of Rome. But the vision never
fades, and to see conflict in a poet's mind differs absolutely
from maintaining that he is vehemently and consciously hostile
to the subject of his poem. Sforza will convince no one that
Virgil wrote his masterpiece in order that his readers might turn
it inside out.[37]

When Sforza refers to Aeneas as "falso, egoista, codardo, assassino,"[38]
or speaks of "the old dotard Evander"[39] he speaks with a strongly

---

[37] Williams (1954) 167. Johnson (1976), 156 n. 10 mentions Sforza's article as almost a
"caricature" of the pessimistic views of the "Harvard school"; cf. also Williams in
Harrison (1990) 22, n. 2, for a passing reference to the "remarkable article of Sforza."
Harrison himself (1990) 4 n. 16 does note that Sforza is an "interesting exception" to
general European positive readings between the two World Wars – "apparently written
against the background of European fascism" – as were many of those positive views, as
we saw!

[38] Sforza (1952) 33.

[39] Sforza (1935) 104.

anti-Augustan voice and gives characterizations that few will recognize, that, in short, seem unfamiliar. Readers who have in mind the piety and compassion of Aeneas (exhibited at certain times), or fatherly love and concern in the case of Evander (how much older is he than Mezentius, who *did* go into battle with *his* son?), will reject Sforza precisely for the same reason that many readers reject the extreme Augustan reading: each tries to close out the other meaning. Whether or not Sforza allowed the Augustan Virgil, he did not do so in print. He thus could not explore ambiguity, insisting instead on open hostility. This failure rendered him an easy target, easily rejected.

Williams, however, made one concession, and in that concession is the heart of the matter, "that the *Aeneid* is not pure panegyric, contains certain elements (the suffering of Dido, of Turnus, of many others) which do not altogether harmonize with the vision of the glory of Rome." As soon as we have agreed to that, we have essentially admitted that the text is an ideologically open one; if panegyric is qualified it becomes susceptible to ambiguous reading. The extent of that ambiguity, i.e., the extent to which its panegyric elements are in conflict with something that is not panegyric, will open space for individual interpretive acts. And as for the claim that "Sforza will convince no one that Virgil wrote his masterpiece in order that his readers might turn it inside out," that involves precisely a hermeneutic circularity of assuming without examination that the genre of Virgilian epic functions as panegyric and that the purpose of the poem is to praise Augustus – that is, the Servian default.

Indeed the safest response to Sforza is to put the focus back onto (a beneficent) Augustus, as R. Rieks does in his *Aufstieg und Niedergang* article on "Vergil und die römische Geschichte."[40] Against the anti-fascist Sforza, Rieks, writing in 1981, presumably for strategic reasons, avoids the more obvious National Socialist encomia of Augustus by Berve and such figures. However, he is nevertheless able to line up a variety of articles from the mid- to late-thirties, chiefly celebratory of Augustus and of the cult of emperor and empire, and comfortable with the idea of Augustan poetry as propaganda. M. P. Charlesworth is the main standard-bearer, and his views, based on no evidence, are used to paint the very opposite picture of that to be found in Sforza:[41]

---

[40] Rieks (1981).
[41] Rieks (1981) 834, quoting Charlesworth (1937) 108, 109.

In any large empire, embracing many languages, nations and cultures, the ruler must somehow persuade his subjects (1) that he is fit to rule them, and (2) that they are being ruled for their own good. He must, in fact, use propaganda.

First of all emperors could call on the services of poets and prose-writers, and Augustus was indeed fortunate in those he found: characteristically he would not risk his name being cheapened by the panegyrics of minor poets.

Rieks even quoted Syme, on the poets, if not on Augustus. There is no evidence that Augustus "could call on the services" of a poet such as Virgil. At least Sforza's evidence existed, and in the text of Virgil. But Rieks, by shifting the focus to Augustus and to the issue of propaganda, immediately limits us to the few lines of the poem we saw used and abused in the last chapter.

Milan to Lucania

Let us observe a final view of the *Aeneid*, embedded in a brief "history" of Italy:

A mythological history must have its root in myth and for this reason Vergil is a great historian. The Phoenician [*sic*] invaders from Troy brought with them a set of values diametrically opposed to those of the ancient peasant civilization. They brought religion and the state, and the religion of the state. The religious tradition or *pietas* of Aeneas could not be understood by the ancient Italians, who lived beside the beasts of the field. The invaders brought also arms and an army, escutcheons, heraldry, and war. Their religion was a violent one, demanding human sacrifice; on the funeral pyre of Pallas the pious Aeneas made a burnt offering of prisoners to the gods of the state. The ancient Italians, meanwhile, lived on the land, knowing neither sacrifice nor religion. The Trojans met with insuperable hostility among the natives, and the two civilizations clashed. Aeneas found his only allies among the Etruscans, city people, like him from the Orient, perhaps of the same Semitic origin, and similarly ruled by a military oligarchy. With these allies, then, he waged war. On one side there was an army in shining armour forged by the gods; on the other, as Vergil describes them, were peasant bands, risen in self-defence, with no god-given weapons but only axes, knives, and scythes, the tools of their daily work in the fields. These, too, were valorous brigands, doomed to defeat. Italy, the humble Italy, was conquered:

> *per cui morì la vergine Cammilla*
> *Eurialo e Turno e Niso di ferute.*

Carlo Levi, Christo si è fermato a Eboli[42]

Levi's words, characterized by N. Horsfall as an interpretation of the second half of the *Aeneid*,[43] like those of his fellow-Italian, Francesco Sforza, were produced under very particular cultural conditions. Levi's book is an account of his exile to Lucania in 1935–6, an exile imposed as a punishment for his opposition to the fascist adventure in Abyssinia. Produced under such conditions, Levi's "interpretation" coincides oddly and precisely with that of Sforza. The victims of fascism readily identified with the victims of Aeneas and his Trojans.

The end

"The *Mostra Augustea* of 1937, staged with much ado by Fascist Italy to mark the bimillenary of Augustus' birth, had the effect of appropriating the Roman *princeps* completely for modern Italian aspirations."[44] But it worked both ways, and this equation also meant that from the perspective of anti-fascism Augustus became a much more ambivalent figure than he had ever been: to the extent that there were questions about Mussolini's manipulation of political systems and use and abuse of power, there could be such questions about Augustus as well. That is in essence why Syme's Augustus can never be restored to the status which had previously seemed so much more benign.

The openly subversive reading of Virgil in a sense only becomes possible after the extreme nationalist one has established itself. Parry's 1963 article was written before the fall of Diem and the Tonkin Gulf Resolution, when the US only had "advisers" in Vietnam, and the

---

[42] Levi (1947) trans. F. Frenaye (1982) 138–9; orig. trans. 1947. Significantly Levi read Nisus and Euryalus as more akin to the tragic Italian victims Camilla and Turnus, with whom both he and Dante combined them.

[43] Horsfall (1991) 86.

[44] Galsterer (1990) 3, n. 5.

radical left (to say nothing of the classical professoriate)[45] was only beginning to look to Indochina. On the other hand, Parry himself, like Clausen, was formed in the course of Europe's crisis.[46] But his study does look ahead to the experience that would end the comfortable hierarchies of American and other societies. 1963 was the same year Oppermann's slightly denazified Virgil volume came out, a volume which reached back into the darkness of National Socialism, in whose cause Virgil was selectively read. Time will tell which works of the last forty years have advanced our understanding of Virgil, but let us not pretend that the Augustan Virgil, whose profile was sharpened in continental Europe in the middle of the twentieth century, is unconstructed by those peculiar ideological and spiritual conditions.

Carlo Levi, Francesco Sforza, Hermann Broch, and Walter Benjamin, even Eduard Fraenkel, all found themselves expelled to the margins of continental Europe or beyond, in Lucania, Nicosia, New York, on the Spanish–French border, even, oddly, in Oxford. Within Europe, there was only room for the "Father of the West," the Augustan Virgil who legitimated the new Augustuses – whether Charlemagne, Louis XIV, Charles II, Bismarck, Mussolini, or Hitler. The other Virgil worked against Augustus, and he did so from the boundaries of Europe, which had no place for him. The *Lives* tell us that Virgil died in Calabria, adjacent to Levi's Lucania, while trying to leave Italy and Europe for Asia, reversing the steps of Aeneas, the proto-European. Augustus brought the poet back; he died, but his poem survived, perhaps against his wishes, as a resource for Augustus and European leader-cult. Perhaps Virgil in leaving Europe was the first to attempt to escape the burden of Augustus and the Augustan reading.

[45] James Halporn tells me that in the late 1960s he and Parry tried, with naive enthusiasm, to bring a resolution condemning the war to the floor of the American Philological Association's annual meeting; the move was killed by the directors.

[46] For an anti-fascist application of Livy, see the 22-year old Clausen (1945) 299: "Today (presumably 1944) a similar conflict of patient sagacity pitted against a once overwhelming force sweeps to a climax in eastern Europe. Another, modern Zama – a complete Russian victory on German soil – will surely soon put an end to this struggle too" (written at Mt. Angel College, St. Benedict, Oregon).

9

Critical end games

"Mr. Prufrock" does not "go off at the end." It is a portrait of
failure, or of a character which fails, and it would be false art to
make it end on a note of triumph.

> *The Letters of Ezra Pound 1907–1941*, ed. D. D. PAIGE
> (New York 1950) pp. 44–5

> I am not quite sure, but I seem to remember that E. Lefèvre
> (in Freiburg) tends to believe that the *Aeneid* is unfinished.
> But as he is a serious scholar he won't publish this. And one
> last thought: Vergil writes in the proem "... dum conderet
> urbem," but Aeneas doesn't found a city, he finishes his poem
> with the death of Turnus. One could say that the foundation
> of Lavinium is implied by the death of his rival, but to me that
> is not convincing. I keep on having my problems with the
> *Aeneid*. Ulrich Schmitzer Universität Erlangen-Nuernberg,
> "Classics list" @uwashington.edu (1996)

Dr. Schmitzer is not alone in having his problems with this poem,
particularly its ending.[1] On May 28, 1996 I was one of three exam-
iners for a "Vergil Academy" at a school in New York City. Each of
us conducted four fifteen-minute public examinations of four students, each of them being responsible for one book. I happened to be
assigned *Aeneid* 12, and I concluded my examination by holding up
the brochure for the event, on which was depicted the body of a
fallen warrior, with another warrior standing alongside, his sword-
point resting on the ground. When I asked "What is wrong with this
picture?" my student quickly responded: "Well, we don't actually see

---

[1] I ignore and contemn the proposition that Virgil died before he could wrap up the
poem with some sort of "happily ever after" coda; those who wish to clutch at that
particular straw will presumably continue to do so.

that moment in the poem." She left it at that, but I was told later that this decision was made because depicting Aeneas with his sword in Turnus' body "would undermine Virgil's presentation of *pius Aeneas*." This is a true story.

There is a famous event in Milton scholarship that will be a guide for us. J. H. Summers put the matter well:[2]

> The eighteenth-century critics' concern with the very last lines
> of [*Paradise Lost*] is symptomatic of their uneasiness with the
> final two books. Addison wished to omit the final two lines
> ("They hand in hand with wand'ring steps and slow, / Through
> *Eden* took their solitary way") because they were not happy
> enough: they "renew" "anguish" "in the mind of the reader."
> Bentley, always more daring, simply rewrote the lines in a
> manner which he believed more "agreeable" to the author's
> "scheme":
>
> > *Then* hand in hand, with *social* steps their way
> > Through Eden took, *with heav'nly comfort chear'd*.

Philological science and critical acumen, on the rise as Bentley was writing, soon corrected his audacity, and left a text that had to be interpreted rather than altered to fit the aesthetic and ideological expectations of the critic. Virgil's text had an infinitely greater space to travel over before it reached such shores (not that they are without their rocks, as we shall see), and the reception of the end has its own turbulent history which is emblematic of larger critical strategies.

Maphaeus Vegius and Aeneid *13*

The following is Thomas Twyne's 1583 translation of some lines written by an Italian poet from the fifteenth century:

> Then Venus through the flittring aire descending down did
> slide,
> And to Laurentum towne she goes, neere where to sea doth
> glide
> Numicie river drenched deepe in reede, and overhid.
> The body of her son to wash, and mortall part she bid
> The water then to clense, and glad the happy soule on hie

---

[2] Summers (1962) 188.

Late losed from the corpse she bare aloft to dwell in skie,
And did amid the starres Aeneas place, whom Iulies line
Their private God doth call, adorning him with rites devine.

The humanist Maphaeus Vegius' ("Vegio") thirteenth book of the *Aeneid* (1427) grafts and expands the closure provided by Ovid, *Metamorphoses* 14.581–608 (Aeneas's death and deification) onto the Virgilian story. Nowadays editors and translators of Virgil have abandoned the practice of including the thirteenth book in their editions, though for a good two centuries that was not the case: this curious work was printed, translated and illustrated along with the "rest" of Virgil.[3] The first "English" translation, that of Gawin Douglas, includes the book, along with a verse prologue narrating the humanist's apparition, somewhat like Lycidas in Theocritus 7, and his exhortation that Douglas include a translation of Book 13. It is also significant that "Maphaeus Vegius was not alone in his aspiration to complete the tale of Aeneas' fortunes."[4] At least four other sequels are known between the fifteenth and seventeenth centuries, and thereafter Vegio himself became an object of satire, but also of emulation: as recently as 1883 one T. Seymour Burt felt the poem should continue until the death of Romulus, and so he mined Livy 1.3–16 for his "Supplement to the *Aeneid*" in blank verse, which he published along with translations of the *Eclogues*, *Georgics* and *Aeneid* (including "Book 13"). He also included a proposal, which fell on deaf ears, that his supplement be the basis for a Fourteenth Book in Latin verse, an accomplishment fortunately beyond his own powers.[5]

This tradition of continuation may be viewed not simply as a detached curiosity of literary history, nor solely as a chapter in the history of Renaissance rhetorical education,[6] but perhaps from a more diachronic perspective, as part of a literary critical collective, of a critical tendency which is alive and well today. The more recent avatars are just more subtle. There will initially be little direct dis-

---

[3] See Brinton (1930) for the text, and 24–40 on the history of this work, both on the way it was accepted by allegorizers as an appropriate appendix, and on its eventual transition "to the realm of historical interest." Also Hijmans (1971–2) 144. Vegio's book appears in almost 50 MSS from the fifteenth and sixteenth century; see Kallendorf (1989) 100.

[4] Cf. Brinton (1930) 1; for details of these see Kallendorf (1989) 204, n. 19.

[5] Cf. Brinton (1930) 39–40.

[6] The thrust of Kallendorf's (1989) interest.

cussion or interpretation of the end of Virgil's *Aeneid*, on which my views, in as far as they are not already clear, will become so.[7] Rather the current focus will be on the alternatives to confronting that ending, on the variety of barriers and diversions that may be constructed in order precisely to divert the reader from returning there.

Throughout Vegio's *Supplement*, the Christian and allegorical element is to the fore, as it is in Sebastian Brant's final woodcut in the six-volume collection devoted to Virgil's (and Vegio's) poem: Aeneas' body reclines on the bank of the river, clad (as is Jupiter, who is also depicted) only in a loin cloth, with a Botticelli-like Venus washing him and – Brant's contribution, it would seem – with the hero's soul as a *parvulus Aeneas* ascending through the corpse's mouth. The apotheosis of Aeneas bridges the pagan and Christian worlds as Venus "leads the blessed soul with her up into heaven" (628 *felicemque animam secum super aera duxit*), where he is worshipped as a god, in what smacks of a blending of pagan catasterism and Christian ascent. Ovid's account of Aeneas' deification is also very much in evidence here (*Met.* 14.596–608), a passage that may be seen as the first attempt to provide the *Aeneid* with the closure it lacks. In Ovid's account (*Met.* 14.605–8) there is no actual ascent; Venus merely turned him into a god (*fecitque deum*) by sprinkling him with perfume and touching his lips with ambrosia and nectar.

It is not just the end of Vegio's book that imposes closure; that is its mission from the very beginning, and the manner is uniform throughout: loose Virgilian strings are tied off, uneasiness quelled, and the radically open Virgilian text is closed off in all possible details, and not just in the final elevation of Aeneas. As soon as Turnus is dead, the Latins are made to lower their weapons and lose their appetite for war (10 *insanumque horrent optati Martis amorem*, "mad love of war, once prayed for, now they hate"). Vegio adapts and advances the complex Virgilian simile of *Aeneid* 12.715–24, where Aeneas and Turnus had been compared to bulls fighting for control of the herd. In that simile the herd's future, like the outcome itself, was uncertain and never resolved in the poem (12.718–19):

> stat pecus omne metu mutum mussantque iuvencae
> quis nemori imperitet, quem tota armenta sequantur.

---

[7] One of the better recent treatments of the finale is that of Quint (1993) 68–83.

The whole herd stands dumb with fear and the heifers mutter
about who will command the woods, whom all the cattle will
follow.

Vegio brilliantly plays off this simile and constructs a legitimization,
even from the Latin perspective, of Trojan rule:

> sicut acerba duo quando in certamina tauri
> concurrunt, largo miscentes sanguine pugnam,
> cuique suum pecus inclinat: sine cesserit uni
> palma duci, mox quae victo pecora ante favebant
> nunc sese imperio subdunt victoris, et ultro,
> quamquam animum dolor altus habet, parere fatentur.
>
> (15–20)

Just as when two bulls rush into bitter contest, joining battle
with copious blood, each one's herd leans towards him: but if
victory goes to one of the leaders, those hearts which just
before favored the vanquished one now submit to the power of
the victor, and though their minds are held in deep grief, they
willingly agree to obey.

The key is in the combination *ultro . . . parere fatentur* ("they willingly
agree to obey"), with which Vegio averts the aura of civil war that
hangs so markedly over the end of the *Aeneid*. The humanist sounds
like the tendentious Augustus of *Res gestae* 25.2: *iuravit in mea verba tota
Italia sponte sua, et me belli quo vici ad Actium ducem depoposcit* ("all Italy
of its own free will took an oath of allegiance to me and demanded
me as leader in the war in which I was victorious at Actium").[8] This
willing submission of the Latins, a resolution at the level of the two
conflicting cultures of the *Aeneid*, sets the stage for a demonstration of
the justice of Aeneas' unresolved actions in *Aeneid* 12, a demonstration effected in large part by revelation of Turnus' "iniquity." This
revelation is one of the chief themes of Book 13 and it comes most
noticeably in the speech of Aeneas that follows at *Supplement* 24–48.
There Vegio insists on Aeneas' mood, in the seconds that follow his
enraged killing of Turnus at *Aeneid* 12.945–52; no longer, as Virgil had
left him, "enflamed by rage and terrible in his anger" (*furiis accensus et
ira | terribilis*), Aeneas is here fully in control and addresses the corpse
of Turnus "calmly" (23 *placido ore*). Closure and damage control are
under way as Vegio in effect contradicts Virgil.

---

[8] For a more sceptical view of *sponte sua*, see Dio 50.6.2–7.3; Suet. *Aug.* 17.2.

In Aeneas' speech over the fallen Turnus, Vegio has the Trojan hero invoke Jupiter in two ways: first Turnus has offended Jupiter by disobeying divine orders; and second, Aeneas informs the corpse of his slain enemy, "even Jupiter gets angry"; Turnus' death is therefore made to serve as an example for posterity, as Vegio puts his triumphant Aeneas in the pulpit (24–35):

> "quae tanta animo dementia crevit,
> ut Teucros superum monitis, summique tonantis
> imperio huc vectos, patereris, Daunia proles,
> Italia et pactis nequiquam expellere tectis?
> disce Iovem revereri et iussa facessere divum.
> magnum etiam capit ira Iovem, memoresque malorum
> sollicitat vindicta deos; en ultima tanti
> meta furoris adest, quo contra iura fidemque
> Iliacam rupto turbasti foedere gentem.
> ecce suprema dies, aliis exempla sub aevum
> venturum missura; Iovem ne temnere frustra
> fas sit, et indignos bellorum accendere motus."

What great madness grew in your mind, son of Daunus, that you saw fit to try to drive the Trojans from Italy and from the houses promised them, they who were brought here by the advice of the gods and the command of mighty Jove? Learn now to revere him and to follow the orders of the gods. Even great Jove is overcome by anger, and the gods remember evil deeds and concern themselves with vengeance; look, here is the final limit of your rage, with which you broke the treaty and aroused the race of Troy against law and faith. See this final day destined to serve as example for ages to come; that it be a sin vainly to scorn Jove, and kindle shameful turmoil of war.

Vegio again shows himself a skillful rhetorician and organizer of facts, as he has Aeneas (perhaps developing the rhetoric of *Aeneid* 8.127–51) present the Trojans as liberators rather than invaders. Although for our tastes it in fact crosses the boundary into the absurd, the didactic stance of Vegio's Aeneas towards the corpse of Turnus (28 *"disce Iovem revereri et iussa facessere divum"*), adapted from the warning of Phlegyas in the Underworld (*Aen.* 6.620 *"discite iustitiam moniti et non temnere divos"* "Take your warning and learn justice and not to spurn the gods"), is intended to present an Aeneas at his most rational and father-like, as in his famous instruction to Ascanius at *Aeneid* 12.435:

disce, puer, virtutem ex me verumque laborem "from me, boy, learn virtue and true toil." Everything conspires to distract from Virgil's close.

At 13.36–48 Vegio's Aeneas first grants return of the corpse of Turnus, so closing out the possibility that it could receive the treatment of a Hector – or a Mezentius, whose fate hangs over the last lines of the real *Aeneid*. He then brilliantly shifts blame for his own actions to the Ausonians: "driven by *your* rage" (47 *vestris actus furiis*) – thereby suppressing his *own furiae*, so prominent at *Aeneid* 12.946.

C. Kallendorf has examined Vegio's *Supplement* within the tradition of early Renaissance epideictic, focusing on its play with the contrast between good (Aeneas), and evil (Turnus) – as other works try to use Aeneas and Dido for the same purpose. In pursuing this program Vegio eradicated precisely the moments at which such easy paradigms are most challenged by Virgil's poem. Where Virgil ended with Aeneas *furiis accensus et ira | terribilis*, Vegio begins, some seconds later in narrative time, not only with a placid Aeneas, but with the hero chastising the Italians for their *furiae*. And so Vegio's larger aim establishes itself, the aim of projecting mitigation and transference onto Virgil. If we accept the closure, as editors and translators who printed Vegio's work implicitly did, we remove the Virgilian Aeneas' final act from the sphere of human shortcoming, and by assigning to Jupiter the anger and rage of Aeneas, we can finally achieve the comfortable banality, denied by Virgil, for which so many have hungered at the poem's end.

The persistent inclusion of Vegio's *Supplement* in editions of Virgil becomes comprehensible as a function of forced closure. Things are nicely wrapped up, and readers of Virgil, aided by the fact that Virgil died with the *Aeneid* "incomplete," can allow themselves to provide the closure denied by the original author. The parallel of Dickens' *Edwin Drood*, a truly unfinished work, and of its subsequent editorial history, comes readily to mind, as do the very real differences: that work was unfinished; Virgil's, at the end of *Aeneid* 12, simply lacked closure.

Ariosto and Tasso

The sixteenth century saw two Italian poets engaging the end of the poem. Ariosto's Virgilian ending is one of the clearest instances of powerful and unmistakable intertextuality (*Orlando Furioso* 46.140):

E due e tre volte ne l' orribili fronte,
alzando, più ch' alzar si possa, il braccio,
il ferro del pugnale a Rodomonte
tutto nascose, e si levò d' impaccio.
Alle squalide ripe d' Acheronte,
sciolta dal corpo più freddo che giaccio,
bestemmiando fuggì l' alma sdegnosa,
che fu sí altiera al mondo e sì orgogliosa.

And two or three times, in Rodomont's horrible face, raising
his arms as high as he could, he hid all the steel of his dagger
and freed himself from straits. To the foul banks of Acheron –
loosed from the body colder than ice – blaspheming fled the
disdainful spirit that was so haughty in the world and so
arrogant. (trans. Fichter)

There has been a great deal of discussion of the degree to which
Ariosto and Virgil provide closure to their epics.[9] But there has not
been great attention to minute difference of detail, so that Fichter, for
instance, can say of these lines: "And so the narrative breaks off,
leaving the anger and frustration of the unregenerate pagan hero to
reverberate in the reader's mind. But if Ariosto has not changed the
ending of the *Aeneid*, he has modified its context."[10] This does not go
far enough, for that modification indeed amounts to a transformation
of the Virgilian model. When the narrator characterizes the vanquished hero, as he does ("the disdainful spirit that was so haughty in
the world and so arrogant"), Ariosto's poem receives, in a single line,
precisely the comforting ethical closure that is so lacking and so
yearned for at the end of the *Aeneid*. Where Turnus lay humbled and
suppliant (*Aen.* 12.930 *ille humilis supplex* ...), seeming to qualify for
the mercy Anchises enjoined upon his son (6.853 *parcere subiectis*),
Ariosto's defeated enemy is by his actions and attitude (*che fu sì altiera
al mondo e sì orgogliosa*) made to suit the other half of Anchises' line
(6.853 *debellare superbos*). In this he is fundamentally distinct from
Turnus; Ariosto has rewritten Virgil as surely as Vegio did.

Another figure who confronted the issue of Virgilian closure, in
fact before Ariosto, was the Italian critic and poet Torquato Tasso,
whose participation is of special interest in that he expressed himself

[9] For Ariosto see (with bibliography) Sitterson (1992) 1–19.
[10] Fichter (1982) 103.

both as a critic and as a poet.[11] First, Tasso the critic, who was involved in a debate with various sixteenth-century Italian scholars, chiefly Antonio Possevino, whose *Dialogo d' honore* (1553) found fault with Aeneas' final act, from the perspective of Christian chivalric codes of honor. Possevino's discussion takes the form of a dialogue between Giberto di Correggio and Giovanni Battista Possevino, and as Seem describes, the following conclusion is reached:

> Giberto asks Giovanni whether it can ever be right for a man
> to kill his adversary in a duel. Giberto explains that he raises the
> question because it has already been established that the goal of
> a duel between two heroes or strong men ("uomini forti")
> should be the recuperation of lost honor and not the death of
> one of the combatants. Possevino's answer is no: killing an
> opponent would be dishonorable since, as Aristotle teaches us
> [Aristotle will be used on both sides of this debate, as we shall
> see], the victory itself is the honorable thing. Giberto then asks
> the pivotal question: how, then, can Aeneas kill the suppliant
> Turnus and yet retain his honor? Possevino answers that indeed
> he cannot: at the poem's conclusion Aeneas is stripped of
> honor.

Tasso responded to this criticism, not without some implicit agreement, by rewriting the end of the *Aeneid* twice in his epic *Gerusalemme liberata*. As Seem shows, in two separate duel scenes, one in Canto 7 (the Christian Raimondo [standing in for Tancredi] vs. the Saracen Argante), the other in the penultimate Canto 19 (Tancredi himself vs. Argante), Tasso explores ways to avoid the final Virgilian outcome. In the first instance, he sets the Virgilian parallelism in motion by having Argante's (i.e. Turnus') sword shatter against Raimondo's (i.e. Aeneas') shield, which like its classical model is given divine strength, though only for this instant in Tasso. Raimondo is then made to reflect about the correct way to proceed, a reflection that directly engages Virgil, Possevino, and other contemporary critics:

> Ma però ch' egli disarmata vede
> la man nemica, si riman sospeso,

[11] In the observations that follow I am indebted almost completely to a superb brief study by a Renaissance scholar, Seem (1990) 116–25.

ché stima ignobil palma e vili spoglie
quelle ch' altrui con tal vantaggio toglie.

"Prendi," volea già dirgli, "un altra spada,"
quando novo pensier nacque nel core,
ch' alto scorno è de' suoi dove egli cada,
che di publica causa è difensore.
Così né indegna a lui vittoria aggrada,
né in dubbio vuol porre il comune onore.

(7.94–5)

But when he saw his enemy's hand disarmed, he stood hesitant,
for he judged the victory base and spoils cheap taken with such
an advantage.

"Take" he meant to say "another sword," when a new thought
sprung up in his heart, that it was a deep dishonour for his
people for him to fall who was defender of the public cause. So
neither did unworthy victory please him nor could he put at
risk the army's honor.

The dilemma is resolved when Argante throws his broken hilt at
Raimondo and so escapes to fight another day. Seem proposes:
"endless repetition is presented as the alternative to the decisive
Vergilian solution."[12] Alternatively we might see the encounter as a
way of drawing attention to the Virgilian solution, which is then put
on hold for more than half the poem. The hesitation of Aeneas
reappears in that of Raimondo (*si riman sospeso*), and it begins to be
replaced by resolve as the Christian hero dwells on duty to God and
the army (*sine ira et furiis*, we will note), but still the moral dilemma
remains and the action is suspended by Argante's distraction and flight.

But this suspension of close and closure is not endless, as the issue
returns in *Canto* 19, where, as Seem notes, "finally the only solution
left open to the Christian knight is the Virgilian one."[13] Tancredi
indeed kills Argante, driving his sword through the Saracen's visor
and on through his eyes. So much for the similarities, but the differences are more notable. Tancredi's act is most immediately in
response to Argante's stabbing him in the heel – Argante, unlike
Turnus, was still capable of combat. Where the disabled Turnus
allows Aeneas his victory and even his vengeance (*"equidem merui nec*

---

[12] Seem (1990) 121.   [13] Seem (1990) 123.

deprecor" inquit | *"utere sorte tua"* "truly I deserve this and I am not pleading my way out," he said, "use what your fortune has given you" 931–2), Tasso has Argante make an intertextual "correction," maintaining the Virgilian rhythm while transforming Turnus' words into a vaunt: *"Usa la sorte tua, ché null' io temo | né lascierò la tua follia impunita"* "Try your luck, for I have no fear of you | nor will I let your foolish pride go unpunished."[14] Likewise, the manner of Argante's eventual death is very different. Where Turnus' shade, like that of Camilla, had departed indignant, with a groan, reminding us of the complex network of loss and death throughout the poem's second half, and and reminding us too of our shared mortality, Argante dies uncomplicatedly villainous (19.26):

> Moriva Argante, e tal moria qual visse:
> minacciava morendo e non languia.
> Superbi, formidabili e feroci
> gli ultimi moti fur, l'ultime voci.

Argante died, and in that death was as in life: still threatening he died and did not fade away. Haughty, formidable and ferocious were his final movements, so his final words.

Such a character, like Ariosto's Rodomont unambiguous in his ferocity and his pride, allows for unproblematic closure, and this time, in "Superbi," we even have the Italian cognate of Anchises' [*debellare*] *superbos*. Precisely because of these differences we feel here none of the sympathy elicited by Turnus in his final moments: Tancredi's act has, as Aeneas' cannot, precisely that moral certitude for which Augustan readers of Virgil have so long tried to argue, but which can be found in the last analysis only outside the text of Virgil.

"The Man is a Thug!" Rhetoric of persuasion

So far we have been dealing with poetic closings to the Virgilian text, clearly external and recognizably imposed on the model. Now it is time to look to parallel critical acts, where interpretation, not adaptation, provides the resolution. When, with the advance of philological rigor and critical sophistication, it became untenable to append Vegio's *Supplement*, and thereby stabilize the ending of the *Aeneid*,

---

[14] Seem (1990) 123.

closure by hermeneutics took over. I here focus on some recent instances, partly to show that while critical strategies may have changed
and developed, the basic goal has not: the mentality behind this
modern effort is really similar to that which created Vegio's *Supplement* – the pressing need to demonstrate the virtue of Aeneas and
villainy of Turnus.

One approach is that of H. P. Stahl, which involves diverting the
critical focus, not forward in time as Vegio allowed with his *Supplement*, but backwards, always away from the final act and to the events
that precede and precipitate that act. This approach is also characterized by intense rhetoric: "Far from being a foreign invader, the
Julian ancestor is duly welcomed by pious Latinus as the carrier of
a divine mission and as a homecomer; but then Aeneas is ruthlessly
attacked by the oracle-defying head of a local faction."[15] And later:
"Repelled by Turnus' unethical, abominable conduct as depicted in
Book 10, the attentive reader will join Aeneas in the end in opting for
revenge rather than mercy ... not only is the reader being impreg-
nated with antipathy against cruel Turnus, he is also preoccupied so
as to feel for Turnus' victim, Aeneas' young friend Pallas, and for
Aeneas himself."[16] The strategy is fairly obvious: Stahl needs to get us
away from that moment at the end of the poem, and if we fail to
follow him back to those selected parts of Book 10 (to Turnus'
atrocities, but not to Aeneas' decapitating, trunk-kicking and human
sacrifice), we are simply being inattentive.

A second critical approach, pursued chiefly by F. Cairns and K.
Galinsky, involves turning away from the text and from Virgil, and
locating various issues that arise from the end of the poem in other
ancient thinkers, generally philosophers. In each case we see critics
reaching for "objective" criteria with which they are then enabled to
close the poem. The motives are parallel to those of Vegio, though
the methods are somewhat more subtle! In *Virgil's Augustan Epic*,
Cairns ranges widely through the ancient sources to collect the evidence which allows him to demonstrate that "Virgil regarded Dido as
a bad example of the genus king, and Aeneas as an excellent one" (2),
and that "in essence Turnus is a bad king" (67). The problem, of
course, is that Aeneas will exhibit precisely those qualities which are
part of the typology of the bad ruler, that is, he becomes angry and

---

enraged (again, *Aen.* 12.946–7 *furiis accensus et ira | terribilis*) precisely at
the moment in question, the poem's end. And Cairns' response to
this inversion of the expected typology exposes the shortcomings of
his overall critical approach.[17] In analyzing the end of the poem he
makes a distinction "between *furor* and *furibundus* on the one hand,
which are always condemnatory, and *furiae* and *furo | furens* on the
other. These latter terms may be condemnatory, but need not be."[18]
The evidence for the rehabilitation of *furiae* over *furor* comes chiefly
from *Aeneid* 8.494, where in response to the atrocities and tortures of
Mezentius Etruria rises up *furiis . . . iustis*. But that merely suggests
that the whole range of such words is generally condemnatory, and
that there when justifiable *furiae* are provoked, in order to be acceptable, it must modified by the adjective *iustus*. In response to
Cairns' argument, D. P. Fowler has noted: "if you want to distinguish
justified anger from irrational rage, you do it more clearly than by
using words from the same root."[19] I should think that is so, but it is
also worth noting that the ancients attempted to make the distinction,
though not in a way that will assuage uneasiness about Aeneas' final
act: *quidam "furorem" pro bono et innocenti motu accipiunt, "furias" semper
pro malo* "some people allow 'furor' to be a good and blameless
emotion, 'furiae,' to be consistently bad" (DServ. ad *Aen.* 4.474). The
observation *per se* is philologically and critically worthless (as *Aen.*
8.494 proves); DServ. or his source just needed at this moment to
formulate a "scientific" rule so as to blame Dido, as some at *Aeneid*
12.946–7 seem to need to do in order to praise Aeneas. And the rule
so formulated was the opposite of that created by Cairns.

Galinsky develops his case for convincing us of the poem's satisfy-
ing closure in a series of articles, to be read as companion pieces, and
the second in part responds to criticisms of the first.[20] Galinsky's mis-

---

[17] What follows is a restatement of Thomas (1991a).
[18] Cf. Cairns (1989) 82–4.
[19] Fowler (1990b) 108.
[20] Galinsky (1988) 321–48; (1994) 191–201; and again, (1997) 89–100, where Galinsky
(who frequently mocks critics for being preoccupied with the problematic end of the
poem) enters the lists for a third time in what is ostensibly a review article – in the final
page reviewing contributions other than those having to do with the end of the *Aeneid*.
He first notes in this, at least his third contribution on the passage "The final scene of
the *Aeneid* for me has never had the importance that it holds for others"[!], then proceeds to establish his credentials as a teacher and discussant of Virgil, implying that the
rest of us have been teaching and discussing something else, and ends up remonstrating

sion is precisely to make us feel comfortable with the fact that Aeneas' final act is carried out under the influence of *furor* and *ira*. The reasons are simple: in the thinking of Aristotle, and even closer to home in the Epicurean philosopher Philodemus, anger may be a legitimate component of the state's administration of punishment. At the same time the anger of Aeneas ("a virtue and not a throwback to primitivism") is an elaboration of that of Achilles in the *Iliad*, with Aeneas, however, the superior figure, "acting in behalf of a civilized society" (343). And so his *ira* turns out to be a virtue, indistinguishable from that of Turnus, for whom the same word constitutes a vice, "a demonic and un-Aristotelian mania" (345). Turnus, then, breaker of treaties and resister to the will of Jove, may be killed "with extreme prejudice," we might say, so that society may be recompensed for all of his violations. And this scholar, who is constantly ridiculing other critics' "modern misconceptions," cheerfully embraces the wording of A. Wlosok, writing in *Gymnasium*, who refers to Turnus as "a breaker of treaties and, therefore, a *war criminal*"[21] (emphasis added).

All of this is, of course, false to the actual end: it is not the breaking of a truce that motivates Aeneas' final act, nor is it concern about the future security of the state, it is the image of the fateful belt, and the vengeance that that evokes. When, in other words, we turn back to the ending of *Aeneid* 12, no matter how comprehensible the vengeance is, we are left with a sense that it might not have happened and therefore might not have needed to happen (Aeneas' hesitation shows the reality of that possibility). We are given a glimpse of a world which might have had a different closure, and no amount of argument which depends on averting the gaze from the actual ending, which is aimed at distracting our gaze from that ending, will plausibly create the missing closure.

In the critical works surveyed above, we have retreated from 1976,

for the third time that we are all getting this unproblematic ending wrong, because we are not following his (obviously correct and only possible) reading of the end of the poem.

[21] Galinsky (1988) 324, referring to Wlosok (1973) 149 "Da ist Turnus zwar auch ein um Gnade flehender Besiegter, aber er ist – modern gesprochen – ein vielfacher Kriegsverbrecher." As for breaking the treaty (7.467 *polluta pace*), you can argue that Allecto's infection of Turnus (the cause of that action *ergo*) is simply a metaphor for the innate criminality of the latter (though there are various obstacles to this view), but you should not simply ignore it, as Galinsky does.

when W. R. Johnson reminded us that any view that saw either
Turnus or Aeneas as a monster (or thug?) failed this poem, and failed
it precisely through critical banality. He was surely right in criticizing
such views for their providing a closure that does not easily emerge
from the text of Virgil.[22] If a more open closure may be tied, among
other things, to "the degree to which questions posed in the work are
answered, tensions released, conflicts resolved,"[23] then the language
preferred by Galinsky is to be seen as part of the rhetoric of enforcing
closure. This is perhaps best exemplified in the following, into which
I have inserted my own rhetorical commentary:[24]

> Today, it takes a Homeric scholar rather than a Vergilian one
> [all Virgilian scholarship is thus rendered suspect] to reject the
> facile escape into arguing for moral ambiguity [inversion of the
> more plausible proposition that arguing for moral resolution
> and closure is the facile escape] and to state bluntly [good,
> honest critic, not likely to deceive] that Turnus cuts off the
> heads of his slain enemies [as had Aeneas at 10.552–6] and
> suspends them from his chariot dripping blood – an action
> reminiscent of the habit of Cacus, the monster of Book 8, who
> used to fix dripping heads to his doorposts. How anyone can
> feel strong sympathy for Turnus in his weakness [door left open
> for *some* degree of sympathy] at the end of Book 12 escapes me
> [opposition isolated as inexplicably stupid]. The man is a thug
> [do you feel sorry for thugs?].

We might wonder about the consistency of a critical stance that
rejects as deluded by their modern sensibility those who find sympa-

---

[22] Johnson (1976) 115–16; his words are particularly worth citing after the ethical solutions of Galinsky: "It is no secret that there is a general dissatisfaction or uneasiness with
this famous closure. One may try to rationalize the dissatisfaction by proving the villainy of Turnus or by showing that the death of Turnus, the manner of his death,
symbolizes the defeat of Juno; for those who are content to read the poem as an ethical
melodrama, such solutions are apparently adequate – once we have separated the good
guys from the bad guys and the bad guys get what is coming to them, the beauty of the
poem is found to be intact." He also warns against simply seeing Aeneas as the monster,
and I would stress that I only bring out the violence of Aeneas (for instance, in Book
10) in order to suggest that neither character is exempt from violent and frenzied action
in this poem.
[23] Fowler (1997), elaborating on his views at Fowler (1989a) 78.
[24] Galinsky (1988) 323.

thy for Turnus at the end of Virgil's poem, but which then depends on such language and presents itself as the pinnacle of critical judgment of these lines.

Virgil and Milton: epic closure

The close of *Paradise Lost* should in terms of the narrative stage it has attained be open and troubling – the expulsion from Eden. But of course the Archangel Michael gives Adam a vision beyond that expulsion, forward again to Christ and to the hope of redemption (602–5):

> That ye may live, which will be many dayes,
> Both in one faith unanimous though sad,
> With cause for evils past, yet much more cheer'd
> With meditation on the happie end.

That hope is allowed by Milton to inform the very end of the poem (the passage with which this chapter began), and with knowledge of it Adam and Eve proceed out into the world with words that look to a final optimistic closure. Eve is assured that woman's body will be the source of salvation (12.621–3 "though all by me is lost, | Such favour I unworthie am vouchsaft, | By mee the Promis'd Seed shall all restore"); she and Adam (625 "well pleas'd") can thus proceed to a destiny initially involving loss of paradise, but they do so secure of the ultimate end (645–9):

> Some natural tears they drop'd, but wip'd them soon;
> The World was all before them, where to choose
> Thir place of rest, and Providence their guide:
> They hand in hand with wandering steps and slow,
> Through *Eden* took thir solitarie way.

How different the end of Virgil, lacking the teleology of Christ and unfocused even on the attainment of Rome. Wendell Clausen has discussed the end of the *Aeneid* in a way that relates to our theme:

> It is a measure of Virgil's greatness that he withstood the
> temptation to sentimentality; for it is a temptation that those
> who write or talk about the *Aeneid* rarely withstand. "All had
> fought well and, according to their best lights, justly. (This is

how one critic [M. Hadas] writes about the end of the *Aeneid*.)
All bitterness and all passion was now laid at rest, and all could
now join hands as comrades and together walk to meet the
shining future." This is sentimental: at the end of the *Aeneid*
there is no clasping of hands, no walking together towards the
shining future. The light is hard and clear: Aeneas has killed
Turnus, and on Turnus' shoulder gleams the sword-belt of
Pallas.[25]

Neither Hadas nor Clausen mentions Milton, but the former critic's
wording ("all could now join hands as comrades and together walk to
meet the shining future"), false to the text and to realities of Virgil,
seems at the same time to be supplied not by Virgil but precisely by
the ending of the poem that succeeds Virgil: "The World was all
before them ... | They hand in hand with wandering steps and
slow, | Through *Eden* took thir solitarie way." It is almost as if Hadas
is thinking of Virgil's greatest English adapter as he turns away from
Virgil in his need to close what the *Aeneid* left open.

We can, I think, look in Milton for the very foundation of the
origins of this "sentimentality," this attempt to achieve closure. To
turn from endings to beginnings, Milton shows, at the very start of his
great epic, what drives him. The invocation and proem are of course
replete with Greco-Roman (and biblical) intertextuality, but the
close of the passage shows the new purpose of poetry (*Paradise Lost*
1.22–6):

> What in me is dark
> Illumin, what is low raise and support;
> That to the highth of this great Argument
> I may assert Eternal Providence,
> And justifie the wayes of God to men.

A strongly Lucretian motif becomes anti-Lucretian, as pagan rationalism is replaced by Christian faith in the justice of the divine order.
"To justifie the ways of God to men" – the words seem almost banal,
so familiar have they become. But we should not impose that familiarity onto Virgil, nor assume, as so many have, that it was in Virgil's
design to assure us of the order of the cosmos.

---

[25] Clausen (1966) 86–7.

Turnus at the end[26]

For those who consider sympathy or even support for Turnus a mark of American post-Vietnam aesthetic *angst*, it is worth quoting a German scholar writing before Vietnam but, more importantly, after he had perhaps had time to reflect on the consequences of his own society's simplistically identifying, *sine humanitate*, enemies of the state:[27]

> There is something of the small and narrow outlook of the
> nineteenth century at the bottom of this downgrading of
> Turnus. There is also something of the political delusion of the
> twentieth century which is always choosing ideological sides
> without the slightest realization of the immense disdain which
> the great geniuses of mankind have for such considerations.

While allowing that from an Augustan point of view, from the point of view of Augustus himself, and of Aeneas himself, with a few minor adjustments, a reading which vilifies Turnus is a possible one, supported much of the time by the text (though not by the whole text), one may insist also on a point of view that allows a competing meaning. Stahl at one point notes "repelled by Turnus' unethical, abominable conduct as depicted in Book 10, the attentive reader will join Aeneas in the end in opting for revenge rather than mercy." Of course it depends on what the reader attends to and what he is discouraged from attending to. Pöschl presents a more balanced view of Turnus. Stahl claims his own paper "concentrates on, and if possible, limits itself to perspectives that can be demonstrated to flow from the epic's text itself."[28] The word "epic" is frequently evoked in Augustan readings, as a device for establishing the monolithic and for validating those readings, but be that as it may I hope my own conclusions have also emerged from the Virgilian text. G. B. Conte's formulation

---

[26] See Thomas (1998b) for a full treatment from the point of view of Turnus.

[27] Pöschl (1962) 94, from Pöschl (1977) 127: "In der herabziehenden Deutung der Turnusgestalt liegt etwas von der kleinen und engen Gesinnung der Wissenschaft des neunzehnten Jahrhunderts und auch der politischen Verblendung des zwanzigsten, die immer nach irgendwelchen Parteinahmen fahndet, ohne zu ahnen, wie unendlich erhaben die grossen Genien der Menschheit solchen Ueberlegungen gegenüberstehen."

[28] Stahl (1990).

reminds us that we must always attend to individual focalizations in this poem; there is no overarching "epic" or other point of view: "The coexistence of the worlds of Aeneas, Dido, Turnus, Mezentius, and Juturna springs from the fact that Vergil allows each of them an autonomous, personal raison d' être which the historico-epic norm had always denied."[29] So I do not deny a Turnus focalized from the Augustan perspective, but rather end by drawing attention to the Turnus who keeps him company, and whose full voice still merits critical attention.[30]

S. G. P. Small, an Augustan reader, has observed of Turnus:[31]

> The torment of his closing days on earth is barren. It only lays bare the fact that he is basically unworthy to participate in the new order of life in Italy. He lives just long enough to discover the shattering truth that all along he has been no more than an impediment to the making of a better world and that as such he is the enemy of Jupiter.

These words seem true to Virgil's account of Turnus at the end of the *Aeneid*, as a version of them was true of Meliboeus at the end of the First *Eclogue*. What is more in doubt is the spiritual and ethical quality of the "new order" of which Turnus is unworthy. It is one of the marks of Virgil's poetic genius that he insists on showing us how it *feels* to be the enemy of Jupiter. We can see the world through the eyes of Tityrus, Aristaeus and Aeneas, or we can choose to look from the very different perspectives of Meliboeus, Orpheus and Turnus. Either way of reading remains an option, and Virgil impels us to neither. It has been our theme that one particular point of view, that of Augustus and the successors of Augustus, necessarily suppresses the point of view of the dispossessed. But in the end Virgil's poetry refuses to succumb to the needs of Augustus and those who follow his standard.

[29] So Conte (1986) 157.
[30] I again refer readers to Thomas (1998b) for fuller treatment of the oppositional reading of Turnus.
[31] Small (1959) 252.

BIBLIOGRAPHY

Adam, U. D. (1972) *Judenpolitik im Dritten Reich*. Düsseldorf

Adams, J. N. (1982) *The Latin Sexual Vocabulary*. London

Ahl, F. M. (1976) *Lucan. An Introduction*. Ithaca and London

  (1984) "The Art of Safe Criticism in Greece and Rome," *AJP* 105: 174–208

  (1989) "Homer, Vergil, and Complex Narrative Structures," *Illinois Classical Studies* 14: 1–31

Ahl, F. M. and Roisman, H. M. (1996) *The* Odyssey *Reformed*. Ithaca

Altevogt, H. (1952) *Labor improbus. Eine Vergilstudie. Orbis antiquus* 8. Münster

Anderson, W. S. (1969) *The Art of the* Aeneid. Englewood Cliffs, N.J.

Arendt, H. (1968) *Men in Dark Times*. New York

Armstrong, M. and Calder, W. M. III (1994), "The Damnatio of Vergil in Theodor Mommsen, *Römische Kaisergeschichte*," *Vergilius* 40: 85–92

Asmis, E. (1992) "An Epicurean Survey of Poetic Terms (Philodemus, *On Poems*, cols. 26–36)," *CQ* 42: 395–415

Austin, R. G. (1955, repr. 1963) *P. Vergili Maronis Aeneidos Liber Quartus*. Oxford

  (1971) *P. Vergili Maronis Aeneidos Liber Primus*. Oxford

  (1977) *P. Vergili Maronis Aeneidos Liber Sextus*. Oxford

Bade, W. (1933) *Joseph Goebbels*. Lübeck

Bakhtin, M. (1981) "Epic and Novel: Toward a Methodology for the Study of the Novel," in *The Dialogic Imagination: Four Essays by M. M. Bakhtin*, ed. M. Holquist, tr. C. Emerson and M. Holquist. Austin: 3–40

Ball, R. J. (1975) "Tibullus 2.5 and Vergil's *Aeneid*," *Vergilius* 21: 33–50

Balot, R. K. (1998) "Pindar, Virgil, and the Proem to *Georgic* 3," *Phoenix* 52: 83–94

Banks, T. H. (1928) *The Poetical Works of Sir John Denham*. New Haven

Barchiesi, A. (1994) *Il poeta e il principe*. Rome and Bari

Barnes, W. R. (1995) "Virgil: The Literary Impact," in Horsfall (1995) 257–92

Basto, R. (1982) "Horace's Propempticon to Vergil: A re-examination," *Vergilius* 28: 30–43

Bell, A. J. (1923) *The Latin Dual and Poetic Diction*. Oxford

Belmont, D. E. (1980) "The Vergilius of Horace, *Ode* 4.12," *TAPhA* 110: 1–20

Benjamin, W. (1932) "Privilegiertes Denken" in *Angelus Novus. Ausgewählte Schriften* 2 (1966). Frankfurt am Main: 467–74

Betensky, A. (1979) "The Farmer's Battles," in Boyle (1979) 108–19

Binder, G. (1971) *Aeneas und Augustus; Interpretationen zum 8. Buch der Aeneis. Beiträge zur klassischen Philologie* 38. Meisenheim am Glan

Bloom, H. (1994) *The Western Canon*. New York

Bottkol, J. M. (1943) "Dryden's Latin Scholarship," *Modern Philology* 40: 241–54

Bowra, C. M. (1933–34) "Aeneas and the Stoic Ideal," *GR* 3: 8–21

Boyd, B. W. (1983) "*Cydonea mala*: Virgilian Word-Play and Allusion," *HSCP* 87: 169–74

Boyle, A. J. (1972) "The Meaning of the *Aeneid*: A Critical Inquiry," *Ramus* 1.1 and 2: 63–90, 113–51

(1979) (ed.), *Virgil's Ascraean Song*. Melbourne

Brandenstein, W. (1943/8) "Tyrrhener," *RE* VII A: 1909–38

Briggs, W. W. Jr. (1980) *Narrative and Simile from the Georgics in the Aeneid. Mnemosyne Supplement* 58. Leiden

Brink, C. O. (1971) *Horace on Poetry. The Ars Poetica*. Cambridge

(1982) *Horace on Poetry. Epistles Book II: The Letters to Augustus and Florus*. Cambridge

Brinton, A. C. (1930) *Maphaeus Vegius and his Thirteenth Book of the Aeneid*. Stanford

Broch, H. (1945) *The Death of Virgil*, tr. J. S. Untermeyer. Berkeley

Burkert, W. (1974) *Structure and History in Greek Mythology and Ritual*. Berkeley and Los Angeles

Burrow, C. (1997) "Virgil in English Translation," in Martindale (1997) 21–37

Butler, E. M. (1935) *The Tyranny of Greece over Germany*. Cambridge

Cairns, F. (1972) *Generic Composition in Greek and Roman Poetry*. Edinburgh

(1989) *Virgil's Augustan Epic*. Cambridge

Calder, W. M. III (1977) "Seventeen Letters of Ulrich von Wilamowitz-Moellendorff to Eduard Fraenkel" *HSCP* 81: 275–97

(1981) rev. of Losemann (1977), *CP* 76: 168

(1985) "Ecce Homo," in Calder, W. M. III, Flashar, H., Lindken, T. (eds.), *Wilamowitz nach 50 Jahren*. Darmstadt: 80–110

(1988) tr. "Wilamowitz' Bimillenary Essay on Vergil," *Vergilius* 34: 112–27

(1995) rev. Ziolkowski (1993), *Journal of English and German Philology* 94: 588–91

(1996) "'Tell it Hitler! Ecco!' Paul Friedländer on Werner Jaeger's *Paideia*," *Quaderni di Storia* 43: 211–48

Callu, J.-P. (1976–78) "'Impius Aeneas'? Echos virgiliens du bas-empire," in R. Chevallier (ed.), *Présence de Virgile*. Paris: 161–74

Cameron, A. (1989) *History as Text. The Writing of Ancient History*. London

Campbell, J. S. (1987) "*Animae Dimidium Meae:* Horace's Tribute to Vergil," *CJ* 82: 314–18

Canfora, L. (1977) *Cultura classica e crisi tedesca. Gli scritti politici di Wilamo-witz*. Bari

Casali, S. (1995) "Altri voci nell' 'Eneide' di Ovidio," *MD* 35: 59–76

Castriota, D. (1995) *The Ara Pacis Augustae and the Imagery of Abundance in Later Greek and Early Roman Imperial Art*. Princeton

Charlesworth, M. P. (1935) "The Virtues of a Roman Emperor," *Proc. British Academy* 23: 105–33

Cichorius, C. (1922) *Römische Studien*. Leipzig and Berlin

Clark, A. F. B. (1925, repr. 1978) *Boileau and the French Classical Critics in England (1660–1830)*. Geneva

Clausen, W. V. (1945) "The Scorched Earth Policy, Ancient and Modern," *CJ* 40: 298–9

(1966) "An Interpretation of the *Aeneid*," 75–88 in Commager (1966) 75–88 = *HSCP* 68 [1964] 139–47

(1987) *Virgil's* Aeneid *and the Tradition of Hellenistic Poetry*. Berkeley

(1994) *Virgil, Eclogues*. Oxford

(1995) "Appendix" to Horsfall (1995) 313–14

Cockburn, G. (1992) "Aeneas and the Gates of Sleep: An Etymological Approach," *Phoenix* 46: 362–4

Coleman, K. M. (1988) *Statius*, Silvae 4. Oxford

Commager, H. S. (1966) (ed.), *Virgil. A Collection of Critical Essays*. Englewood Cliffs, N.J.

Conington (1898) (ed.), *The Works of Virgil*. London

Conte, G. B. (1986) *The Rhetoric of Imitation: Genre and Poetic Memory in Virgil and Other Latin Poets*. Ithaca

(1993) rev. of Harrison (1991), *JRS* 83: 208–12

(1994) *Latin Literature. A History*. Baltimore

Corse, T. (1991) *Dryden's* Aeneid. *The English Virgil*. Newark, London and Toronto

Courtney, E. (1993) *The Fragmentary Latin Poets*. Oxford

Cova, P. V. (1989) *Il poeta Vario*. Milan

Cramer, R. (1998) *Vergils Weltsicht. Optimismus und Pessimismus in Vergils Georgica. Untersuchungen zur antiken Literatur und Geschichte* 51. Berlin and New York

Curtius, E. (1890–97) *Olympia. Die Ergebnisse der von dem deutschen Reich veranstalteten Ausgrabung.* Berlin

D'Agostino, V. (1971) "Verso il 'Nuovo Virgilio,' " 124–36 in H. Bardon and R. Verdière (eds.) *Vergiliana.* Leiden

Dietz, H. (1984) "Political Classical Studies by Leading German Scholars of the Third Reich," *Quaderni di Storia* 19: 255–70

Drexler, H. (1939) *Tacitus: Grundzüge einer politischen Pathologie. Auf dem Wege zum nationalpolitischen Gymnasium* 8. Frankfurt am Main = Darmstadt 1970

Duckworth, G. E. (1956) "*Animae Dimidium Meae*: Two Poets of Rome," *TAPhA* 87: 281–316

Eagleton, T. (1983) *Literary Theory: An Introduction.* Minneapolis

Eberhardt, W. (1935) "Die Antike und Wir," *Nationalsozialistische Monatshefte* 6: 115–27

Edmunds, E. L. (1994) "*Textus receptus*," rev. of Martindale (1993a), *CR* 44: 38–40

Ehrenberg, V. (1965) "Mommsens Kolleg über römische Kaisergeschichte," in K. F. Stroheker and A. J. Graham (eds.), *Polis und Imperium.* Zürich and Stuttgart: 613–30

Elder, J. P. (1952) "Horace, *C.*, I, 3," *AJP* 73: 140–58

Eliot, T. S. (1944) "What is a Classic?" in F. Kermode (ed.), *Selected prose of T. S. Eliot.* New York (1975) 115–31

(1951) "Virgil and the Christian World" in *On Poetry and Poets.* New York (1957): 135–48

Elsner, J. (1995) *Art and the Roman Viewer.* Cambridge

Ernout, A., and Meillet, A. (1979) *Dictionnaire étymologique de la langue latine. Histoire des mots.* Paris

Erskine-Hill, H. (1983) *The Augustan Idea in English Literature.* London
(1996) *Poetry and the Realm of Politics. Shakespeare to Dryden.* Oxford

Faber, R. (1983) " 'Présence de Virgile': seine (pro-)faschistische Rezeption," *Quaderni di Storia* 18: 233–71

Fahrner, R. (1964) (ed.), *Denkmal.* Düsseldorf and Munich = Stanffenberg (1964)

Fantham, R. E. (1991) Rev. of Thomas (1988a), *CP* 86: 163–7

Fantuzzi, M. (1980) "'Εκ Διὸς ἀρχώμεσθα. Arat. *Phaen.* 1 e Theocr. XVII 1," *MD* 5: 163–72

Farrell, J. (1982) "Dialogue of Genres in Ovid's 'Lovesong of Polyphemus' (*Metamorphoses* 13.719–897)," *AJP* 113: 235–68
(1990) "Which *Aeneid* in Whose Nineties?" *Vergilius* 66: 74–80

Feeney, D. C. (1986) "History and Revelation in Vergil's Underworld," *PCPS* 32: 1–24
(1988) "The Paradoxical Country," rev. of Ross (1987), *TLS* April 29: 476

(1991) *The Gods in Epic. Poets and Critics of the Classical Tradition.* Oxford

Fichter, A. (1982) *Poets Historical. Dynastic Epic in the Renaissance.* New Haven and London

Fish, S. (1981) "*Lycidas*: A Poem Finally Anonymous," *Glyph* 8: 1–18

Fordyce, C. J. (1977) *P. Vergili Maronis Aeneidos Libri VII–VIII.* Oxford and Glasgow

Foss C. (1998) "Augustus and the Poets in Mussolini's Rome," in P. Knox and C. Foss, *Style and Tradition. Studies in Honor of Wendell Clausen. Beiträge zur Altertumskunde* 92: 306–25

Fowler, D. P. (1989a) "First Thoughts on Closure: Problems and Prospects," *MD* 22: 75–122

(1989b) "Roman Literature" (rev.), *GR* 36: 234–41

(1990a) "Deviant Focalisation in Virgil's *Aeneid*," *PCPS* 36: 42–63

(1990b) "Roman Literature" (rev.), *GR* 37: 104–11

(1991) "Roman Literature" (rev.), *GR* 38: 86–97

(1997) "Second Thoughts on Closure," in D. H. Roberts, F. M. Dunn, and D. P. Fowler, *Classical Closure: Reading the End in Greek and Latin Literature.* Princeton: 3–22

Fowler, R. L. (1991) "Four (Five) Stages of Greek Religion," in W. M. Calder III (ed.), *The Cambridge Ritualists Revisited, ICS* 1: 79–95

Fraenkel, E. (1930) *Gedanken zu einer deutschen Vergilfeier.* Berlin

(1930–31) "Nebengedanken bei dem Jubiläum Vergils," *Süddeutsche Monatshefte* 38: 43–6 = *Kleine Schriften* 6.375–81

(1948) "The Latin Studies of Hermann and Wilamowitz," *JRS* 38: 28–34 = *Kleine Beiträge zur klassischen Philologie* II (Rome 1964) 563–76

(1957) *Horace.* Oxford

Frost, W. (1955) *Dryden and the Art of Translation.* New Haven and London

Frost, W. and Dearing, V. A. (1987) *The Works of John Dryden. Volumes 5–6: The Works of Virgil in English.* Berkeley, Los Angeles and London

Gaines, R. N. (1982) "Qualities of Rhetorical Expression in Philodemus," *TAPhA* 112: 71–81

Galinsky, K. (1975) *Ovid's Metamorphoses. An Introduction to the Basic Aspects.* Berkeley and Los Angeles

(1988) "The Anger of Aeneas," *AJP* 109: 321–48

(1991) Rev. of Perkell (1989), *CW* 84: 478

(1992) "Introduction: The Current State of the Interpretation of Roman Poetry and the Contemporary Critical Scene," in K. Galinsky (ed.), *The Interpretation of Roman Poetry: Empiricism or Hermeneutics.* Frankfurt am Main, Bern, New York, Paris

(1994) "How to be Philosophical about the End of the *Aeneid*," *ICS* 19: 191–201

(1996) *Augustan Culture.* Princeton

(1997) "Damned If You Do, Damned If You Don't: Aeneas and the Passions," rev. of S. M. Braund and C. Gill (eds.), *The Passions in Roman Thought and Literature* (Cambridge 1997), *Vergilius* 43 (1997) 89–100

Galsterer, H. (1990) "A Man, a Book, and a Method: Sir Ronald Syme's *Roman Revolution* after Fifty Years," in Raaflaub and Toher (1990) 1–20

Gardiner, E. N. (1925) *Olympia. Its History and Remains*. Oxford

Garrison, J. D. (1992) *"Pietas" from Vergil to Dryden*. University Park, Penn.

Getty, R. J. (1950) "Romulus, Roma, and Augustus in the Sixth Book of the Aeneid," *CP* 45: 1–12

Geymonat, M. (1973) *P. Vergili Maronis Opera*. Paravia

(1984) "Cornuto," *Enciclopedia Virgiliana* 1. Rome: 897–98

(1990) "Urbano," *Enciclopedia Virgiliana* 5. Rome: 400–1

Gigante, M. (1989) "Il ritorno di Virgilio a Ercolano," *SIFC* 7: 3–6

(1990) "La brigata virgiliana ad Ercolano," in M. Gigante (ed.), *Virgilio e gli Augustei*. Naples: 10–13

Gillis, D. (1983) *Eros and Death in the* Aeneid. Rome

Goebbels, P. J. (1923) *Wilhelm von Schütz als Dramatiker. Ein Beitrag zur Geschichte des Dramas der romantischen Schule*. Diss. [1921] Heidelberg

Goold, G. P. (1970) "Servius and the Helen Episode," *HSCP* 74: 101–68

Gordon, L. (1998) *T. S. Eliot. An Imperfect Life*. New York and London

Görler, W. (1984–91) "Cacozelia," *Enciclopedia Virgiliana* 1. Rome: 596–97

Gransden, K. W. (1976) *Virgil, Aeneid* VIII. Cambridge

(1984) *Virgil's Iliad*. Cambridge

Graves, R. (1962), "The Virgil Cult," *Virginia Quarterly Review* 38: 13–35.

Griffin, J. (1979) "The Fourth *Georgic*, Virgil and Rome," *GR* 26: 61–80 = *Latin Poets and Roman Life*. London (1985) 163–82

(1981) "Haec super arvorum cultu," *CR* 31: 23–37

(1984) "Caesar qui cogere posset," in F. Millar and E. Segal (eds.), *Caesar Augustus: Seven Aspects*. Oxford and New York

(1994) Rev. of Conte (1994) in *New York Review of Books*, Oct. 6: 42–4

Grube, G. M. A. (1961) *A Greek Critic. Demetrius on Style*. Toronto

Gurval, R. (1995) *Actium and Augustus. The Politics and Emotions of Civil War*. Ann Arbor

Haarhof, T. J. (1949) *Vergil the Universal*. Oxford

Habinek. T. (1990) "Sacrifice, Society, and Vergil's Ox-born Bees," in M. Griffith and D. J. Mastronarde (eds.), *Cabinet of the Muses. Essays on Classical and Comparative Literature in Honor of Thomas G. Rosenmeyer*. Atlanta: 209–23

Haecker, T. (1934) *Virgil, Father of the West* (trans. from the 1931 German version). London and New York

Hagendahl, H. (1967) *Augustine and the Latin Classics. Studia Graeca et Latina Gothoburgensia* 20. Göteborg

Hahn, E. A. (1945) "Horace's Odes to Vergil," *TAPhA* 76: xxxii–xxxiii

Hammond M. (1965) "The Sincerity of Augustus," *HSCP* 69: 139–62

Hammond P. (1999) *Dryden and the Traces of Classical Rome.* Oxford

Hardie, P. R. (1986) *Virgil's* Aeneid: *Cosmos and Imperium.* Oxford
(1993) *The Epic Successors of Virgil. A Study in the Dynamics of a Tradition.* Cambridge
(1994) *Virgil, Aeneid IX.* Cambridge

Harrison, S. J. (1990) "Some Views of the *Aeneid* in the Twentieth Century," in S. J. Harrison (ed.), *Oxford Readings in Vergil's* Aeneid. Oxford: 1–20
(1991) *Vergil, Aeneid 10.* Oxford

Harrison, T. W. (1967) "English Virgil: The *Aeneid* in the XVIII Century," *Philologica Pragensia* 10: 1–11, 80–92
(1969), "Dryden's *Aeneid*," in B. King (ed.), *Dryden's Mind and Art,* Edinburgh: 143–67

Heinze, R. (1903) *Virgil's Epic Technique,* trans. (1993) H. and D. Harvey and F. Robertson. Berkeley and Los Angeles

Heißer, H. (1962) *Goebbels.* Berlin, trans. [1972] John K. Dickinson. New York

Henderson, J. (1988) "Lucan / The Word at War," 122–64 in A. J. Boyle (ed.), *The Imperial Muse: Ramus Essays on Roman Literature of the Empire to Juvenal through Ovid.* Victoria
(1995) "Pump up the Volume: Juvenal, *Satires* 1.1–21." *PCPS* 41: 101–37
(1998) "*Exemploque suo mores reget*," rev. of Galinsky (1996), *Hermathena* 164: 101–16

Herzog, R. (1939) "Der englische Krieg," *Gymnasium* 50: 153–4.

Heyne, C. G. (1830–41) *P. Virgilius Maro varietate lectionis et perpetua adnotatione illustratus* (4th ed.). Leipzig

Hijmans, B. L. Jr. (1971–2) "*Aeneia Virtus*: Vegio's *Supplementum* to the *Aeneid*," *CJ* 67: 144–55

Hoffmann, P. (1995) *Stauffenberg. A Family History, 1905–1944.* Cambridge

Hollis, A. S. (1977) "L. Varius Rufus, *De Morte* (frs. 1–4 Morel)," *CQ* 27: 187–90

Hooley, D. M. (1988) *The Classics in Paraphrase.* Selinsgrove, London and Toronto

Hopkins, D. (1986) *John Dryden.* Cambridge

Horsfall, N. M. (1987) "The Enciclopedia Virgiliana," *Vergilius* 33: 146
(1988a), "Afterword" to Calder (1988), *Vergilius* 34: 128–30
(1988b) rev. of R. O. A. M. Lyne (1987) *CR* 38: 243
(1991) *Virgilio: l' epopea in alambicco.* Naples
(1994) Rev. of A. Wlosok (1990), *Vergilius* 40: 133–5
(1995) (ed.), *A Companion to the Study of Virgil. Mnemosyne Supplement* 151. Leiden

Housman, A. E. (1926) *M. Annaei Lucani Belli Civilis Libri Decem*. Oxford

Hutchinson, G. O. (1988) *Hellenistic Poetry*. Oxford

Jenkyns, R. (1998) *Virgil's Experience. Nature and History: Times, Names and Places*. Oxford

Jocelyn, H. D. (1979) "Vergilius Cacozelus (Donatus, *Vita Vergilii* 44)," *PLLS* 2: 67–142

(1980) "The Fate of Varius' *Thyestes*," *CQ* 30: 387–400

Johnson, W. R. (1970) "The Problem of the Counter-Classical Sensibility and its Critics," *CSCA* 3: 123–51

(1976) *Darkness Visible. A Study of Virgil's* Aeneid. Berkeley, Los Angeles and London

(1981) "The Broken World: Virgil and his Augustus," *Arethusa* 14: 49–56

Jönsson, A., and Roos, B.-A. (1996) "A Note on *Aeneid* 6.893–8," *Eranos* 94: 21–8

Jungnickel, M. (1933) *Goebbels*. Leipzig

Kallendorf, C. (1989) *In Praise of Aeneas. Virgil and Epideictic Rhetoric in the Early Renaissance*. Hanover, N.H. and London

(1994) "Philology, the Reader, and the *Nachleben* of Classical Texts," *Modern Philology* 92.2: 137–56

Kavanagh, J. (1990) "Ideology" in F. Lentricchia and T. McLaughlin (eds.), *Critical Terms for Literary Study*. Chicago: 306–20

Kellum, B. A. (1990) "The City Adorned: Programmatic Display at the Aedes Concordiae Augustae," in Raaflaub and Toher (1990) 276–307

Kennedy, D. F. (1992) " 'Augustan' and 'Anti-Augustan': Reflections on Terms of Reference," in A. Powell (ed.), *Roman Poetry and Propaganda in the Age of Augustus*. London: 26–58

(1995) "Tradition and Appropriation: T. S. Eliot and Virgil's *Aeneid*," *Hermathena* 158: 73–94

Kenney, E. J. (1968) "Eduard Norden," *CR* 18: 105–7

Kermode, F. (1975) (ed.), *Selected Prose of T. S. Eliot*. London

Kinsley, J. (1961) (ed.), *The Works of Virgil, translated by John Dryden*. Oxford

Klingner, F. (1967) *Virgils Bucolica Georgica Aeneis*. Zürich

Knight, W. F. Jackson (1966) *Roman Vergil*. Harmondsworth

Knox, B. (1989) *Essays Ancient and Modern*. Baltimore

Knox, P. E. (1995) *Ovid, Heroides. Select Epistles*. Cambridge

(1997) "Savagery in the *Aeneid* and Virgil's Ancient Commentators," *CJ* 92: 225–33

Korfmacher, W. C. (1955–6) "Vergil, Spokesman for the Augustan Reforms," *CJ* 51: 329–34

Kraggerud, E. (1992) "Which Julius Caesar? On *Aen*. 1.286–96," *SO* 67: 103–12

(1994) "Caesar Versus Caesar Again: A Reply," *SO* 69: 83–93

Kürschner, J. (1980) *Deutscher Gelehrten-Kalender*. Berlin and New York

Kytzler, B. (1961) "Das früheste Aeneis-Zitat," in G. Radke (ed.), *Gedenkenschrift f. G. Rohde*. Tübingen: 151–67

Lamacchia, R. (1969) "Precisiazioni su alcuni aspetti dell' epica ovidiana," *AR* 14: 1–20

Lefevere, A. (1977) (ed. and tr.), *Translating Literature: The German Tradition from Luther to Rosenzweig*. Assen

Linderski, J. (1990) "Mommsen and Syme: Law and Power in the Principate of Augustus," in Raaflaub and Toher (1990) Berkeley: 42–53

Livingstone, R. et al. (1999) (tr.), *Walter Benjamin. Selected Writings*, Volume 2. Cambridge, Mass. and London

Lloyd-Jones, H. (1971) "Eduard Fraenkel †," *Gnomon* 43: 634–40

Long, J. D. (1879) *Virgil*, Aeneid (trans.). Boston
(1895) *After-Dinner and Other Speeches*. Boston and New York
(1908–9) "Reminiscences of My Seventy Years' Education," *Proc. Mass. Hist. Soc.* 42: 348–58
(1956) *The Journal of John D. Long*, ed. M. Long. Rindge, N.H.

Long, J. D. (*MHS* papers) Archive of John Davis Long, Massachusetts Historical Society, Boston

Losemann, V. (1977) *Nationalsozialismus und Antike: Studien zur Entwicklung des Faches Alte Geschichte 1933–1945*. Hamburg

Løsnes, A. (1963) "Dryden's *Aeneis*," in M.-S. Rostvig (ed.), *The Hidden Sense*. Oslo: 115–57

Lyne, R. O. A. M. (1987) *Further Voices in Vergil's* Aeneid. Oxford
(1995) *Horace. Behind the Public Poetry*. New Haven

MacCormack, S. (1998) *The Shadows of Poetry. Virgil in the Mind of Augustine*. Berkeley, Los Angeles and London

Mackail, J. W. (1922) *Virgil and his Meaning to the World Today*. Boston

Macleod, C. (1970) "Eduard David Mortier Fraenkel," *The Oxford Magazine* 8: 209–10 = *Collected Papers* (Oxford 1983): 115–57

MacPherson, C. (1910) *Über die Vergil-Übersetzung des John Dryden*. diss. Berlin

Magoffin, R. V. D. (1930) *The Tribute of Mussolini to Vergil, and the Vergilian Bimillennial in the United States*, American Classical League Publication No. 30. Reprint of an article in the *New York Herald Tribune*, Feb. 23, 1930

Malitz, J. (1998) "Römertum im 'Dritten Reich': Hans Oppermann," in P. Kneissl and V. Losemann (eds.), *Imperium Romanum. Studien zu Geschichte und Rezeption. Festschrift für Karl Christ zum 75. Geburtstag*. Stuttgart: 519–43

Manvell, R. and Fraenkel, H. (1960) *Doctor Goebbels. His Life and Death*. London, Melbourne and Toronto

Markland, J. (1827) *P. Papini Statii Libri Quinque Silvarum*. London

Martindale, C. (1993a) *Redeeming the Text*. Cambridge

(1993b) "Descent into Hell: Reading Ambiguity, or Virgil and the Critics," *PVS* 21: 111–50

(1997) (ed.), *The Cambridge Companion to Virgil*. Cambridge

Masters, J. (1992) *Poetry and Civil War in Lucan's Bellum Civile*. Cambridge

Mayo, L. S. (1923) (ed.), *America of Yesterday, as Reflected in the Journal of John Davis Long*. Boston

Meister, K. (1952) in H. Haas and K. Meister (eds.), *Cornelius Tacitus, Germania. Heidelberger Texte, Lateinische Reihe* 23

Mensching, E. (1991) *Nugae zur Philologie-Geschichte* IV. Berlin

Milbourne, L. (1698) *Notes on Dryden's Virgil*. London

Miles, G. B. (1980) *Virgil's Georgics: A New Interpretation*. Berkeley and Los Angeles

Miller, H. (1991) *Theory Now and Then*. New York and London

Minadeo, R. (1975–6) "Vergil in Horace's *Odes* 4.12," *CJ* 71: 161–4

Molyviati-Toptsis, U. (1995) "*Sed falsa ad caelum mittunt insomnia Manes*," *AJP* 116: 639–52

Momigliano, A. (1971) "Eduard Fraenkel" in *Encounter*, Feb. 1971: 55–6

Morgan, L. (1999) *Patterns of Redemption in Virgil's Georgics*. Cambridge

Moritz, L. A. (1969) "Horace's Virgil," *GR* 16: 174–93

Morrison, P. (1996) *The Poetics of Fascism. Ezra Pound, T. S. Eliot, Paul de Man*. New York and Oxford

Müller, G.-W. (1939) (ed.), *Wetterleuchten. Aufsätze aus der Kampfzeit*. Munich

Mynors, R. A. B. (1990) *Virgil, Georgics*. Oxford

Näf, B. (1986) *Von Perikles zu Hitler? Die athenische Demokratie und die deutsche Althistorie bis 1945*. Bern, Frankfurt am Main and New York

Narducci, E. (1979) *La provvidenza crudele. Lucano e la distruzione dei miti augustei*. Pisa

Nauck, A. (1867, repr. 1965) *Lexicon Vindobonense*. Petersburg

(1869–74) "Kritische Bemerkungen," *Mélanges Gréco-Romains* 3: 9–102

Nethercut, W. R. (1968) "Invasion in the *Aeneid*," *GR* 15: 82–95

Nisbet, R. G. M. and Hubbard, M. (1970) *A Commentary on Horace Odes Book 1*. Oxford

(1978) *A Commentary on Horace Odes Book 2*. Oxford

Norden, E. (1899) "Ein Panegyricus auf Augustus in Vergils *Aeneis*," *RhM* 54: 466–82 = (1966) *Kleine Schriften zum klassischen Altertum* (Berlin 1966): 422–36

(1924, repr. 1931) *Die Geburt des Kindes: Geschichte einer religiösen Idee, Studien der Bibliothek Warburg* 3. Berlin and Leipzig

(1970) *P. Vergilius Maro Aeneis Buch* VI. 5th ed. Stuttgart

O'Hara, J. J. (1990) *Death and the Optimistic Prophecy in Virgil's* Aeneid. Princeton

(1994) "Temporal Distortions, 'Fatal' Ambiguity, and *Iulius Caesar* at *Aeneid* 1.286–96," *SO* 69: 72–82

(1996) "An Unconvincing Etymological Argument about Aeneas and the Gates of Sleep," *Phoenix* 50: 331–4

(1997) "Virgil's Style," in Martindale (1996) 241–58

O Hehir, B. (1968) *Harmony from Discords. A Life of Sir John Denham.* Berkeley and Los Angeles

Oppermann, H. (1934) "Cäsar als Führergestalt," *Vergangenheit und Gegenwart* 24: 641–52

(1935) "Altertumswissenschaft und politische Erziehung," *Neue Jahrbücher für Wissenschaft und Jugendbildung* 11: 367–72

(1936) "Die Bevölkerungspolitik des Augustus," *Neue Jahrbücher für Wissenschaft und Jugendbildung* 12: 116–33

(1937a) "Volk, Geschichte, Dichtung (Schiller und Vergil)," *Historische Schriften* 156: 71–81

(1937b) "Neuordnung des höheren Schulwesens und Altertumswissenschaft," *Neue Jahrbücher für deutsche Wissenschaft* 15: 263–73

(1938a) "Die alten Sprachen in der Neuordnung des höheren Schulwesens," *NJAB* 3: 127–36

(1938b) *Probleme der augusteischen Erneuerung. Auf dem Wege zum nationalpolitischen Gymnasium* 6. Frankfurt am Main

(1941) "Das römische Schicksal und die Zeit des Augustus," *Historische Schriften* 164: 1–20

(1943) *Der Jude im griechisch-römischen Altertum.* Munich

(1963) *Wege zu Vergil. Drei Jahrzehnte Begegnungen in Dichtung und Wissenschaft.* Darmstadt

Otis, B. (1959) "Three Problems of *Aeneid* 6," *TAPhA* 90: 165–79

(1995) *Virgil: A Study in Civilized Poetry.* 2nd ed. Norman, Okla.

Otto, W. F. (1931), *Vergil. Schriften der Strassburger Wissenschaftlichen Gesellschaft an der Universität Frankfurt am Main* 13. Berlin and Leipzig; cited from Oppermann (1963) 69–92

Page, T. E. (1883, repr. 1977) *Q. Horatii Flacci Carminum Libri* IV. London

(1894) *The Aeneid of Virgil. Books* I–VI. London

Paratore, E. (1950) *Storia della letteratura latina.* Florence

Parkes-Perret, F. B. (1984) *Hanns Johst's Nazi Drama Schlageter.* Stuttgart

Parry, A. (1963) "The Two Voices of Virgil's *Aeneid*," *Arion* 2: 66–80

Pascal, C. B. (1990) "The Dubious *Devotio* of Turnus," *TAPhA* 120: 251–68

Peerlkamp, P. H. (1843) *P. Virgilii Maronis Aeneidos Libri* VII–XII. Leiden

Perkell, C. (1981) "On Creusa, Dido, and the Quality of Victory in Virgil's *Aeneid*," *Women's Studies* 8: 201–23

(1989) *The Poet's Truth. A Study of the Poet in Virgil's* Georgics. Berkeley and Los Angeles

(1994) "Ambiguity and Irony: The Last Resort?" *Helios* 21: 63–74

(1997) "The Lament of Juturna: Pathos and Interpretation in the *Aeneid*," *TAPhA* 127: 257–86

Petrini, M. (1997) *The Child and the Hero: Coming of Age in Catullus and Vergil.* Ann Arbor

Phillips, O. C. (1968) "Lucan's Grove," *CP* 63: 296–300

Picht, G. (1980) in *Hier und Jetzt: Philosophieren nach Auschwitz und Hiroshima* 1: Stuttgart = "Gewitterlandschaft. Erinnerung an Martin Heidegger," *Merkur* 31 (1977) 962

Pöschl, V. (1962) *The Art of Vergil. Image and Symbol in the Aeneid* (trans. G. Seligson). Ann Arbor

(1977) *Die Dichtkunst Virgils.* 3rd ed. (1st ed. 1950) Berlin and New York

Preisendanz, K. and Meister, R. (1948) (eds.), *P. Vergilius Maro. Bucolica / Georgica / Aeneis. Heidelberger Texte. Lateinische Reihe* 4

Proudfoot, L. (1960) *Dryden's* Aeneid *and its Seventeenth Century Predecessors.* Manchester

Pucci, J. (1991) "The Dilemma of Writing: Augustine, *Confessions* 4.6 and Horace, *Odes* 1.3," *Arethusa* 24: 257–81

Putnam, M. C. J. (1965) *The Poetry of the* Aeneid. Cambridge, Mass.

(1979) *Virgil's Poem of the Earth.* Princeton

(1986) *Artifices of Eternity. Horace's Fourth Book of Odes.* Ithaca, N.Y.

(1990) "Horace, *carm.* 2.9: Augustus and the Ambiguities of Encomium," in Raaflaub and Toher (1990) 212–38

Quinn, K. (1972) "Did Virgil Fail?", in J. R. C. Martyn (ed.), *Cicero and Virgil: Studies in Honor of Harold Hunt.* Amsterdam

Quint, D. (1993) *Epic and Empire. Politics and Generic Form from Virgil to Milton.* Princeton

Raaflaub, K. A. and Toher, M. (1990) (eds.), *Between Republic and Empire. Interpretations of Augustus and his Principate.* Berkeley

Ramsey, J. T. (1984) *Sallust's* Bellum Catilinae, *APA Textbooks* 9

Reckford, K. J. (1974) "Some Trees in Virgil and Tolkien," in G. K. Galinsky (ed.), *Perspectives of Roman Poetry.* Austin: 57–91

Ribbeck, O. (1966) *Prolegomena Critica ad P. Vergili Maronis Opera Maiora.* Leipzig

Rieks, R. (1981) "Vergil und die römische Geschichte," *Aufstieg und Niedergang* 31.2: 728–864

Riess, C. (1948) *Joseph Goebbels.* New York

Ritter, F. (1856) *Q. Horatius Flaccus.* Leipzig

Ross, A. (1984) "Virgil and the Augustans," in C. Martindale (ed.), *Virgil and his Influence.* Bristol

Ross, D. O. Jr. (1979) "Ancient Logs and Old Saws (Horace, *Epode* 2.43)," *AJP* 100: 241–4

(1987) *Virgil's Elements. Physics and Poetry in the* Georgics. Princeton

Rudd, N. (1989) *Horace*, Epistles II *and* Epistle to the Pisones. Cambridge

Rutherford, I. (1988) "ΕΜΦΑΣΙΣ in Ancient Literary Criticism and *Tractatus Coislinianus c. 7*," *Maia* 40: 125–9

Ryberg, I. S. (1958) "Vergil's Golden Age," *TAPhA* 89: 112–31

Schadewaldt, W. (1931) "Sinn und Werden der vergilischen Dichtung," *Das Erbe der Alten* 2.20: 67–95; cited from Oppermann (1963) 43–68

Schaefer, H. (1936) "Horaz und Vergil im dritten Reich," *Das humanistische Gymnasium* 47: 204–9

Schenkeveld, D. M. (1964) *Studies in Demetrius on Style*. Amsterdam

Schiesaro, A. (1983) Rev. of O'Hara (1990), *CP* 88: 258–65

Schmidt, P. L. (1985) "Wilamowitz und die Geschichte der lateinischen Literatur," in W. M. Calder III, H. Flashar, T. Lindken, (eds.) *Wilamowitz nach 50 Jahren*. Darmstadt: 358–99

Schulte R, and Biguenet, J. (1992) *Theories of Translation. An Anthology of Essays from Dryden to Derrida*. Chicago and London

Seem, L. S. (1990) "The Limits of Chivalry: Tasso and the End of the *Aeneid*," *Comparative Literature* 42: 116–25

Serpa, F. (1987) *Il punto su Virgilio*. Rome and Bari

Sforza, F. (1935) "The Problem of Virgil," *CR* 49: 97–108

(1952) *Il più prezioso tesoro spirituale d' Italia: L'*Eneide. Milan

Shackleton Bailey, D. R. (1982) *Profile of Horace*. London

Sitterson, J. J. Jr. (1992) "Allusive and Elusive Meaning: Reading Ariosto's Vergilian Ending," *Renaissance Quarterly* 45: 1–19

Sloman, J. (1985) *Dryden: The Poetics of Translation*. Toronto

Small, S. G. P. (1959) "The Arms of Turnus: *Aeneid* 7.783–92," *TAPhA* 92: 243–52

Smith, B. H. (1968) *Poetic Closure. A Study of How Poems End*. Chicago

Smolenaars, J. J. L. (1987) "Labour in the Golden Age. A Unifying Theme in Vergil's Poems," *Mnemosyne* 40: 391–405

Stahl, H. P. (1990) "The Death of Turnus: Augustan Vergil and the Political Rival," in Raaflaub and Toher (1990) 174–211

Stauffenberg, A. Schenk, Count von (1943) "Vergil und der augusteische Staat," *Die Welt als Geschichte* 9: 55–67; cited from Oppermann (1963) 177–98

(1964) *Denkmal*. Düsseldorf = Fahrner (1964)

Steiner, G. (1975) *After Babel. Aspects of Language and Translation*. Oxford

Suerbaum, W. (1981) *Vergils Aeneis. Beiträge zu ihrer Rezeption in Geschichte und Gegenwart*. Bamberg

Sullivan, J. P. (1964–5) *Ezra Pound and Sextus Propertius: A Study in Creative Translation*. Austin and London

Summers, J. H. (1962) *The Muse's Methods. An Introduction to* Paradise Lost. Cambridge, Mass.

Syme, R. (1939) *The Roman Revolution*. Oxford

  (1950) *A Roman Post-Mortem. An Inquest on the Fall of the Roman Republic*. Todd Memorial Lecture 3. Sydney

  (1979) "Imperator Caesar: A Study in Nomenclature," *Roman Papers* vol. 1. Oxford: 361–77

Tarrant, R. J. (1982) "Aeneas and the Gates of Sleep," *CP* 77: 51–5

Thomas, R. F. (1979) "Theocritus, Calvus and *Eclogue* 6," *CP* 74: 337–9 = Thomas (1999) 297–9

  (1982) *Lands and Peoples in Roman Poetry. The Ethnographical Tradition*, *PCPhS*. Supp. 7. Cambridge

  [1983] "Virgil's Ecphrastic Centrepieces," *HSCP* 87: 175–84 = Thomas (1999) 310–20

  (1988a) *Virgil, Georgics*. 2 vols. Cambridge

  (1988b) "Tree Violation and Ambivalence in Virgil," *TAPhA* 118: 261–73

  (1990) "Ideology, Influence, and Future Studies in the *Georgics*," *Vergilius* 66: 64–70

  (1991a) "*Furor* and *furiae* in Virgil," *AJP* 112: 261

  (1991b) "The 'Sacrifice' at the End of the *Georgics*, Aristaeus, and Virgilian Closure," *CP* 86: 211–18

  (1992) Rev. of Harrison (1991), *Vergilius* 38: 134–44

  (1993) "Callimachus back in Rome," *Hellenistica Groningana* 1: 197–215 = Thomas (1999) 206–28

  (1995) "Browsing in the Western Stacks," *Harvard Library Bulletin* n.s. 6.3: 27–33

  (1996) "Genre through Intertextuality: Theocritus to Virgil and Propertius," *HG* 2: 227–46 = Thomas (1999) 246–66

  (1997) "Virgil, Theodore Roosevelt, and John Davis Long: Neighbors in the Widener Stacks," *Harvard Library Bulletin* 8.1: 31–48

  (1998a) "Virgil's Pindar?" in P. Knox. and C. Foss (eds.), *Style and Tradition. Studies in Honor of Wendell Clausen. Beiträge zur Altertumskunde* 92: 99–120 = Thomas (1999) 267–87

  (1998b) "The Isolation of Turnus," in H. P. Stahl (ed.), *Vergil's* Aeneid: *Augustan Epic and Political Context*. London and Swansea: 271–302

  (1999) *Reading Virgil and his Texts. Studies in Intertextuality*. Ann Arbor.

  (2000a) Rev. of Cramer (1998), *Gnomon* 72

  (2000b) "A Trope by Any Other Name: 'Polysemy,' Ambiguity and *Significatio* in Virgil," *HSCP* 100

Thompson, L. and Bruère, R. T. (1968) "Lucan's Use of Vergilian Reminiscence," *CP* 63: 1–21

Timpanaro, S. (1986) *Per la storia della filologia virgiliana antica. Quaderni di "Filologia e Critica"* 6

Todd, R. W. (1980) "Lavinia Blushed," *Vergilius* 26: 27–33

Traina, A. (1988) "Superbia," *Enciclopedia Virgiliana* 4. Rome: 1072–6

Trevor-Roper, H. R. (repr. 1973) (ed.), *Hitler's Table Talk 1941–44*. London

Usener, H. (1875) "Italische Mythen," *RhM* 30: 182–229

Venuti, L. (1995) *The Translator's Invisibility. A History of Translation*. London and New York

Vogt, J. (1943) *Rom und Karthago*. Leipzig

von Humboldt, W. (1816) "From the Introduction of His Translation of *Agamemnon*," trans. S. Sloan, in Schulte and Biguenet (1992) 55–9

Vretska, K. (1938) "Der Weg ins neue Gymnasium. Bekenntnis eines Ostmarkdeutschen zu Erziehung und Unterricht in der höheren Schule," *Gymnasium* 49: 113–20

Waite, R. G. L. (1952) *Vanguard of Nazism. The Free Corps Movement in Post-War Germany 1918–1923*. Cambridge, Mass.

Warren, D. (1996) *Radio Priest. Charles Coughlin, the Father of Hate Radio*. New York

Watkins, J. (1995) *The Specter of Dido. Spenser and Virgilian Epic*. New Haven and London

Watson, G. (1962) (ed.), *John Dryden. Of Dramatic Poesy and Other Critical Essays*. 2 vols. London

Weinbrot, H. D. (1978) *Augustus Caesar in "Augustan" England. The Decline of a Classical Norm*. Princeton

Weinstock, S. (1971) *Divus Julius*. Oxford

West, D. (1993a) "On Serial Narration and on the Julian Star," *PVS* 21: 1–16

(1993b) "The Pageant of Heroes as Panegyric (Virgil, *Aen.* 6.760–886)," in H. D. Jocelyn (ed.), *Tria Lustra. Essays and Notes Presented to John Pinsent*. Liverpool: 283–96

White, P. (1988) "Julius Caesar in Augustan Rome," *Phoenix* 42: 334–56

(1993) *Promised Verse. Poets in the Society of Augustan Rome*. Cambridge

Wilamowitz-Moellendorff, U. von (1885) "An den Quellen des Clitumnus," in *Reden und Vorträge* (1925) 1. Berlin: 333–59

(1928). *Erinnerungen: 1848–1914*. Leipzig

Wilkinson, L. P. (1969) *The Georgics of Virgil. A Critical Survey*. Cambridge

(1970) "Pindar and the Proem to the Third Georgic," in W. Wimmel (ed.), *Forschungen zur römischen Literatur*. Wiesbaden: 286–90

Williams, G. (1968) *Tradition and Originality in Roman Poetry*. Oxford

(1980) *Figures of Thought in Roman Poetry*. New Haven and London

Williams, R. D. (1954) Rev. of Sforza (1952), *CR* 4: 167

(1973) *The* Aeneid *of Virgil*. 2 volumes. Glasgow

(1990) "The Sixth Book of the *Aeneid*," in S. J. Harrison (ed.), *Oxford Readings in Vergil's* Aeneid. Oxford: 191–207 = *GR* 11 (1964) 48–63

Wimmel, W. (1970) *Kallimachos in Rom. Die Nachfolge seines apologetischen Dichtens in der Augusteerzeit. Hermes Einzelschriften* 16. Wiesbaden

Wiseman, T. P. (1992) *Talking to Virgil: A Miscellany*. Exeter

Wlosok, A. (1973), "Vergil in der neueren Forschung," *Gymnasium* 80: 129–50 = Wlosok (1990) 279–300

(1990) *Res Humanae-Res Divinae. Kleine Schriften*, ed. E. Heck and E. A. Schmidt. Heidelberg

Yavetz, Z. (1984) "The *Res Gestae* and Augustus' Public Image," in F. Millar and E. Segal (eds.), *Caesar Augustus. Seven Aspects*. Oxford: 1–36

(1990) "The Personality of Augustus," in Raaflaub and Toher (1990) 21–41

Zanker, P. (1988) *The Power of Images in the Age of Augustus*. Ann Arbor

Zetzel, J. E. G. (1989) "ROMANE, MEMENTO: Justice and Judgement in *Aeneid* 6," *TAPhA* 119: 263–84

(1997) "Rome and its Traditions," in Martindale (1997) 188–203

Zimmermann, O. (1943–4) "Gedanken zur Aeneïs," *Das Gymnasium* 54/55: 42–53

Ziolkowski, J. M. (1990) " 'What is Philology': Introduction," *Comparative Literature Studies* 27: 1–12

Ziolkowski, T. (1993) *Virgil and the Moderns*. Princeton

Zwicker, S. N. (1984) *Politics and Language in Dryden's Poetry. The Arts of Disguise*. Princeton

Zwierlein, O. (1999) *Die Ovid- und Vergil-Revision in tiberischer Zeit, I. Prolegomena. Untersuchungen zur antiken Literatur und Geschichte* 57. Berlin

INDEX

313